POEMS WITH POWER

TO

STRENGTHEN THE SOUL

COMPILED AND EDITED BY

JAMES MUDGE

Author of

THE BEST OF BROWNING, ETC.

REVISED AND ENLARGED EDITION

New York: EATON & MAINS

Cincinnati: JENNINGS & GRAHAM

TO ALL
WHO ARE AT THE SAME TIME
OVERS OF GOOD POETRY AND LOVERS OF GOOD CHARACTER,
DEVOTED TO GOD AND THEIR FELLOW-MEN, AS WELL AS TO
LITERATURE, THE COMPILER, WHO CLAIMS A LITTLE
PLACE IN THIS LARGE COMPANY,
DEDICATES THE RESULT OF HIS PLEASANT LABORS

CONTENTS

PREFACE

This is not like other collections of religious verse; still less is it a hymnal. The present volume is directed to a very specific and wholly practical end, the production of high personal character; and only those poems which have an immediate bearing in this direction have been admitted. We know of no other book published which has followed this special line. There are fine hymnals, deservedly dear to the Church, but they are necessarily devoted in large measure to institutional and theological subjects, are adapted to the wants of the general congregation and to purposes of song; while many poetical productions that touch the heart the closest are for that very reason unsuited to the hymnal. There are many anthologies and plentiful volumes of religious poetry, but not one coming within our ken has been made up as this has been. We have sought far and wide, through many libraries, carefully conning hundreds of books and glancing through hundreds more, to find just those lines which would have the most tonic and stimulating effect in the direction of holier, nobler living. We have coveted verses whose influence would be directly on daily life and would help to form the very best habits of thought and conduct, which would have intrinsic spiritual value and elevating power; those whose immediate tendency would be to make people better, toughening their moral fibre and helping them heavenward; those which they could hardly read attentively without feeling an impulse toward the things which are pure and true and honorable and lovely and of good report, things virtuous and praiseworthy.

It is surprising to one who has not made the search how very many poets there are whose voluminous and popular works yield nothing, or scarcely anything, of this sort. We have looked carefully through many scores of volumes of poetry without finding a line that could be of the slightest use in this collection. They were taken up altogether with other topics. They contained many pretty conceits, pleasant descriptions, lovely or lively narrations—these in abundance, but words that would send the spirit heavenward, or even earthward with any added love for humanity, not one. On the other hand, in papers and periodicals, even in books, are great multitudes of verses, unexceptionable in sentiment and helpful in influence, which bear so little of the true poetic afflatus, are so careless in construction or so faulty in diction, so imperfect in rhyme or rhythm, so much mingled with colloquialisms or so hopelessly commonplace in thought, as to be unworthy of a permanent place in a book like this. They would not bear reading many times. They would offend a properly educated taste. They would not so capture the ear as to linger on the memory with compelling persistence, nor strike the intellect as an exceptional presentation of important truth. The combination of fine form and deep or inspiring thought is by no means common, but, when found, very precious. We will not claim that this has been secured in all the poems here presented. Not all will approve our choice in all respects. There is nothing in which tastes more differ than in matters of this kind. And we will admit that in some cases we have let in—because of the important truth which they so well voiced—stanzas not fully up to the mark in point of poetic merit. Where it has not been possible to get the two desirable things together, as it has not always, we have been more solicitous for the sentiment that would benefit than for mere prettiness or perfection of form. Helpfulness has been the test oftener than a high literary standard. The labored workmanship of the vessel has not weighed so much with us as its perfect fitness to convey the water of life wherewith the thirsty soul of man has been or may be refreshed. If poets are properly judged, as has been alleged, by the frame of mind they induce, then some who have not gained great literary fame may still hold up their heads and claim a worthy crown.

Some poems fully within the scope of the book—like Longfellow's "Psalm of Life"—have been omitted because of their exceeding commonness and their accessibility. Many hymns of very high value—like "Jesus, Lover of my soul," "My faith looks up to thee," "Nearer, my God, to thee," "When all thy mercies, O my God," "How firm a foundation"—have also been omitted because they are found in all the hymnals, and to include them would unduly swell the size of the book. A few others, although similarly familiar, like "Jesus, I my cross have taken," and "God moves in a mysterious way," have been inserted from a feeling that even yet their depth and richness are not properly appreciated and that they can never be sufficiently pondered. A few poems we have been unable to procure permission to use; but in nearly all cases we have met with most generous treatment from both authors and publishers owning copyrights, and we take this occasion to express our hearty thanks for the kindness afforded in the following instances:

Houghton, Mifflin & Company, for the use of the poems and stanzas here found from Henry Wadsworth Longfellow, James Russell Lowell, John Greenleaf Whittier, Ralph Waldo Emerson, Oliver Wendell Holmes, Edward Rowland Sill, Celia Thaxter, Caroline Atherton Mason, Edna Dean Proctor, Edmund Clarence Stedman, John Burroughs, John Hay, William Dean Howells, Harriet Beecher Stowe, Lucy Larcom, Margaret E. Sangster, Francis Bret Harte, James Freeman Clarke, Samuel Longfellow, Samuel Johnson, Christopher Pearse Cranch, Thomas Wentworth Higginson, Elizabeth Stuart Phelps and John Vance Cheney.

Little, Brown & Company, for poems by Helen Hunt Jackson, Louise Chandler Moulton, William Rounseville Alger, "Susan Coolidge" [Sarah Chauncey Woolsey], and John White Chadwick.

Lothrop, Lee & Shepard Company, for poems by Sam Walter Foss.

D. Appleton & Company, for poems by William Cullen Bryant.

T. Y. Crowell & Company, for poems by Sarah Knowles Bolton.

Charles Scribner's Sons, for poems by Josiah Gilbert Holland.

The Century Company, for poems by Richard Watson Gilder.

The Bobbs-Merrill Company, for poems by James Whitcomb Riley.

Harper & Brothers, for poems by Edward Sandford Martin.

Small, Maynard & Co., for poems by Charlotte Perkins Gilman.

The Rev. D. C. Knowles, for poems by Frederic Lawrence Knowles, especially from "Love Triumphant," published by Dana, Estes & Company.

The Rev. Frederic Rowland Marvin, for poems from his "Flowers of Song from Many Lands."

Professor Amos R. Wells, for poems from his "Just to Help."

Mr. Nixon Waterman, for poems from "In Merry Mood," published by Forbes & Co., of Chicago.

The selections from the above American authors are used by special arrangements with the firms mentioned, who are the only authorized publishers of their works. Many other poems used have been found in papers or other places which gave no indication of the original source. In spite of much effort to trace these things it is quite likely we have failed in some cases to give due credit or obtain the usual permission; and we hope that if such omissions, due to ignorance or inadvertence, are noticed they will be pardoned. Many unknown writers have left behind them some things of value, but their names have become detached from them or perhaps never were appended. Many volumes consulted have been long out of print.

We are glad to record our large indebtedness to the custodians of the Boston, Cambridge, Malden, Natick, Brookline, Jamaica Plain, Somerville, and Newton Public Libraries, the Boston Athenæum, the Congregational Library, the General Theological Library, and the Library of Harvard College, for free access to their treasures.

By far the greater part of the contents are from British and other foreign authors, such as William Wordsworth, Alfred Tennyson, Robert Browning, Elizabeth Barrett Browning, Dinah Maria Mulock Craik, Mrs. S. F. Adams, Anna Letitia Barbauld, Mrs. Charles, Frances Ridley Havergal, Anna Letitia Waring, Jean Ingelow, Adelaide Anne Procter, Mme. Guyon, Theodore Monod, Matthew Arnold, Edwin Arnold, William Shakespeare, John Milton, George Gordon Byron, Robert Burns, William Cowper, George Herbert, Robert Herrick, Francis Quarles, Frederick W. Faber, John Keble, Charles Kingsley, Alexander Pope, Joseph Addison, John Gay, Edward Young, Thomas Moore, John Newton, John Bunyan, H. Kirke White, Horatius Bonar, James Montgomery, Charles Wesley, Richard Baxter, Norman Macleod, George Heber, Richard Chenevix Trench, Henry Alford, Charles Mackay, Gerald Massey, Alfred Austin, Robert Louis Stevenson, Arthur Hugh Clough, Henry Burton, Samuel Taylor Coleridge, Hartley Coleridge, Joseph Anstice, George Macdonald, Robert Leighton, John Henry Newman, John Sterling, Edward H. Bickersteth, Dante Gabriel Rossetti, and many others. Of German authors there are not a few, including Johann W. von Goethe, Johann C. F. Schiller, George A. Neumarck, Paul Gerhardt, Benjamin Schmolke, S. C. Schoener, Scheffler, Karl Rudolf Hagenbach, S. Rodigast, Novalis, Wolfgang C. Dessler, L. Gedicke, Martin Luther, and Johann G. von Herder.

The number of American poets drawn upon is small compared with this list. It is the case in all such collections. According to an analysis of the hymns contained in the most widely used American hymnals down to 1880 the average number of hymns of purely American origin was not quite one in seven; the proportion would be a little larger now. And the number of Methodist poets is almost nil, in spite of the fact that the compiler is a Methodist and the volume is issued from the official Methodist Publishing House. But if we thought that this would be any barrier to its wide circulation in Methodist homes we should be deeply ashamed for our church. We are confident it will not be. For mere denominational tenets do not at all enter into these great matters of the soul's life. A book like this speaks loudly for the real oneness, not only of all branches of the Christian Church, but of all religions, in some respects. Not only do we find the various Protestant denominations amply represented here; not only have we most inspiring words from Roman Catholic writers like Francis Xavier, Madame Guyon, Alexander Pope, John Henry Newman, Frederick W. Faber, and Adelaide Anne Procter; but from Mohammèdan sources, from Sufi saints of Persia, and the Moslem devotees of Arabia, and even from Hinduism, there are utterances of noblest truth which we cannot read without a kindling heart. These are all brought together from the ends of the earth into a delightful "upper chamber," where the warring discords of opinion cease and an exceedingly precious peace prevails.

It should be said, though it is perhaps hardly necessary, that this is by no means a book to be read at a sitting. It furnishes very concentrated nourishment. It can be taken with largest profit only a little at a time, according as the mood demands and circumstances appoint. There should be very much meditation mingled with the perusal, an attempt to penetrate the deep meaning of the lines and have them enter into the soul for practical benefit. Some of these hymns have great histories: they are the war cries of combatants on hard-fought battle fields; they are living words of deep experience pressed out of the heart by strong feeling; they are the embodiment of visions caught on some Pisgah's glowing top. Here will be found and furnished hope for the faint-hearted, rest for the weary, courage for the trembling, cheer for the despondent, power for the weak, comfort for the afflicted, guidance in times of difficulty, wise counsel for moments of perplexity, a stimulant to faithfulness, a cure for the blues, exhilaration, jubilation. Everything of a depressing nature has been scrupulously ruled out. The keynote, persistently followed through all the pages, is optimistic, bright, buoyant. Trumpet calls and bugle notes are furnished in abundance, but no dirges or elegies. Large space, it will be seen, is given to such topics as Heroism, True Greatness, the Care and Presence of God, the blessings of Brotherliness, the privilege of Service, the path of Peace, the secret of Contentment, the mission of Prayer, the joy of Jesus, the meaning of Life, the glory of Love, the promise of Faith, the happy aspect of old Age and Death; for these subjects come very close home to the heart, and are illustrated in daily experience. Anyone who feels a special need in any of these directions is confidently recommended to turn to the proper sections and read the selections.

Very much that is here may easily and suitably be committed to memory, that thus it may the more permanently penetrate into the inmost depth of being. It may be used with most telling effect in sermons to give point and pungency to the thought of the preacher. Alike in popular discourse and public testimony or in private meditation these gems of sentiment and thought will come into play with great advantage. The benefit which may be derived from them can scarcely be overestimated. President Eliot, of Harvard University, has said: "There are bits of poetry in my mind learned in infancy that have stood by me in keeping me true to my ideas of duty and life. Rather than lose these I would have missed all the sermons I have ever heard." Many another can say substantially the same, can trace his best deeds very largely to the influence of some little stanza or couplet early stored away in his memory and coming ever freshly to mind in after years as the embodiment of truest wisdom.

We cannot guarantee in all cases the absolute correctness of the forms of the poems given, though much pains have been taken to ensure accuracy; but authors themselves make changes in their productions at different times in different editions. Nor have we always been able to trace the poem to its source. Slips and errors of various kinds can hardly be avoided in such matters. Even so competent an editor as John G. Whittier, in his "Songs of Three Centuries," ascribes "Love divine, all love excelling" to that bitter Calvinist, Augustus M. Toplady, giving it as the sole specimen of his verse; when it was really written by the ardent Arminian, Charles Wesley, with whom Toplady was on anything but friendly terms. If Whittier could make a blunder of this magnitude we may be pardoned if possibly a keen-eyed critic spies something in our book almost as grossly incorrect. In some cases we have been obliged to change the titles of poems so as to avoid reduplication in our index, or to adapt them the better to the small extract taken from the much longer form in the original. In a few cases we have made (indicated) alterations in poems to fit them more fully to the purpose of the book.

The volume will be found not only a readable one, we think, but also an uncommonly useful one for presentation by those who would do good and give gratification to their serious-minded friends with a taste for religious poetry and a love for wandering in the "holy land of song." He who would put before another the essential elements of religion would do better to give him such a book as this than a treatise on theology. He who would himself get a clear idea of what the religious life really is will do better to pore over these pages than to dip into some philosophical discussion. Here the best life is expressed rather than analyzed, exhibited rather than explained. Mrs. Browning has well said, "Plant a poet's word deep enough in any man's breast, looking presently for offshoots, and you have done more for the man than if you dressed him in a broadcloth coat and warmed his Sunday pottage at your fire." We who, by preparing or circulating such volumes, aid the poets in finding a larger circle to whom to give their message, may claim a part of the blessing which comes to those who in any way aid humanity. George Herbert has said,

> "A verse may find him who a sermon flies,
> And turn delight into a sacrifice."

He himself most excellently illustrated the sentiment by bequeathing to the world many beautiful verses that are sermons of the most picturesque sort.

One definition of poetry is "a record of the best thoughts and best moments of the best and happiest minds." This in itself would almost be sufficient to establish the connection between poetry and religion. It is certain that the two have very close and vital relations. Dr. Washington Gladden has admirably remarked, "Poetry is indebted to religion for its largest and loftiest inspirations, and religion is indebted to poetry for its subtlest and most luminous interpretations." No doubt a man may be truly, deeply religious who has little or no development on the æsthetic side, to whom poetry makes no special appeal. But it is certain that he whose soul is deaf to the "concord of sweet sounds" misses a mighty aid in the spiritual life. For a hymn is a wing by which the spirit soars above earthly cares and trials into a purer air and a clearer sunshine. Nothing can better scatter the devils of melancholy and gloom or doubt and fear. When praise and prayer, trust and love, faith and hope, and similar sentiments, have passed into and through some poet's passionate soul, until he has become so charged with them that he has been able to fix them in a form of expression where beauty is united to strength, where concentration and ornamentation are alike secured, then the deepest needs of great numbers are fully met. What was vague and dim is brought into light. What was only half conceived, and so but half felt, is made to grip the soul with power. Poetry is of the very highest value for the inspiration and guidance of life, for calling out the emotions and opening up spiritual visions. It carries truths not only into the understanding, but into the heart, where they are likely to have the most direct effect on conduct.

In the language of Robert Southey, I commit these pages to the Christian public, with a sincere belief that much benefit will result to all who shall read them:

"Go forth, little book, from this my solitude;
  I cast thee on the waters,—go thy ways;
And if, as I believe, thy vein be good,
  The world will find thee after many days.
Be it with thee according to thy worth;
Go, little book! in faith I send thee forth."

JAMES MUDGE.

Malden, Mass.

HEROISM

CHIVALRY, NOBILITY, HONOR, TRUTH

THE INEVITABLE

I like the man who faces what he must,
With step triumphant and a heart of cheer;
Who fights the daily battle without fear;
Sees his hopes fail, yet keeps unfaltering trust
That God is God; that somehow, true and just,
His plans work out for mortals; not a tear
Is shed when fortune, which the world holds dear,
Falls from his grasp: better, with love, a crust
Than living in dishonor: envies not,
Nor loses faith in man; but does his best,
Nor ever murmurs at his humbler lot,
But, with a smile and words of hope, gives zest
To every toiler: he alone is great
Who by a life heroic conquers fate.
—Sarah Knowles Bolton.

DEFEATED YET TRIUMPHANT

They never fail who die
In a great cause. The block may soak their gore;
Their heads may sodden in the sun; their limbs
Be strung to city gates and castle walls;
But still their spirit walks abroad.
Though years
Elapse and others share as dark a doom,
They but augment the deep and sweeping thoughts
Which overpower all others and conduct
The world, at last, to freedom.
—George Gordon Byron.

A HERO GONE

He has done the work of a true man—
Crown him, honor him, love him;
Weep over him, tears of woman,
Stoop, manliest brows, above him!

For the warmest of hearts is frozen;
The freest of hands is still;
And the gap in our picked and chosen
The long years may not fill.

No duty could overtask him,
No need his will outrun:
Or ever our lips could ask him,
His hands the work had done.

He forgot his own life for others,
Himself to his neighbor lending.
Found the Lord in his suffering brothers,
And not in the clouds descending.

And he saw, ere his eye was darkened,
The sheaves of the harvest-bringing;
And knew, while his ear yet hearkened,
The voice of the reapers singing.

Never rode to the wrong's redressing
A worthier paladin.
He has heard the Master's blessing,
"Good and faithful, enter in!"
—John Greenleaf Whittier.

THE CHARGE

They outtalked thee, hissed thee, tore thee?
Better men fared thus before thee;
Fired their ringing shot and pass'd,
Hotly charged—and sank at last.
Charge once more, then, and be dumb!
Let the victors, when they come,
When the forts of folly fall,
Find thy body by the wall!
—Matthew Arnold.

THE REFORMER

Before the monstrous wrong he sets him down—
One man against a stone-walled city of sin.
For centuries those walls have been a-building;
Smooth porphyry, they slope and coldly glass
The flying storm and wheeling sun. No chink,
No crevice, lets the thinnest arrow in.
He fights alone, and from the cloudy ramparts
A thousand evil faces gibe and jeer him.
Let him lie down and die: what is the right,
And where is justice, in a world like this?
But by and by earth shakes herself, impatient;
And down, in one great roar of ruin, crash
Watch-tower and citadel and battlements.
When the red dust has cleared, the lonely soldier
Stands with strange thoughts beneath the friendly stars.

—Edward Rowland Sill.

LIFE AND DEATH

So he died for his faith. That is fine—
More than most of us do.
But, say, can you add to that line
That he lived for it, too?
In his death he bore witness at last
As a martyr to truth.
Did his life do the same in the past
From the days of his youth?
It is easy to die. Men have died
For a wish or a whim—
From bravado or passion or pride.
Was it harder for him?
But to live—every day to live out
All the truth that he dreamt,
While his friends met his conduct with doubt
And the world with contempt.
Was it thus that he plodded ahead,
Never turning aside?
Then we'll talk of the life that he lived.
Never mind how he died.

—Ernest Crosby.

THE RED PLANET MARS

The star of the unconquered will,
He rises in my breast,
Serene, and resolute, and still,
And calm, and self-possessed.

And thou, too, whosoe'er thou art,
That readest this brief psalm,
As one by one thy hopes depart,
Be resolute and calm.

Oh, fear not in a world like this,
And thou shalt know erelong,—
Know how sublime a thing it is
To suffer and be strong.

—Henry Wadsworth Longfellow.

THE NOBLE ARMY OF MARTYRS PRAISE THEE

Not they alone who from the bitter strife
Came forth victorious, yielding willingly
That which they deem most precious, even life,
Content to suffer all things, Christ, for Thee;
Not they alone whose feet so firmly trod
The pathway ending in rack, sword and flame,
Foreseeing death, yet faithful to their Lord,
Enduring for His sake the pain and shame;
Not they alone have won the martyr's palm,
Not only from their life proceeds the eternal psalm.

For earth hath martyrs now, a saintly throng;
Each day unnoticed do we pass them by;
'Mid busy crowds they calmly move along,
Bearing a hidden cross, how patiently!
Not theirs the sudden anguish, swift and keen,
Their hearts are worn and wasted with small cares,
With daily griefs and thrusts from foes unseen;
Troubles and trials that take them unawares;
Theirs is a lingering, silent martyrdom;
They weep through weary years, and long for rest to come.

They weep, but murmur not; it is God's will,
And they have learned to bend their own to his;
Simply enduring, knowing that each ill
Is but the herald of some future bliss;
Striving and suffering, yet so silently
They know it least who seem to know them best.
Faithful and true through long adversity
They work and wait until God gives them rest;
These surely share with those of bygone days
The palm-branch and the crown, and swell their song of praise.

THE HAPPY WARRIOR

'Tis, finally, the man, who, lifted high,
Conspicuous object in a nation's eye,
Or left unthought of in obscurity,
Who, with a toward or untoward lot,
Prosperous or adverse, to his wish or not,—
Plays, in the many games of life, that one
Where what he most doth value must be won;
Whom neither shape of danger can dismay,
Nor thought of tender happiness betray;
Who, not content that former work stand fast,
Looks forward, persevering to the last,
From well to better, daily self-surpast;
Who, whether praise of him must walk the earth
Forever, and to noble deeds give birth,
Or he must fall, to sleep without his fame,
And leave a dead, unprofitable name—
Finds comfort in himself and in his cause,
And, while the mortal mist is gathering, draws
His breath in confidence of Heaven's applause:
This is the happy warrior; this is he
That every man in arms should wish to be. —William Wordsworth.

Around the man who seeks a noble end
Not angels but divinities attend.
—Ralph Waldo Emerson.

ROBERT BROWNING'S MESSAGE

Grow old along with me!
The best is yet to be,
The last of life, for which the first was made;
Our times are in His hand
Who saith, "A whole I planned,
Youth shows but half; trust God: see all, nor be afraid!"

Poor vaunt of life indeed,
Were man but formed to feed
On joy, to solely seek and find and feast;
Such feasting ended, then
As sure an end to men:
Irks care the crop-full bird? Frets doubt the maw-crammed beast?

Then welcome each rebuff
That turns earth's smoothness rough,
Each sting that bids nor sit nor stand, but go!
Be our joys three parts pain!
Strive, and hold cheap the strain;
Learn, nor account the pang; dare, never grudge the throe!

For thence—a paradox
Which comforts while it mocks—
Shall life succeed in that it seems to fail:
What I aspired to be,
And was not, comforts me:
A brute I might have been, but would not sink i' the scale.

* * * * * * * * * *

Not on the vulgar mass
Called "work" must sentence pass,
Things done, that took the eye and had the price;
O'er which, from level stand,
The low world laid its hand,
Found straightway to its mind, could value in a trice:

But all, the world's coarse thumb
And finger failed to plumb,
So passed in making up the main account;
All instincts immature,
All purposes unsure,
That weighed not as his work, yet swelled the man's amount:

Thoughts hardly to be packed
Into a narrow act,
Fancies that broke through language and escaped;
All I could never be,
All, men ignored in me,
This I was worth to God, whose wheel the pitcher shaped.
* * * * * * * * * * *
Fool! All that is, at all,
Lasts ever, past recall;
Earth changes, but thy soul and God stand sure:
What entered into thee
That was, is, and shall be:
Time's wheel runs back or stops;
Potter and clay endure.
—From "Rabbi Ben Ezra."

TRUTH AND FALSEHOOD

Once to every man and nation comes the moment to decide,
In the strife of Truth with Falsehood, for the good or evil side;
Some great cause, God's new Messiah, offering each the bloom or blight,
Parts the goats upon the left hand, and the sheep upon the right,
And the choice goes by forever 'twixt that darkness and that light.

Careless seems the great Avenger; history's pages but record
One death-grapple in the darkness 'twixt old systems and the Word;
Truth forever on the scaffold, Wrong forever on the throne—
Yet that scaffold sways the future, and, behind the dim unknown,
Standeth God within the shadow, keeping watch above his own.

Then to side with Truth is noble when we share her wretched crust,
Ere her cause bring fame and profit, and 'tis prosperous to be just;
Then it is the brave man chooses, while the coward stands aside,
Doubting in his abject spirit, till his Lord is crucified,
And the multitude make virtue of the faith they had denied.

Count me o'er earth's chosen heroes—they were souls that stood alone
While the men they agonized for hurled the contumelious stone;
Stood serene, and down the future saw the golden beam incline
To the side of perfect justice, mastered by their faith divine,
By one man's plain truth to manhood and to God's supreme design.

By the light of burning heretics Christ's bleeding feet I track,
Toiling up new Calvaries ever with the cross that turns not back,
And these mounts of anguish number how each generation learned
One new word of that grand *Credo* which in prophet-hearts hath burned
Since the first man stood God-conquered with his face to heaven upturned.

For Humanity sweeps onward: where to-day the martyr stands,
On the morrow crouches Judas with the silver in his hands;
Far in front the cross stands ready and the crackling fagots burn,
While the hooting mob of yesterday in silent awe return
To glean up the scattered ashes into History's golden urn.

'Tis as easy to be heroes as to sit the idle slaves
Of a legendary virtue carved upon our fathers' graves;
Worshipers of light ancestral make the present light a crime;—
Was the Mayflower launched by cowards, steered by men behind their time?
Turn those tracks toward Past or Future that make Plymouth Rock sublime?

They have rights who dare maintain them; we are traitors to our sires,
Smothering in their holy ashes Freedom's new-lit altar-fires;
Shall we make their creed our jailer? shall we in our haste to slay,
From the tombs of the old prophets steal the funeral lamps away
To light up the martyr-fagots round the prophets of to-day?

New occasions teach new duties; Time makes ancient good uncouth;
They must upward still, and onward, who would keep abreast of Truth;
Lo, before us gleam her camp-fires! we ourselves must Pilgrims be,
Launch our Mayflower, and steer boldly through the desperate winter sea,
Nor attempt the Future's portal with the Past's blood-rusted key.
James Russell Lowell.

COLUMBUS

Behind him lay the gray Azores,
  Behind the Gates of Hercules;
Before him not the ghost of shores,
  Before him only shoreless seas.
The good mate said: "Now, we must pray,
  For lo! the very stars are gone.
Speak, Admiral, what shall I say?"
  "Why say, 'Sail on! sail on! and on!'"

"My men grow mutinous day by day;
  My men grow ghastly wan and weak."
The stout mate thought of home; a spray
  Of salt wave washed his swarthy cheek.
"What shall I say, brave Admiral, say,
  If we sight naught but seas at dawn?"
"Why, you shall say at break of day,
  'Sail on! sail on! sail on! and on!'"

They sailed and sailed, as winds might blow,
  Until at last the blanched mate said:
"Why, now not even God would know
  Should I and all my men fall dead.
These very winds forget their way,
  For God from these dread seas is gone.
Now speak, brave Admiral, speak and say—"
  He said, "Sail on! sail on! and on!"

They sailed. They sailed. Then spoke the mate:
  "This mad sea shows its teeth to-night.
He curls his lip, he lies in wait,
  With lifted teeth, as if to bite!
Brave Admiral, say but one good word.
  What shall we do when hope is gone?"
The words leapt as a leaping sword,
  "Sail on! sail on! sail on! and on!"

Then, pale and worn, he kept his deck,
  And peered through darkness. Ah, that night
Of all dark nights! And then a speck—
  A light! A light! A light!
It grew, a starlit flag unfurled!
  It grew to be Time's burst of dawn:
He gained a world; he gave that world
  Its grandest lesson: "On, and on!"

—Joaquin Miller.

THE CHOSEN FEW

The Son of God goes forth to war,
  A kingly crown to gain;
His blood-red banner streams afar;
  Who follows in his train?

Who best can drink His cup of woe,
  And triumph over pain,
Who patient bears His cross below—
  He follows in His train.

A glorious band, the chosen few,
  On whom the Spirit came;
Twelve valiant saints, their hope they knew,
  And mocked the cross and flame.

They climbed the dizzy steep to heaven
  Through peril, toil and pain;
O God! to us may grace be given
  To follow in their train!

—Reginald Heber.

HOW DID YOU DIE?

Did you tackle that trouble that came your way
  With a resolute heart and cheerful,
Or hide your face from the light of day
  With a craven soul and fearful?
O, a trouble is a ton, or a trouble is an ounce,
  Or a trouble is what you make it,
And it isn't the fact that you're hurt that counts,
  But only—how did you take it?

You are beaten to earth? Well, well, what's that?
  Come up with a smiling face.
It's nothing against you to fall down flat,
  But to lie there—that's disgrace.
The harder you're thrown, why, the higher you bounce;
  Be proud of your blackened eye!
It isn't the fact that you're licked that counts;
  It's how did you fight—and why?

And though you be done to the death, what then?
  If you battled the best you could.
If you played your part in the world of men,
  Why, the Critic will call it good.
Death comes with a crawl or comes with a pounce,
  And whether he's slow or spry,
It isn't the fact that you're dead that counts,
  But only—how did you die?

—Edmund Vance Cooke.

LUTHER

That which he knew he uttered,
Conviction made him strong;
And with undaunted courage
He faced and fought the wrong.
No power on earth could silence him
Whom love and faith made brave;
And though four hundred years have gone
Men strew with flowers his grave.

A frail child born to poverty,
A German miner's son;
A poor monk searching in his cell,
What honors he has won!
The nations crown him faithful,
A man whom truth made free;
God give us for these easier times
More men as real as he!
—Marianne Farningham.

THE MARTYRS

Flung to the heedless winds,
Or on the waters cast,
The martyrs' ashes, watched,
Shall gathered be at last;
And from that scattered dust,
Around us and abroad,
Shall spring a plenteous seed
Of witnesses for God.

The Father hath received
Their latest living breath;
And vain is Satan's boast
Of victory in their death;
Still, still, though dead, they speak,
And, trumpet-tongued, proclaim
To many a wakening land,
The one availing name.
—Martin Luther, tr. by John A. Messenger.

Stainless soldier on the walls,
Knowing this—and knows no more—
Whoever fights, whoever falls,
Justice conquers evermore,
Justice after as before;
And he who battles on her side,
God, though he were ten times slain,
Crowns him victor glorified,
Victor over death and pain.
—Ralph Waldo Emerson.

ETERNAL JUSTICE

The man is thought a knave, or fool,
Or bigot, plotting crime,
Who, for the advancement of his kind,
Is wiser than his time.
For him the hemlock shall distil;
For him the axe be bared;
For him the gibbet shall be built;
For him the stake prepared.
Him shall the scorn and wrath of men
Pursue with deadly aim;
And malice, envy, spite, and lies,
Shall desecrate his name.
But Truth shall conquer at the last,
For round and round we run;
And ever the Right comes uppermost,
And ever is Justice done.

Pace through thy cell, old Socrates,
Cheerily to and fro;
Trust to the impulse of thy soul,
And let the poison flow.
They may shatter to earth the lamp of clay
That holds a light divine,
But they cannot quench the fire of thought
By any such deadly wine.
They cannot blot thy spoken words
From the memory of man
By all the poison ever was brewed
Since time its course began.
To-day abhorred, to-morrow adored,
For round and round we run,
And ever the Truth comes uppermost,
And ever is Justice done.

Plod in thy cave, gray anchorite;
Be wiser than thy peers;
Augment the range of human power,
And trust to coming years.
They may call thee wizard, and monk accursed,
And load thee with dispraise;
Thou wert born five hundred years too soon
For the comfort of thy days;
But not too soon for human kind.
Time hath reward in store;
And the demons of our sires become
The saints that we adore.
The blind can see, the slave is lord,
So round and round we run;
And ever the Wrong is proved to be wrong
And ever is Justice done.

Keep, Galileo, to thy thought,
  And nerve thy soul to bear;
They may gloat o'er the senseless words they wring
  From the pangs of thy despair;
They may veil their eyes, but they cannot hide
  The sun's meridian glow;
The heel of a priest may tread thee down
  And a tyrant work thee woe;
But never a truth has been destroyed;
  They may curse it and call it crime;
Pervert and betray, or slander and slay
  Its teachers for a time.
But the sunshine aye shall light the sky,
  As round and round we run;
And the Truth shall ever come uppermost,
  And Justice shall be done.

And live there now such men as these—
  With thoughts like the great of old?
Many have died in their misery,
  And left their thought untold;
And many live, and are ranked as mad,
  And are placed in the cold world's ban,
For sending their bright, far-seeing souls
  Three centuries in the van.
They toil in penury and grief,
  Unknown, if not maligned;
Forlorn, forlorn, bearing the scorn
  Of the meanest of mankind!
But yet the world goes round and round,
  And the genial seasons run;
And ever the Truth comes uppermost,
  And ever is Justice done.
—Charles Mackay.

We cannot kindle when we will
  The fire which in the heart resides.
The spirit bloweth and is still;
  In mystery our soul abides:
But tasks in hours of insight willed
Can be through hours of gloom fulfilled.

With aching hands and bleeding feet
  We dig and heap, lay stone on stone;
We bear the burden and the heat
  Of the long day, and wish 'twere done.
Not till the hours of light return,
All we have built do we discern.
—Matthew Arnold.

WHAT MAKES A HERO?

What makes a hero?—not success, not fame,
Inebriate merchants, and the loud acclaim
  Of glutted avarice—caps tossed up in air,
  Or pen of journalist with flourish fair;
Bells pealed, stars, ribbons, and a titular name—
  These, though his rightful tribute, he can spare;
His rightful tribute, not his end or aim,
  Or true reward; for never yet did these
  Refresh the soul, or set the heart at ease.
What makes a hero?—An heroic mind,
Expressed in action, in endurance proved.
  And if there be preëminence of right,
  Derived through pain well suffered, to the height
Of rank heroic, 'tis to bear unmoved
Not toil, not risk, not rage of sea or wind,
Not the brute fury of barbarians blind,
  But worse—ingratitude and poisonous darts,
  Launched by the country he had served and loved.
This, with a free, unclouded spirit pure,
This, in the strength of silence to endure,
  A dignity to noble deeds imparts
  Beyond the gauds and trappings of renown;
  This is the hero's complement and crown;
This missed, one struggle had been wanting still—
One glorious triumph of the heroic will,
  One self-approval in his heart of hearts.
—Henry Taylor.

As the bird trims her to the gale
  I trim myself to the storm of time;
I man the rudder, reef the sail,
  Obey the voice at eve obeyed at prime;
"Lowly faithful banish fear,
  Right onward drive unharmed;
The port, well worth the cruise, is near,
  And every wave is charmed."
—Ralph Waldo Emerson.

DEMAND FOR MEN

The world wants men—large-hearted, manly men;
Men who shall join its chorus and prolong
The psalm of labor, and the psalm of love.
The times want scholars—scholars who shall shape
The doubtful destinies of dubious years,
And land the ark that bears our country's good
Safe on some peaceful Ararat at last.
The age wants heroes—heroes who shall dare
To struggle in the solid ranks of truth;
To clutch the monster error by the throat;
To bear opinion to a loftier seat;
To blot the era of oppression out,
And lead a universal freedom on.
And heaven wants souls—fresh and capacious souls;
To taste its raptures, and expand, like flowers,
Beneath the glory of its central sun.
It wants fresh souls—not lean and shrivelled ones;
It wants fresh souls, my brother, give it thine.
If thou indeed wilt be what scholars should;
If thou wilt be a hero, and wilt strive
To help thy fellow and exalt thyself,
Thy feet at last shall stand on jasper floors;
Thy heart, at last, shall seem a thousand hearts—
Each single heart with myriad raptures filled—
While thou shalt sit with princes and with kings,
Rich in the jewel of a ransomed soul.

Blessed are they who die for God,
And earn the martyr's crown of light;
Yet he who lives for God may be
A greater conqueror in his sight.

Better to stem with heart and hand
The roaring tide of life than lie,
Unmindful, on its flowery strand,
Of God's occasions drifting by!

TRUTH

Truth will prevail, though men abhor
The glory of its light;
And wage exterminating war
And put all foes to flight.

Though trodden under foot of men,
Truth from the dust will spring,
And from the press—the lip—the pen—
In tones of thunder ring.

Beware—beware, ye who resist
The light that beams around,
Lest, ere you look through error's mist,
Truth strike you to the ground.

—D. C. Colesworthy.

TO A REFORMER

Nay, now, if these things that you yearn to teach
Bear wisdom, in your judgment, rich and strong,
Give voice to them though no man heed your speech,
Since right is right though all the world go wrong.

The proof that you believe what you declare
Is that you still stand firm though throngs pass by;
Rather cry truth a lifetime to void air
Than flatter listening millions with one lie!

—Edgar Fawcett.

TEACH ME THE TRUTH

Teach me the truth, Lord, though it put to flight
My cherished dreams and fondest fancy's play;
Give me to know the darkness from the light,
The night from day.

Teach me the truth, Lord, though my heart may break
In casting out the falsehood for the true;
Help me to take my shattered life and make
Its actions new.

Teach me the truth, Lord, though my
feet may fear
The rocky path that opens out to me;
Rough it may be, but let the way be
clear
That leads to thee.

Teach me the truth, Lord. When
false creeds decay,
When man-made dogmas vanish
with the night,
Then, Lord, on thee my darkened soul
shall stay,
Thou living Light.
—Frances Lockwood Green.

HEROISM

It takes great strength to train
To modern service your ancestral
brain;
To lift the weight of the unnumbered
years
Of dead men's habits, methods, and
ideas;
To hold that back with one hand, and
support
With the other the weak steps of the
new thought.

It takes great strength to bring your
life up square
With your accepted thought and hold
it there;
Resisting the inertia that drags back
From new attempts to the old habit's
track.
It is so easy to drift back, to sink;
So hard to live abreast of what you
think.

It takes great strength to live where
you belong
When other people think that you are
wrong;
People you love, and who love you, and
whose
Approval is a pleasure you would
choose.
To bear this pressure and succeed at
length
In living your belief—well, it takes
strength,

And courage, too. But what does
courage mean
Save strength to help you face a pain
foreseen?
Courage to undertake this lifelong
strain
Of setting yours against your grand-
sire's brain;
Dangerous risk of walking lone and
free
Out of the easy paths that used to be,
And the fierce pain of hurting those
we love
When love meets truth, and truth
must ride above.

But the best courage man has ever
shown
Is daring to cut loose and think alone.
Dark are the unlit chambers of clear
space
Where light shines back from no re-
flecting face.
Our sun's wide glare, our heaven's
shining blue,
We owe to fog and dust they fumble
through;
And our rich wisdom that we treasure
so
Shines from the thousand things that
we don't know.
But to think new—it takes a courage
grim
As led Columbus over the world's
rim.
To think it cost some courage. And
to go—
Try it. It takes every power you
know.

It takes great love to stir the human
heart
To live beyond the others and apart.
A love that is not shallow, is not small,
Is not for one or two, but for them
all.
Love that can wound love for its higher
need;
Love that can leave love, though the
heart may bleed;
Love that can lose love, family and
friend,
Yet steadfastly live, loving, to the
end.
A love that asks no answer, that can
live
Moved by one burning, deathless
force—to give.
Love, strength, and courage; courage,
strength, and love.
The heroes of all time are built thereof.
—Charlotte Perkins Stetson.

TO TRUTH

O star of truth down shining
  Through clouds of doubt and fear,
I ask but 'neath your guidance
  My pathway may appear.
However long the journey
  How hard soe'er it be,
Though I be lone and weary,
  Lead on, I'll follow thee.

I know thy blessed radiance
  Can never lead astray,
However ancient custom
  May trend some other way.
E'en if through untried deserts,
  Or over trackless sea,
Though I be lone and weary,
  Lead on, I'll follow thee.

The bleeding feet of martyrs
  Thy toilsome road have trod.
But fires of human passion
  May light the way to God.
Then, though my feet should falter,
  While I thy beams can see,
Though I be lone and weary,
  Lead on, I'll follow thee.

Though loving friends forsake me,
  Or plead with me in tears—
Though angry foes may threaten
  To shake my soul with fears—
Still to my high allegiance
  I must not faithless be.
Through life or death, forever,
  Lead on, I'll follow thee.

—Minot J. Savage.

NOBLESSE OBLIGE

Not ours nobility of this world's giving
  Granted by monarchs of some earthly throne;
Not this life only which is worth the living,
  Nor honor here worth striving for alone.

Princes are we, and of a line right royal;
  Heirs are we of a glorious realm above;
Yet bound to service humble, true, and loyal,
  For thus constraineth us our Monarch's love.

And looking to the joy that lies before us,
  The crown held out to our once fallen race;
Led by the light that ever shineth o'er us,
  Man is restored to nature's noblest place.

Noblesse oblige—(our very watchword be it!)
  To raise the fallen from this low estate,
To boldly combat wrong whene'er we see it,
  To render good for evil, love for hate.

Noblesse oblige—to deeds of valiant daring
  In alien lands which other lords obey,
And into farthest climes our standard bearing,
  To lead them captive 'neath our Master's sway.

Noblesse oblige—that, grudging not our treasure,
  Nor seeking any portion to withhold,
We freely give it, without stint or measure,
  Whate'er it be—our talents, time, or gold.

Noblesse oblige—that, looking upward ever,
  We serve our King with courage, faith, and love,
Till, through that grace which can from death deliver,
  We claim our noble heritage above!

OUR HEROES

The winds that once the Argo bore
  Have died by Neptune's ruined shrines,
And her hull is the drift of the deep sea floor,
  Though shaped of Pelion's tallest pines.
You may seek her crew in every isle,
  Fair in the foam of Ægean seas,
But out of their sleep no charm can wile
  Jason and Orpheus and Hercules.

And Priam's voice is heard no more
  By windy Ilium's sea-built walls;
From the washing wave and the lonely shore
  No wail goes up as Hector falls.
On Ida's mount is the shining snow,
  But Jove has gone from its brow away,
And red on the plain the poppies grow
  Where Greek and Trojan fought that day.

Mother Earth! Are thy heroes dead?
  Do they thrill the soul of the years no more?
Are the gleaming snows and the poppies red
  All that is left of the brave of yore?
Are there none to fight as Theseus fought,
  Far in the young world's misty dawn?
Or teach as the gray-haired Nestor taught?
  Mother Earth! Are thy heroes gone?

Gone?—in a nobler form they rise;
  Dead?—we may clasp their hands in ours,
And catch the light of their glorious eyes,
  And wreathe their brows with immortal flowers.
Whenever a noble deed is done,
  There are the souls of our heroes stirred;
Whenever a field for truth is won,
  There are our heroes' voices heard.

Their armor rings in a fairer field
  Than Greek or Trojan ever trod,
For Freedom's sword is the blade they wield,
  And the light above them the smile of God!
So, in his Isle of calm delight,
  Jason may dream the years away,
But the heroes live, and the skies are bright,
  And the world is a braver world to-day.
—Edna Dean Proctor.

The hero is not fed on sweets,
Daily his own heart he eats;
Chambers of the great are jails,
And head winds right for royal sails.
—Ralph Waldo Emerson.

TRIUMPH OF THE MARTYRS

They seemed to die on battle-field,
  To die with justice, truth, and law;
The bloody corpse, the broken shield,
  Were all that senseless folly saw.
But, like Antæus from the turf,
  They sprung refreshed, to strive again,
Where'er the savage and the serf
  Rise to the rank of men.

They seemed to die by sword and fire,
  Their voices hushed in endless sleep;
Well might the noblest cause expire
  Beneath that mangled, smouldering heap;
Yet that wan band, unarmed, defied
  The legions of their pagan foes;
And in the truths they testified,
  From out the ashes rose.

WORTH WHILE

I pray thee, Lord, that when it comes to me
To say if I will follow truth and Thee,
Or choose instead to win, as better worth
My pains, some cloying recompense of earth—

Grant me, great Father, from a hard-fought field,
Forspent and bruised, upon a battered shield,
Home to obscure endurance to be borne
Rather than live my own mean gains to scorn.
—Edward Sandford Martin.

WILL

O, well for him whose will is strong!
He suffers, but he will not suffer long;
He suffers, but he cannot suffer wrong.
For him nor moves the loud world's random mock,
Nor all Calamity's hugest waves confound,
Who seems a promontory of rock,
That, compassed round with turbulent sound,
In middle ocean meets the surging shock,
Tempest-buffeted, citadel-crowned.
—Alfred Tennyson.

NOBLE DEEDS

Whene'er a noble deed is wrought,
Whene'er is spoken a noble thought,
 Our hearts in glad surprise,
 To higher levels rise.

The tidal wave of deeper souls
Into our inmost being rolls,
 And lifts us unawares
 Out of all meaner cares.

Honor to those whose words or deeds
Thus help us in our daily needs,
 And by their overflow
 Raise us from what is low!
 —Henry Wadsworth Longfellow.

GOD'S HEROES

Not on the gory field of fame
 Their noble deeds were done;
Not in the sound of earth's acclaim
 Their fadeless crowns were won.
Not from the palaces of kings,
 Nor fortune's sunny clime,
Came the great souls, whose life-work flings
 Luster o'er earth and time.

For truth with tireless zeal they sought;
 In joyless paths they trod—
Heedless of praise or blame they wrought,
 And left the rest to God.
The lowliest sphere was not disdained;
 Where love could soothe or save,
They went, by fearless faith sustained,
 Nor knew their deeds were brave.

The foes with which they waged their strife
 Were passion, self, and sin;
The victories that laureled life
 Were fought and won within.
Not names in gold emblazoned here,
 And great and good confessed,
In Heaven's immortal scroll appear
 As noblest and as best.

No sculptured stone in stately temple
 Proclaims their rugged lot;
Like Him who was their great example,
 This vain world knew them not.
But though their names no poet wove
 In deathless song or story,
Their record is inscribed above;
 Their wreaths are crowns of glory.
 —Edward Hartley Dewart.

WORLDLY PLACE

"Even in a palace, life may be led well!"
So spoke the imperial sage, purest of men,
Marcus Aurelius. But the stifling den
Of common life, where, crowded up pell-mell,
Our freedom for a little bread we sell,
And drudge under some foolish master's ken,
Who rates us if we peer outside our pen—
Matched with a palace, is not this a hell?
"Even in a palace!" On his truth sincere,
Who spoke these words no shadow ever came;
And when my ill-schooled spirit is aflame
Some nobler, ampler stage of life to win,
I'll stop and say: "There were no succor here!
The aids to noble life are all within."
 —Matthew Arnold.

THE VICTORY

To do the tasks of life, and be not lost;
 To mingle, yet dwell apart;
To be by roughest seas how rudely tossed,
 Yet bate no jot of heart;

To hold thy course among the heavenly stars,
 Yet dwell upon the earth;
To stand behind Fate's firm-laid prison bars,
 Yet win all Freedom's worth.
 —Sydney Henry Morse.

'Twere sweet indeed to close our eyes with those we cherish near,
And wafted upward by their sighs soar to some calmer sphere;
But whether on the scaffold high or in the battle's van
The fittest place where man can die is where he dies for man.
 —Michael Joseph Barry.

A TRUE HERO

(James Braidwood of the London Fire Brigade; died June, 1861.)

Not at the battle front, writ of in story,
Not in the blazing wreck, steering to glory;

Not while in martyr-pangs soul and flesh sever,
Died he—this Hero now; hero forever.

No pomp poetic crowned, no forms enchained him;
No friends applauding watched, no foes arraigned him;

Death found him there, without grandeur or beauty.
Only an honest man doing his duty;

Just a God-fearing man, simple and lowly,
Constant at kirk and hearth, kindly as holy;

Death found—and touched him with finger in flying—
Lo! he rose up complete—hero undying.

Now all men mourn for him, lovingly raise him,
Up from his life obscure, chronicle, praise him;

Tell his last act; done 'midst peril appalling,
And the last word of cheer from his lips falling;

Follow in multitudes to his grave's portal;
Leave him there, buried in honor immortal.

So many a Hero walks unseen beside us,
Till comes the supreme stroke sent to divide us.

Then the Lord calls his own—like this man, even,
Carried, Elijah-like, fire-winged, to heaven.

—Dinah Maria Mulock Craik.

Unless above himself he can
Erect himself, how poor a thing is man.

—Samuel Daniel.

BATTLES

Nay, not for place, but for the right,
To make this fair world fairer still—
Or lowly lily of the night,
Or sun topped tower of a hill,
Or high or low, or near or far,
Or dull or keen, or bright or dim,
Or blade of grass, or brightest star—
All, all are but the same to him.

O pity of the strife for place!
O pity of the strife for power!
How scarred, how marred a mountain's face!
How fair the face of a flower!
The blade of grass beneath your feet
The bravest sword—aye, braver far
To do and die in mute defeat
Than bravest conqueror of war!

When I am dead, say this, but this:
"He grasped at no man's blade or shield.
Or banner bore, but helmetless,
Alone, unknown, he held the field;
He held the field, with sabre drawn,
Where God had set him in the fight;
He held the field, fought on and on,
And so fell, fighting for the right!"

—Joaquin Miller.

While thus to love he gave his days
In loyal worship, scorning praise,
How spread their lures for him in vain,
Thieving Ambition and paltering Gain!
He thought it happier to be dead,
To die for Beauty than live for bread.

—Ralph Waldo Emerson.

Whether we climb, whether we plod,
Space for one task the scant years lend,
To choose some path that leads to God,
And keep it to the end.

—Lizette Woodworth Reese.

Bravely to do whate'er the time demands,
Whether with pen or sword, and not to flinch,
This is the task that fits heroic hands;
So are Truth's boundaries widened, inch by inch.

—James Russell Lowell.

COURAGE

CONSTANCY, CONFIDENCE, STRENGTH, VALOR

THE BATTLEFIELD

Once this soft turf, this rivulet's sands,
 Were trampled by a hurrying crowd,
And fiery hearts and armed hands
 Encountered in the battle cloud.

Ah! never shall the land forget
 How gushed the life-blood of her brave—
Gushed, warm with life and courage yet,
 Upon the soil they fought to save.

Now all is calm and fresh and still,
 Alone the chirp of flitting bird,
And talks of children on the hill,
 And bell of wandering kine are heard.

No solemn host goes trailing by
 The black-mouthed gun and staggering wain;
Men start not at the battle-cry;
 Oh, be it never heard again!

Soon rested those who fought; but thou
 Who minglest in the harder strife
For truths which men receive not now,
 Thy warfare only ends with life.

A friendless warfare! lingering long
 Through weary day and weary year;
A wild and many-weaponed throng
 Hang on thy front, and flank, and rear.

Yet nerve thy spirit to the proof.
 And blench not at thy chosen lot;
The timid good may stand aloof,
 The sage may frown—yet faint thou not.

Nor heed the shaft too surely cast,
 The foul and hissing bolt of scorn;
For with thy side shall dwell at last
 The victory of endurance born.

Truth, crushed to earth, shall rise again;
 The eternal years of God are hers;
But Error, wounded, writhes in pain,
 And dies among his worshipers.

Yea, though thou lie upon the dust,
 When they who helped thee flee in fear,
Die full of hope and manly trust,
 Like those who fell in battle here.

Another hand thy sword shall wield,
 Another hand the standard wave,
Till from the trumpet's mouth is pealed,
 The blast of triumph o'er thy grave.

—William Cullen Byrant.

DARE YOU?

Doubting Thomas and loving John,
Behind the others walking on:

"Tell me now, John, dare you be
One of the minority?
To be lonely in your thought,
Never visited nor sought,
Shunned with secret shrug, to go
Through the world esteemed its foe;
To be singled out and hissed,
Pointed at as one unblessed,
Warned against in whispers faint,
Lest the children catch a taint;
To bear off your titles well,—
Heretic and infidel?
If you dare, come now with me,
Fearless, confident and free."

"Thomas, do you dare to be
Of the great majority?
To be only, as the rest,
With Heaven's common comforts blessed;

To accept, in humble part,
Truth that shines on every heart;
Never to be set on high,
Where the envious curses fly;
Never name or fame to find,
Still outstripped in soul and mind;
To be hid, unless to God,
As one grass-blade in the sod;
Underfoot with millions trod?
If you dare, come with us, be
Lost in love's great unity."
—Edward Rowland Sill.

SENSITIVENESS

Time was I shrank from what was right,
From fear of what was wrong;
I would not brave the sacred fight
Because the foe was strong.

But now I cast that finer sense
And sorer shame aside;
Such dread of sin was indolence,
Such aim at heaven was pride.

So when my Saviour calls I rise,
And calmly do my best;
Leaving to Him, with silent eyes
Of hope and fear, the rest.

I step, I mount, where He has led;
Men count my haltings o'er;
I know them; yet, though self I dread,
I love His precept more.
—John Henry Newman.

COURAGE

Because I hold it sinful to despond,
And will not let the bitterness of life
Blind me with burning tears, but look beyond
Its tumult and its strife;
Because I lift my head above the mist,
Where the sun shines and the broad breezes blow,
By every ray and every rain-drop kissed
That God's love doth bestow;

Think you I find no bitterness at all?
No burden to be borne, like Christian's pack?
Think you there are no ready tears to fall
Because I keep them back?

Why should I hug life's ills with cold reserve,
To curse myself and all who love me? Nay!
A thousand times more good than I deserve
God gives me every day.

And in each one of these rebellious tears
Kept bravely back He makes a rainbow shine;
Gratefully I take His slightest gift, no fears
Nor any doubts are mine.

Dark skies must clear, and when the clouds are past
One golden day redeems a weary year;
Patient I listen, sure that sweet at last
Will sound his voice of cheer.

Then vex me not with chiding. Let me be.
I must be glad and grateful to the end.
I grudge you not your cold and darkness,—me
The powers of light befriend.
—Celia Thaxter.

DO AND BE BLEST

Dare to think, though others frown;
Dare in words your thoughts express;
Dare to rise, though oft cast down;
Dare the wronged and scorned to bless.

Dare from custom to depart;
Dare the priceless pearl possess;
Dare to wear it next your heart;
Dare, when others curse, to bless.

Dare forsake what you deem wrong;
Dare to walk in wisdom's way;
Dare to give where gifts belong,
Dare God's precepts to obey.

Do what conscience says is right,
Do what reason says is best,
Do with all your mind and might;
Do your duty and be blest.

A PLACE WITH HIM

O tired worker, faltering on life's rugged way,
With faithful hands so full they may not rest,
Forget not that the weak of earth have one sure stay,
And humblest ones by God himself are blest,
Who work for Him!

Then courage take, faint heart! and though the path be long
God's simple rule thy steps will safely guide:—
"Love Him, thy neighbor as thyself, and do no wrong";
In calm content they all shall surely bide
Who walk with Him!

So banish every fear, each daily task take up,
God's grace thy failing strength shall build anew;
His mercy, in thy sorrows, stay the flowing cup:
And His great love keep for thy spirit true
A place with him!

—J. D. Seabury.

GOD A FORTRESS

A mighty fortress is our God,
A bulwark never failing:
Our Helper, he, amid the flood
Of mortal ills prevailing.
For still our ancient foe
Doth seek to work us woe;
His craft and power are great,
And, armed with cruel hate,
On earth is not his equal.

Did we in our own strength confide,
Our striving would be losing;
Were not the right man on our side,
The man of God's own choosing.
Dost ask who that may be?
Christ Jesus, it is he;
Lord Sabaoth is his name,
From age to age the same,
And he must win the battle.

And though this world, with devils filled,
Should threaten to undo us;
We will not fear, for God hath willed
His truth to triumph through us.
The Prince of darkness grim—
We tremble not for him;
His rage we can endure,
For lo! his doom is sure,
One little word shall fell him.

That word above all earthly powers—
No thanks to them—abideth;
The Spirit and the gifts are ours
Through him who with us sideth.
Let goods and kindred go,
This mortal life also;
The body they may kill:
God's truth abideth still,
His kingdom is forever.

—Martin Luther, tr. by Frederick H. Hedge.

STRENGTH

Be strong to hope, O heart!
Though day is bright,
The stars can only shine
In the dark night.
Be strong, O heart of mine,
Look toward the light.

Be strong to bear, O heart!
Nothing is vain:
Strive not, for life is care,
And God sends pain.
Heaven is above, and there
Rest will remain.

Be strong to love, O heart!
Love knows not wrong;
Didst thou love creatures even,
Life were not long;
Didst thou love God in heaven
Thou wouldst be strong.

Why comes temptation but for man to meet
And master and make crouch beneath his foot,
And so be pedestaled in triumph? Pray,
"Lead us into no such temptation, Lord!"
Yea, but, O thou whose servants are the bold,
Lead such temptations by the head and hair,
Reluctant dragons, up to who dares fight,
That so he may do battle and have praise.

—Robert Browning.

BE JUST AND FEAR NOT

Speak thou the truth. Let others fence,
And trim their words for pay:
In pleasant sunshine of pretense
Let others bask their day.

Guard thou the fact; though clouds of night
Down on thy watch tower stoop:
Though thou shouldst see thine heart's delight
Borne from thee by their swoop.

Face thou the wind. Though safer seem
In shelter to abide:
We were not made to sit and dream:
The safe must first be tried.

Where God hath set His thorns about,
Cry not, "The way is plain":
His path within for those without
Is paved with toil and pain.

One fragment of His blessed Word,
Into thy spirit burned,
Is better than the whole half-heard
And by thine interest turned.

Show thou thy light. If conscience gleam,
Set not thy bushel down;
The smallest spark may send his beam
O'er hamlet, tower, and town.

Woe, woe to him, on safety bent,
Who creeps to age from youth,
Failing to grasp his life's intent
Because he fears the truth.

Be true to every inmost thought,
And as thy thought, thy speech:
What thou hast not by suffering bought,
Presume thou not to teach.

Hold on, hold on—thou hast the rock,
The foes are on the sand:
The first world tempest's ruthless shock
Scatters their drifting strand:

While each wild gust the mist shall clear
We now see darkly through,
And justified at last appear
The true, in Him that's True.

—Henry Alford.

COURAGE DEFINED

The brave man is not he who feels no fear,
For that were stupid and irrational;
But he whose noble soul its fear subdues,
And bravely dares the danger nature shrinks from.
As for your youth whom blood and blows delight,
Away with them! there is not in their crew
One valiant spirit.

—Joanna Baillie.

DEMAND FOR COURAGE

Thy life's a warfare, thou a soldier art;
Satan's thy foeman, and a faithful heart
Thy two-edged weapon; patience is thy shield,
Heaven is thy chieftain, and the world thy field.
To be afraid to die, or wish for death,
Are words and passions of despairing breath.
Who doth the first the day doth faintly yield;
And who the second basely flies the field.

—Francis Quarles.

When falls the hour of evil chance—
And hours of evil chance will fall—
Strike, though with but a broken lance!
Strike, though you have no lance at all!

Shrink not, however great the odds;
Shrink not, however dark the hour—
The barest possibility of good
Demands your utmost power.

They are slaves who fear to speak
For the fallen and the weak;
They are slaves who will not choose
Hatred, scoffing and abuse,
Rather than in silence shrink
From the truth they needs must think;
They are slaves who dare not be
In the right with two or three.

—James Russell Lowell.

TRUST IN GOD AND DO THE RIGHT

Courage, brother, do not stumble,
  Though thy path be dark as night;
There's a star to guide the humble—
  Trust in God and do the right.
Though the road be long and dreary,
  And the end be out of sight;
Foot it bravely, strong or weary—
  Trust in God and do the right.

Perish "policy" and cunning,
  Perish all that fears the light;
Whether losing, whether winning,
  Trust in God and do the right.
Shun all forms of guilty passion,
  Fiends can look like angels bright;
Heed no custom, school, or fashion—
  Trust in God and do the right.

Some will hate thee, some will love thee,
  Some will flatter, some will slight;
Cease from man and look above thee,
  Trust in God and do the right.
Simple rule and safest guiding—
  Inward peace and shining light—
Star upon our path abiding—
  TRUST IN GOD AND DO THE RIGHT.
—Norman Macleod.

THE PRESENT CRISIS

We are living, we are dwelling, in a grand and awful time.
In an age on ages telling to be living is sublime.
Hark! the waking up of nations; Gog and Magog to the fray.
Hark! what soundeth? 'Tis creation groaning for its latter day.

Will ye play, then, will ye dally, with your music and your wine?
Up! it is Jehovah's rally; God's own arm hath need of thine;
Hark! the onset! will ye fold your faith-clad arms in lazy lock?
Up! O up, thou drowsy soldier! Worlds are charging to the shock.

Worlds are charging—heaven beholding; thou hast but an hour to fight;
Now the blazoned cross unfolding, on, right onward for the right!
On! let all the soul within you for the truth's sake go abroad!
Strike! let every nerve and sinew tell on ages; tell for God!
—Arthur Cleveland Coxe.

BRAVERY

We will speak on; we will be heard;
  Though all earth's systems crack,
We will not bate a single word,
  Nor take a letter back.

We speak the truth; and what care we
  For hissing and for scorn
While some faint gleaming we can see
  Of Freedom's coming morn!

Let liars fear; let cowards shrink;
  Let traitors turn away;
Whatever we have dared to think,
  That dare we also say.
—James Russell Lowell.

NO ENEMIES

He has no enemies, you say?
  My friend, your boast is poor;
He who hath mingled in the fray
  Of duty, that the brave endure,
Must have made foes. If he has none
Small is the work that he has done.
He has hit no traitor on the hip;
He has cast no cup from tempted lip;
He has never turned the wrong to right;
He has been a coward in the fight.

One deed may mar a life,
  And one can make it.
Hold firm thy will for strife,
  Lest a quick blow break it!
Even now from far, on viewless wing,
Hither speeds the nameless thing
  Shall put thy spirit to the test.
Haply or e'er yon sinking sun
  Shall drop behind the purple West
All shall be lost—or won!
—Richard Watson Gilder.

In spite of sorrow, loss, and pain,
  Our course be onward still;
We sow on Burmah's barren plain,
  We reap on Zion's hill.
—Adoniram Judson.

I find no foeman in the road but Fear.
To doubt is failure and to dare success.
—Frederic Lawrence Knowles.

DARE TO DO RIGHT

Dare to do right! dare to be true!
You have a work that no other can do,
Do it so bravely, so kindly, so well,
Angels will hasten the story to tell.

Dare to do right! dare to be true!
Other men's failures can never save you;
Stand by your conscience, your honor, your faith;
Stand like a hero, and battle till death.

Dare to do right! dare to be true!
God, who created you, cares for you too;
Treasures the tears that his striving ones shed,
Counts and protects every hair of your head.

Dare to do right! dare to be true!
Keep the great judgment-seat always in view;
Look at your work as you'll look at it then—
Scanned by Jehovah, and angels, and men.

Dare to do right! dare to be true!
Cannot Omnipotence carry you through?
City, and mansion, and throne all in sight—
Can you not dare to be true and do right?

Dare to do right! dare to be true!
Prayerfully, lovingly, firmly pursue
The path by apostles and martyrs once trod,
The path of the just to the city of God.

—George Lansing Taylor.

PLUCK WINS

Pluck wins! It always wins! though days be slow,
And nights be dark 'twixt days that come and go,
Still pluck will win; its average is sure,
He gains the prize who will the most endure;
Who faces issues; he who never shirks;
Who waits and watches, and who always works.

BE NEVER DISCOURAGED

Be never discouraged!
Look up and look on;
When the prospect is darkest
The cloud is withdrawn.
The shadows that blacken
The earth and the sky,
Speak to the strong-hearted,
Salvation is nigh.

Be never discouraged!
If you would secure
The earth's richest blessings,
And make heaven sure,
Yield not in the battle,
Nor quail in the blast;
The brave and unyielding
Win nobly at last.

Be never discouraged!
By day and by night
Have glory in prospect
And wisdom in sight;
Undaunted and faithful,
You never will fail,
Though kingdoms oppose you
And devils assail.

—D. C. Colesworthy.

NEVER SAY FAIL

Keep pushing—'tis wiser than sitting aside
And dreaming and sighing and waiting the tide.
In life's earnest battle they only prevail
Who daily march onward, and never say fail.

With an eye ever open, a tongue that's not dumb,
And a heart that will never to sorrow succumb,
You'll battle—and conquer, though thousands assail;
How strong and how mighty, who never say fail.

In life's rosy morning, in manhood's firm pride,
Let this be the motto your footsteps to guide:
In storm and in sunshine, whatever assail,
We'll onward and conquer, and never say fail.

ONLY ONE WAY

However the battle is ended,
Though proudly the victor comes,
With fluttering flags and prancing nags
And echoing roll of drums,
Still truth proclaims this motto,
In letters of living light:
No question is ever settled
Until it is settled right.

Though the heel of the strong oppressor
May grind the weak in the dust,
And the voices of fame with one acclaim
May call him great and just,
Let those who applaud take warning,
And keep this motto in sight:
No question is ever settled
Until it is settled right.

Let those who have failed take courage;
Though the enemy seemed to have won,
Though his ranks are strong, if in the wrong
The battle is not yet done.
For, sure as the morning follows
The darkest hour of the night,
No question is ever settled
Until it is settled right.

FORTITUDE AMID TRIALS

O, never from thy tempted heart
Let thine integrity depart!
When Disappointment fills thy cup,
Undaunted, nobly drink it up;
Truth will prevail and Justice show
Her tardy honors, sure, though slow.
Bear on—bear bravely on!

Bear on! Our life is not a dream,
Though often such its mazes seem;
We were not born for lives of ease,
Ourselves alone to aid and please.
To each a daily task is given,
A labor which shall fit for Heaven;
When Duty calls, let Love grow warm;
Amid the sunshine and the storm,
With Faith life's trials boldly breast,
And come a conqueror to thy rest.
Bear on—bear bravely on!

He that feeds men serveth few;
He serves all who dares be true.
—Ralph Waldo Emerson.

PLUCK

Be firm. One constant element in luck
Is genuine, solid, old Teutonic pluck.
See yon tall shaft? It felt the earthquake's thrill,
Clung to its base, and greets the sunlight still.

Stick to your aim; the mongrel's hold will slip,
But only crow-bars loose the bulldog's grip;
Small as he looks, the jaw that never yields
Drags down the bellowing monarch of the fields.

Yet, in opinions look not always back;
Your wake is nothing,—mind the coming track;
Leave what you've done for what you have to do,
Don't be "consistent," but be simply true.
—Oliver Wendell Holmes.

Do thy little; do it well;
Do what right and reason tell;
Do what wrong and sorrow claim:
Conquer sin and cover shame.
Do thy little, though it be
Dreariness and drudgery;
They whom Christ apostles made
Gathered fragments when he bade.

Is the work difficult?
Jesus directs thee.
Is the path dangerous?
Jesus protects thee.

Fear not and falter not;
Let the word cheer thee:
All through the coming year
He will be near thee.

Well to suffer is divine.
Pass the watchword down the line,
Pass the countersign, Endure!
Not to him who rashly dares,
But to him who nobly bears,
Is the victor's garland sure.
—John Greenleaf Whittier.

'f thou canst plan a noble deed
\nd never flag till thou succeed,
Though in the strife thy heart shall bleed,
Whatever obstacles control,
Thine hour will come; go on, true soul!
Thou'lt win the prize; thou'lt reach the goal.

---

 honor the man who is willing to sink
Half his present repute for freedom to think;
And when he has that, be his cause strong or weak,
Will risk t'other half for freedom to speak. —James Russell Lowell.

The word is great, and no deed is greater
When both are of God, to follow or lead;
But alas! for the truth when the word comes later,
With questioned steps, to sustain the deed. —John Boyle O'Reilly.

Stand upright, speak thy thought, declare
The truth thou hast that all may share;
Be bold, proclaim it everywhere;
They only live who dare.
—Lewis Morris.

There is no duty patent in the world
Like daring try be good and true myself,
Leaving the shows of things to the Lord of show
And Prince o' the power of the air.
—Robert Browning.

Tender-handed stroke a nettle,
And it stings you for your pains;
Grasp it like a man of mettle,
And it soft as silk remains.
—Aaron Hill (1685–1750).

On the red rampart's slippery swell,
With heart that beat a charge, he fell
Foeward, as fits a man;
But the high soul burns on to light men's feet
Where death for noble ends makes dying sweet.
—James Russell Lowell.

I do not ask that Thou shalt front the fray.
And drive the warring foeman from my sight:
I only ask, O Lord, by night, by day,
Strength for the fight!

No coward soul is mine,
No trembler in the world's storm-troubled sphere;
I see Heaven's glories shine,
And faith shines equal, arming me from fear. —Emily Brontë.

You will find that luck
Is only pluck
To try things over and over;
Patience and skill,
Courage and will,
Are the four leaves of luck's clover.

The chivalry
That dares the right and disregards alike
The yea and nay o' the world.
—Robert Browning.

God has his best things for the few
Who dare to stand the test;
He has his second choice for those
Who will not have his best.

Dare to be true; nothing can need a lie;
A fault which needs it most grows two thereby. —George Herbert.

INDEPENDENCE

MANHOOD, FIRMNESS, EARNESTNESS, RESOLUTION

WANTED

God give us men! A time like this
demands
Strong minds, great hearts, true faith,
and ready hands;
Men whom the lust of office does not
kill;
Men whom the spoils of office cannot
buy;
Men who possess opinions and a will;
Men who have honor—men who will
not lie.
Men who can stand before a demagogue
And damn his treacherous flatteries
without winking;
Tall men, sun-crowned, who live above
the fog
In public duty and in private think-
ing;
For while the rabble, with their thumb-
worn creeds,
Their large professions and their little
deeds,
Mingle in selfish strife, lo! Freedom
weeps,
Wrong rules the land, and waiting
Justice sleeps.

—Josiah Gilbert Holland.

TO THINE OWN SELF BE TRUE

By thine own soul's law learn to live,
And if men thwart thee take no
heed;
And if men hate thee have no care;
Sing thou thy song, and do thy deed;
Hope thou thy hope, and pray thy
prayer,
And claim no crown they will not
give,
Nor bays they grudge thee for thy hair.

Keep thou thy soul-won, steadfast oath,
And to thy heart be true thy heart;
What thy soul teaches learn to know,
And play out thine appointed part,
And thou shalt reap as thou shalt sow,
Nor helped nor hardened in thy
growth,
To thy full stature thou shalt grow.

Fix on the future's goal thy face,
And let thy feet be lured to stray
Nowhither, but be swift to run,
And nowhere tarry by the way,
Until at last the end is won,
And thou mayst look back from thy
place
And see thy long day's journey done.

—Pakenham Beatty.

LORD OF HIMSELF

How happy is he born and taught
That serveth not another's will;
Whose armor is his honest thought,
And simple truth his utmost skill.

Whose passions not his masters are,
Whose soul is still prepared for death;
Not tied unto the world with care
Of public fame or private breath.

Who envies none that chance doth
raise,
Or vice; who never understood
How deepest wounds are given by
praise,
Nor rules of state but rules of good.

Who hath his life from rumors freed,
Whose conscience is his strong retreat;
Whose state can neither flatterers feed,
Nor ruin make accusers great.

Who God doth late and early pray
More of his grace than gifts to lend;
And entertains the harmless day
With a well-chosen book or friend.

This man is freed from servile bands,
Of hope to rise or fear to fall;
Lord of himself, though not of lands,
And having nothing, yet hath all.

—Henry Wotton.

High above hate I dwell;
O storms, farewell!

UNCONQUERED

Out of the night that covers me,
Black as the pit from pole to pole,
I thank whatever gods may be
For my unconquerable soul.

Beyond this place of wrath and tears
Looms but the horror of the shade,
And yet the menace of the years
Finds and shall find me unafraid.

In the fell clutch of circumstance
I have not winced nor cried aloud;
Under the bludgeonings of chance
My head is bloody, but unbowed.

It matters not how strait the gate,
How charged with punishments the scroll;
I am the master of my fate,
I am the captain of my soul.

—William Ernest Henley.

RELIGION AND DOCTRINE

He stood before the Sanhedrim:
The scowling rabbis gazed at him.
He recked not of their praise or blame;
There was no fear, there was no shame,
For one upon whose dazzled eyes
The whole world poured its vast surprise.
The open heaven was far too near
His first day's light too sweet and clear,
To let him waste his new-gained ken
On the hate-clouded face of men.

But still they questioned, Who art thou?
What hast thou been? What art thou now?
Thou art not he who yesterday
Sat here and begged beside the way,
For he was blind.
"*And I am he;*
For I was blind, but now I see."

He told the story o'er and o'er;
It was his full heart's only lore;
A prophet on the Sabbath day
Had touched his sightless eyes with clay,
And made him see who had been blind.
Their words passed by him like the wind
Which raves and howls, but cannot shock
The hundred-fathom-rooted rock.

Their threats and fury all went wide;
They could not touch his Hebrew pride.
Their sneers at Jesus and his band,
Nameless and homeless in the land,
Their boasts of Moses and his Lord,
All could not change him by one word.

"*I know not what this man may be,*
Sinner or saint; but as for me
One thing I know: that I am he
Who once was blind, and now I see."

They were all doctors of renown,
The great men of a famous town
With deep brows, wrinkled, broad, and wise
Beneath their wide phylacteries;
The wisdom of the East was theirs,
And honor crowned their silvery hairs.
The man they jeered, and laughed to scorn
Was unlearned, poor, and humbly born;
But he knew better far than they
What came to him that Sabbath day;
And what the Christ had done for him
He knew, and not the Sanhedrim.

—John Hay.

THE OLD STOIC

Riches I hold in light esteem,
And Love I laugh to scorn;
And lust of fame was but a dream,
That vanished with the morn.

And, if I pray, the only prayer
That moves my lips for me
Is, "Leave the heart that now I bear,
And give me liberty!"

Yes, as my swift days near their goal,
'Tis all that I implore,
In life and death a chainless soul
And courage to endure.

—Emily Brontë.

Keep to the right, within and without,
With stranger and pilgrim and friend;
Keep to the right and you need have no doubt
That all will be well in the end.
Keep to the right in whatever you do,
Nor claim but your own on the way;
Keep to the right, and hold on to the true,
From the morn to the close of life's day!

FOR A' THAT

Is there for honest poverty
 That hangs his head, and a' that?
The coward slave, we pass him by,
 We dare be poor for a' that;
 For a' that and a' that;
 Our toils obscure and a' that;
The rank is but the guinea-stamp,
 The man's the gowd for a' that.

What though on hamely fare we dine,
 Wear hodden gray, and a' that:
Gie fools their silks and knaves their wine,
 A man's a man for a' that;
 For a' that and a' that,
 Their tinsel show, and a' that,
The honest man, though e'er sae poor,
 Is king o' men, for a' that.

You see yon birkie ca'd a lord,
 Wha struts and stares, and a' that:
Though hundreds worship at his word
 He's but a coof for a' that.
 For a' that and a' that,
 His riband, star, and a' that,
The man of independent mind,
 He looks and laughs at a' that.

A prince can mak a belted knight,
 A marquis, duke, and a' that;
But an honest man's aboon his might,
 Guid faith, he maunna fa' that,
 For a' that and a' that,
 Their dignities, and a' that,
The pith of sense and pride o' worth,
 Are higher ranks than a' that.

Then let us pray that come it may,
 As come it will, for a' that,
That sense and worth o'er a' the earth,
 May bear the gree and a' that;
 For a' that and a' that,
 It's comin' yet for a' that,
That man to man, the warld o'er,
 Shall brothers be, for a' that.

—Robert Burns.

Stone walls do not a prison make,
 Nor iron bars a cage;
Minds innocent and quiet take
 That for a hermitage;
If I have freedom in my love,
 And in my soul am free,
Angels alone, that soar above,
 Enjoy such liberty.

—Richard Lovelace.

"A MAN'S A MAN FOR A' THAT"

(A new song to an old tune.)

"A man's a man," says Robert Burns,
 "For a' that and a' that";
But though the song be clear and strong
 It lacks a note for a' that.
The lout who'd shirk his daily work,
 Yet claim his wage and a' that,
Or beg when he might earn his bread,
 Is *not* a man for a' that.

If all who "dine on homely fare"
 Were true and brave and a' that,
And none whose garb is "hodden gray"
 Was fool or knave and a' that,
The vice and crime that shame our time
 Would disappear and a' that,
And plowmen be as great as kings,
 And churls as earls for a' that.

But 'tis not so; yon brawny fool,
 Who swaggers, swears, and a' that,
And thinks because his strong right arm
 Might fell an ox, and a' that,
That he's as noble, man for man,
 As duke or lord, and a' that,
Is but an animal at best
 But *not* a man for a' that.

A man may own a large estate,
 Have palace, park, and a' that,
And not for birth, but honest worth,
 Be thrice a man for a' that.
And Sawnie, herding on the moor,
 Who beats his wife and a' that,
Is nothing but a brutal boor,
 Nor half a man for a' that.

It comes to this, dear Robert Burns,
 The truth is old, and a' that,
The rank *is* but the guinea's stamp,
 The man's the gowd for a' that.
And though you'd put the self-same mark
 On copper, brass, and a' that,
The lie is gross, the cheat is plain,
 And will not pass for a' that.

"For a' that and a' that"
 'Tis soul and heart and a' that
That makes a king a gentleman,
 And not his crown for a' that.
And whether he be rich or poor
 The best is he, for a' that,
Who stands erect in self-respect,
 And acts the man for a' that.

—Charles Mackay.

ESSE QUAM VIDERI

The knightly legend on thy shield betrays
The moral of thy life; a forecast wise,
And that large honor that deceit defies,
Inspired thy fathers in the elder days,
Who decked thy scutcheon with that sturdy phrase,
To be, rather than seem. As eve's red skies
Surpass the morning's rosy prophecies,
Thy life to that proud boast its answer pays,
Scorning thy faith and purpose to defend.
The ever-mutable multitude at last
Will hail the power they did not comprehend—
Thy fame will broaden through the centuries;
As, storm and billowy tumult overpast,
The moon rules calmly o'er the conquered seas. —John Hay.

THE HIGHER LAW

Man was not made for forms, but forms for man,
And there are times when law itself must bend
To that clear spirit always in the van,
Outspeeding human justice. In the end
Potentates, not humanity, must fall.
Water will find its level, fire will burn,
The winds must blow around the earthly ball,
The earthly ball by day and night must turn;
Freedom is typed in every element,
Man must be free, if not through law, why then
Above the law, until its force be spent
And justice brings a better. But, O, when,
Father of Light, when shall the reckoning come
To lift the weak, and strike the oppressor dumb.—Christopher Pearse Cranch.

What I am, what I am not, in the eye
Of the world, is what I never cared for much. —Robert Browning.

I RESOLVE

To keep my health;
To do my work;
To live;
To see to it that I grow and gain and give;
Never to look behind me for an hour;
To wait in meekness, and to walk in power;
But always fronting onward, to the light,
Always and always facing toward the right.
Robbed, starved, defeated, fallen, wide-astray—
On, with what strength I have—
Back to the way.
—Charlotte Perkins Stetson.

IN MYSELF

I do not ask for any crown
But that which all may win;
Nor try to conquer any world
Except the one within.
Be thou my guide until I find
Led by a tender hand,
The happy kingdom in myself
And dare to take command.
—Louisa May Alcott.

HIDE NOT THY HEART

This is my creed,
This is my deed:
"Hide not thy heart!"
Soon we depart;
Mortals are all;
A breath, then the pall;
A flash on the dark—
All's done—stiff and stark.
No time for a lie;
The truth, and then die.
Hide not thy heart!

Forth with thy thought!
Soon 'twill be naught,
And thou in thy tomb.
Now is air, now is room.
Down with false shame;
Reck not of fame;
Dread not man's spite;
Quench not thy light.
This be thy creed,
This be thy deed:
"Hide not thy heart!"

If God is, he made
Sunshine and shade,
Heaven and hell;
This we know well.
Dost thou believe?
Do not deceive;
Scorn not thy faith—
If 'tis a wraith
Soon it will fly.
Thou who must die,
Hide not thy heart!

This is my creed,
This be my deed:
Faith, or a doubt,
I shall speak out—
And hide not my heart.
—Richard Watson Gilder.

A GENTLEMAN

(Psa. xv.)

'Tis he whose every thought and deed
By rule of virtue moves;
Whose generous tongue disdains to speak
The thing his heart disproves.

Who never did a slander forge
His neighbor's fame to wound;
Nor hearken to a false report
By malice whispered round.

Who vice in all its pomp and power
Can treat with just neglect;
And piety, though clothed in rags,
Religiously respect.

Who to his plighted word of truth
Has ever firmly stood;
And, though he promised to his loss,
Still makes his promise good.

Whose soul in usury disdains
His treasure to employ;
Whom no reward can ever bribe
The guiltless to destroy.

I hold it as a changeless law,
From which no soul can sway or swerve,
We have that in us which will draw
Whate'er we need or most deserve.

BE TRUE THYSELF

Thou must be true thyself
If thou the truth wouldst teach;
Thy soul must overflow if thou
Another's soul wouldst reach.
It needs the overflow of heart
To give the lips full speech.

Think truly, and thy thoughts
Shall the world's famine feed;
Speak truly, and each word of thine
Shall be a fruitful seed;
Live truly, and thy life shall be
A great and noble creed.
—Horatius Bonar.

Keep pure thy soul!
Then shalt thou take the whole
Of delight;
Then, without a pang,
Thine shall be all of beauty whereof the poet sang—
The perfume and the pageant, the melody, the mirth,
Of the golden day and the starry night;
Of heaven and of earth.
Oh, keep pure thy soul!
—Richard Watson Gilder.

Somebody did a golden deed;
Somebody proved a friend in need;
Somebody sang a beautiful song;
Somebody smiled the whole day long;
Somebody thought, "'Tis sweet to live."
Somebody said, "I'm glad to give";
Somebody fought a valiant fight;
Somebody lived to shield the right;
Was it you?

Then draw we nearer, day by day,
Each to his brethren, all to God;
Let the world take us as she may,
We must not change our road;
Not wondering, though in grief, to find
The martyr's foe still keep her mind;
But fixed to hold Love's banner fast,
And by submission win at last.
—John Keble.

Knowing, what all experience serves to show,
No mud can soil us but the mud we throw.
—James Russell Lowell.

Be no imitator; freshly act thy part;
Through this world be thou an independent ranger;
Better is the faith that springeth from thy heart
Than a better faith belonging to a stranger. —From the Persian.

None but one can harm you,
None but yourself who are your greatest foe,
He that respects himself is safe from others,
He wears a coat of mail that none can pierce.
—Henry Wadsworth Longfellow.

And some innative weakness there must be
In him that condescends to victory
Such as the *present* gives, and cannot wait—
Safe in himself as in a fate.
—James Russell Lowell.

To be the thing we seem,
To do the thing we deem
Enjoined by duty;
To walk in faith, nor dream
Of questioning God's scheme
Of truth and beauty.

To live by law, acting the law we live by without fear,
And, because right is right, to follow right,
Were wisdom, in the scorn of consequence. —Alfred Tennyson.

Though love repine, and reason chafe,
There came a voice without reply:
"'Tis man's perdition to be safe,
When for the truth he ought to die."
—Ralph Waldo Emerson.

Whatever you are—be that;
Whatever you say—be true;
Straightforwardly act—
Be honest—in fact
Be nobody else but you.

If thou *hast* something, bring thy goods;
A fair exchange be thine!
If thou *art* something, bring thy soul,
And interchange with mine.
—Schiller, tr. by Edward Bulwer Lytton.

However others act toward thee,
Act thou toward them as seemeth right;
And whatsoever others be,
Be thou the child of love and light.

This above all: to thine own self be true,
And it must follow, as the night the day,
Thou canst not then be false to any man. —William Shakespeare.

My time is short enough at best,
I push right onward while I may;
I open to the winds my breast,
And walk the way.
—John Vance Cheney.

Not in the clamor of the crowded street,
Not in the shouts and plaudits of the throng,
But in ourselves are triumph and defeat.
—Henry Wadsworth Longfellow.

It becomes no man to nurse despair,
But in the teeth of clenched antagonisms
To follow up the worthiest till he die.
—Alfred Tennyson.

GREATNESS

FAME, SUCCESS, PROGRESS, VICTORY

A GREAT MAN

That man is great, and he alone,
Who serves a greatness not his own,
For neither praise nor pelf;
Content to know and be unknown:
Whole in himself.

Strong is that man, he only strong,
To whose well-ordered will belong,
For service and delight,
All powers that, in the face of Wrong,
Establish Right.

And free is he, and only he,
Who, from his tyrant passions free,
By Fortune undismayed,
Hath power upon himself, to be
By himself obeyed.

If such a man there be, where'er
Beneath the sun and moon he fare,
He cannot fare amiss;
Great Nature hath him in her care,
Her cause is his;

Who holds by everlasting law
Which neither chance nor change can flaw,
Whose steadfast course is one
With whatsoever forces draw
The ages on;

Who hath not bowed his honest head
To base Occasion; nor, in dread
Of Duty, shunned her eye;
Nor truckled to loud times; nor wed
His heart to a lie;

Nor feared to follow, in the offense
Of false opinion, his own sense
Of justice unsubdued;
Nor shrunk from any consequence
Of doing good;

He looks his Angel in the face
Without a blush; nor heeds disgrace
Whom naught disgraceful done
Disgraces. Who knows nothing base
Fears nothing known.

Not morseled out from day to day
In feverish wishes, nor the prey
Of hours that have no plan,
His life is whole, to give away
To God and man.

For though he live aloof from ken,
The world's unwitnessed denizen,
The love within him stirs
Abroad, and with the hearts of men
His own confers.

The judge upon the justice-seat;
The brown-backed beggar in the street;
The spinner in the sun;
The reapers reaping in the wheat;
The wan-checked nun

In cloisters cold; the prisoner lean
In lightless den, the robèd queen;
Even the youth who waits,
Hiding the knife, to glide unseen
Between the gates—

He nothing human alien deems
Unto himself, nor disesteems
Man's meanest claim upon him.
And where he walks the mere sunbeams
Drop blessings on him.

Because they know him Nature's friend,
One whom she doth delight to tend
With loving kindness ever:
Helping and heartening to the end
His high endeavor.

—Edward Bulwer Lytton.

FAME AND DUTY

What shall I do lest life in silence pass?
"And if it do,
And never prompt the bray of noisy brass,
What need'st thou rue?
Remember, aye the ocean-deeps are mute—
The shallows roar;
Worth is the ocean—fame is but the bruit
Along the shore."

What shall I do to be forever known?
  "Thy duty ever!"
This did full many who yet slept unknown.
  "O never, never!
Think'st thou perchance that they remain unknown
  Whom thou know'st not?
By angel trumps in heaven their praise is blown—
  Divine their lot."

What shall I do, an heir of endless life?
  "Discharge aright
The simple dues with which each day is rife,
  Yea, with thy might.
Ere perfect scheme of action thou devise
  Will life be fled,
While he who ever acts as conscience cries,
  Shall live, though dead."
—Johann C. F. Schiller.

NOBLE LIVES

There are hearts which never falter
  In the battle for the right;
There are ranks which never alter
  Watching through the darkest night;
And the agony of sharing
  In the fiercest of the strife
Only gives a nobler daring,
  Only makes a grander life.

There are those who never weary
  Bearing suffering and wrong;
Though the way is long and dreary
  It is vocal with their song,
While their spirits in God's furnace,
  Bending to His gracious will,
Are fashioned in a purer mold
  By His loving, matchless skill.

There are those whose loving mission
  'Tis to bind the bleeding heart;
And to teach a calm submission
  When the pain and sorrow smart.
They are angels, bearing to us
  Love's rich ministry of peace,
While the night is nearing to us
  When life's bitter trials cease.

There are those who battle slander,
  Envy, jealousy and hate;
Who would rather die than pander
  To the passions of earth's great;
No earthly power can ever crush them,
  They dread not the tyrant's frown;
Fear or favor cannot hush them,
  Nothing bind their spirits down.

These, these alone are truly great;
These are the conquerors of fate;
These truly live, they never die;
But, clothed with immortality,
When they lay their armor down
Shall enter and receive the crown.

THE HIGHER LIFE

To play through life a perfect part,
  Unnoticed and unknown;
To seek no rest in any heart
  Save only God alone;
In little things to own no will,
  To have no share in great;
To find the labor ready still
  And for the crown to wait.

Upon the brow to bear no trace
  Of more than common care;
To write no secret in the face
  For men to read it there;
The daily cross to clasp and bless
  With such familiar zeal
As hides from all that not the less
  The daily weight you feel;

In toils that praise will never pay,
  To see your life go past;
To meet in every coming day
  Twin sister of the last;
To hear of high heroic things,
  And yield them reverence due,
But feel life's daily sufferings
  Are far more fit for you;

To own no secret, soft disguise
  To which self-love is prone,
Unnoticed by all other eyes,
  Unworthy in your own;
To yield with such a happy art,
  That no one thinks you care,
And say to your poor bleeding heart,
  "How little you can bear!"

O 'tis a pathway hard to choose,
  A struggle hard to share;
For human pride would still refuse
  The nameless trials there.
But since we know the gate is low
  That leads to heavenly bliss,
What higher grace could God bestow
  Than such a life as this?
—Adelaide Anne Procter.

NOBILITY OF GOODNESS

My fairest child, I have no song to give you;
No lark could pipe to skies so dull and gray;
Yet, ere we part, one lesson I can leave you,
For every day.
Be good, sweet maid, and let who will be clever;
Do noble things, not dream them all day long;
And so make life, death, and that vast forever,
One grand, sweet song!

—Charles Kingsley.

THE GLORY OF FAILURE

We who have lost the battle
To you who have fought and won:
Give ye good cheer and greeting!
Stoutly and bravely done!

Reach us a hand in passing,
Comrades—and own the name!
Yours is the thrill and the laurel:
Ours is the smart and shame.

Though we were nothing skillful,
Pity us not nor scorn!
Send us a hail as hearty—
"Stoutly and bravely borne!"

Others may scorn or pity;
You who are soldiers know.
Where was the joy of your battle
Save in the grip with the foe?

Did we not stand to the conflict?
Did we not fairly fall?
Is it your crowns ye care for?
Nay, to have fought is all.

Humbled and sore we watch you,
Cheerful and bruised and lamed.
Take the applause of the conquered—
Conquered and unashamed!

—Alice Van Vliet.

He is brave whose tongue is silent
Of the trophies of his word.
He is great whose quiet bearing
Marks his greatness well assured.

—Edwin Arnold.

THE LOSING SIDE

Helmet and plume and saber, banner and lance and shield,
Scattered in sad confusion over the trampled field;
And the band of broken soldiers, with a weary, hopeless air,
With heads in silence drooping, and eyes of grim despair.
Like foam-flakes left on the drifting sand
In the track of a falling tide,
On the ground where their cause has failed they stand,
The last of the losing side.

Wisdom of age is vanquished, and generous hopes of youth,
Passion of faith and honor, fire of love and truth;
And the plans that seemed the fairest in the fight have not prevailed,
The keenest blades are broken, and the strongest arms have failed.
But souls that know not the breath of shame,
And tongues that have never lied,
And the truest hearts, and the fairest fame,
Are here—on the losing side.

The conqueror's crown of glory is set with many a gem,
But I join not in their triumph—there are plenty to shout for *them;*
The cause is the most applauded whose warriors gain the day,
And the world's best smiles are given to the victors in the fray.
But dearer to me is the darkened plain,
Where the noblest dreams have died,
Where hopes have been shattered and heroes slain
In the ranks of the losing side.

—Arthur E. J. Legge.

IO VICTIS

I sing the hymn of the conquered, who fell in the battle of life,
The hymn of the wounded and beaten, who died overwhelmed in the strife;
Not the jubilant song of the victors, for whom the resounding acclaim
Of nations was lifted in chorus, whose brows wore the chaplet of fame,

But the hymn of the low and the humble, the weary and broken in heart,
Who strove and who failed, acting bravely a silent and desperate part;
Whose youth bore no flower on its branches, whose hopes burned in ashes away,
From whose hands slipped the prize they had grasped at, who stood at the dying of day
With the wreck of their life all around them, unpitied, unheeded, alone,
With death swooping down o'er their failure, and all but their faith overthrown.

While the voice of the world shouts its chorus—its pean for those who have won;
While the trumpet is sounding triumphant, and high to the breeze and the sun
Glad banners are waving, hands clapping, and hurrying feet
Thronging after the laurel-crowned victors, I stand on the field of defeat,
In the shadow, with those who are fallen, and wounded, and dying, and there
Chant a requiem low, place my hand on their pain-knotted brows, breathe a prayer,
Hold the hand that is helpless, and whisper, "They only the victory win,
Who have fought the good fight and have vanquished the demon that tempts us within;
Who have held to their faith unseduced by the prize that the world holds on high;
Who have dared for a high cause to suffer, resist, fight—if need be, to die."

Speak, History! who are Life's victors? Unroll thy long annals and say,
Are they those whom the world called the victors? who won the success of a day?
The martyrs, or Nero? The Spartans who fell at Thermopylæ's tryst,
Or the Persians and Xerxes? His judges, or Socrates? Pilate, or Christ?
—William M. Story.

He makes no friend who never made a foe.
—Alfred Tennyson.

THE TRUE KING

'Tis not wealth that makes a king,
Nor the purple coloring;
Nor the brow that's bound with gold,
Nor gate on mighty hinges rolled.

The king is he who, void of fear,
Looks abroad with bosom clear;
Who can tread ambition down,
Nor be swayed by smile or frown,
Nor for all the treasure cares,
That mine conceals or harvest wears,
Or that golden sands deliver
Bosomed in the glassy river.

What shall move his placid might?
Not the headlong thunder's light,
Nor all the shapes of slaughter's trade,
With onward lance or fiery blade.
Safe, with wisdom for his crown,
He looks on all things calmly down,
He welcomes Fate when Fate is near,
Nor taints his dying breath with fear.

No; to fear not earthly thing,
That it is that makes the king;
And all of us, whoe'er we be,
May carve us out that royalty.

With comrade Duty, in the dark or day,
To follow Truth—wherever it may lead;
To hate all meanness, cowardice or greed;
To look for Beauty under common clay;
Our brothers' burden sharing, when they weep,
But, if we fall, to bear defeat alone;
To live in hearts that loved us, when we're gone
Beyond the twilight (till the morning break!)—to sleep—
That is Success!
—Ernest Neal Lyon.

The common problem, yours, mine, every one's,
Is, not to fancy what were fair in life
Provided it could be, but, finding first
What may be, then find out how to make it fair
Up to our means; a very different thing.
—Robert Browning.

BETTER THAN GOLD

Better than grandeur, better than gold,
Than rank and titles a thousandfold,
Is a healthy body, a mind at ease,
And simple pleasures that always please;
A heart that can feel for another's woe,
That has learned with love's deep fires
to glow,
With sympathy large enough to enfold
All men as brothers, is better than gold.

Better than gold is a conscience clear,
Though toiling for bread in a humble
sphere;
Doubly blest is content and health
Untried by the lusts and the cares of
wealth.
Lowly living and lofty thought
Adorn and ennoble the poor man's cot;
For mind and morals in nature's plan
Are the genuine tests of the gentleman.

Better than gold is the sweet repose
Of the sons of toil when labors close;
Better than gold is the poor man's sleep
And the balm that drops on his slum-
bers deep.
Bring sleeping draughts to the downy
bed,
Where luxury pillows its aching head;
The toiler a simple opiate deems
A shorter route to the land of dreams.

Better than gold is a thinking mind
That in the realm of books can find
A treasure surpassing Australian ore,
And live with the great and good of yore;
The sage's lore and the poet's lay;
The glories of empires passed away;
The world's great dream will thus unfold
And yield a pleasure better than gold.

Better than gold is a peaceful home,
Where all the fireside characters come,
The shrine of love, the heaven of life,
Hallowed by mother or by wife.
However humble the home may be,
Or tried with sorrow by heaven's decree,
The blessings that never were bought or
sold
And center there, are better than gold.
—Abram J. Ryan.

When success exalts thy lot
God for thy virtue lays a plot.
—Ralph Waldo Emerson.

MAXIMUS

I hold him great who, for Love's sake,
Can give with generous, earnest will;
Yet he who takes for Love's sweet sake
I think I hold more generous still.

I bow before the noble mind
That freely some great wrong forgives;
Yet nobler is the one forgiven,
Who bears that burden well and lives.

It may be hard to gain, and still
To keep a lowly, steadfast heart;
Yet he who loses has to fill
A harder and a truer part.

Glorious it is to wear the crown
Of a deserved and pure success;
He who knows how to fail has won
A crown whose luster is not less.

Great may he be who can command
And rule with just and tender sway;
Yet is Diviner wisdom taught
Better by him who can obey.

Blessed are those who die for God,
And earn the martyr's crown of light;
Yet he who lives for God may be
A greater conqueror in his sight.
—Adelaide Anne Procter.

'Tis phrase absurd to call a villain great:
Who wickedly is wise, or madly brave,
Is but the more a fool, the more a knave.
Who noble ends by noble means obtains,
Or, failing, smiles in exile or in chains;
Like good Aurelius, let him reign, or
bleed
Like Socrates—that man is great indeed.
One self-approving hour whole years
outweighs
Of stupid starers and of loud huzzas;
And more true joy Marcellus exiled
feels,
Than Cæsar with a senate at his heels.
—Alexander Pope.

Though world on world in myriad
myriads roll
Round us, each with different powers,
And other forms of life than ours,
What know we greater than the soul?
On God and Godlike men we build our
trust. —Alfred Tennyson.

THE GOOD, GREAT MAN

How seldom, friend, a good, great man inherits
Honor and wealth, with all his worth and pains!
It seems a story from the world of spirits
When any man obtains that which he merits,
Or any merits that which he obtains.

For shame, my friend; renounce this idle strain!
What would'st thou have a good, great man obtain?
Wealth, title, dignity, a golden chain,
Or heap of corses which his sword hath slain?
Goodness and greatness are not means, but ends.
Hath he not always treasurer, always friends,
The great, good man? Three treasures—love, and light,
And calm thoughts, equable as infants' breath;
And three fast friends, more sure than day or night—
Himself, his Maker, and the angel Death.

—Samuel Taylor Coleridge.

THE POEM OF THE UNIVERSE

The poem of the universe
Nor rhythm has nor rhyme;
For God recites the wondrous song
A stanza at a time.

Great deeds is he foredoomed to do—
With Freedom's flag unfurled—
Who hears the echo of that song
As it goes down the world.

Great words he is compelled to speak
Who understands the song;
He rises up like fifty men,
Fifty good men and strong.

A stanza for each century:
Now heed it all who can!
Who hears it, he, and only he,
Is the elected man.

—Charles Weldon.

When faith is lost, when honor dies,
The man is dead!

—John Greenleaf Whittier.

FAILURE AND SUCCESS

He fails who climbs to power and place
Up the pathway of disgrace.
He fails not who makes truth his cause,
Nor bends to win the crowd's applause.
He fails not, he who stakes his all
Upon the right, and dares to fall;
What though the living bless or blame,
For him the long success of fame.

—Richard Watson Gilder.

WHAT DOES IT MATTER?

It matters little where I was born,
Or if my parents were rich or poor;
Whether they shrunk at the cold world's scorn,
Or walked in the pride of wealth secure.
But whether I live an honest man
And hold my integrity firm in my clutch
I tell you, brother, as plain as I can,
It matters much.

It matters little how long I stay
In a world of sorrow, sin, and care;
Whether in youth I am called away
Or live till my bones and pate are bare.
But whether I do the best I can
To soften the weight of Adversity's touch
On the faded cheek of my fellow man,
It matters much.

It matters little where be my grave—
Or on the land or in the sea,
By purling brook or 'neath stormy wave,
It matters little or naught to me;
But whether the Angel Death comes down,
And marks my brow with his loving touch,
As one that shall wear the victor's crown,
It matters much.

—Noah Barker.

For I am 'ware it is the seed of act
God holds appraising in his hollow palm,
Not act grown great thence in the world below;
Leafage and branchage vulgar eyes admire.

—Robert Browning.

OBSCURE MARTYRS

"The world knows nothing of its greatest men."

They have no place in storied page;
 No rest in marble shrine;
They are past and gone with a perished age,
 They died and "made no sign."
But work that shall find its wages yet,
And deeds that their God did not forget,
 Done for their love divine—
These were their mourners, and these shall be
The crowns of their immortality.

O, seek them not where sleep the dead,
 Ye shall not find their trace;
No graven stone is at their head,
 No green grass hides their face;
But sad and unseen is their silent grave;
It may be the sand or the deep sea wave,
 Or a lonely desert place;
For they needed no prayers and no mourning-bell—
They were tombed in true hearts that knew them well.

They healed sick hearts till theirs were broken,
 And dried sad eyes till theirs lost light;
We shall know at last by a certain token
 How they fought and fell in the fight.
Salt tears of sorrow unbeheld,
Passionate cries unchronicled,
 And silent strifes for the right—
Angels shall count them, and earth shall sigh
That she left her best children to battle and die.

—Edwin Arnold.

THY BEST

Before God's footstool to confess
 A poor soul knelt and bowed his head.
 "I failed," he wailed. The Master said,
"Thou did'st thy best—that is success."

—Henry Coyle.

 Aspire, break bounds, I say;
Endeavor to be good and better still,
And best! Success is naught, endeavor's all.

—Robert Browning.

FAILURE

He cast his net at morn where fishers toiled,
 At eve he drew it empty to the shore;
He took the diver's plunge into the sea,
 But thence within his hand no pearl he bore.

He ran a race, but never reached his goal;
 He sped an arrow, but he missed his aim;
And slept at last beneath a simple stone,
 With no achievements carved about his name.

Men called it failure; but for my own part
 I dare not use that word, for what if Heaven
Shall question, ere its judgment shall be read,
 Not, "Hast thou won?" but only, "Hast thou striven?"

—Kate Tucker Goode.

THE BEGGAR'S REVENGE

The king's proud favorite at a beggar threw a stone.
He picked it up as if it had for alms been thrown.

He bore it in his bosom long with bitter ache,
And sought his time revenge with that same stone to take.

One day he heard a street mob's hoarse, commingled cry:
The favorite comes!—but draws no more the admiring eye.

He rides an ass, from all his haughty state disgraced;
And by the rabble's mocking gibes his way is traced.

The stone from out his bosom swift the beggar draws,
And flinging it away, exclaims: "A fool I was!

'Tis madness to attack, when in his power, your foe,
And meanness then to strike when he has fallen low."

—From the Persian.

A THOUGHT

Hearts that are great beat never loud;
They muffle their music, when they come;
They hurry away from the thronging crowd
With bended brows and lips half dumb.

And the world looks on and mutters—"Proud."
But when great hearts have passed away,
Men gather in awe and kiss their shroud,
And in love they kneel around their clay.

Hearts that are great are always lone;
They never will manifest their best;
Their greatest greatness is unknown,
Earth knows a little—God the rest.
—Abram J. Ryan.

HIS MONUMENT

He built a house, time laid it in the dust;
He wrote a book, its title now forgot;
He ruled a city, but his name is not
On any tablet graven, or where rust
Can gather from disuse, or marble bust.

He took a child from out a wretched cot;
Who on the State dishonor might have brought;
And reared him in the Christian's hope and trust.
The boy, to manhood grown, became a light
To many souls and preached to human need
The wondrous love of the Omnipotent.
The work has multiplied like stars at night
When darkness deepens; every noble deed
Lasts longer than a granite monument.
—Sarah Knowles Bolton.

It is not the wall of stone without
That makes a building small or great,
But the soul's light shining round about,
And the faith that overcometh doubt,
And the love that stronger is than hate.
—Henry Wadsworth Longfellow.

THE NOBLY BORN

Who counts himself as nobly born
Is noble in despite of place;
And honors are but brands to one
Who wears them not with nature's grace.

The prince may sit with clown or churl
Nor feel himself disgraced thereby;
But he who has but small esteem
Husbands that little carefully.

Then, be thou peasant, be thou peer,
Count it still more thou art thine own.
Stand on a larger heraldry
Than that of nation or of zone.

Art thou not bid to knightly halls?
Those halls have missed a courtly guest;
That mansion is not privileged
Which is not open to the best.

Give honor due when custom asks,
Nor wrangle for this lesser claim;
It is not to be destitute
To have the thing without the name.

Then, dost thou come of gentle blood,
Disgrace not thy good company;
If lowly born, so bear thyself
That gentle blood may come of thee.

Strive not with pain to scale the height
Of some fair garden's petty wall;
But climb the open mountain side
Whose summit rises over all.

And, for success, I ask no more than this:
To bear unflinching witness to the truth.
All true whole men succeed; for what is worth
Success's name unless it be the thought,
The inward surety, to have carried out
A noble purpose to a noble end,
Although it be the gallows or the block?
'Tis only Falsehood that doth ever need
These outward shows of gain to bolster her.
—James Russell Lowell.

Greatly begin! though thou have time
But for a line, be that sublime—
Not failure, but low aim is crime.
—James Russell Lowell.

THE BURIAL OF MOSES

By Nebo's lonely mountain,
On this side Jordan's wave,
In a vale in the land of Moab,
There lies a lonely grave.
But no man dug that sepulchre,
And no man saw it e'er;
For the angels of God upturned the sod,
And laid the dead man there.

That was the grandest funeral
That ever passed on earth;
But no man heard the trampling,
Or saw the train go forth.
Noiselessly as the daylight
Comes when the night is done,
And the crimson streak on ocean's cheek
Grows into the great sun—

Noiselessly as the springtime
Her crest of verdure weaves,
And all the trees on all the hills
Open their thousand leaves—
So, without sound of music,
Or voice of them that wept,
Silently down from the mountain crown
The great procession swept.

Perchance some bald old eagle
On gray Beth-peor's height,
Out of his rocky eyrie
Looked on the wondrous sight.
Perchance some lion, stalking,
Still shuns the hallowed spot,
For beast and bird have seen and heard
That which man knoweth not.

But when the warrior dieth
His comrades in the war,
With arms reversed and muffled drums
Follow the funeral car;
They show the banners taken,
They tell his battles won,
And after him lead his matchless steed
While peals the minute gun.

Amid the noblest of the land
They lay the sage to rest;
And give the bard an honored place,
With costly marble drest,
In the great minster's transept height,
Where lights like glory fall,
While the sweet choir sings and the organ rings
Along the emblazoned wall.

This was the bravest warrior
That ever buckled sword;
This the most gifted poet
That ever breathed a word;
And never earth's philosopher
Traced, with his golden pen,
On the deathless page, truths half so sage
As he wrote down for men.

And had he not high honor?
The hillside for his pall;
To lie in state while angels wait
With stars for tapers tall;
And the dark rock pines, like tossing plumes,
Over his bier to wave;
And God's own hand, in that lonely land,
To lay him in his grave;

In that deep grave without a name,
Whence his uncoffined clay
Shall break again—most wondrous thought!—
Before the judgment day,
And stand, with glory wrapt around,
On the hills he never trod,
And speak of the strife that won our life
Through Christ, the incarnate God.

O lonely tomb in Moab's land,
O dark Beth-peor's hill,
Speak to these curious hearts of ours,
And teach them to be still.
God hath his mysteries of grace—
Ways that we cannot tell;
He hides them deep, like the secret sleep
Of him he loved so well.

—Cecil Frances Alexander.

O, blessed is that man of whom some soul can say,
"He was an inspiration along life's toilsome way,
A well of sparkling water, a fountain flowing free,
Forever like his Master, in tenderest sympathy."

Truths would you teach, or save a sinking land?
All fear, none aid you, and few understand.
Painful pre-eminence!—yourself to view
Above life's weakness, and its comforts too.

—Alexander Pope.

EMIR HASSAN

Emir Hassan, of the prophet's race,
Asked with folded hands the Almighty's grace,
Then within the banquet-hall he sat,
At his meal, upon the embroidered mat.

There a slave before him placed the food,
Spilling from the charger, as he stood,
Awkwardly upon the Emir's breast
Drops that foully stained the silken vest.

To the floor, in great remorse and dread,
Fell the slave, and thus, beseeching, said:
"Master, they who hasten to restrain
Rising wrath, in paradise shall reign."

Gentle was the answer Hassan gave:
"I am not angry." "Yet," pursued the slave,
"Yet doth higher recompense belong
To the injured who forgives a wrong."

"I forgive," said Hassan. "Yet we read,"
So the prostrate slave went on to plead,
"That a higher seat in glory still
Waits the man who renders good for ill."

"Slave, receive thy freedom; and, behold,
In thy hand I lay a purse of gold.
Let me never fail to heed, in aught,
What the prophet of our God hath taught."

TRUE GREATNESS

Who is as the Christian great?
Bought and washed with sacred blood,
Crowns he sees beneath his feet.
Soars aloft and walks with God.

Lo, his clothing is the sun,
The bright sun of righteousness;
He hath put salvation on,
Jesus is his beauteous dress.

Angels are his servants here;
Spread for him their golden wings;
To his throne of glory bear,
Seat him by the King of kings.
—Charles Wesley.

The glory is not in the task, but in
The doing it for Him.
—Jean Ingelow.

MENCIUS

Three centuries before the Christian age
China's great teacher, Mencius, was born;
Her teeming millions did not know that morn
Had broken on her darkness; that a sage,
Reared by a noble mother, would her page
Of history forevermore adorn.
For twenty years, from court to court, forlorn
He journeyed, poverty his heritage,
And preached of virtue, but none cared to hear.
Life seemed a failure, like a barren rill;
He wrote his books, and lay beneath the sod:
When, lo! his work began; and far and near
Adown the ages Mencius preaches still:
Do thy whole duty, trusting all to God.
—Sarah Knowles Bolton.

He stood, the youth they called the Beautiful,
At morning, on his untried battle-field,
And laughed with joy to see his stainless shield,
When, with a tender smile, but doubting sigh,
His lord rode by.

When evening fell, they brought him, wounded sore,
His battered shield with sword-thrusts gashed and rent,
And laid him where the king stood by his tent.
"Now art thou Beautiful," the master said,
And bared his head.
—Annie M. L. Hawes.

Great men grow greater by the lapse of time;
We know those least whom we have seen the latest;
And they, 'mongst those whose names have grown sublime,
Who worked for human liberty are greatest.
—John Boyle O'Reilly.

It is enough—
Enough—just to be good;
To lift our hearts where they are understood;
To let the thirst for worldly power and place
Go unappeased; to smile back in God's face
With the glad lips our mothers used to kiss.
Ah! though we miss
All else but this,
To be good is enough!
—James Whitcomb Riley.

He who ascends to mountain tops shall find
Their loftiest peaks most wrapped in clouds and snow;
He who surpasses or subdues mankind
Must look down on the hate of those below.
Though high above the sun of glory glow,
And far beneath the earth and ocean spread,
Round him are icy rocks, and loudly blow
Contending tempests on his naked head.
—George Gordon Byron.

Good name in man and woman, dear my lord,
Is the immediate jewel of their souls:
Who steals my purse steals trash; 'tis something, nothing;
'Twas mine, 'tis his, and has been slave to thousands;
But he that filches from me my good name
Robs me of that which not enriches him,
And makes me poor indeed.
—William Shakespeare.

That man may last, but never lives,
Who much receives but nothing gives;
Whom none can love, whom none can thank;
Creation's blot; creation's blank!

But he who marks, from day to day,
In generous acts his radiant way
Treads the same path his Saviour trod:
The path to glory and to God.

The eye with seeing is not filled,
The ear with hearing not at rest;
Desire with having is not stilled,
With human praise no heart is blest.

Vanity, then, of vanities,
All things for which men grasp and grope!
The precious things in heavenly eyes
Are love, and truth, and trust, and hope.

A gem which falls within the mire will still a gem remain;
Men's eyes turn downward to the earth and search for it with pain.
But *dust*, though whirled aloft to heaven, continues dust alway,
More base and noxious in the air than when on earth it lay.
—Saadi, tr. by James Freeman Clarke.

It was not anything she said;
It was not anything she did;
It was the movement of her head,
The lifting of her lid.
And as she trod her path aright
Power from her very garments stole;
For such is the mysterious might
God grants a noble soul.

True worth is in being, not seeming;
In doing, each day that goes by,
Some little good, not in dreaming,
Of great things to do by and by.
For whatever men say in their blindness,
And spite of the fancies of youth,
There's nothing so kingly as kindness,
And nothing so royal as truth.
—Alice Cary.

The wisest man could ask no more of Fate
Than to be simple, modest, manly, true,
Safe from the Many, honored by the Few;
To count as naught in world of church or state
But inwardly in secret to be great.
—James Russell Lowell.

And only the Master shall praise us, and only the Master shall blame;
And no one shall work for money, and no one shall work for fame;
But each for the joy of the working, and each, in his separate star,
Shall draw the Thing as he sees it, for the God of Things as they are.
—Rudyard Kipling.

In life's small things be resolute and great
To keep thy muscle trained; knowest thou when Fate
Thy measure takes? or when she'll say to thee,
"I find thee worthy; do this deed for me"? —James Russell Lowell.

'Tis a life-long toil till our lump be leaven.
The better! What's come to perfection perishes.
Things learned on earth we shall practice in heaven.
Work done least rapidly Art most cherishes. —Robert Browning.

Let come what will, I mean to bear it out,
And either live with glorious victory
Or die with fame, renowned in chivalry.
He is not worthy of the honey-comb
That shuns the hive because the bees have stings.
—William Shakespeare.

One by one thy duties wait thee,
Let thy whole strength go to each.
Let no future dreams elate thee,
Learn thou first what these can teach.
—Adelaide Anne Procter.

Give me heart-touch with all that live
And strength to speak my word;
But if that is denied me, give
The strength to live unheard.
—Edwin Markham.

Honor and shame from no condition rise;
Act well your part, there all the honor lies. —Alexander Pope.

How wretched is the man with honors crowned,
Who, having not the one thing needful found,
Dies, known to all, but to himself unknown.
—Henry Wadsworth Longfellow.

He fought a thousand glorious wars,
And more than half the world was his,
And somewhere, now, in yonder stars,
Can tell, mayhap, what greatness is.
—William Makepeace Thackeray.

Howe'er it be, it seems to me
'Tis only noble to be good;
Kind hearts are more than coronets,
And simple faith than Norman blood.
—Alfred Tennyson.

I've learned to prize the quiet, lightning deed,
Not the applauding thunder at its heels
Which men call fame.
—Alexander Smith.

It is worth while to live!
Be of good cheer;
Love casts out fear;
Rise up, achieve.
—Christina G. Rossetti.

No endeavor is in vain;
Its reward is in the doing,
And the rapture of pursuing
Is the prize the vanquished gain.
—Henry Wadsworth Longfellow.

Far better in its place the lowliest bird
Should sing aright to Him the lowliest song,
Than that a seraph strayed should take the word
And sing His glory wrong.
—Jean Ingelow.

Often ornateness
Goes with greatness.
Oftener felicity
Comes of simplicity.
—William Watson.

A jewel is a jewel still, though lying in the dust,
And sand is sand, though up to heaven by the tempest thrust.
—From the Persian.

Vulgar souls surpass a rare one in the headlong rush;
As the hard and worthless stones a precious pearl will crush.
—From the Persian.

Be noble! and the nobleness that lies
In other men, sleeping, but never dead,
Will rise in majesty to meet thine own.
—James Russell Lowell.

The mean of soul are sure their faults to gloss,
And find a secret gain in others' loss.
—John Boyle O'Reilly.

Ah, a man's reach should exceed his grasp,
Or what's heaven for?
—Robert Browning.

Though thy name be spread abroad,
Like winged seed, from shore to shore,
What thou art before thy God,
That thou art and nothing more.

My business is not to remake myself,
But make the absolute best of what God made.
—Robert Browning.

For never land long lease of empire won
Whose sons sat silent when base deeds were done.
—James Russell Lowell.

He that would free from malice pass his days
Must live obscure and never merit praise. —John Gay.

Wearing the white flower of a blameless life,
Before a thousand peering littlenesses.
—Alfred Tennyson.

The aim, if reached or not, makes great the life,
Try to be Shakespeare—leave the rest to fate. —Robert Browning.

Unblemished let me live, or die unknown;
O, grant an honest fame, or grant me none. —Alexander Pope.

With fame in just proportion envy grows;
The man that makes a character makes foes. —Edward Young.

'Tis not what man does which exalts him,
But what man would do.
—Robert Browning.

Better have failed in the high aim, as I,
Than vulgarly in the low aim succeed.
—Robert Browning.

The simple, silent, selfless man
Is worth a world of tonguesters.
—Alfred Tennyson.

DUTY

LOYALTY, FAITHFULNESS, CONSCIENCE, ZEAL

ODE TO DUTY

Stern daughter of the voice of God!
O Duty! if that name thou love
Who art a light to guide, a rod
To check the erring and reprove;
Thou who art victory and law
When empty terrors overawe;
From vain temptation dost set free;
And calm'st the weary strife of frail humanity!

There are who ask not if thine eye
Be on them; who, in love and truth,
Where no misgiving is, rely
Upon the genial sense of youth;
Glad hearts, without reproach or blot,
Who do thy work and know it not:
Oh! if through confidence misplaced
They fail, thy saving arms, dread Power, around them cast.

Serene will be our days, and bright
And happy will our nature be,
When love is an unerring light,
And joy its own security;
And they a blissful course may hold
Even now, who, not unwisely bold,
Live in the spirit of this creed;
Yet seek thy firm support according to their need.

I, loving freedom, and untried,
No sport of every random gust,
Yet being to myself a guide,
Too blindly have reposed my trust;
And oft, when in my heart was heard
Thy timely mandate, I deferred
The task, in smoother walks to stray;
But thee I now would serve more strictly, if I may.

Through no disturbance of my soul,
Or strong compunction in me wrought,
I supplicate for thy control,
But in the quietness of thought.
Me this unchartered freedom tires;
I feel the weight of chance desires:
My hopes no more must change their name,
I long for a repose that ever is the same.

Stern Lawgiver! Yet thou dost wear
The Godhead's most benignant grace;
Nor know we anything so fair
As is the smile upon thy face:
Flowers laugh before thee on their beds
And fragrance in thy footing treads;
Thou dost preserve the stars from wrong;
And the most ancient heavens, through Thee, are fresh and strong.

To humbler functions, awful Power!
I call thee; I myself commend
Unto thy guidance from this hour;
Oh, let my weakness have an end!
Give unto me, made lowly wise,
The spirit of self-sacrifice;
The confidence of reason give;
And in the light of truth thy bondman let me live.

—William Wordsworth.

THE LADDER OF SAINT AUGUSTINE

Saint Augustine! well hast thou said,
That of our vices we can frame
A ladder, if we will but tread
Beneath our feet each deed of shame!

All common things, each day's events,
That with the hour begin and end,
Our pleasures and our discontents,
Are rounds by which we may ascend.

The longing for ignoble things;
The strife for triumph more than truth;
The hardening of the heart, that brings
Irreverence for the dreams of youth;

All thoughts of ill, all evil deeds
That have their root in thoughts of ill;
Whatever hinders or impedes
The action of the nobler will;—

All these must first be trampled down
Beneath our feet, if we would gain
In the bright fields of fair renown
The right of eminent domain.

We have not wings, we cannot soar;
But we have feet to scale and climb
By slow degrees, by more and more,
The cloudy summits of our time.

The heights by great men reached and kept
Were not attained by sudden flight,
But they while their companions slept
Were toiling upward in the night.

Standing on what too long we bore
With shoulders bent and downcast eyes,
We may discern—unseen before—
A path to higher destinies,

Nor deem the irrevocable Past
As wholly wasted, wholly vain,
If, rising on its wrecks, at last
To something nobler we attain.
—Henry Wadsworth Longfellow.

REWARD OF FAITHFULNESS

The deeds which selfish hearts approve
And fame's loud trumpet sings
Secure no praise where truth and love
Are counted noblest things;
And work which godless folly deems
Worthless, obscure, and lowly,
To Heaven's ennobling vision seems
Most god-like, grand, and holy.

Then murmur not if toils obscure
And thorny paths be thine;
To God be true—they shall secure
The joy of life divine
Who in the darkest, sternest sphere
For Him their powers employ;
The toils contemned and slighted here
Shall yield the purest joy.

When endless day dispels the strife
Which blinds and darkens now,
Perchance the brightest crown of life
Shall deck some lowly brow.
Then learn, despite thy boding fears,
From seed with sorrow sown,
In love, obscurity and tears
The richest sheaves are grown.
—Edward Hartley Dewart.

"DOE THE NEXTE THYNGE"

From an old English parsonage
Down by the sea,
There came in the twilight
A message to me;
Its quaint Saxon legend
Deeply engraven,
Hath as it seems to me
Teaching for heaven;
And on through the hours
The quiet words ring,
Like a low inspiration,
"Doe the nexte thynge."

Many a questioning,
Many a fear,
Many a doubt,
Hath guiding here.
Moment by moment
Let down from heaven,
Time, opportunity,
Guidance are given.
Fear not to-morrow,
Child of the King;
Trust it with Jesus,
"Doe the nexte thynge."

O He would have thee
Daily more free,
Knowing the might
Of thy royal degree;
Ever in waiting,
Glad for his call,
Tranquil in chastening,
Trusting through all.
Comings and goings
No turmoil need bring:
His all thy future—
"Doe the nexte thynge."

Do it immediately,
Do it with prayer,
Do it reliantly,
Casting all care:
Do it with reverence,
Tracing His hand
Who hath placed it before thee
With earnest command.
Stayed on Omnipotence,
Safe, 'neath his wing,
Leave all resultings,
"Doe the nexte thynge."

Looking to Jesus,
Ever serener,
Working or suffering,
Be thy demeanor!
In the shade of his presence,
The rest of his calm,

The light of his countenance,
  Live out thy psalm:
Strong in his faithfulness.
  Praise him and sing,
Then as he beckons thee,
  "Doe the nexte thynge."

ZEAL IN LABOR

Go, labor on; spend and be spent,
  Thy joy to do the Father's will;
It is the way the Master went;
  Should not the servant tread it still?

Go, labor on; 'tis not for naught;
  Thine earthly loss is heavenly gain;
Men heed thee, love thee, praise thee not;
  The Master praises—what are men?

Go, labor on; your hands are weak;
  Your knees are faint, your soul cast down;
Yet falter not; the prize you seek
  Is near—a kingdom and a crown!

Toil on, faint not; keep watch, and pray!
  Be wise the erring soul to win;
Go forth into the world's highway;
  Compel the wanderer to come in.

Toil on, and in thy toil rejoice:
  For toil comes rest, for exile home;
Soon shalt thou hear the Bridegroom's voice,
  The midnight peal, "Behold, I come!"

—Horatius Bonar.

THE EVANGELIST

Walking with Peter, Christ his footsteps set
On the lake shore, hard by Gennesaret,
At the hour when noontide's burning rays down pour.
When they beheld at a mean cabin's door,
A fisher's widow in her mourning clad,
Who, on the threshold seated, silent, sad,
The tear that wet them kept her lids within,
Her child to cradle and her flax to spin;
Near by, behind the fig-trees' leafy screen,
The Master and His friend could see, unseen.
An old man ready for his earthly bed,
A beggar with a jar upon his head,
Came by, and to the mourning spinner there
Said, "Woman, I this vase of milk should bear
Unto a dweller in the hamlet near;
But I am weak and bent with many a year;
More than a thousand paces yet to go
Remain, and, without help, I surely know
I cannot end my task and earn its fee."

The woman rose, and not a word said she,
Without a pause her distaff laid aside,
And left the cradle where the orphan cried,
Took up the jar, and with the beggar went.

"Master, 'tis well to be benevolent,"
Said Peter, "but small sense that woman showed,
In leaving thus her child and her abode
For the chance-comer that first sought her out;
The beggar some one would have found, no doubt,
To ease him of his load upon the way."

The Lord made answer unto Peter, "Nay,
Thy Father, when the poor assists the poorer,
Will keep her cot, and her reward assure her.
She went at once, and wisely did in that."

And Jesus, having finished speaking, sat
Down on a bench was in the humble place,
And with His blest hands for a moment's space,
He touched the distaff, rocked the little one.
Rose, signed to Peter, and they gat them gone.

When she to whom the Lord had given this proof
Of good-will came back to her humble roof,
She found, nor knew what Friend the deed had done,
The baby sleeping and the flax all spun!

—Francois Coppee.

THE BEST THAT I CAN

"I cannot do much," said a little star,
"To make the dark world bright;
My silver beams cannot struggle far
Through the folding gloom of night:
But I am a part of God's great plan,
And I'll cheerfully do the best that I can."

"What is the use," said a fleecy cloud,
"Of these dew-drops that I hold?
They will hardly bend the lily proud,
Though caught in her cup of gold;
Yet I am a part of God's great plan,
My treasures I'll give as well as I can."

A child went merrily forth to play,
But a thought, like a silver thread,
Kept winding in and out all day
Through the happy, busy head,
"Mother said, 'Darling, do all you can,
For you are a part of God's great plan.'"

So she helped a younger child along,
When the road was rough to the feet;
And she sang from her heart a little song,
A song that was passing sweet;
And her father, a weary, toil-worn man,
Said, "I too will do the best that I can."

WORK LOYALLY

Just where you stand in the conflict,
There is your place!
Just where you think you are useless
Hide not your face!
God placed you there for a purpose,
Whate'er it be;
Think He has chosen you for it—
Work loyally.

Gird on your armor! Be faithful
At toil or rest,
Whiche'er it be, never doubting
God's way is best.
Out in the fight, or on picket,
Stand firm and true;
This is the work which your Master
Gives you to do.

Who does the best his circumstance allows,
Does well, acts nobly; angels could no more.

—Edward Young.

LOYALTY

When courage fails and faith burns low,
And men are timid grown,
Hold fast thy loyalty and know
That Truth still moveth on.

For unseen messengers she hath,
To work her will and ways,
And even human scorn and wrath
God turneth to her praise.

She can both meek and lordly be,
In heavenly might secure;
With her is pledge of victory,
And patience to endure.

The race is not unto the swift,
The battle to the strong,
When dawn her judgment-days that sift
The claims of right and wrong.

And more than thou canst do for Truth
Can she on thee confer,
If thou, O heart, but give thy youth
And manhood unto her.

For she can make thee inly bright,
Thy self-love purge away,
And lead thee in the path whose light
Shines to the perfect day.

Who follow her, though men deride,
In her strength shall be strong;
Shall see their shame become their pride,
And share her triumph song!

—Frederick Lucian Hosmer.

LIBERTY

I am Liberty—God's daughter!
My symbols—a law and a torch;
Not a sword to threaten slaughter,
Nor a flame to dazzle or scorch;
But a light that the world may see,
And a truth that shall make men free.

I am the sister of Duty,
And I am the sister of Faith;
To-day adored for my beauty,
To-morrow led forth for death.
I am she whom ages prayed for;
Heroes suffered undismayed for;
Whom the martyrs were betrayed for.

—John Boyle O'Reilly.

THE NEAREST DUTY

My soul was stirred; I prayed, "Let me
Do some great work, so purely,
To right life's wrongs, that I shall know
That I have loved Thee surely."
My lips sent forth their eager cry,
The while my heart beat faster,
"For some great deed to prove my love
Send me; send me, my Master!"

From out the silence came a voice,
Saying: "If God thou fearest,
Rise up and do, thy whole life through,
The duty that lies nearest.
The friendly word, the kindly deed,
Though small the act in seeming,
Shall in the end unto thy soul
Prove mightier than thy dreaming.

The cup of water to the faint,
Or rest unto the weary,
The light thou giv'st another's life,
Shall make thine own less dreary.
And boundless realms of faith and love
Will wait for thy possessing;
Not creeds, but deeds, if thou wouldst win
Unto thy soul a blessing."

And so I wait with peaceful heart,
Content to do His pleasure;
Not caring if the world shall mock
At smallness of the measure
Of thoughts or deeds or daily life.
He knows the true endeavor—
To do His will, to seek His face—
And He will fail me never.

—Sarah A. Gibbs.

THE ONE TALENT

Hide not thy talent in the earth;
However small it be,
Its faithful use, its utmost worth,
God will require of thee.

The humblest service rendered here
He will as truly own
As Paul's in his exalted sphere,
Or Gabriel's near the throne.

The cup of water kindly given,
The widow's cheerful mites,
Are worthier in the eye of heaven
Than pride's most costly rites.

His own, which He hath lent on trust,
He asks of thee again;
Little or much, the claim is just,
And thine excuses vain.

Go, then, and strive to do thy part—
Though humble it may be;
The ready hand, the willing heart,
Are all heaven asks of thee.

—William Cutler.

ONE TALENT ✓

(Matt. xxv. 18)

In a napkin smooth and white,
Hidden from all mortal sight,
My one talent lies to-night.

Mine to hoard, or mine to use;
Mine to keep, or mine to lose;
May I not do what I choose?

Ah! the gift was only lent
With the Giver's known intent
That it should be wisely spent.

And I know he will demand
Every farthing at my hand,
When I in his presence stand.

What will be my grief and shame
When I hear my humble name
And cannot repay his claim!

One poor talent—nothing more!
All the years that have gone o'er
Have not added to the store.

Some will double what they hold,
Others add to it tenfold
And pay back the shining gold.

Would that I had toiled like them!
All my sloth I now condemn;
Guilty fears my soul o'erwhelm.

Lord, oh teach me what to do.
Make me faithful, make me true,
And the sacred trust renew.

Help me, ere too late it be,
Something yet to do for Thee,
Thou who hast done all for me.

Art thou little? Do thy little well;
And for thy comfort know
Great men can do their greatest work
No better than just so.

—Johann W. von Goethe.

RESPONSIBILITY FOR TALENTS

Thou that in life's crowded city art arrived, thou knowest not how—
By what path or on what errand—list and learn thine errand now.

From the palace to the city on the business of thy King
Thou wert sent at early morning, to return at evening.

Dreamer, waken; loiterer, hasten; what thy task is understand:
Thou art here to purchase substance, and the price is in thine hand.

Has the tumult of the market all thy sense confused and drowned?
Do its glittering wares entice thee, or its shouts and cries confound?

Oh, beware lest thy Lord's business be forgotten, while thy gaze
Is on every show and pageant which the giddy square displays.

Barter not his gold for pebbles; do not trade in vanities;
Pearls there are of price and jewels for the purchase of the wise.

And know this—at thy returning thou wilt surely find the King
With an open book before Him, waiting to make reckoning.

Thus large honors will the faithful, earnest service of one day
Reap of Him; but one day's folly largest penalties will pay.

—Richard Chenevix Trench.

Not once or twice in our fair island-story
The path of duty was the way to glory.
He, that ever following her commands,
On with toil of heart and knees and hands,
Thro' the long gorge to the far light has won
His path upward, and prevailed,
Shall find the toppling crags of Duty scaled
Are close upon the shining table-lands
To which our God himself is moon and sun.

—Alfred Tennyson.

GO RIGHT ON WORKING

Ah, yes! the task is hard, 'tis true,
But what's the use of sighing?
They're soonest with their duties through
Who bravely keep on trying.
There's no advantage to be found
In sorrowing or shirking;
They with success are soonest crowned
Who just go right on working.

Strive patiently and with a will
That shall not be defeated;
Keep singing at your task until
You see it stand completed.
Nor let the clouds of doubt draw near,
Your sky's glad sunshine murking;
Be brave, and fill your heart with cheer,
And just go right on working.

—Nixon Waterman.

JUSTICE ONLY

Be not too proud of good deeds wrought!
When thou art come from prayer, speak truly!
Even if he wrongeth thee in aught,
Respect thy Guru. Give alms duly.

But let none wist! Live, day by day,
With little and with little swelling
Thy tale of duty done—the way
The wise ant-people build their dwelling;

Not harming any living thing;
That thou may'st have—at time of dying—
A Hand to hold thee, and to bring
Thy footsteps safe; and, so relying,

Pass to the farther world. For none
Save Justice leads there! Father, mother,
Will not be nigh; nor wife, nor son,
Nor friends, nor kin; nor any other

Save only Justice! All alone
Each entereth here, and each one leaveth
This life alone; and every one
The fruit of all his deeds receiveth

Alone—alone; bad deeds and good!
That day when kinsmen, sadly turning,
Forsake thee, like the clay or wood,
A thing committed to the burning.

But Justice shall not quit thee then,
If thou hast served her, therefore never
Cease serving; that shall hold thee when
The darkness falls which falls forever,

Which hath no star, nor way and guide.
But Justice knows the road; and midnight
Is noon to her. Man at her side
Goes, through the gloom, safe to the hid light.

And he who loved her more than all,
Who purged by sorrow his offenses,
Shall shine, in realms celestial,
With glory, quit of sins and senses.
—Edwin Arnold, from the Sanskrit.

GOD'S VENGEANCE

Saith the Lord, "Vengeance is mine;"
"I will repay," saith the Lord;
Ours be the anger divine,
Lit by the flash of his word.

How shall his vengeance be done?
How, when his purpose is clear?
Must he come down from the throne?
Hath he no instruments here?

Sleep not in imbecile trust,
Waiting for God to begin;
While, growing strong in the dust,
Rests the bruised serpent of sin.

Right and Wrong—both cannot live
Death-grappled. Which shall we see?
Strike! Only Justice can give
Safety to all that shall be.

Shame! to stand faltering thus,
Tricked by the balancing odds;
Strike! God is waiting for us!
Strike! for the vengeance is God's!
—John Hay.

Bear a lily in thy hand;
Gates of brass cannot withstand
One touch of that magic wand.

Bear through sorrow, wrong, and ruth,
In thy heart the dew of youth,
On thy lips the smile of truth.
—Henry Wadsworth Longfellow.

A SINGLE STITCH

One stitch dropped as the weaver drove
His nimble shuttle to and fro,
In and out, beneath, above,
Till the pattern seemed to bud and grow
As if the fairies had helping been;
One small stitch which could scarce be seen,
But the one stitch dropped pulled the next stitch out,
And a weak place grew in the fabric stout;
And the perfect pattern was marred for aye
By the one small stitch that was dropped that day.

One small life in God's great plan,
How futile it seems as the ages roll,
Do what it may or strive how it can
To alter the sweep of the infinite whole!
A single stitch in an endless web,
A drop in the ocean's flood and ebb!
But the pattern is rent where the stitch is lost,
Or marred where the tangled threads have crossed;
And each life that fails of its true intent
Mars the perfect plan that its Master meant.
—Susan Coolidge.

THE BLESSINGS

An angel came from the courts of gold,
With gifts and tidings manifold;
With blessings many to crown the one
Whose work of life was the noblest done.

He came to a rich man's gilded door;
Where a beautiful lady stood before
His vision, fair as the saints are fair,
With smile as sweet as the seraphs wear.

He needed not to be told her life—
The pure young mother, the tender wife;
He needed not to be told that she,
In home of sorrow and poverty,

Was giving wealth with a lavish hand;
He thought her worthy in heaven to stand.
"No! no!" a voice to the angel heart
Spoke low: "Seek on in the busy mart."

He found a door that was worn and old;
The night was damp and the wind was cold.
A pale-faced girl at her sewing bent;
The midnight lamp to her features lent

A paler look as she toiled the while,
But yet the mouth had a restful smile.
Doing her duty with honest pride;
Breasting temptation on every side.

"For her the blessings," the angel said,
And touched with pity the girlish head.
"No time nor money for alms has she,
But duty is higher than charity."
—Sarah Knowles Bolton.

DUTIES

I reach a duty, yet I do it not,
And therefore see no higher; but, if done,
My view is brightened and another spot
Seen on my moral sun.

For, be the duty high as angels' flight,
Fulfill it, and a higher will arise
E'en from its ashes. Duty is infinite—
Receding as the skies.

And thus it is the purest most deplore
Their want of purity. As fold by fold,
In duties done, falls from their eyes, the more
Of duty they behold.

Were it not wisdom, then, to close our eyes
On duties crowding only to appal?
No; duty is our ladder to the skies,
And, climbing not, we fall.
—Robert Leighton (1611–1684).

WHAT SHE COULD

"And do the hours step fast or slow?
And are ye sad or gay?
And is your heart with your liege lord, lady,
Or is it far away?"

The lady raised her calm, proud head,
Though her tears fell, one by one:
"Life counts not hours by joy or pangs,
But just by duties done.

"And when I lie in the green kirkyard,
With the mould upon my breast,
Say not that 'She did well—or ill,'
Only, 'She did her best.'"
—Dinah Maria Mulock Craik.

UNWASTED DAYS

The longer on this earth we live
And weigh the various qualities of men,
Seeing how most are fugitive
Or fitful gifts at best, of now and then—
Wind-favored corpse-lights, daughters of the fen—
The more we feel the high, stern-featured beauty
Of plain devotedness to duty,
Steadfast and still, nor paid with mortal praise,
But finding amplest recompense
For life's ungarlanded expense
In work done squarely and unwasted days.
—James Russell Lowell.

TRIFLES THAT MAKE SAINTS

A tone of pride or petulance repressed
A selfish inclination firmly fought,
A shadow of annoyance set at naught,
A measure of disquietude suppressed;
A peace in importunity possessed,
A reconcilement generously sought,
A purpose put aside, a banished thought,
A word of self-explaining unexpressed:
Trifles they seem, these petty soul-restraints,
Yet he who proves them so must needs possess
A constancy and courage grand and bold;
They are the trifles that have made the saints.
Give me to practice them in humbleness
And nobler power than mine doth no man hold.

The world is full of beauty,
As other worlds above;
And if we did our duty
It might be full of love.
—Gerald Massey.

What stronger breastplate than a heart
untainted?
Thrice is he armed that hath his quarrel
just;
And he but naked, though locked up in
steel,
Whose conscience with injustice is corrupted.
—William Shakespeare.

I slept, and dreamed that life was
Beauty;
I woke, and found that life was Duty.
Was thy dream then, a shadowy lie?
Toil on, sad heart, courageously,
And thou shalt find that dream to be
A noonday light and truth to thee.
—Ellen Sturgis Hooper.

Do thy duty; that is best;
Leave unto thy Lord the rest.
—James Russell Lowell.

While I sought Happiness she fled
Before me constantly.
Weary, I turned to Duty's path,
And Happiness sought me,
Saying, "I walk this road to-day,
I'll bear thee company."

So nigh is grandeur to our dust,
So near is God to man,
When Duty whispers low, "Thou must,"
The youth replies, "I can."
Ralph Waldo Emerson.

Faithfully faithful to every trust,
Honestly honest in every deed,
Righteously righteous and justly just;
This is the whole of the good man's
creed.

Find out what God would have you do,
And do that little well;
For what is great and what is small
'Tis only he can tell.

SERVICE

USEFULNESS, BENEVOLENCE, LABOR

WAKING

I have done at length with dreaming;
  Henceforth, O thou soul of mine!
Thou must take up sword and buckler,
  Waging warfare most divine.

Life is struggle, combat, victory!
  Wherefore have I slumbered on
With my forces all unmarshaled,
  With my weapons all undrawn?

O how many a glorious record
  Had the angels of me kept
Had I done instead of doubted,
  Had I warred instead of wept!

But begone, regret, bewailing!
  Ye had weakened at the best;
I have tried the trusty weapons
  Resting erst within my breast.

I have wakened to my duty,
  To a knowledge strong and deep,
That I recked not of aforetime,
  In my long inglorious sleep.

For the end of life is service,
  And I felt it not before,
And I dreamed not how stupendous
  Was the meaning that it bore.

In this subtle sense of being,
  Newly stirred in every vein,
I can feel a throb electric—
  Pleasure half allied with pain.

'Tis so sweet, and yet so awful,
  So bewildering, yet brave,
To be king in every conflict
  Where before I crouched a slave!

'Tis so glorious to be conscious
  Of a growing power within
Stronger than the rallying forces
  Of a charged and marshaled sin!

Never in those old romances
  Felt I half the thrill of life
That I feel within me stirring,
  Standing in this place of strife.

O those olden days of dalliance,
  When I wantoned with my fate;
When I trifled with the knowledge
  That had well-nigh come too late.

Yet, my soul, look not behind thee;
  Thou hast work to do at last;
Let the brave toil of the present
  Overarch the crumbling past.

Build thy great acts high and higher;
  Build them on the conquered sod
Where thy weakness first fell bleeding,
  And thy first prayer rose to God.
      —Caroline Atherton Mason.

SMALL BEGINNINGS

A traveler through a dusty road strewed acorns on the lea;
And one took root and sprouted up, and grew into a tree.
Love sought its shade, at evening time, to breathe its early vows;
And age was pleased, in heat of noon, to bask beneath its boughs;
The dormouse loved its dangling twigs the birds sweet music bore;
It stood a glory in its place, a blessing evermore.

A little spring had lost its way amid the grass and fern,
A passing stranger scooped a well where weary men might turn;
He walled it in, and hung with care a ladle at the brink;
He thought not of the deed he did, but judged that toil might drink.

He passed again, and lo! the well, by summers never dried,
Had cooled ten thousand parching tongues, and saved a life beside.

A dreamer dropped a random thought; 'twas old, and yet 'twas new;
A simple fancy of the brain, but strong in being true.
It shone upon a genial mind, and lo! its light became
A lamp of life, a beacon ray, a monitory flame.
The thought was small; its issue great; a watchfire on the hill,
It shed its radiance far adown, and cheers the valley still!

A nameless man, amid the crowd that thronged the daily mart,
Let fall a word of Hope and Love, unstudied, from the heart;
A whisper on the tumult thrown—a transitory breath—
It raised a brother from the dust; it saved a soul from death.
O germ! O fount! O word of love! O thought at random cast!
Ye were but little at the first, but mighty at the last!

—Charles Mackay.

THE CHOIR INVISIBLE

O may I join the choir invisible
Of those immortal dead who live again
In minds made better by their presence; live
In pulses stirred to generosity,
In deeds of daring rectitude, in scorn
For miserable aims that end with self,
In thoughts sublime that pierce the night like stars,
And with their mild persistence urge man's search
To vaster issues.
So to live is heaven:
To make undying music in the world,
Breathing as beauteous order that controls
With growing sway the growing life of man.
So we inherit that sweet purity
For which we struggled, failed and agonized,
With widening retrospect that bred despair.
Rebellious flesh that would not be subdued,
A vicious parent shaming still its child
Poor, anxious penitence, is quick dissolved;
Its discords, quenched by meeting harmonies,
Die in the large and charitable air.
And all our rarer, better, truer, self,
That sobbed religiously in yearning song,
That watched to ease the burden of the world,
Laboriously tracing what must be,
And what may yet be better—saw within
A worthier image for the sanctuary,
And shaped it forth before the multitude
Divinely human, raising worship so
To higher reverence more mixed with love—
That better self shall live till human Time
Shall fold its eyelids, and the human sky
Be gathered like a scroll within the tomb,
Unread forever.
This is life to come,
Which martyred men have made more glorious
For us who strive to follow. May I reach
That purest heaven, be to other souls
The cup of strength in some great agony,
Enkindle generous ardor, feed pure love,
Beget the smiles that have no cruelty—
Be the sweet presence of a good diffused,
And in diffusion ever more intense.
So shall I join the choir invisible
Whose music is the gladness of the world.

—George Eliot.

MY TASK

To love some one more dearly ev'ry day,
To help a wandering child to find his way,
To ponder o'er a noble thought, and pray,
And smile when evening falls.

To follow truth as blind men long for light,
To do my best from dawn of day till night,
To keep my heart fit for His holy sight,
And answer when He calls.

—Maude Louise Ray.

"IT IS MORE BLESSED"

Give! as the morning that flows out of heaven;
Give! as the waves when their channel is riven;
Give! as the free air and sunshine are given;
  Lavishly, utterly, joyfully give!
Not the waste drops of thy cup overflowing;
Not the faint sparks of thy hearth ever glowing;
Not a pale bud from the June roses blowing:
  Give as He gave thee who gave thee to live.

Pour out thy love like the rush of a river,
Wasting its waters, forever and ever,
Through the burnt sands that reward not the giver:
  Silent or songful, thou nearest the sea.
Scatter thy life as the summer's shower pouring;
What if no bird through the pearl rain is soaring?
What if no blossom looks upward adoring?
  Look to the life that was lavished for thee!

So the wild wind strews its perfumed caresses:
Evil and thankless the desert it blesses;
Bitter the wave that its soft pinion presses;
  Never it ceaseth to whisper and sing.
What if the hard heart give thorns for thy roses?
What if on rocks thy tired bosom reposes?
Sweeter is music with minor-keyed closes,
  Fairest the vines that on ruin will cling.

Almost the day of thy giving is over;
Ere from the grass dies the bee-haunted clover
Thou wilt have vanished from friend and from lover:
  What shall thy longing avail in the grave?
Give as the heart gives whose fetters are breaking—
Life, love, and hope, all thy dreams and thy waking;
Soon, heaven's river thy soul-fever slaking,
  Thou shalt know God and the gift that he gave.

—Rose Terry Cooke.

ALONG THE WAY

There are so many helpful things to do
  Along life's way
(Helps to the helper, if we did but know),
  From day to day.
So many troubled hearts to soothe,
So many pathways rough to smooth,
So many comforting words to say,
To the hearts that falter along the way.

Here is a lamp of hope gone out
  Along the way.
Some one stumbled and fell, no doubt—
  But, brother, stay!
Out of thy store of oil refill;
Kindle the courage that smoulders still;
Think what Jesus would do to-day
For one who had fallen beside the way.

How many lifted hands still plead
  Along life's way!
The old, sad story of human need
  Reads on for aye.
But let us follow the Saviour's plan—
Love unstinted to every man;
Content if, at most, the world should say:
"He helped his brother along the way!"

SAVED TO SERVE

Is thy cruse of comfort failing?
  Rise and share it with another,
And through all the years of famine
  It shall serve thee and thy brother.

Love divine will fill thy storehouse
  Or thy handful still renew;
Scanty fare for one will often
  Make a royal feast for two.

For the heart grows rich in giving—
  All its wealth is living gain;
Seeds which mildew in the garner
  Scattered fill with gold the plain.

Is thy burden hard and heavy?
  Do thy steps drag wearily?
Help to bear thy brother's burden;
  God will bear both it and thee.

Numb and weary on the mountains,
  Wouldst thou sleep amidst the snow?
Chafe that frozen form beside thee,
  And together both shall glow.

Art thou stricken in life's battle?
Many wounded round thee moan:
Lavish on their wounds thy balsam,
And that balm shall heal thine own.

Is thy heart a well left empty?
None but God the void can fill.
Nothing but the ceaseless Fountain
Can its ceaseless longings still.

Is the heart a living power?
Self-entwined its strength sinks low.
It can only live in loving,
And by serving love will grow.

BY DOING GOOD WE LIVE

A certain wise man, deeply versed
In all the learning of the East,
Grew tired in spirit, and athirst
From life to be released.

So to Eliab, holy man
Of God he came: "Ah, give me, friend,
The herb of death, that now the span
Of my vain life may end."

Eliab gently answered: "Ere
The soul may free itself indeed,
This herb of healing thou must bear
To seven men in need;

"When thou hast lightened each man's grief,
And brought him hope and joy again,
Return; nor shalt thou seek relief
At Allah's hands in vain."

The wise man sighed, and humbly said:
"As Allah willeth, so is best."
And with the healing herb he sped
Away upon his quest.

And as he journeyed on, intent
To serve the sorrowing in the land
On deeds of love and mercy bent,
The herb bloomed in his hand,

And through his pulses shot a fire
Of strength and hope and happiness;
His heart leaped with a glad desire
To live and serve and bless.

Lord of all earthly woe and need,
Be this, life's flower, mine!
To love, to comfort, and to heal—
Therein is life divine!

—Josephine Troup.

FOR STRENGTH WE ASK

For strength we ask
For the ten thousand times repeated task,
The endless smallnesses of every day.

No, not to lay
My life down in the cause I cherish most,
That were too easy. But, whate'er it cost,
To fail no more
In gentleness toward the ungentle, nor
In love toward the unlovely, and to give,

Each day I live,
To every hour with outstretched hand, its meed
Of not-to-be-regretted thought and deed.

—Agnes Ethelwyn Wetherald.

MARTHA OR MARY?

I cannot choose; I should have liked so much
To sit at Jesus' feet—to feel the touch
Of his kind gentle hand upon my head
While drinking in the gracious words he said.

And yet to serve Him!—Oh, divine employ—
To minister and give the Master joy;
To bathe in coolest springs his weary feet,
And wait upon Him while He sat at meat!

Worship or service—which? Ah, that is best
To which he calls us, be it toil or rest;
To labor for Him in life's busy stir,
Or seek His feet, a silent worshiper.

—Caroline Atherton Mason.

This is the gospel of labor—ring it, ye bells of the kirk—
The Lord of Love came down from above to live with the men who work.
This is the rose that he planted, here in the thorn-cursed soil;
Heaven is blest with perfect rest, but the blessing of earth is toil.

—Henry van Dyke.

MARTHA

Yes, Lord, Yet some must serve!
Not all with tranquil heart,
Even at Thy dear feet,
Wrapped in devotion sweet,
May sit apart!

Yes, Lord! Yet some must bear
The burden of the day,
Its labor and its heat,
While others at Thy feet
May muse and pray.

Yes, Lord! Yet some must do
Life's daily task-work; some
Who fain would sing must toil
Amid earth's dust and moil,
While lips are dumb!

Yes, Lord! Yet man must earn
And woman bake the bread;
And some must watch and wake
Early for others' sake,
Who pray instead!

Yes, Lord! Yet even thou
Hast need of earthly care;
I bring the bread and wine
To Thee a Guest divine—
Be this my prayer!
—Julia Caroline Ripley Dorr.

If we sit down at set of sun
And count the things that we have done,
And counting, find
One self-denying act, one word
That eased the heart of him who heard,
One glance most kind,
That fell like sunshine where it went,
Then we may count the day well spent.

But if through all the livelong day
We've eased no heart by yea or nay;
If through it all
We've nothing done that we can trace
That brought the sunshine to a face,
No act most small
That helped some soul, and nothing cost,
Then count that day as worse than lost.

This for the day of life I ask:
Some all-absorbing, useful task;
And when 'tis wholly, truly done,
A tranquil rest at set of sun.

SERVICE

Ah! grand is the world's work, and noble, forsooth,
The doing one's part, be it ever so small!
You, reaping with Boaz, I, gleaning with Ruth,
Are honored by serving, yet servants of all.

No drudge in his corner but speeds the world's wheels;
No serf in the field but is sowing God's seed—
More noble, I think, in the dust though he kneels,
Than the pauper of wealth, who makes scorn of the deed.

Is toil but a treadmill? Think not of the grind,
But think of the grist, what is done and to do,
The world growing better, more like to God's mind,
By long, faithful labor of helpers like you.

The broom or the spade or the shuttle, that plies
Its own honest task in its own honest way,
Serves heaven not less than a star in the skies—
What more could the Pleiades do than obey? —James Buckham.

SUMMER AND WINTER

If no kindly thought or word
We can give, some soul to bless,
If our hands, from hour to hour,
Do no deeds of gentleness;
If to lone and weary ones
We no comfort will impart—
Tho' 'tis summer in the sky,
Yet 'tis winter in the heart!

If we strive to lift the gloom
From a dark and burdened life;
If we seek to lull the storm
Of our fallen brother's strife;
If we bid all hate and scorn
From the spirit to depart—
Tho' 'tis winter in the sky,
Yet 'tis summer in the heart!

THE ELEVENTH-HOUR LABORER

Idlers all day about the market-place
They name us, and our dumb lips answer not,
Bearing the bitter while our sloth's disgrace,
And our dark tasking whereof none may wot.

Oh, the fair slopes where the grape-gatherers go!—
Not they the day's fierce heat and burden bear,
But we who on the market-stones drop slow
Our barren tears, while all the bright hours wear.

Lord of the vineyard, whose dear word declares
Our one hour's labor as the day's shall be,
What coin divine can make our wage as theirs
Who had the morning joy of work for Thee?

—L. Gray Noble.

"THY LABOR IS NOT IN VAIN"

"I have labored in vain," a preacher said,
And his brow was marked with care;
"I have labored in vain." He bowed down his head,
And bitter and sad were the tears he shed
In that moment of dark despair.

"I am weary and worn, and my hands are weak,
And my courage is well-nigh gone;
For none give heed to the words I speak,
And in vain for a promise of fruit I seek
Where the seed of the Word is sown."

And again with a sorrowful heart he wept,
For his spirit with grief was stirred,
Till the night grew dark, and at last he slept,
And a silent calm o'er his spirit crept,
And a whisper of "peace" was heard.

And he thought in his dream that his soul took flight
To a blessed and bright abode;
He saw a throne of dazzling light,
And harps were ringing, and robes were white—
Made white in a Saviour's blood.

And he saw such a countless throng around
As he never had seen before,
Their brows with jewels of light were crowned,
And sorrow and sighing no place had found—
The troubles of time were o'er.

Then a white-robed maiden came forth and said,
"Joy! Joy! for the trials are passed!
I am one that thy gentle words have led
In the narrow pathway of life to tread—
I welcome thee home at last!"

And the preacher gazed on the maiden's face—
He had seen that face on earth,
Where, with anxious heart, in his wonted place
He had told his charge of a Saviour's grace,
And their need of a second birth.

Then the preacher smiled, and the angel said,
"Go forth to thy work again;
It is not in vain that the seed is shed—
If only ONE soul to the cross is led,
Thy labor is not in vain."

And at last he woke, and his knee he bent
In grateful, childlike prayer,
And he prayed till an answer of peace was sent,
And Faith and Hope as a rainbow bent
O'er the clouds of his earthly care.

And he rose in joy, and his eye was bright,
His sorrow and grief had fled,
And his soul was calm and his heart was light,
For his hands were strong in his Saviour's might
As forth to his work he sped.

Whatever dies, or is forgot—
Work done for God, it dieth not.

FOLLOWING THE MASTER

I asked the Lord that I might worthier be,
Might grow in faith and hope and charity;
And straight, "Go feed my lambs!" he answered me.

"Nay, Lord!" I cried. "Can outward deeds avail
To cleanse my spirit? Heart and courage fail
And sins prevent, and foes and fears assail."

And still, "Go, feed my lambs!" was all I heard.
But should I rest upon that simple word?
Was that, indeed, my message from my Lord?

Behold, I thought that he his hand would lay
On my sick soul, and words of healing say,
And charm the plague-spot from my heart away.

Half wroth, I turned to go; but oh! the look
He on me cast—a gaze I could not brook;
With deep relentings all my spirit shook.

"O dearest Lord," I cried, "I will obey,
Say what thou wilt! only lead thou the way;
For, following thee, my footsteps shall not stray."

He took me at my word. He went before;
He led me to the dwellings of the poor,
Where wolf-eyed Want keeps watch beside the door.

He beckoned me, and I essayed to go
Where Sin and Crime, more sad than Want and Woe,
Hold carnival, and Vice walks to and fro.

And when I faltered at the sight, He said,
"Behold, I died for such! These hands have bled,
This side for such has pierced been," he said.

"Is the disciple greater than his Lord?
The servant than his Master?" Oh, that word!
It smote me like a sharp, two-edged sword!

And since that hour, if any work of mine
Has been accepted by my Lord as sign
That I was following in his steps divine;

If, serving others (though imperfectly),
My own poor life has worthier come to be,
And I have grown in faith and charity,

Dear Lord, be thine the glory! Thou hast wrought,
All unaware, the blessing that I sought.
O that these lips might praise thee as they ought!

BE ALWAYS GIVING

The sun gives ever; so the earth—
What it can give so much 'tis worth;
The ocean gives in many ways—
Gives baths, gives fishes, rivers, bays;
So, too, the air, it gives us breath.
When it stops giving, comes in death.
Give, give, be always giving;
Who gives not is not living;
The more you give
The more you live.

God's love hath in us wealth unheaped
Only by giving it is reaped;
The body withers, and the mind
Is pent up by a selfish rind.
Give strength, give thought, give deeds, give pelf,
Give love, give tears, and give thyself.
Give, give, be always giving,
Who gives not is not living;
The more we give
The more we live.

Slightest actions often meet the sorest needs,
For the world wants daily little kindly deeds;
O, what care and sorrow you may help remove
With your song and courage, sympathy and love.

NOT LOST

The look of sympathy; the gentle word
Spoken so low that only angels heard;
The secret act of pure self-sacrifice,
Unseen by men, but marked by angels' eyes;
These are not lost.

The silent tears that fall at dead of night
Over soiled robes that once were pure and white;
The prayers that rise like incense from the soul,
Longing for Christ to make it clean and whole;
These are not lost.

The happy dreams that gladdened all our youth,
When dreams had less of self and more of truth;
The childhood's faith, so tranquil and so sweet,
Which sat like Mary at the Master's feet;
These are not lost.

The kindly plans devised for others' good,
So seldom guessed, so little understood;
The quiet, steadfast love that strove to win
Some wanderer from the ways of sin;
These are not lost.

Not lost, O Lord! for in Thy city bright
Our eyes shall see the past by clearer light,
And things long hidden from our gaze below
Thou wilt reveal, and we shall surely know
They were not lost.

There's never a rose in all the world
But makes some green spray sweeter;
There's never a wind in all the sky
But makes some bird wing fleeter;
There's never a star but brings to heaven
Some silver radiance tender;
And never a rosy cloud but helps
To crown the sunset splendor;
No robin but may thrill some heart,
His dawn like gladness voicing;
God gives us all some small sweet way
To set the world rejoicing.

A BROADER FIELD

O thou who sighest for a broader field
Wherein to sow the seeds of truth and right—
Who fain a fuller, nobler power would wield
O'er human souls that languish for the light—

Search well the realm that even now is thine!
Canst not thou in some far-off corner find
A heart sin-bound, like tree with sapping vine,
Waiting for help its burdens to unbind?

Some human plant, perchance beneath thine eyes,
Pierced through with hidden thorns of idle fears;
Or drooping low for need of light from skies
Obscured by doubt-clouds raining poison tears?

Some bruisèd soul the balm of love would heal;
Some timid spirit faith would courage give;
Or maimèd brother, who, though brave and leal,
Still needeth thee, to rightly walk and live?

O while one soul thou findest which hath not known
The fullest help thy soul hath power to give,
Sigh not for fields still broader than thine own,
But, steadfast in thine own, more broadly live.

—Julia Anna Wolcott.

Be it health or be it leisure,
Be it skill we have to give,
Still in spending it for others
Christians only really live.

Not in having or receiving,
But in giving, there is bliss;
He who has no other pleasure
Ever may rejoice in this.

WHAT CHRIST SAID

I said, "Let me walk in the fields."
He said, "No, walk in the town."
I said, "There are no flowers there."
He said, "No flowers, but a crown."

I said, "But the skies are black;
There is nothing but noise and din."
And He wept as he sent me back;
"There is more," He said; "there is sin."

I said, "But the air is thick,
And fogs are veiling the sun."
He answered, "Yet souls are sick,
And souls in the dark undone."

I said, "I shall miss the light,
And friends will miss me, they say."
He answered, "Choose to-night
If *I* am to miss you, or they."

I pleaded for time to be given.
He said, "Is it hard to decide?
It will not seem hard in heaven
To have followed the steps of your Guide."

I cast one look at the fields,
Then set my face to the town;
He said, "My child, do you yield?
Will you leave the flowers for the crown?"

Then into His hand went mine,
And into my heart came He;
And I walk in a light divine
The path I had feared to see.
—George Macdonald.

MY SERVICE

I asked the Lord to let me do
Some mighty work for Him;
To fight amid His battle hosts,
Then sing the victor's hymn.
I longed my ardent love to show,
But Jesus would not have it so.

He placed me in a quiet home,
Whose life was calm and still,
And gave me little things to do,
My daily round to fill;
I could not think it good to be
Just put aside so silently.

Small duties gathered round my way,
They seemed of earth alone;
I, who had longed for conquests bright
To lay before His throne,
Had common things to do and bear,
To watch and strive with daily care.

So then I thought my prayer unheard,
And asked the Lord once more
That He would give me work for Him
And open wide the door;
Forgetting that my Master knew
Just what was best for me to do.

Then quietly the answer came,
"My child, I hear thy cry;
Think not that mighty deeds alone
Will bring the victory.
The battle has been planned by Me,
Let daily life thy conquests see."

PASS IT ON

Have you had a kindness shown?
Pass it on.
It was not given to you alone,
Pass it on.
Let it travel through the years;
Let it wipe another's tears;
Till in heaven the deed appears,
Pass it on.

Have you found the heavenly light?
Pass it on.
Souls are groping in the night,
Daylight gone.
Lift your lighted lamp on high,
Be a star in some one's sky,
He may live who else would die.
Pass it on.

GIVING AND TAKING

Who gives, and hides the giving hand,
Nor counts on favor, fame, or praise,
Shall find his smallest gift outweighs
The burden of the sea and land.

Who gives to whom hath naught been given,
His gift in need, though small indeed
As is the grass-blade's wind-blown seed,
Is large as earth and rich as heaven.
—John Greenleaf Whittier, from Tinnevaluna of India.

ONE PATH TO LIGHT

What is the world? A wandering maze,
Where sin hath tracked a thousand ways
Her victims to ensnare.
All broad and winding and aslope,
All tempting with perfidious hope,
All ending in despair.
Millions of pilgrims throng those roads,
Bearing their baubles or their loads
Down to eternal night.
One only path that never bends,
Narrow and rough and steep, ascends
Through darkness into light.
Is there no guide to show that path?
The Bible. He alone that hath
The Bible need not stray.
But he who hath and will not give
That light of life to all that live,
Himself shall lose the way.

IF WE COULD ONLY SEE

It were not hard, we think, to serve Him
If we could only see!
If he would stand with that gaze intense
Burning into our bodily sense,
If we might look on that face most tender,
The brows where the scars are turned to splendor,
Might catch the light of his smile so sweet,
And view the marks on his hands and feet,
How loyal we should be!
It were not hard, we think, to serve him,
If we could only see!

It were not hard, he says, to see him,
If we would only serve;
"He that doeth the will of Heaven,
To him shall knowledge and sight be given."
While for his presence we sit repining,
Never we see his countenance shining;
They who toil where his reapers be
The glow of his smile may always see,
And their faith can never swerve.
It were not hard, he says, to see him,
If we would only serve.

Think not in sleep to fold thy hands,
Forgetful of thy Lord's commands,
From Duty's claims no life is free,
Behold! To-day has need of thee.

WHEN YOU DO AN ACT

You can never tell when you do an act
Just what the result will be;
But with every deed you are sowing a seed,
Though its harvest you may not see.
Each kindly act is an acorn dropped
In God's productive soil;
Though you may not know, yet the tree shall grow
And shelter the brows that toil.

YOUR MISSION

If you cannot on the ocean
Sail among the swiftest fleet,
Rocking on the highest billows,
Laughing at the storms you meet;
You can stand among the sailors
Anchored yet within the bay;
You can lend a hand to help them
As they launch their boat away.

If you are too weak to journey
Up the mountain steep and high,
You can stand within the valley
While the multitudes go by;
You can chant in happy measure
As they slowly pass along;
Though they may forget the singer
They will not forget the song.

If you have not gold and silver
Ever ready to command;
If you cannot toward the needy,
Reach an ever-open hand;
You can visit the afflicted,
O'er the erring you can weep;
You can be a true disciple
Sitting at the Saviour's feet.

If you cannot in the harvest
Garner up the richest sheaves,
Many a grain both ripe and golden
Will the careless reapers leave;
Go and glean among the briers
Growing rank against the wall,
For it may be that their shadow
Hides the heaviest wheat of all.

If you cannot in the conflict
Prove yourself a soldier true,
If where fire and smoke are thickest
There's no work for you to do;
When the battle-field is silent
You can go with careful tread:
You can bear away the wounded,
You can cover up the dead.

If you cannot be the watchman,
  Standing high on Zion's wall,
Pointing out the path to heaven,
  Offering life and peace to all;
With your prayers and with your bounties
  You can do what Heaven demands,
You can be like faithful Aaron,
  Holding up the prophet's hands.

Do not, then, stand idly waiting
  For some greater work to do;
Fortune is a lazy goddess—
  She will never come to you.
Go and toil in any vineyard,
  Do not fear to do or dare;
If you want a field of labor
  You can find it anywhere.
—G. M. Grannis.

THE FAITHFUL MONK

Golden gleams of noonday fell
On the pavement of the cell,
And the monk still lingered there
In the ecstasy of prayer;
Fuller floods of glory streamed
Through the window, and it seemed
Like an answering glow of love
From the countenance above.

On the silence of the cell
Break the faint tones of a bell.
'Tis the hour when at the gate
Crowds of poor and hungry wait,
Wan and wistful, to be fed
With the friar of mercy's bread.

Hark! that chime of heaven's far bells!
On the monk's rapt ear it swells,
No! fond, flattering dream, away!
Mercy calls; no longer stay!
Whom thou yearnest here to find
In the musings of thy mind,
God and Jesus, lo, they wait
Knocking at thy convent gate!

From his knees the monk arose;
With full heart and hand he goes,
At his gate the poor relieves,
Gains a blessing and receives;
To his cell returned, and there
Found the angel of his prayer,
Who with radiant features said,
"Hadst thou stayed I must have fled."
—Charles Timothy Brooks.

THE HEAVENLY PRESENCE

Somewhere I have read of an aged monk
  Who, kneeling one day in his cell,
Beheld in a glorious vision the form
  Of the dear Lord Christ; and there fell

Upon him a rapture, wondrously sweet,
  And his lips could frame no word,
As he gazed on the form and noted the love
  That beamed from the face of his Lord.

There came to his ears the sound of a bell
  Which called him early and late
To carry loaves to the wretched poor
  Who lingered about the gate.

Could he leave his cell now glorified
  By the presence of the Christ,
The Blessed Son, the Holy One,
  His Saviour, the Sacrificed?

He went to his act of mercy, and when
  He returned to his cell, the dim
Gay light was dispelled as the loving Christ
  Re-entered to welcome him.

And the Blessed One remained, more fair,
  More glorious than before,
And the heart of the aged monk was glad,
  And his cell was dim no more.

"Draw nigh and abide with me, O Christ,
  All through this day," is the prayer
Which sounds from my heart, and my lips repeat
  Each morning, and Christ, the Fair,

Seems very near as his words I hear,
  Though his form I do not see;
"When you care for the least of these, dear child,
  You have done it unto me.

"With loving service fill all this day,
  Do good in the name of your Lord,
And I will be near, your heart to cheer,
  According to my word."
—William Norris Burr.

ONLY

It was *only* a blossom,
Just the merest bit of bloom,
But it brought a glimpse of summer
To the little darkened room.

It was *only* a glad "good morning,"
As she passed along the way;
But it spread the morning's glory
Over the livelong day.

Only a song; but the music,
Though simply pure and sweet,
Brought back to better pathways
The reckless roving feet.

"*Only*," in our blind wisdom,
How dare we say at all?
Since the ages alone can tell us
Which is the great or small.

SOMETHING YOU CAN DO

Hark! the voice of Jesus calling,
"Who will go and work to-day?
Fields are white and harvests waiting,
Who will bear the sheaves away?"
Loud and long the Master calleth,
Rich reward he offers free;
Who will answer, gladly saying,
"Here am I, send me, send me."

If you cannot cross the ocean
And the heathen lands explore,
You can find the heathen nearer,
You can help them at your door;
If you cannot give your thousands
You can give the widow's mite;
And the least you give for Jesus
Will be precious in his sight.

If you cannot speak like angels,
If you cannot preach like Paul,
You can tell the love of Jesus,
You can say he died for all.
If you cannot rouse the wicked
With the Judgment's dread alarms,
You can lead the little children
To the Saviour's waiting arms.

Let none hear you idly saying
"There is nothing I can do,"
While the sons of men are dying,
And the Master calls for you.
Take the task he gives you gladly,
Let his work your pleasure be;
Answer quickly, when he calleth,
"Here am I, send me, send me."
—Daniel March.

SEEDTIME

Sow thou thy seed!
Glad is the light of Spring—the sun is glowing.
Do thou thy deed:
Who knows when flower or deed shall cease its growing?

Thy seed may be
Bearer of thousands scattered far and near;
Eternity
May feel the impress of the deed done here.
—Arthur L. Salmon.

TOIL A BLESSING

The toil of brain, or heart, or hand,
Is man's appointed lot;
He who God's call can understand
Will work and murmur not.
Toil is no thorny crown of pain,
Bound round man's brow for sin;
True souls, from it, all strength may gain,
High manliness may win.

O God! who workest hitherto,
Working in all we see,
Fain would we be, and bear, and do,
As best it pleaseth thee.
Where'er thou sendest we will go,
Nor any questions ask,
And that thou biddest we will do,
Whatever be the task.

Our skill of hand, and strength of limb,
Are not our own, but thine;
We link them to the work of Him
Who made all life divine.
Our brother-friend, thy holy Son,
Shared all our lot and strife;
And nobly will our work be done
If molded by his life.
—Thomas W. Freckelton.

No service in itself is small;
None great, though earth it fill;
But that is small that seeks its own,
And great that seeks God's will.

Then hold my hand, most gracious God,
Guide all my goings still;
And let it be my life's one aim,
To know and do thy will.

EASILY GIVEN

It was only a sunny smile,
And little it cost in the giving;
But it scattered the night
Like morning light,
And made the day worth living.
Through life's dull warp a woof it wove,
In shining colors of light and love,
And the angels smiled as they watched above,
Yet little it cost in giving.

It was only a kindly word,
And a word that was lightly spoken;
Yet not in vain,
For it stilled the pain
Of a heart that was nearly broken.
It strengthened a fate beset by fears
And groping blindly through mists of tears
For light to brighten the coming years,
Although it was lightly spoken.

It was only a helping hand,
And it seemed of little availing;
But its clasps were warm,
And it saved from harm
A brother whose strength was failing.
Its touch was tender as angels' wings,
But it rolled the stone from the hidden springs,
And pointed the way to higher things,
Though it seemed of little availing.

A smile, a word, a touch,
And each is easily given;
Yet one may win
A soul from sin
Or smooth the way to heaven.
A smile may lighten a falling heart,
A word may soften pain's keenest smart,
A touch may lead us from sin apart—
How easily each is given!

WORKING WITH CHRIST

O matchless honor, all unsought,
High privilege, surpassing thought
That thou shouldst call us, Lord, to be
Linked in work-fellowship with thee!
To carry out *thy* wondrous plan,
To bear *thy* messages to man;
"In trust," with Christ's own word of grace
To every soul of human race.

THE "NEW LOGION"

"Jesus saith," and His deep Saying who shall rightly understand,
Rescued from the grasp of ages, risen from its grave of sand?
Who shall read its mystic meaning, who explain its import high:
"Raise the stone and thou shalt find Me, cleave the wood and there am I"?

Does it mean the stone-built altar, and the cleft-wood for its fire,
That with sacrificial offering shall the soul to God aspire,
Purged and pure from sin's defilement, lifting holy hands on high,
"Raise the stone and thou shalt find Me, cleave the wood and there am I"?

Does it mean that toil and action are the price that man shall pay,
Striving the strait gait to enter, pressing on the narrow way,
Clearing it from shade and hindrance, with strong arm and purpose high,
"Raise the stone and thou shalt find Me, cleave the wood and there am I"?

Does it mean that he who seeketh may Thy presence always see
In the common things around him, in the stone and in the tree,
Underlying, all-pervading, Soul of Nature, ever nigh,
"Raise the stone and thou shalt find Me, cleave the wood and there am I"?

Yea, in all our work and worship, in our quiet, in our strife,
In the daily, busy handwork, in the soul's most ardent life,
Each may read his own true meaning of the Saying deep and high,
"Raise the stone and thou shalt find Me, cleave the wood and there am I."

—Mrs. Henry B. Smith.

He's true to God, who's true to man; wherever wrong is done,
To the humblest and the weakest, 'neath the all-beholding sun,
That wrong is also done to us; and they are slaves most base
Whose love of right is for themselves, and not for all their race.

—James Russell Lowell.

HER CREED

She stood before a chosen few,
With modest air and eyes of blue;
A gentle creature, in whose face
Were mingled tenderness and grace.

"You wish to join our fold," they said;
"Do you believe in all that's read
From ritual and written creed,
Essential to our human need?"

A troubled look was in her eyes;
She answered, as in vague surprise,
As though the sense to her were dim.
"I only strive to follow Him."

They knew her life, how oft she stood,
Pure in her guileless maidenhood,
By dying bed, in hovel lone,
Whose sorrow she had made her own.

Oft had her voice in prayer been heard,
Sweet as the note of any bird;
Her hand been open in distress;
Her joy to brighten and to bless.

Yet still she answered, when they sought
To know her inmost, earnest thought,
With look as of the seraphim
"I only strive to follow Him."

—Sarah Knowles Bolton.

WAKING THOUGHTS

Another day God gives me, pure and white.
How can I make it holy in his sight?
Small means have I and but a narrow sphere,
Yet work is round me, for he placed me here.
How can I serve thee, Lord? Open mine eyes;
Show me the duty that around me lies.

"The house is small, but human hearts are there,
And for this day at least beneath thy care.
Someone is sad—then speak a word of cheer;
Someone is lonely—make him welcome here;
Someone has failed—protect him from despair;
Someone is poor—there's something you can spare!
"Thine own heart's sorrow mention but in prayer,
And carry sunshine with thee everywhere.
The little duties do with all thine heart
And from things sordid keep a mind apart;
Then sleep, my child, and take a well-earned rest,
In blessing others thou thyself art blest!"

LONELY SERVICE

Methought that in a solemn church I stood;
Its marble acres, worn with knees and feet,
Lay spread from door to door, from street to street.
Midway the form hung high upon the rood
Of Him who gave his life to be our good.
Beyond, priests flitted, bowed, and murmured meet
Among the candles, shining still and sweet.
Men came and went, and worshipped as they could—
And still their dust a woman with her broom,
Bowed to her work, kept sweeping to the door.
Then saw I, slow through all the pillared gloom,
Across the church a silent figure come;
"Daughter," it said, "thou sweepest well my floor."
"It is the Lord!" I cried, and saw no more. —George Macdonald.

SHARE YOUR BLESSINGS

Dig channels for the streams of love,
 Where they may broadly run,
And love has overflowing streams
 To fill them every one.
But if at any time thou cease
 Such channels to provide,
The very founts of love to thee
 Will soon be parched and dried.
For thou must share if thou wouldst keep
 That good thing from above;
Ceasing to share you cease to have;
 Such is the law of love.

ONLY A LITTLE

Only a seed—but it chanced to fall
In a little cleft of a city wall,
And taking root, grew bravely up
Till a tiny blossom crowned its top.

Only a thought—but the work it wrought
Could never by tongue or pen be taught;
For it ran through a life like a thread of gold,
And the life bore fruit—a hundred fold.

Only a word—but 'twas spoken in love,
With a whispered prayer to the Lord above;
And the angels in heaven rejoiced once more,
For a new-born soul "entered in by the door."

PAUL AT MELITA

Secure in his prophetic strength,
The water peril o'er,
The many-gifted man at length
Stepped on the promised shore.

He trod the shore; but not to rest,
Nor wait till angels came;
Lo! humblest pains the saint attest,
The firebrands and the flame.

But when he felt the viper's smart,
Then instant aid was given.
Christian, hence learn to do thy part,
And leave the rest to Heaven.

—John Henry Newman.

All service ranks the same with God;
If now, as formerly He trod
Paradise, His presence fills
Our earth, each only as God wills
Can work—God's puppets, best and worst,
Are we; there is no last nor first.

Say not "a small event!" Why "small"?
Costs it more pain that this, ye call
A "great event," should come to pass
Than that? Untwine me, from the mass
Of deeds which make up life, one deed
Power shall fall short in, or exceed.

—Robert Browning.

What will it matter in a little while
That for a day
We met and gave a word, a touch, a smile,
Upon the way?
These trifles! Can they make or mar
Human life?
Are souls as lightly swayed as rushes are
By love or strife?
Yea, yea, a look the fainting heart may break,
Or make it whole,
And just one word, if said for love's sweet sake,
May save a soul.

Get leave to work
In this world—'tis the best you get at all;
For God in cursing gives us better gifts
Than men in benediction. God says, "Sweat
For foreheads;" men say "crowns;" and so we are crowned—
Ay, gashed by some tormenting circle of steel
Which snaps with a secret spring. Get work; get work;
Be sure 'tis better than what you work to get.

—Elizabeth Barrett Browning.

Be useful where thou livest, that they may
Both want and wish thy pleasing presence still;
Kindness, good parts, great places, are the way
To compass this. Find out men's wants and will,
And meet them there. All worldly joys go less
To the one joy of doing kindnesses.

—George Herbert.

When He who, sad and weary, longing sore
For love's sweet service sought the sisters' door,
One saw the heavenly, one the human guest;
But who shall say which loved the Master best?

—John Greenleaf Whittier.

Oft, when the Word is on me to deliver,
Opens the heaven, and the Lord is there.

. . . .

Then with a rush the intolerable craving
Shivers throughout me like a trumpet call—
Oh to save these! to perish for their saving,
Die for their life, be offered for them all!

No man is born into the world whose work
Is not born with him; there is always work,
And tools to work withal, for those who will;
And blessed are the horny hands of toil!
—James Russell Lowell.

The Holy Supper is kept, indeed,
In whatso we share with another's need;
Not what we give, but what we share,
For the gift without the giver is bare;
Who gives himself with his alms feeds three:
Himself, his hungering neighbor, and Me.
—James Russell Lowell.

Look not beyond the stars for heaven,
Nor 'neath the sea for hell;
Know thou, who leads a useful life
In Paradise doth dwell.
—Hafiz, tr. by Frederic Rowland Marvin.

Small service is true service while it lasts:
Of humblest friends, bright creature, scorn not one;
The daisy, by the shadow that it casts,
Protects the lingering dewdrop from the sun. —William Wordsworth.

Mechanic soul, thou must not only do
With Martha, but with Mary ponder too;
Happy's the home where these fair sisters vary;
But most, when Martha's reconciled to Mary. —Francis Quarles.

If thou hast the gift of strength, then know
Thy part is to uplift the trodden low;
Else, in the giant's grasp, until the end
A hopeless wrestler shall thy soul contend. —George Meredith.

The best men doing their best
Know, peradventure, least of what they do.
Men usefullest i' the world are simply used.
—Elizabeth Barrett Browning.

New words to speak, new thoughts to hear,
New love to give and take;
Perchance new burdens I may bear
To-day for love's sweet sake,

He doth good work whose heart can find
The spirit 'neath the letter;
Who makes his kind of happier mind,
Leaves wiser men and better.

Work for some good, be it ever so slowly,
Cherish some flower, be it ever so lowly,
Labor—all labor is noble and holy.
—Frances Sargent Osgood.

In silence mend what ills deform the mind;
But all thy good impart to all thy kind.
—John Sterling.

God gave me something very sweet to be mine own this day:
A precious opportunity a word for Christ to say.

That best portion of a good man's life—
His little, nameless, unremembered acts
Of kindness and of love.
—William Wordsworth.

Wouldst thou go forth to bless, be sure of thine own ground,
Fix well thy center first, then draw thy circle round.
—Richard Chenevix Trench.

BROTHERHOOD

CHARITY, SYMPATHY, EXAMPLE, INFLUENCE

THE HOUSE BY THE SIDE OF THE ROAD

There are hermit souls that live withdrawn
  In the peace of their self-content;
There are souls, like stars, that dwell apart
  In a fellowless firmament;
There are pioneer souls that blaze their paths
  Where highways never ran—
But let me live by the side of the road
  And be a friend to man.

Let me live in a house by the side of the road,
  Where the race of men go by—
The men who are good and the men who are bad,
  As good and as bad as I.
I would not sit in the scorner's seat,
  Or hurl the cynic's ban—
Let me live in a house by the side of the road,
  And be a friend to man.

I see from my house by the side of the road,
  By the side of the highway of life,
The men who press with the ardor of hope
  The men who are faint with the strife.
But I turn not away from their smiles nor their tears—
  Both parts of an infinite plan—
Let me live in a house by the side of the road
  And be a friend to man.

I know there are brook-gladdened meadows ahead
  And mountains of wearisome height;
And the road passes on through the long afternoon
  And stretches away to the night.
But still I rejoice when the travelers rejoice,
  And weep with the strangers that moan,
Nor live in my house by the side of the road
  Like a man who dwells alone.

Let me live in my house by the side of the road
  Where the race of men go by—
They are good, they are bad, they are weak, they are strong,
  Wise, foolish—so am I.
Then why should I sit in the scorner's seat
  Or hurl the cynic's ban?
Let me live in my house by the side of the road
  And be a friend to man.

—Sam Walter Foss.

IS YOUR LAMP BURNING?

Say, is your lamp burning, my brother?
  I pray you look quickly and see;
For if it were burning, then surely
  Some beams would fall brightly on me.

Straight, straight is the road, but I falter.
  And oft I fall out by the way;
Then lift your lamp higher, my brother,
  Lest I should make fatal delay.

There are many and many around you
  Who follow wherever you go;
If you thought that they walked in the shadow
  Your lamp would burn brighter, I know.

Upon the dark mountains they stumble,
  They are bruised on the rocks, and they lie
With their white pleading faces turned upward
  To the clouds and the pitiful sky.

There is many a lamp that is lighted,
We behold them anear and afar,
But not many among them, my brother,
Shine steadily on, like a star.

I think, were they trimmed night and morning,
They would never burn down or go out,
Though from the four quarters of heaven
The winds were all blowing about.

If once all the lamps that are lighted
Should steadily blaze in a line,
Wide over the land and the ocean,
What a girdle of glory would shine!

How all the dark places would brighten!
How the mists would roll up and away!
How the earth would laugh out in her gladness
To hail the millennial day!

Say, is your lamp burning, my brother?
I pray you look quickly and see;
For if it were burning, then surely
Some beams would fall brightly on me.

IF I SHOULD DIE TO-NIGHT

If I should die to-night,
My friends would look upon my quiet face
Before they laid it in its resting-place,
And deem that death had left it almost fair,
And laying snow-white flowers upon my hair,
Would smooth it down with tearful tenderness,
And fold my hands with lingering caress—
Poor hands, so empty and so cold to-night!

If I should die to-night,
My friends would call to mind, with loving thought,
Some kindly deed the icy hand had wrought,
Some gentle word the frozen lips had said—
Errands on which the willing feet had sped;
The memory of my selfishness and pride,
My hasty words, would all be put aside,
And so I should be loved and mourned to-night.

If I should die to-night,
Even hearts estranged would turn once more to me,
Recalling other days remorsefully.
The eyes that chill me with averted glance
Would look upon me as of yore, perchance,
And soften in the old familiar way;
For who would war with dumb, unconscious clay?
So I might rest, forgiven of all to-night.

O friends, I pray to-night,
Keep not your kisses for my dead cold brow.
The way is lonely; let me feel them now.
Think gently of me; I am travel-worn,
My faltering feet are pierced with many a thorn.
Forgive! O hearts estranged, forgive, I plead!
When ceaseless bliss is mine I shall not need
The tenderness for which I long to-night.
—Belle Eugenia Smith.

FRUITION

We scatter seeds with careless hand
And dream we ne'er shall see them more,
But for a thousand years
Their fruit appears
In weeds that mar the land
Or helpful store.

The deeds we do, the words we say—
Into still air they seem to fleet;
We count them ever past;
But they shall last—
In the dread judgment they
And we shall meet.

I charge thee by the years gone by,
For the love's sake of brethren dear,
Keep thou the one true way,
In work and play,
Lest in that world their cry
Of woe thou hear. —John Keble.

Still shines the light of holy lives
Like star beams over doubt;
Each sainted memory, Christlike, drives
Some dark possession out.
—John Greenleaf Whittier.

HAVE CHARITY

Then gently scan your brother man,
Still gentler sister woman;
Though they may gang a kennin' wrang
To step aside is human:
One point must still be greatly dark,
The moving *why* they do it:
And just as lamely can ye mark
How far, perhaps, they rue it.

Who made the heart, 'tis He alone
Decidedly can try us;
He knows each chord—its various tone,
Each spring—its various bias;
Then at the balance let's be mute,
We never can adjust it;
What's done we partly may compute,
But know not what's resisted.
—Robert Burns.

THE VOICE OF PITY

Couldst thou boast, O child of weakness,
O'er the sons of wrong and strife,
Were their strong temptations planted
In thy path of life?

He alone whose hand is bounding
Human power and human will,
Looking through each soul's surrounding,
Knows its good or ill.

Earnest words must needs be spoken
When the warm heart bleeds or burns
With its scorn of wrong, or pity
For the wronged, by turns.

But, by all thy nature's weakness,
Hidden faults and follies known,
Be thou, in rebuking evil,
Conscious of thine own.

Not the less shall stern-eyed Duty
To thy lips her trumpet set,
But with harsher blasts shall mingle
Wailings of regret.

So when thoughts of evil-doers
Waken scorn or hatred move,
Shall a mournful fellow-feeling
Temper all with love.
—John Greenleaf Whittier.

'Tis the Almighty's gracious plan,
That man shall be the joy of man.
—From the Scandinavian, tr. by Frederic Rowland Marvin.

JUDGE NOT

Judge not; the workings of his brain
And of his heart thou canst not see;
What looks to thy dim eyes a stain
In God's pure light may only be
A scar—brought from some well-won field
Where thou wouldst only faint and yield.

The look, the air, that frets thy sight
May be a token that, below,
The soul has closed in deadly fight
With some infernal fiery foe—
Whose glance would scorch thy smiling grace
And cast thee shuddering on thy face!

The fall thou darest to despise—
May be the angel's slackened hand
Has suffered it, that he may rise
And take a firmer, surer stand;
Or, trusting less to earthly things,
May henceforth learn to use his wings.

And judge none lost; but wait and see,
With hopeful pity, not disdain,
The depth of the abyss may be
The measure of the height of pain,
And love and glory that may raise
This soul to God in after days.
—Adelaide Anne Procter.

THINK GENTLY OF THE ERRING

Think gently of the erring;
Ye know not of the power
With which the dark temptation came,
In some unguarded hour;
Ye may not know how earnestly
They struggled, or how well,
Until the hour of weakness came
And sadly thus they fell.

Think gently of the erring;
Oh, do not thou forget,
However darkly stained by sin,
He is thy brother yet;
Heir of the self-same heritage,
Child of the self-same God,
He has but stumbled in the path
Thou hast in weakness trod.

Speak gently to the erring;
For is it not enough
That innocence and peace have gone,
Without thy censure rough?

It sure must be a weary lot,
That sin-stained heart to bear,
And those who share a happier fate
Their chidings well may spare.

Speak gently to the erring;
Thou yet mayst lead them back,
With holy words and tones of love,
From misery's thorny track;
Forget not thou hast often sinned,
And sinful yet must be;
Deal gently with the erring, then,
As God has dealt with thee.
—Julia A. Fletcher.

HARSH JUDGMENTS

O God! whose thoughts are brightest light,
Whose love runs always clear,
To whose kind wisdom sinning souls
Amidst their sins are dear,

Sweeten my bitter-thoughted heart
With charity like thine,
Till self shall be the only spot
On earth which does not shine.

I often see in my own thoughts,
When they lie nearest Thee,
That the worst men I ever knew
Were better men than me.

He whom no praise can reach is aye
Men's least attempts approving;
Whom justice makes all-merciful
Omniscience makes all-loving.

How thou canst think so well of us
Yet be the God thou art,
Is darkness to my intellect,
But sunshine to my heart.

Yet habits linger in the soul;
More grace, O Lord! more grace!
More sweetness from thy loving heart!
More sunshine from thy face!

The discord is within, which jars
So sadly in life's song;
'Tis we, not they, who are in fault,
When others seem so wrong.

'Tis we who weigh upon ourselves;
Self is the irksome weight;
To those who can see straight themselves,
All things look always straight.

My God, with what surpassing love
Thou lovest all on earth;
How good the least good is to thee,
How much each soul is worth!

All bitterness is from ourselves;
All sweetness is from thee;
Sweet God! for evermore be thou
Fountain and fire in me!
—Frederick William Faber.

HOW TO JUDGE

"Judge the people by their actions''—'tis a rule you often get—
"Judge the actions by their people" is a wiser maxim yet.
Have I known you, brother, sister? Have I looked into your heart?
Mingled with your thoughts my feelings, taken of your life my part?
Through the warp of your convictions sent the shuttle of my thought
Till the web became the Credo, for us both, of Should and Ought?
Seen in thousand ways your nature, in all act and look and speech?
By that large induction only I your law of being reach.
Now I hear of this wrong action—what is that to you and me?
Sin within you may have done it—fruit not nature to the tree.
Foreign graft has come to bearing—mistletoe grown on your bough—
If I ever really knew you, then, my friend, I know you now.
So I say, "He never did it," or, "He did not so intend";
Or, "Some foreign power o'ercame him"—so I judge the action, friend.
Let the mere outside observer note appearance as he can;
We, more righteous judgment passing, test each action by its man.
—James Freeman Clarke.

"TO KNOW ALL IS TO FORGIVE ALL"

If I knew you and you knew me,
If both of us could clearly see,
And with an inner sight divine
The meaning of your heart and mine,
I'm sure that we would differ less,
And clasp our hands in friendliness;
Our thoughts would pleasantly agree
If I knew you and you knew me.
—Nixon Waterman.

KINDNESS

A little word in kindness spoken,
  A motion, or a tear,
Has often healed the heart that's broken
  And made a friend sincere.

A word, a look, has crushed to earth
  Full many a budding flower,
Which, had a smile but owned its birth,
  Would bless life's darkest hour.

Then deem it not an idle thing
  A pleasant word to speak;
The face you wear, the thought you bring,
  A heart may heal or break.
—John Greenleaf Whittier.

IF WE KNEW

If we knew the cares and sorrows
  Crowded round our neighbor's way,
If we knew the little losses,
  Sorely grievous, day by day,
Would we then so often chide him
  For the lack of thrift and gain,
Leaving on his heart a shadow
  Leaving on our hearts a stain?

If we knew the clouds above us,
  Held by gentle blessings there,
Woud we turn away, all trembling,
  In our blind and weak despair?
Would we shrink from little shadows
  Lying on the dewy grass
While 'tis only birds of Eden
  Just in mercy flying past?

Let us reach within our bosoms
  For the key to other lives,
And with love to erring natures
  Cherish good that still survives;
So that when our disrobed spirits
  Soar to realms of light again,
We may say, "Dear Father, judge us
  As we judged our fellow men."

Time to me this truth hath taught,
  'Tis a truth that's worth revealing:
More offend from want of thought
  Than from want of feeling.
If advice we would convey,
  There's a time we should convey it;
If we've but a word to say,
  There's a time in which to say it.

HONOR ALL MEN

Great Master! teach us how to hope in man:
  We lift our eyes upon his works and ways,
  And disappointment chills us as we gaze,
Our dream of him so far the truth outran,
So far his deeds are ever falling short.
  And then we fold our graceful hands and say,
  "The world is vulgar." Didst thou turn away,
O Sacred Spirit, delicately wrought,
Because the humble souls of Galilee
  Were tuned not to the music of thine own
  And chimed not to the pulsing undertone
Which swelled Thy loving bosom like the sea?
Shame thou our coldness, most benignant Friend,
  When we so daintily do condescend.
—Martha Perry Howe.

BROTHERHOOD

That plenty but reproaches me
  Which leaves my neighbor bare.
Not wholly glad my heart can be
  While his is bowed with care.

If I go free, and sound, and stout,
  While his poor fetters clank,
Unsated still, I'll still cry out,
  And plead with Whom I thank.

Almighty, thou who Father be
  Of him, of me, of all,
Draw us together, him and me,
  That, whichsoever fall,

The other's hand may fail him not—
  The other's strength decline
No task of succor that his lot
  May claim from son of thine.

I would be fed. I would be clad.
  I would be housed and dry.
But if so be my heart is sad—
  What benefit have I?

Best he whose shoulders best endure
  The load that brings relief;
And best shall be his joy secure
  Who shares that joy with grief.
—Edward Sandford Martin.

THE LIFE I SEEK

Not in some cloistered cell
Dost thou, Lord, bid me dwell
My love to show,
But 'mid the busy marts,
Where men with burdened hearts
Do come and go.

Some tempted soul to cheer
When breath of ill is near
And foes annoy;
The sinning to restrain,
To ease the throb of pain—
Be such my joy.

Lord, make me quick to see
Each task awaiting me,
And quick to do;
Oh, grant me strength, I pray,
With lowly love each day,
And purpose true,

To go as Jesus went,
Spending and being spent,
Myself forgot;
Supplying human needs
By loving words and deeds—
Oh, happy lot!

—Robert M. Offord.

THY BROTHER

When thy heart with joy o'erflowing
Sings a thankful prayer,
In thy joy, O let thy brother
With thee share.

When the harvest sheaves ingathered
Fill thy barns with store,
To thy God and to thy brother
Give the more.

If thy soul with power uplifted
Yearns for glorious deed,
Give thy strength to serve thy brother
In his need.

Hast thou borne a secret sorrow
In thy lonely breast?
Take to thee thy sorrowing brother
For a guest.

Share with him thy bread of blessing,
Sorrow's burden share;
When thy heart enfolds a brother,
God is there.

—Theodore Chickering Williams.

ALL'S WELL

Sweet-voiced Hope, thy fine discourse
Foretold not half life's good to me:
Thy painter, Fancy, hath not force
To show how sweet it is to be!
Thy witching dream
And pictured scheme
To match the fact still want the power:
Thy promise brave—
From birth to grave—
Life's boon may beggar in an hour.

"Ask and receive," 'tis sweetly said;
Yet what to plead for know I not;
For wish is wasted, hope o'ersped,
And aye to thanks returns my thought.
If I would pray,
I've naught to say
But this, that God may be God still;
For him to live
Is still to give,
And sweeter than my wish, his will.

O wealth of life beyond all bound!
Eternity each moment given!
What plummet may the Present sound
Who promises a future heaven?
Or glad or grieved,
Oppressed, relieved,
In blackest night or brightest day,
Still pours the flood
Of golden good,
And more than heartful fills me aye.

My wealth is common; I possess
No petty province, but the whole.
What's mine alone is mine far less
Than treasure shared by every soul.
Talk not of store,
Millions or more—
Of values which the purse may hold—
But this divine!
I own the mine
Whose grains outweigh a planet's gold.

I have a stake in every star,
In every beam that fills the day;
All hearts of men my coffers are,
My ores arterial tides convey;
The fields and skies
And sweet replies
Of thought to thought are my gold-dust,
The oaks and brooks
And speaking looks
Of lovers' faith and friendship's trust.

Life's youngest tides joy-brimming flow
 For him who lives above all years;
Who all-immortal makes the Now,
 And is not ta'en in Time's arrears;
  His life's a hymn
  The seraphim
Might stop to hear or help to sing,
  And to his soul
  The boundless whole
Its bounty all doth daily bring.

"All mine is thine," the sky-soul saith;
 "The wealth I am must then become
Richer and richer, breath by breath—
 Immortal gain, immortal room!"
  And since all his
  Mine also is,
Life's gift outruns my fancies far,
 And drowns the dream
 In larger stream,
As morning drinks the morning star.
—David Atwood Wasson.

HOW DOTH DEATH SPEAK OF OUR BELOVED?

How doth death speak of our beloved
 When it has laid them low,
When it has set its hallowing touch
 On speechless lip and brow?

It clothes their every gift and grace
With radiance from the holiest place,
With light as from an angel's face,

Recalling with resistless force
And tracing to their hidden source
Deeds scarcely noticed in their course—

This little loving fond device,
That daily act of sacrifice,
Of which too late we learned the price.

Opening our weeping eyes to trace
Simple unnoticed kindnesses,
Forgotten tones of tenderness,

Which evermore to us must be
Sacred as hymns in infancy
Learnt listening at a mother's knee.

Thus doth death speak of our beloved
 When it has laid them low.
Then let love antedate the work of
 death,
 And speak thus now.

* * * * * *

How does death speak of our beloved
 When it has laid them low,
When it has set its hallowing touch
 On speechless lip and brow?

It sweeps their faults with heavy hand
As sweeps the sea the trampled sand,
Till scarce the faintest print is scanned.

It shows how much the vexing deed
Was but a generous nature's weed
Or some choice virtue run to seed;

How that small fretting fretfulness
Was but love's overanxiousness,
Which had not been had love been less;

This failing at which we repined
But the dim shade of day declined
Which should have made us doubly
 kind.

It takes each failing on our part
And brands it in upon the heart
With caustic power and cruel art.

The small neglect that may have pained
A giant stature will have gained
When it can never be explained;

The little service which had proved
How tenderly we watched and loved,
And those mute lips to smiles had
 moved;

The little gift from out our store
Which might have cheered some cheer-
 less hour
When they with earth's poor needs were
 poor.

It shows our faults like fires at night;
It sweeps their failings out of sight;
It clothes their good in heavenly light.

O Christ, our life, foredate the work of
 death
 And do this now;
Thou, who art love, thus hallow our be-
 loved;
 Not death, but Thou!
—Elizabeth Rundle Charles.

God gives each man one life, like a lamp,
 then gives
That lamp due measure of oil: Lamp
 lighted—hold high, wave wide,
Its comfort for others to share!
—Muleykeh.

THE NEW ERA

It is coming! it is coming! The day is just a-dawning
When man shall be to fellow-man a helper and a brother;
When the mansion, with its gilded hall, its tower and arch and awning,
Shall be to hovel desolate a kind and foster-mother.

When the men who work for wages shall not toil from morn till even,
With no vision of the sunlight, nor flowers, nor birds a-singing;
When the men who hire the workers, blest with all the gifts of heaven,
Shall the golden rule remember, its glad millennium bringing.

The time is coming when the man who cares not for another
Shall be accounted as a stain upon a fair creation;
Who lives to fill his coffers full, his better self to smother,
As blight and mildew on the fame and glory of a nation.

Tho hours are growing shorter for the millions who are toiling,
And the homes are growing better for the millions yet to be;
And the poor shall learn the lesson, how that waste and sin are spoiling
The fairest and the finest of a grand humanity.

It is coming! it is coming! and men's thoughts are growing deeper;
They are giving of their millions as they never gave before;
They are learning the new gospel, man must be his brother's keeper,
And right, not might, shall triumph, and the selfish rule no more.
—Sarah Knowles Bolton.

To a darning-needle once exclaimed the kitchen sieve,
"You've a hole right through your body, and I wonder how you live."
But the needle (who was sharp) replied, "I too have wondered
That you notice my *one* hole, when in you there are a hundred!"
—Saadi, tr. by James Freeman Clarke.

LOOKING FOR PEARLS

The Master came one evening to the gate
Of a fair city; it was growing late,
And sending his disciples to buy food,
He wandered forth intent on doing good,
As was his wont. And in the market-place
He saw a crowd, close gathered in one space,
Gazing with eager eyes upon the ground,
Jesus drew nearer, and thereon he found
A noisome creature, a bedraggled wreck—
A dead dog with a halter round his neck,
And those who stood by mocked the object there,
And one said, scoffing, "It pollutes the air!"
Another, jeering, asked, "How long to-night
Shall such a miscreant cur offend our sight?"
"Look at his torn hide," sneered a Jewish wit,
"You could not cut even a shoe from it,"
And turned away. "Behold his ears that bleed,"
A fourth chimed in, "an unclean wretch indeed!"
"He hath been hanged for thieving," they all cried.
And spurned the loathsome beast from side to side.
Then Jesus, standing by them in the street,
Looked on the poor, spent creature at his feet,
And, bending o'er him, spake unto the men,
"*Pearls are not whiter than his teeth.*" And then
The people at each other gazed, asking,
"Who is this stranger pitying this vile thing?"
Then one exclaimed, with awe-abated breath,
"This surely is the Man of Nazareth;
This must be Jesus, for none else but he
Something to praise in a dead dog could see!"
And, being ashamed, each scoffer bowed his head,
And from the sight of Jesus turned and fled.

Vice is a monster of so frightful mien
As, to be hated, needs but to be seen;
Yet seen too oft, familiar with her face,
We first endure, then pity, then embrace.
—Alexander Pope.

WHAT MIGHT BE DONE

What might be done if men were wise—
What glorious deeds, my suffering brother,
Would they unite
In love and right,
And cease their scorn of one another!

Oppression's heart might be imbued
With kindling drops of loving-kindness,
And knowledge pour
From shore to shore
Light on the eyes of mental blindness.

All slavery, warfare, lies, and wrongs,
All vice and crime, might die together;
And wine and corn
To each man born
Be free as warmth in summer weather.

The meanest wretch that ever trod,
The deepest sunk in guilt and sorrow,
Might stand erect
In self-respect,
And share the teeming world to-morrow.

What might be done? This might be done.
And more than this, my suffering brother;
More than the tongue
E'er said or sung
If men were wise and loved each other.

—Charles Mackay.

If I could see
A brother languishing in sore distress,
And I should turn and leave him comfortless,
When I might be
A messenger of hope and happiness—
How could I ask to have that I denied
In my own hour of bitterness supplied?

If I might share
A brother's load along the dusty way,
And I should turn and walk alone that day,
How could I dare—
When in the evening watch I kneel to pray—
To ask for help to bear my pain and loss,
If I had heeded not my brother's cross?

SHARED

I said it in the meadow path,
I say it on the mountain-stairs:
The best things any mortal hath
Are those which every mortal shares.

The air we breathe—the sky—the breeze—
The light without us and within—
Life with its unlocked treasuries—
God's riches, are for all to win.

The grass is softer to my tread
For rest it yields unnumbered feet;
Sweeter to me the wild-rose red
Because she makes the whole world sweet.

Into your heavenly loneliness
Ye welcomed me, O solemn peaks!
And me in every guest you bless
Who reverently your mystery seeks.

And up the radiant peopled way
That opens into worlds unknown
It will be life's delight to say,
"Heaven is not heaven for me alone."

Rich through my brethren's poverty!
Such wealth were hideous! I am blest
Only in what they share with me,
In what I share with all the rest.

—Lucy Larcom.

UNCHARITABLENESS NOT CHRISTIAN

I know not if 'twas wise or well
To give all heathens up to hell—
Hadrian—Aurelius—Socrates—
And others wise and good as these;
I know not if it is forbid,
But this I know —Christ never did.

May every soul that touches mine—
Be it the slightest contact—get therefrom some good,
Some little grace, one kindly thought,
One inspiration yet unfelt, one bit of courage
For the darkening sky, one gleam of faith
To brave the thickening ills of life,
One glimpse of brighter skies beyond the gathering mists,
To make this life worth while,
And heaven a surer heritage.

SOCIAL CHRISTIANITY

O for a closer walk with man!
  Sweet fellowship of soul,
Where each is to the other bound,
  Parts of one living whole.

Our Father, God, help us to see
  That all in thee are one;
O warm our hearts with thy pure love,
  Strong as your glorious sun.

Pride, envy, selfishness will melt
  Beneath that kindling fire;
Our brother's faults we scarce shall see,
  But good in all admire.

No bitter cry of misery
  Shall ever pass unheard;
But gentle sympathy spring forth
  In smile and strengthening word.

And when our brother's voice shall call
  From lands beyond the sea,
Our hearts in glad response will say,
  "Here, Lord, am I, send me."

O Jesus Christ, thou who wast man,
  Grant us thy face to see;
In thy light shall we understand
  What human life may be.

Then daily with thy Spirit filled,
  According to thy word,
New power shall flow through us to all,
  And draw men near our Lord.

Thus will the deep desire be met
  With which our prayer began;
A closer walk with Thee will mean
  A closer walk with man.

If any little word of mine may make a
    life the brighter,
If any little song of mine may make a
    heart the lighter,
God help me speak the little word, and
    take my bit of singing,
And drop it in some lonely vale to set
    the echoes ringing.
If any little love of mine may make a
    life the sweeter,
If any little care of mine make other life
    completer,
If any lift of mine may ease the burden
    of another,
God give me love and care and strength
    to help my toiling brother.

CHARITY NOT JUSTICE

Outwearied with the littleness and spite,
  The falsehood and the treachery of
    men,
  I cried, "Give me but justice!" think-
    ing then
I meekly craved a common boon which
    might
Most easily be granted; soon the light
  Of deeper truth grew on my wonder-
    ing ken,
  (Escaping baneful damps of stagnant
    fen),
And then I saw that in my pride bedight
I claimed from erring man the gift of
    Heaven—
  God's own great vested right; and I
    grew calm,
With folded hands, like stone, to
    patience given,
  And pitying, of pure love distilling
    balm;
And now I wait in quiet trust to be
All known to God—and ask of men
    sweet charity.

—Elizabeth Oakes Smith.

GOD SAVE THE PEOPLE

When wilt thou save the people,
  O God of mercy, when?
Not kings alone, but nations?
  Not thrones and crowns, but men?
Flowers of thy heart, O God, are they:
Let them not pass, like weeds, away—
Their heritage a sunless day.
    God save the people!

Shall crime bring crime forever,
  Strength aiding still the strong?
Is it thy will, O Father,
  That man shall toil for wrong?
"No," say thy mountains, "No,"
    thy skies;
Man's clouded sun shall brightly rise,
And songs ascend instead of sighs.
    God save the people!

When wilt thou save the people?
  O God of mercy, when?
The people, Lord, the people,
  Not thrones and crowns, but men?
God save the people; thine they are,
Thy children, as thine angels fair;
From vice, oppression, and despair,
    God save the people!

—Ebenezer Elliott.

HYMN OF THE CITY

Not in the solitude
Alone may man commune with Heaven, or see
Only in savage wood
And sunny vale the present Deity;
Or only hear his voice
Where the winds whisper and the waves rejoice.

Even here do I behold
Thy steps, Almighty!—here, amidst the crowd
Through the great city rolled
With everlasting murmurs deep and loud—
Choking the ways that wind
'Mongst the proud piles, the work of human kind.

The golden sunshine comes
From the round heaven, and on their dwellings lies
And lights their inner homes;
For them thou fill'st with air the unbounded skies
And givest them the stores
Of ocean, and the harvest of its shores.

Thy spirit is around,
Quickening the restless mass that sweeps along;
And this eternal sound—
Voices and footfalls of the numberless throng—
Like the resounding sea,
Or like the rainy tempest, speaks of Thee.

And when the hour of rest
Comes like a calm upon the mid-sea brine,
Hushing its billowy breast—
The quiet of that moment too is Thine
It breathes of Him who keeps
The vast and helpless city while it sleeps.
—William Cullen Bryant.

No one is so accursed by fate,
No one so utterly desolate,
But some heart, though unknown,
Responds unto his own.
—Henry Wadsworth Longfellow.

Believe not each accusing tongue,
As most weak people do;
But still believe that story wrong
Which ought not to be true.
—Richard Brinsley Sheridan.

CHRIST IN THE CITY

Where cross the crowded ways of life,
Where sound the cries of race and clan,
Above the noise of selfish strife,
We hear thy voice, O Son of man.

In haunts of wretchedness and need,
On shadowed thresholds dark with fears,
From paths where hide the lures of greed
We catch the vision of thy tears.

From tender childhood's helplessness,
From woman's grief, man's burdened toil,
From famished souls, from sorrow's stress,
Thy heart has never known recoil.

The cup of water given for Thee
Still holds the freshness of thy grace;
Yet long these multitudes to see
The sweet compassion of thy face.

O Master, from the mountain side
Make haste to heal these hearts of pain,
Among these restless throngs abide,
O tread the city's streets again,

Till sons of men shall learn thy love
And follow where thy feet have trod;
Till glorious from thy heaven above
Shall come the city of our God.
—Frank Mason North.

Who seeks for heaven alone to save his soul
May keep the path, but will not reach the goal;
While he who walks in love may wander far,
But God will bring him where the blessed are. —Henry van Dyke.

Persuasion, friend, comes not by toil or art,
Hard study never made the matter clearer;
'Tis the live fountain in the preacher's heart
Sends forth the streams that melt the ravished hearer.
—Johann Wolfgang von Goethe.

SPEAK OUT

If you have a friend worth loving,
  Love him. Yes, and let him know
That you love him, ere life's evening
  Tinge his brow with sunset glow.
Why should good words ne'er be said
Of a friend—till he is dead?

If you hear a song that thrills you,
  Sung by any child of song,
Praise it. Do not let the singer
  Wait deserved praises long.
Why should one who thrills your heart
Lack the joy you may impart?

If you hear a prayer that moves you
  By its humble, pleading tone.
Join it. Do not let the seeker
  Bow before his God alone.
Why should not thy brother share
The strength of "two or three" in prayer?

If your work is made more easy
  By a friendly, helping hand,
Say so. Speak out brave and truly,
  Ere the darkness veil the land.
Should a brother workman dear
Falter for a word of cheer?

Scatter thus your seeds of kindness
  All enriching as you go—
Leave them. Trust the Harvest-Giver;
  He will make each seed to grow.
So, until the happy end,
Your life shall never lack a friend.

INFLUENCE

The smallest bark on life's tumultuous ocean
  Will leave a track behind forevermore;
The lightest wave of influence, once in motion,
  Extends and widens to the eternal shore.
  We should be wary, then, who go before
A myriad yet to be, and we should take
  Our bearings carefully where breakers roar
And fearful tempests gather: one mistake
May wreck unnumbered barks that follow in our wake.

—Sarah Knowles Bolton.

TELL HIM SO

If you have a word of cheer
That may light the pathway drear,
Of a brother pilgrim here,
  Let him know.
Show him you appreciate
What he does, and do not wait
Till the heavy hand of fate
  Lays him low.
If your heart contains a thought
That will brighter make his lot,
Then, in mercy, hide it not;
  Tell him so.

Bide not till the end of all
Carries him beyond recall
When beside his sable pall,
  To avow
Your affection and acclaim
To do honor to his name
And to place the wreath of fame
  On his brow.
Rather speak to him to-day;
For the things you have to say
May assist him on his way:
  Tell him now.

Life is hard enough, at best:
But the love that is expressed
Makes it seem a pathway blest
  To our feet;
And the troubles that we share
Seem the easier to bear,
Smile upon your neighbor's care,
  As you greet.
Rough and stony are our ways,
Dark and dreary are our days;
But another's love and praise
  Make them sweet.

Wait not till your friend is dead
Ere your compliments are said;
For the spirit that has fled,
  If it know,
Does not need to speed it on
Our poor praise; where it has gone
Love's eternal, golden dawn
  Is aglow.
But unto our brother here
That poor praise is very dear;
If you've any word of cheer
Tell him so. —J. A. Egerton.

So when a great man dies,
  For years beyond our ken
The light he leaves behind him lies
  Upon the paths of men.

—Henry Wadsworth Longfellow.

THE MAN WITH A GRUDGE

There once was a man who bore a grudge.
Stoutly he bore it many a year.
"Beware!" said the parson. He answered, "Fudge!
Well it becomes me, never fear.

"Men for this world, and saints for heaven;
Too much of meekness shows a fool;
My loaf shall rise with a livelier leaven;
'Give as you get,' is a good old rule."

The longer he bore it, the more it grew,
Grew his grudge, as he trudged along;
Till in sight of a pearly gate he drew,
And he heard within it a wondrous song.

The shining porter said, "Walk in."
He sought to do so; the gate was strait:
Hard he struggled his way to win,
The way was narrow, the grudge was great.

He turned in haste to lay it down;
He strove to tear it away—to cut—
But it had fast to his heart strings grown,
"O wait," he cried; but the door was shut.

Through windows bright and clear he saw
The blessed going with their Lord to sup.
But Satan clapped on his grudge a claw;
Hell opened her mouth and swallowed him up.
—Sara Hammond Palfrey.

Man judges from a partial view,
None ever yet his brother knew;
The Eternal Eye that sees the whole
May better read the darkened soul,
And find, to outward sense denied,
The flower upon its inward side.
—John Greenleaf Whittier.

O brothers! are ye asking how
The hills of happiness to find?
Then know they lie beyond the vow—
"God helping me, I will be kind."
—Nixon Waterman.

A BLESSING

Not to the man of dollars,
Not to the man of deeds,
Not unto craft and cunning,
Not unto human creeds;
Not to the one whose passion
Is for the world's renown,
Not in the form of fashion
Cometh a blessing down.

But to the one whose spirit
Yearns for the great and good;
Unto the one whose storehouse
Yieldeth the hungry food;
Unto the one who labors
Fearless of foe or frown;
Unto the kindly-hearted,
Cometh a blessing down.
—Mary Frances Tucker.

WEAPONS

Both swords and guns are strong, no doubt,
And so are tongue and pen,
And so are sheaves of good bank notes,
To sway the souls of men.
But guns and swords and piles of gold,
Though mighty in their sphere,
Are sometimes feebler than a smile,
And poorer than a tear.
—Charles Mackay.

Enough to know that, through the winter's frost
And summer's heat, no seed of truth is lost,
And every duty pays at last its cost.
—John Greenleaf Whittier.

A kindly act is a kernel sown
That will grow to a goodly tree,
Shedding its fruit when time is flown
Down the gulf of Eternity.
—John Boyle O'Reilly.

The kindly word unspoken is a sin—
A sin that wraps itself in purest guise,
And tells the heart that, doubting, looks within,
That, not in speech, but thought, the virtue lies.
—John Boyle O Reilly.

CONSECRATION

SUBMISSION, DEVOTION, PURITY

THE CHARIOTEER

O God, take the reins of my life!
I have driven it blindly, to left and to right,
In mock of the rock, in the chasm's despite,
Where the brambles were rife,
In the blaze of the sun and the deadliest black of the night.
O God, take the reins of my life!

For I am so weary and weak.
My hands are a-quiver and so is my heart,
And my eyes are too tired for the tear-drops to start,
And the worn horses reek
With the anguishing pull and the hot, heavy harness's smart,
While I am all weary and weak.

But Thou wilt be peace, wilt be power.
Thy hand on the reins and thine eye on the way
Shall be wisdom to guide and controlling to stay,
And my life in that hour
Shall be led into leading, and rest when it comes to obey;
For thou wilt be peace and all power.

Now, Lord, without tarrying, now!
While eyes can look up and while reason remains,
And my hand yet has strength to surrender the reins,
Ere death stamp my brow
And pour coldness and stillness through all the mad course of my veins—
Come, Lord, without tarrying, now!

I yield Thee my place, which is thine.
Appoint me to lie on the chariot floor;
Yea, appoint me to lie at thy feet, and no more,
While the glad axles shine,
And the happy wheels run on their course to the heavenly door,—
Now thou hast my place, which is thine.

—Amos R. Wells.

WHOLLY THE LORD'S

My whole though broken heart, O Lord
From henceforth shall be thine;
And here I do my vow record—
This hand, these words are mine:
All that I have, without reserve,
I offer here to thee:
Thy will and honor all shall serve
That thou bestow'st on me.

All that exceptions save I lose;
All that I lose I save;
The treasures of thy love I choose,
And Thou art all I crave.
My God, thou hast my heart and hand;
I all to thee resign;
I'll ever to this covenant stand,
Though flesh hereat repine.

I know that Thou wast willing first,
And then drew my consent;
Having thus loved me at the worst
Thou wilt not now repent.
Now I have quit all self-pretense,
Take charge of what's thine own:
My life, my health, and my defense,
Now lie on thee alone.

—Richard Baxter.

THE LAST WISH

To do or not to do; to have
Or not to have, I leave to thee;
To be or not to be I leave;
Thy only will be done in me.
All my requests are lost in one:
Father, thy only will be done.

Suffice that, for the season past,
Myself in things divine I sought,
For comforts cried with eager haste,
And murmured that I found them not.
I leave it now to Thee alone:
Father, thy only will be done.

Thy gifts I clamor for no more,
  Or selfishly thy grace require
An evil heart to varnish o'er;
  Jesus, the Giver, I desire,
After the flesh no longer known:
  Father, thy only will be done.

Welcome alike the crown or cross;
  Trouble I cannot ask, nor peace,
Nor toil, nor rest, nor gain, nor loss,
  Nor joy, nor grief, nor pain, nor ease,
Nor life, nor death, but ever groan,
  Father, thy only will be done.
—Charles Wesley.

MORNING HYMN

O God! I thank thee for each sight
  Of beauty that thy hand doth give;
For sunny skies and air and light;
  O God, I thank thee that I live!

That life I consecrate to Thee;
  And ever as the day is born,
On wings of joy my soul would flee
  And thank thee for another morn;

Another day in which to cast
  Some silent deed of love abroad,
That, greatening as it journeys past,
  May do some earnest work for God;

Another day to do and dare;
  To tax anew my growing strength;
To arm my soul with faith and prayer,
  And so reach heaven and Thee at length.
—Caroline Atherton Mason.

"INTO THY HANDS"

Into Thy guiding hands;
Along a way thy love and care forefend
Gladly I fare, or rough or smooth may bend
The longest road that leads at life's far end
  Into thy hands.

Into thy chastening hands:
If e'er I yield to weakness or to sin,
Blind to the guerdon Thou dost bid me win,
Bring Thou me back, by Love's sweet discipline,
  Into thy hands.

Into Thy healing hands;
No hurt of soul or body long enthralls,
The bruisèd heart that for thy succor calls
When, far from doubting as from fear, it falls
  Into thy hands.

Into thy saving hands:
Despite assoil, infirmity, mistake,
My life a perfect whole thy power can make,
If Thou my shards of broken purpose take
  Into thy hands.

Into Thy keeping hands;
As safe as Heaven kept the guarded Grail—
So safe, so pure, so compassed as with mail—
The soul committed, e'en through Death's dark vale,
  Into thy hands.

Into thy loving hands;
Who made my heart to love made Thee my guest;
Who made the world to tire made thee my rest;
My joyful heart I give, at thy behest,
  Into thy hands.
—Louise Manning Hodgkins.

HERE AM I

My will would like a life of ease,
  And power to do, and time to rest,
And health and strength my will would please,
  But, Lord, I know thy will is best.

If I have strength to do thy will
  That should be power enough for me,
Whether to work or to sit still
  The appointment of the day may be.

And if by sickness I may grow
  More patient, holy and resigned,
Strong health I need not wish to know,
  And greater ease I cannot find.

And rest—I need not seek it here;
  For perfect rest remaineth still;
When in thy presence we appear
  Rest shall be given by thy will.

Lord, I have given my life to thee,
And every day and hour is thine;
What thou appointest let them be:
Thy will is better, Lord, than mine.
—Anna B. Warner.

THE SACRIFICE OF THE WILL

Laid on thine altar, O my Lord Divine,
Accept my will this day, for Jesus' sake;
I have no jewels to adorn thy shrine—
Nor any world-proud sacrifice to make;
But here I bring within my trembling hand,
This will of mine—a thing that seemeth small,
And Thou alone, O God, canst understand
How, when I yield Thee this, I yield mine all.
Hidden therein, thy searching gaze can see
Struggles of passion—visions of delight—
All that I love, and am, and fain would be,
Deep loves, fond hopes, and longings infinite.
It hath been wet with tears and dimmed with sighs,
Clinched in my grasp, till beauty hath it none—
Now, from thy footstool where it vanquished lies,
The prayer ascendeth, "May thy will be done."
Take it, O Father, ere my courage fail,
And merge it so in thine own Will, that e'en
If, in some desperate hour, my cries prevail,
And thou give back my will, it may have been
So changed, so purified, so fair have grown,
So one with thee, so filled with peace divine,
I may not see nor know it as my own,
But, gaining back my will, may find it thine.

Manlike is it to fall into sin,
Fiendlike is it to dwell therein,
Christlike is it for sin to grieve,
Godlike is it all sin to leave.
—Friedrich von Logau.

O GOD OF TRUTH

O God of Truth, whose living word
Upholds whate'er hath breath,
Look down on thy creation, Lord,
Enslaved by sin and death.

Set up thy standard, Lord, that they
Who claim a heavenly birth
May march with thee to smite the lies
That vex thy ransomed earth.

Ah! would we join that blest array,
And follow in the might
Of Him, the Faithful and the True,
In raiment clean and white.

We fight for truth, *we* fight for God—
Poor slaves of lies and sin!
He who would fight for thee on earth
Must first be true within.

Thou God of Truth for whom we long—
Thou who wilt hear our prayer—
Do thine own battle in our hearts;
And slay the falsehood there.

Still smite! still burn! till naught is left
But God's own truth and love;
Then, Lord, as morning dew come down,
Rest on us from above.

Yea, come! then, tried as in the fire,
From every lie set free,
Thy perfect truth shall dwell in us,
And we shall live in Thee.
—Thomas Hughes.

GOD ONLY

Lord, in the strength of grace,
With a glad heart and free,
Myself, my residue of days,
I consecrate to Thee.

Thy ransomed servant, I
Restore to thee thine own;
And from this moment live or die
To serve my God alone.
—Charles Wesley.

In full and glad surrender we give ourselves to thee,
Thine utterly and only and evermore to be!
O Son of God, who lovest us, we will be thine alone,
And all we are and all we have shall henceforth be thine own.
—Frances Ridley Havergal.

GOD IS EVERYWHERE

A little bird I am,
  Shut from the fields of air;
And in my cage I sit and sing
  To him who placed me there;
Well pleased a prisoner to be,
Because, my God, it pleaseth thee.

Naught have I else to do;
  I sing the whole day long;
And He whom most I love to please
  Doth listen to my song;
He caught and bound my wandering
    wing,
But still he bends to hear me sing.

My cage confines me round,
  Abroad I cannot fly;
But though my wings are closely bound
  My heart's at liberty.
My prison walls cannot control
The flight, the freedom of my soul.

Oh, it is grand to soar
  These bolts and bars above
To Him whose purpose I adore,
  Whose providence I love!
And in thy mighty will to find
The joy, the freedom of the mind.

—Madame Guyon.

A CONSECRATED LIFE

Take my life and let it be
Consecrated, Lord, to thee.
Take my moments and my days;
Let them flow in ceaseless praise.

Take my hands, and let them move
At the impulse of thy love.
Take my feet and let them be
Swift and "beautiful" for Thee.

Take my voice, and let me sing
Always, only, for my King.
Take my lips, and let them be
Filled with messages from Thee.

Take my silver and my gold;
Not a mite would I withhold.
Take my intellect, and use
Every power as Thou shalt choose.

Take my will and make it Thine;
It shall be no longer mine.
Take my heart; it *is* thine own;
It shall be thy royal throne.

Take my love; my Lord, I pour
At thy feet its treasure-store.
Take myself, and I will be
Ever, *only*, ALL for Thee.

—Frances Ridley Havergal.

UNION WITH GOD

Strong are the walls around me,
  That hold me all the day;
But they who thus have bound me
  Cannot keep God away:
My very dungeon walls are dear,
Because the God I love is here.

They know, who thus oppress me,
  'Tis hard to be alone;
But know not One can bless me
  Who comes through bars and stone.
He makes my dungeon's darkness bright
And fills my bosom with delight.

Thy love, O God! restores me
  From sighs and tears to praise;
And deep my soul adores thee
  Nor thinks of time or place:
I ask no more, in good or ill,
  But union with thy holy will.

'Tis that which makes my treasure,
  'Tis that which brings my gain;
Converting woe to pleasure,
  And reaping joy from pain.
Oh, 'tis enough, whate'er befall,
To know that God is All in All.

—Madame Guyon.

DEDICATED

O Lord, thy heavenly grace impart,
And fix my frail, inconstant heart;
Henceforth my chief desire shall be
To dedicate myself to thee.

Whate'er pursuits my time employ,
One thought shall fill my soul with joy:
That silent, secret thought shall be
That all my hopes are fixed on thee.

Thy glorious eye pervadeth space;
Thy presence, Lord, fills every place;
And wheresoe'er my lot may be
Still shall my spirit cleave to thee.

Renouncing every worldly thing,
And safe beneath thy spreading wing,
My sweetest thought henceforth shall be
That all I want I find in thee.

—Jean F. Oberlin.

LEAVING ALL

Jesus, I my cross have taken,
All to leave and follow thee;
Naked, poor, despised, forsaken,
Thou, from hence, my all shalt be:
Perish every fond ambition,
All I've sought, and hoped, and known;
Yet how rich is my condition,
God and heaven are still my own!

Let the world despise and leave me,
They have left my Saviour too;
Human hearts and looks deceive me;
Thou art not, like man, untrue;
And while thou shalt smile upon me,
God of wisdom, love, and might,
Foes may hate, and friends may shun me;
Show thy face, and all is bright.

Go, then, earthly fame and treasure!
Come, disaster, scorn, and pain!
In Thy service, pain is pleasure;
With thy favor, loss is gain.
I have called thee, "Abba, Father";
I have stayed my heart on thee:
Storms may howl, and clouds may gather,
All must work for good to me.

Man may trouble and distress me,
'Twill but drive me to Thy breast;
Life with trials hard may press me,
Heaven will bring me sweeter rest.
O 'tis not in grief to harm me,
While thy love is left to me;
O 'twere not in joy to charm me,
Were that joy unmixed with thee.

Know, my soul, thy full salvation;
Rise o'er sin, and fear, and care;
Joy to find in every station
Something still to do or bear.
Think what Spirit dwells within thee;
What a Father's smile is thine;
What a Saviour died to win thee:
Child of heaven, shouldst thou repine?

Haste thee on from grace to glory,
Armed by faith, and winged by prayer;
Heaven's eternal day's before thee,
God's own hand shall guide thee there.
Soon shall close thy earthly mission,
Swift shall pass thy pilgrim days,
Hope shall change to glad fruition,
Faith to sight, and prayer to praise.
—Henry F. Lyte.

CHOOSE THOU

Thy way, not mine, O Lord!
However dark it be;
Lead me by Thine own hand,
Choose out the path for me.

Smooth let it be, or rough,
It will be still the best;
Winding or straight it matters not,
It leads me to Thy rest.

I dare not choose my lot,
I would not if I might;
Choose Thou for me, O God!
So shall I walk aright.

The kingdom that I seek
Is Thine; so let the way
That leads to it be thine
Else I must surely stray.

Take Thou my cup, and it
With joy or sorrow fill;
As best to Thee may seem;
Choose Thou my good or ill.

Choose Thou for me my friends
My sickness or my health;
Choose thou my cares for me,
My poverty or wealth.

Not mine, not mine the choice
In things or great or small;
Be Thou my guide, my strength,
My wisdom and my all.
—Horatius Bonar.

ONLY TO-DAY

Only to-day is mine,
And that I owe to Thee;
Help me to make it thine;
As pure as it may be;
Let it see something done,
Let it see something won,
Then at the setting sun
I'll give it back to thee.

What if I cannot tell
The cares the day may bring?
I know that I shall dwell
Beneath Thy sheltering wing;
And there the load is light;
And there the dark is bright,
And weakness turns to might,
And so I trust and sing.

What shall I ask to-day?
  Naught but Thine own sweet will;
The windings of the way
  Lead to thy holy hill;
And whether here or there
Why should I fear or care?
Thy heavens are everywhere,
  And they are o'er me still.

Give me Thyself to-day,
  I dare not walk alone;
Speak to me by the way,
  And "all things are my own";
The treasures of thy grace,
The secret hiding place,
The vision of thy face,
  The shadow of thy throne!

—Henry Burton.

THE OFFERING

No more my own, Lord Jesus,
  Bought with thy precious blood,
I give thee but thine own, Lord,
  That long thy love withstood.

I give the life thou gavest,
  My present, future, past;
My joys, my fears, my sorrows,
  My first hope and my last.

I give thee up my weakness
  That oft distrust hath bred,
That thy indwelling power
  May thus be perfected.

I give the love the sweetest
  Thy goodness grants to me;
Take it, and make it meet, Lord,
  For offering to thee.

Smile, and the very shadows
  In thy blest light shall shine;
Take thou my heart, Lord Jesus,
  For thou hast made it thine.

Thou knowest my soul's ambition,
  For thou hast changed its aim
(The world's reproach I fear not)
  To share a Saviour's shame.

Outside the camp to suffer;
  Within the veil to meet,
And hear Thy softest whisper
  From out the mercy-seat.

Thou bear'st me in thy bosom,
  Amidst thy jewels worn,
Upon thy hands deep graven
  By arms of love upborne.

Rescued from sin's destruction,
  Ransomed from death and hell;
Complete in Thee, Lord Jesus:
  Thou hast done all things well.

Oh, deathless love that bought me!
  Oh, price beyond my ken!
Oh, Life that hides my own life
  E'en from my fellow-men!

Now fashion, form and fill me
  With light and love divine;
So, one with Thee, Lord Jesus,
  I'm thine—forever thine!

I IN THEE AND THOU IN ME

I am but clay in thy hands, but Thou art the all-loving artist;
  Passive I lie in thy sight, yet in my self-hood I strive
So to embody the life and the love thou ever impartest,
  That in my sphere of the finite I may be truly alive.

Knowing Thou needest this form, as I thy divine inspiration,
  Knowing thou shapest the clay with a vision and purpose divine,
So would I answer each touch of thy hand in its loving creation,
  That in my conscious life thy power and beauty may shine.

Reflecting the noble intent Thou hast in forming thy creatures;
  Waking from sense into life of the soul, and the image of thee;
Working with thee in thy work to model humanity's features
  Into the likeness of God, myself from myself I would free.

One with all human existence, no one above or below me;
  Lit by Thy wisdom and love, as roses are steeped in the morn;
Growing from clay to a statue, from statue to flesh, till thou know me
  Wrought into manhood celestial, and in thine image reborn.

So in thy love will I trust, bringing me sooner or later
Past the dark screen that divides these shows of the finite from Thee.
Thine, thine only, this warm dear life, O loving Creator!
Thine the invisible future, born of the present, must be.
—Christopher Pearse Cranch.

ON THEE MY HEART IS RESTING

On Thee my heart is resting:
Ah! this is rest indeed!
What else, Almighty Saviour,
Can a poor sinner need?
Thy light is all my wisdom,
Thy love is all my stay;
Our Father's home in glory
Draws nearer every day.

Great is my guilt, but greater
The mercy Thou dost give;
Thyself, a spotless offering,
Hast died that I should live.
With Thee my soul unfettered
Has risen from the dust;
Thy blood is all my treasure;
Thy word is all my trust.

Through me, thou gentle Master,
Thy purposes fulfill:
I yield myself forever
To thy most holy will.
What though I be but weakness
My strength is not in me;
The poorest of thy people
Has all things, having Thee.

When clouds are darkest round me,
Thou, Lord, art then most near,
My drooping faith to quicken,
My weary soul to cheer.
Safe nestling in thy bosom,
I gaze upon thy face.
In vain my foes would drive me
From Thee, my hiding-place.

'Tis Thou hast made me happy;
'Tis thou hast set me free.
To whom shall I give glory
Forever but to Thee!
Of earthly love and blessing
Should every stream run dry,
Thy grace shall still be with me—
Thy grace to live and die!
—Theodore Monod.

WHOM HAVE I IN HEAVEN BUT THEE?

I love, and have some cause to love, the earth;
She is my Maker's creature, therefore good;
She is my mother, for she gave me birth;
She is my tender nurse, she gives me food;
But what's a creature, Lord, compared with Thee?
Or what's my mother or my nurse to me?

The highest honors that the world can boast
Are subjects far too low for my desire;
The brightest beams of glory are, at most,
But dying sparkles of thy living fire;
The proudest flames that earth can kindle be
But nightly glowworms if compared to Thee.

Without thy presence, wealth are bags of cares;
Wisdom, but folly; joy, disquiet, sadness;
Friendship is treason, and delights are snares;
Pleasure's but pain, and mirth but pleasing madness:
Without Thee, Lord, things be not what they be,
Nor have their being when compared with Thee.

In having all things, and not Thee, what have I?
Not having Thee, what have my labors got?
Let me enjoy but Thee, what further crave I?
And having Thee alone, what have I not?
I wish nor sea nor land; nor would I be
Possess'd of heaven, heaven unpossess'd of thee.
—Francis Quarles.

Only for Jesus! Lord, keep it ever
Sealed on the heart, and engraved on the life;
Pulse of all gladness, and nerve of endeavor,
Secret of rest and the strength of our strife.
—Frances Ridley Havergal.

SINCE FIRST THY WORD AWAKED MY HEART

Since first thy word awaked my heart,
Like new life dawning o'er me,
Where'er I turn my eyes, Thou art
All light and love before me.
Nought else I feel or hear or see,
All bonds of earth I sever,
Thee, O God, and only thee,
I live for now and ever.

Like him whose fetters dropped away
When light shone o'er his prison,
My spirit, touched by mercy's ray,
Hath from her chains arisen.
And shall a soul Thou bid'st be free
Return to bondage? Never!
Thee, O God, and only thee,
I live for now and ever.
—Thomas Moore.

WE GIVE ALL

And now we only ask to serve,
We do not ask to rest;
We would give all without reserve,
Our life, our love, our best.

We only ask to see His face,
It is enough for us;
We only ask the lowest place,
So he may smile on us.
—Mary E. Townsend.

THE TWO WORLDS

Unveil, O Lord, and on us shine
In glory and in grace;
The gaudy world grows pale before
The beauty of thy face.

Till Thou art seen, it seems to be
A sort of fairy ground,
Where suns unsetting light the sky,
And flowers and fruits abound

But when Thy keener, purer beam
Is poured upon our sight,
It loses all its power to charm,
And what was day is night.

Its noblest toils are then the scourge
Which made Thy blood to flow;
Its joys are but the treacherous thorns
Which circled round thy brow.

And thus, when we renounce for Thee
Its restless aims and fears,
The tender memories of the past,
The hopes of coming years,

Poor is our sacrifice, whose eyes
Are lighted from above;
We offer what we cannot keep,
What we have ceased to love.
—John Henry Newman.

SELF-SURRENDER

Saviour, who died for me,
I give myself to thee;
Thy love, so full, so free,
Claims all my powers.
Be this my purpose high,
To serve Thee till I die,
Whether my path shall lie
'Mid thorns or flowers.

But, Lord, the flesh is weak;
Thy gracious aid I seek,
For thou the word must speak
That makes me strong.
Then let me hear thy voice,
Thou art my only choice;
O bid my heart rejoice;
Be thou my song.

May it be joy to me
To follow only Thee;
Thy faithful servant be,
Thine to the end.
For Thee I'll do and dare,
For thee the cross I'll bear,
To thee direct my prayer,
On thee depend.

Saviour, with me abide;
Be ever near my side;
Support, defend, and guide.
I look to thee.
I lay my hand in thine,
And fleeting joys resign,
If I may call thee mine
Eternally.
—Mary J. Mason.

For all the sins that cling to thee
Let wide the gates of pardon be;
But hope not thou shalt smuggle through
The little sin thou clingest to.
—F. Langbridge.

GOD ALONE LOVED

Do I not love thee, Lord most high,
  In answer to thy love for me!
I seek no other liberty
  But that of being bound to Thee.

May memory no thought suggest
  But shall to thy pure glory tend;
May understanding find no rest
  Except in Thee, its only end.

My God, I here protest to Thee
  No other will I have than thine;
Whatever thou hast given me
  I here again to Thee resign.

All mine is thine, say but the word;
  Whate'er Thou willest—be it done;
I know thy love, all-gracious Lord—
  I know it seeks my good alone.

Apart from Thee all things are naught;
  Then grant, O my supremest bliss!
Grant me to love Thee as I ought;
  Thou givest all in giving this.
—Ignatius Loyola, tr. by Edward Caswall.

THE ACQUIESCENCE OF PURE LOVE

To me 'tis equal whether love ordain
  My life or death, appoint me pain or ease
My soul perceives no real ill in pain,
  In ease or health no real good she sees.

One good she covets, and that good alone,
  To choose thy will, from selfish bias free;
And to prefer a cottage to a throne,
  And grief to comfort, if it pleases Thee.

That we should bear the cross is Thy command,
  Die to the world and live to self no more;
Suffer unmoved beneath the rudest hand
  When shipwrecked pleased as when upon the shore.
—Madame Guyon.

I preached as never sure to preach again,
And as a dying man to dying men.
—Richard Baxter.

PRESSING TOWARD THE MARK

Thee will I love, my strength and tower,
  Thee will I love, my joy and crown,
Thee will I love with all my power,
  In all my works, and Thee alone.
Thee will I love, till that pure fire
Fills my whole soul with strong desire.

Give to mine eyes refreshing tears;
  Give to my heart chaste, hallowed fires;
Give to my soul, with filial fears
  The love that all heaven's host inspires;
That all my powers, with all their might,
In thy sole glory may unite.

Thee will I love, my joy, my crown,
  Thee will I love, my Lord, my God;
Thee will I love beneath thy frown
  Or smile, thy scepter or thy rod;
What though my head and flesh decay?
Thee shall I love in endless day.
—Johann A. Scheffler, tr. by John Wesley.

DWELL DEEP

Dwell deep! The little things that chafe and fret,
  O waste not golden hours to give them heed!
The slight, the thoughtless wrong, do thou forget,
  Be self-forgot in serving others' need.
Thou faith in God through love for man shalt keep.
  Dwell deep, my soul, dwell deep.

Dwell deep! Forego the pleasure if it bring
  Neglect of duty; consecrate each thought;
Believe thou in the good of everything,
  And trust that all unto the wisest end is wrought.
Bring thou this comfort unto all who weep:
  Dwell deep, my soul, dwell deep.
—James Buckham.

Out from thyself, thyself depart;
God then shall fill thine empty heart;
Cast from thy soul life's selfish dream—
In flows the Godhead's living stream.
—Scheffler, tr. by Frederic Rowland Marvin.

PEACE

REST, CALM, STILLNESS

THE PEACE OF GOD

When winds are raging o'er the upper
ocean,
And billows wild contend with angry
roar,
'Tis said, far down beneath the wild commotion,
That peaceful stillness reigneth evermore.

Far, far beneath the noise of tempest
dieth,
And silver waves chime ever peacefully;
And no rude storm, how fierce soe'er he
flieth,
Disturbs the Sabbath of that deeper
sea.

So to the soul that knows thy love, O
Purest,
There is a temple peaceful evermore.
And all the babble of life's angry voices
Dies hushed in stillness at its sacred
door.

Far, far away the noise of passion dieth,
And loving thoughts rise ever peacefully;
And no rude storm, how fierce soe'er
he flieth,
Disturbs that deeper rest, O Lord, in
thee.

O rest of rest! O peace serene, eternal!
Thou ever livest, and thou changest
never;
And in the secret of thy presence dwelleth
Fullness of joy, forever and forever.
—Harriet Beecher Stowe.

Life's burdens fall, its discords cease,
I lapse into the glad release
Of Nature's own exceeding peace.
—John Greenleaf Whittier.

BE STILL

Let nothing make thee sad or fretful,
Or too regretful;
Be still.
What God hath ordered must be right;
Then find in it thy own delight,
My will!

Why shouldst thou fill to-day with sorrow
About to-morrow,
My heart?
God watcheth all with care most true;
Doubt not that he will give thee too
Thy part. —Paul Fleming.

SIT STILL

(Ruth 3. 18.)

Sit still, my child. 'Tis no great thing I
ask,
No glorious deed, no mighty task;
But just to sit and patiently abide.
Wait in my presence, in my word confide,

"But oh! dear Lord, I long the sword to
wield,
Forward to go, and in the battle field
To fight for thee, thine enemies o'erthrow,
And in thy strength to vanquish every
foe.

"The harvest-fields spread out before
me lie,
The reapers toward me look, and vainly
cry—
'The field is white, the laborers are few;
Our Lord's command is also sent to
you,'"

My child, it is a sweet and blessed thing
To rest beneath the shadow of my wing;
To feel thy doings and thy words are
naught,
To trust to me each restless, longing
thought.

"Dear Lord, help me this lesson sweet
to learn,
To sit at thy pierced feet and only yearn
To love thee better, Lord, and feel that
still
Waiting is working, if it be thy will."

THE QUIET MIND

I have a treasure which I prize;
The like I cannot find;
There's nothing like it in the earth:
It is a quiet mind.

But 'tis not that I'm stupefied,
Or senseless, dull, or blind:
'Tis God's own peace within my soul
Which forms my quiet mind.

I found this treasure at the Cross.
'Tis there to every kind
Of heavy-laden, weary souls
Christ gives a quiet mind.

My Saviour's death and risen life
To give this were designed;
And that's the root and that's the
branch,
Of this my quiet mind.

The love of God within my heart
My heart to his doth bind;
This is the mind of heaven on earth;
This is my quiet mind.

I've many a cross to take up now,
And many left behind;
But present trials move me not,
Nor shake my quiet mind.

And what may be to-morrow's cross
I never seek to find;
My Saviour says, Leave that to Me,
And keep a quiet mind.

And well I know the Lord hath said,
To make my heart resigned,
That mercy still shall follow such
As have this quiet mind.

I meet with pride of wit and wealth,
And scorn and looks unkind,
It matters naught: I envy not,
For I've a quiet mind.

I'm waiting now to see the Lord,
Who's been to me so kind:
I want to thank him face to face
For this my quiet mind.

MY HEART IS RESTING

My heart is resting, O my God;
I will give thanks and sing:
My heart is at the secret source
Of every precious thing.

Now the frail vessel Thou hast made
No hand but thine shall fill—
The waters of the earth have failed,
And I am thirsty still.

I thirst for springs of heavenly life,
And here all day they rise;
I seek the treasure of Thy love,
And close at hand it lies.

And a "new song" is in my mouth,
To long-loved music set—
Glory to Thee for all the grace
I have not tasted yet.

I have a heritage of joy
That yet I must not see;
The hand that bled to make it mine
Is keeping it for me.

There is a certainty of love
That sets my heart at rest;
A calm assurance for to-day
That to be poor is best!

A prayer reposing on His truth,
Who hath made all things mine;
That draws my captive will to him,
And makes it one with thine.
—Anna Letitia Waring.

KEPT IN PERFECT PEACE

Peace, perfect peace, in this dark world
of sin?
The voice of Jesus whispers Peace with-
in.

Peace, perfect peace, by thronging duties
pressed?
To do the will of Jesus, this is rest.

Peace, perfect peace, with sorrow surg-
ing round?
On Jesus' bosom naught but rest is
found.

Peace, perfect peace, with loved ones
far away?
In Jesus' keeping we are safe, and they.

Peace, perfect peace, our future all unknown?
Jesus we know, and he is on the throne.

Peace, perfect peace, death shadowing us and ours?
Jesus has vanquished death and all its powers.

It is enough: earth's struggles now do cease,
And Jesus calls us to heaven's perfect peace.

—Edward Henry Bickersteth.

PERFECT PEACE

Like a river glorious is God's perfect peace;
Over all victorious in its bright increase;
Perfect, yet it floweth fuller every day,
Perfect, yet it groweth deeper all the way.

Hidden in the hollow of His blessed hand,
Never foe can follow, never traitor stand;
Not a surge of worry, not a shade of care,
Not a blast of hurry touch the spirit there.

Every joy or trial falleth from above,
Traced upon our dial by the Sun of Love,
We may trust him fully, all for us to do;
They who trust him wholly find him wholly true.

—Frances Ridley Havergal.

ABIDING

In heavenly love abiding,
No change my heart shall fear
And safe is such confiding,
For nothing changes here.
The storm may roar without me,
My heart may low be laid,
But God is round about me,
And can I be dismayed?

Whenever he may guide me,
No want shall turn me back;
My Shepherd is beside me,
And nothing can I lack.
His wisdom ever waketh,
His sight is never dim,
He knows the way he taketh,
And I will walk with him.

Green pastures are before me,
Which yet I have not seen;
Bright skies will soon be o'er me,
Where darkest clouds have been.
My hope I cannot measure,
My path to life is free,
My Saviour has my treasure,
And he will walk with me.

—Anna Letitia Waring.

CALM

I stand upon the Mount of God
With sunlight in my soul;
I hear the storms in vales beneath,
I hear the thunders roll.

But I am calm with thee, my God,
Beneath these glorious skies;
And to the height on which I stand,
No storms, nor clouds, can rise.

O, THIS is life! O, this is joy!
My God, to find thee so;
Thy face to see, thy voice to hear,
And all thy love to know.

—Horatius Bonar.

DIVINE PEACE

Peace upon peace, like wave upon wave,
This the portion that I crave;
The peace of God which passeth thought,
The peace of Christ which changeth not.

Peace like the river's gentle flow,
Peace like the morning's silent glow,
From day to day, in love supplied,
An endless and unebbing tide.

Peace flowing on without decrease,
From him who is our joy and peace,
Who, by his reconciling blood,
Hath made the sinner's peace with God.

Peace through the night and through the day,
Peace through the windings of our way;
In pain, and toil, and weariness,
A deep and everlasting peace.

O King of peace, this peace bestow
Upon a stranger here below;
O God of peace, thy peace impart,
To every sad and troubled heart.

Peace from the Father and the Son,
Peace from the Spirit, all his own;
Peace that shall never more be lost,
Of Father, Son, and Holy Ghost.
—Horatius Bonar.

A QUIET HEART

Quiet, Lord, my froward heart:
Make me teachable and mild;
Upright, simple, free from art;
Make me as a weanèd child,
From distrust and envy free,
Pleased with all that pleaseth thee.

What thou shalt to-day provide
Let me as a child receive;
What to-morrow may betide
Calmly to thy wisdom leave.
'Tis enough that thou wilt care:
Why should I the burthen bear?

As a little child relies
On a care beyond his own;
Knows he's neither strong nor wise,
Fears to stir a step alone;
Let me thus with thee abide,
As my Father, Guard and Guide.
—John Newton.

REST WHERE YOU ARE

When, spurred by tasks unceasing or undone,
You would seek rest afar,
And can not, though repose be rightly won—
Rest where you are.

Neglect the needless; sanctify the rest;
Move without stress or jar;
With quiet of a spirit self-possessed
Rest where you are.

Not in event, restriction, or release,
Not in scenes near or far,
But in ourselves are restlessness or peace,
Rest where you are.

Where lives the soul lives God; his day, his world,
No phantom mists need mar;
His starry nights are tents of peace unfurled:
Rest where you are.

BE ALL AT REST

Be all at rest, my soul toward God; from him comes my salvation. Psa. 62. 1.

"Be all at rest, my soul." Oh! blessed secret
Of the true life that glorifies thy Lord:
Not always doth the busiest soul best serve him,
But he who resteth on his faithful word.

"Be all at rest,"—"let not your heart be rippled,"
For tiny wavelets mar the image fair
Which the still pool reflects of heaven's glory—
And thus the Image he would have you bear.

"Be all at rest,"—for rest is highest service;
To the still heart God doth his secrets tell:
Thus shall thou learn to wait, and watch, and labor,
Strengthened to bear, since Christ in thee doth dwell.

For what is service but the life of Jesus
Lived through a vessel of earth's fragile clay;
Loving and giving; poured forth for others;
"A living sacrifice" from day to day?

And what shall meet the deep unrest around thee
But the calm peace of God that filled his breast?
For still a living voice must call the weary
To him who said, "Come unto me and rest."

Therefore "be all at rest, my soul," toward him,
If thou a revelation of the Lord would'st be;
For in the quiet confidence that never doubts him,
Others his truth and faithfulness shall see.

"Be all at rest," for rest alone becometh
The soul that casts on him its every care;
"Be all at rest"—so shall thy life proclaim him
A God who worketh and who heareth prayer.

"Be all at rest"—so shalt thou be an answer
To those who question, "Who is God, and where?"
For God is rest, and where he dwells is stillness,
And they who dwell in him that rest shall share.
—Freda Hanbury Allen.

REST

Sweet is the pleasure
Itself cannot spoil!
Is not true leisure
One with true toil?

Thou that wouldst taste it,
Still do thy best;
Use it, not waste it,
Else 'tis no rest.

Wouldst behold beauty
Near thee all round?
Only hath duty
Such a sight found.

Rest is not quitting
The busy career;
Rest is the fitting
Of self to its sphere.

'Tis the brook's motion,
Clear without strife,
Fleeing to ocean
After its life.

Deeper devotion
Nowhere hath knelt;
Fuller emotion
Heart never felt.

'Tis loving and serving
The Highest and Best!
'Tis onwards, unswerving,
And that is true rest.
—John Sullivan Dwight.

There is peace in power; the men who speak
With the loudest tongues do least;
And the surest sign of a mind that is weak
Is its want of the power to rest.
—John Boyle O'Reilly.

EQUANIMITY

Tost on a sea of troubles, Soul, my Soul,
Thyself do thou control;
And to the weapons of advancing foes
A stubborn breast oppose;
Undaunted 'mid the hostile might
Of squadrons burning for the fight
Thine be no boasting when the victor's crown
Wins thee deserved renown;
Thine no dejected sorrow, when defeat
Would urge a base retreat;
Rejoice in joyous things—nor overmuch
Let grief thy bosom touch
'Midst evil, and still bear in mind
How changeful are the ways of humankind.
—Archilochos, tr. by William Hay.

GOD'S PEACE

Grant us Thy peace, down from thy presence falling,
As on the thirsty earth cool night-dews sweet;
Grant us thy peace, to thy pure paths recalling,
From devious ways, our worn and wandering feet.

Grant us Thy peace, through winning and through losing,
Through gloom and gladness of our pilgrim way;
Grant us thy peace, safe in thy love's enclosing,
Thou who all things in heaven and earth dost sway.

Give us Thy peace, not as the world has given,
In momentary rays that fitful gleamed,
But calm, deep, sure, the peace of spirits shriven,
Of hearts surrendered and of souls redeemed.

Grant us thy peace, that like a deepening river
Swells ever outward to the sea of praise.
O thou of peace the only Lord and Giver,
Grant us thy peace, O Saviour, all our days.
—Eliza Scudder.

THE INNER CALM

Calm me, my God, and keep me calm,
While these hot breezes blow;
Be like the night-dew's cooling balm
Upon earth's fevered brow.

Calm me, my God, and keep me calm,
Soft resting on thy breast;
Soothe me with holy hymn and psalm
And bid my spirit rest.

Yes, keep me calm, though loud and rude
The sounds my ear that greet;
Calm in the closet's solitude,
Calm in the bustling street;

Calm in the hour of buoyant health,
Calm in my hour of pain,
Calm in my poverty or wealth,
Calm in my loss or gain;

Calm when the great world's news with power
My listening spirit stir;
Let not the tidings of the hour
E'er find too fond an ear;

Calm as the ray of sun or star
Which storms assail in vain;
Moving unruffled through earth's war,
The eternal calm to gain.
—Horatius Bonar.

Father, take not away
The burden of the day,
But help me that I bear it
As Christ his burden bore
When cross and thorn he wore
And none with him could share it;
In his name help I pray!

I only ask for grace
To see that patient face
And my impatient one;
Ask that mine grow like His—
Sign of an inward peace
From trust in thee alone,
Unchanged by time or place.

And they who do their souls no wrong,
But keep at eve the faith of morn,
Shall daily hear the angel-song,
To-day the Prince of Peace is born.
—James Russell Lowell.

Drop thy still dews of quietness,
Till all our strivings cease;
Take from our souls the strain and stress,
And let our ordered lives confess
The beauty of thy peace.

Breathe through the heats of our desire
Thy coolness and thy balm;
Let sense be dumb, let flesh retire;
Speak through the earthquake, wind, and fire,
O still, small voice of calm!
—John Greenleaf Whittier.

As flows the river calm and deep,
In silence toward the sea,
So floweth ever, and ceaseth never,
The love of God to me.

What peace He bringeth to my heart,
Deep as the soundless sea;
How sweetly singeth the soul that clingeth,
My loving Lord, to thee.

He fails never.
If He cannot work by us He will work through us.
Let our souls be calm.
We should be ashamed to sit beneath those stars,
Impatient that we're nothing.
Get work, get work; be sure 'tis better
Than what you work to get.
—Elizabeth Barrett Browning.

Calm Soul of all things, make it mine
To feel amid the city's jar,
That there abides a peace of thine
Man did not make and cannot mar.
The will to neither strive nor cry,
The power to feel with others give;
Calm, calm me more, nor let me die
Before I have begun to live.
—Matthew Arnold.

What secret trouble stirs thy heart?
Why all this fret and flurry?
Dost thou not know that what is best
In this too restless world is rest
From over-work and hurry?
—Henry Wadsworth Longfellow.

We bless thee for thy peace, O God,
Deep as the boundless sea,
It falls like sunshine on the road,
Of those who trust in thee;
That peace which suffers and is strong,
Trusts where it cannot see;
Deems not the trial way too long,
But leaves the end with thee.

Be calm in arguing: for fierceness makes
Error a fault, and truth discourtesy.
Why should I feel another man's mistakes
More than his sicknesses or poverty?
In love I should; but anger is not love,
Nor wisdom, neither; therefore gently move.
—George Herbert.

Why fret thee, soul,
For things beyond thy small control?
But do thy part, and thou shalt see
Heaven will have charge of them and thee.
Sow then thy seed, and wait in peace
The Lord's increase.

What is the use of worrying
And flurrying and scurrying
And breaking up one's rest;
When all the world is teaching us
And praying and beseeching us
That quiet ways are best.

I feel within me
A peace above all earthly dignities
A still and quiet conscience.
—William Shakespeare.

The stormy blast is strong, but mightier still
The calm that binds the storm beneath its peaceful will.
—John Sterling.

As running water cleanseth bodies dropped therein
So heavenly truth doth cleanse the secret heart from sin.
—From the Sanskrit, tr. by Frederic Rowland Marvin.

From our ill-ordered hearts we oft are fain to roam,
As men go forth who find unquietness at home.
—Richard Chenevix Trench.

A mind from every evil thought set free
I count the noblest gift of Deity.
—Æschylus, tr. by Frederic Rowland Marvin.

A stone makes not great rivers turbid grow;
When saints are vexed their shallowness they show.
—Saadi.

Yes, Lord, one great eternal yes
To all my Lord shall say;
To what I know, or yet shall know,
In all the untried way.

Good striving
Brings thriving.
Better a dog who works
Than a lion who shirks.
—From the Persian.

HUMILITY

MEEKNESS, WEAKNESS, SELFLESSNESS

✓A LAST PRAYER

Father, I scarcely dare to pray,
So clear I see, now it is done,
That I have wasted half my day
And left my work but just begun.

So clear I see that things I thought
Were right, or harmless, were a sin;
So clear I see that I have sought
Unconscious, selfish aims to win;

So clear I see that I have hurt
The souls I might have helped to save;
That I have slothful been, inert,
Deaf to the calls Thy leaders gave.

In outskirts of thy kingdom vast,
Father, the humblest spot give me;
Set me the lowliest task thou hast;
Let me, repentant, work for thee.
—Helen Hunt Jackson.

A LOWLY HEART

Thy home is with the humble, Lord!
The simplest are the best,
Thy lodging is in child-like hearts:
Thou makest there thy rest.

Dear Comforter! Eternal Love!
If thou wilt stay with me,
Of lowly thoughts and simple ways
I'll build a house for thee.

Who made this beating heart of mine
But Thou, my heavenly guest?
Let no one have it, then, but thee,
And let it be thy rest.
—Lyra Catholica.

Before the eyes of men let duly shine
thy light,
But ever let thy life's best part be out
of sight.
—Richard Chenevix Trench.

KNOWLEDGE AND WISDOM

I.

The Man who Loved the Names of
Things
Went forth beneath the skies
And named all things that he beheld,
And people called him wise.
An unseen presence walked with him
Forever by his side,
The wedded mistress of his soul—
For Knowledge was his bride;
She named the flowers, the weeds, the
trees,
And all the growths of all the seas.

She told him all the rocks by name,
The winds and whence they blew;
She told him how the seas were formed,
And how the mountains grew.
She numbered all the stars for him;
And all the rounded skies
Were mapped and charted for the gaze
Of his devouring eyes.
Thus, taught by her, he taught the
crowd;
They praised—and he was very proud.

II.

The Man who Loved the Soul of Things
Went forth serene and glad,
And mused upon the mighty world,
And people called him mad.
An unseen presence walked with him
Forever by his side,
The wedded mistress of his soul—
For Wisdom was his bride.
She showed him all this mighty frame,
And bade him feel—but named no name.

She stood with him upon the hills
Ringed by the azure sky,
And shamed his lowly thought with stars
And bade it climb as high.
And all the birds he could not name,
The nameless stars that roll,
The unnamed blossoms at his feet
Talked with him soul to soul;
He heard the Nameless Glory speak
In silence—and was very meek.
—Sam Walter Foss.

THE INQUIRY

I wonder if ever a song was sung but the singer's heart sang sweeter!
I wonder if ever a rhyme was rung but the thought surpassed the meter!
I wonder if ever a sculptor wrought till the cold stone echoed his ardent thought!
Or if ever the painter with light and shade the dream of his inmost heart portrayed!

I wonder if ever a rose was found and there might not be a fairer!
Or if ever a glittering gem was ground and we dreamed not of a rarer!
Ah! never on earth do we find the best; but it waits for us in the land of rest,
And a perfect thing we shall never behold till we pass the portals of shining gold.

A SONG OF LOW DEGREE

He that is down need fear no fall;
He that is low, no pride;
He that is humble ever shall
Have God to be his guide.

I am content with what I have,
Little be it, or much;
And, Lord, contentment still I crave,
Because thou savest such.

Fullness to such a burden is
That go on pilgrimage;
Here little, and hereafter bliss,
Is best from age to age.
—John Bunyan.

NOT YET PREPARED

O thou unpolished shaft, why leave the quiver?
O thou blunt axe, what forests canst thou hew?
Untempered sword, canst thou the oppressed deliver?
Go back to thine own maker's forge anew.

Submit thyself to God for preparation,
Seek not to teach thy Master and thy Lord;
Call it not zeal; it is a base temptation.
Satan is pleased when man dictates to God.

Down with thy pride! with holy vengeance trample
On each self-flattering fancy that appears;
Did not the Lord himself, for our example,
Lie hid in Nazareth for thirty years?

RECESSIONAL

God of our fathers, known of old—
Lord of our far-flung battle-line—
Beneath whose awful hand we hold
Dominion over palm and pine—
Lord God of hosts, be with us yet,
Lest we forget—lest we forget.

The tumult and the shouting dies—
The Captains and the Kings depart—
Still stands thine ancient sacrifice,
An humble and a contrite heart.
Lord God of hosts, be with us yet,
Lest we forget—lest we forget.

Far-called our navies melt away—
On dune and headland sinks the fire—
Lo, all our pomp of yesterday
Is one with Nineveh and Tyre.
Judge of the nations, spare us yet,
Lest we forget—lest we forget.

If, drunk with sight of power, we loose
Wild tongues that have not thee in awe—
Such boastings as the Gentiles use,
Or lesser breeds without the Law—
Lord God of hosts, be with us yet,
Lest we forget—lest we forget.

For heathen heart that puts her trust
In reeking tube and iron shard—
All valiant dust that builds on dust,
And guarding calls not Thee to guard.
For frantic boast and foolish word,
Thy mercy on thy people, Lord.
—Rudyard Kipling.

In humbleness, O Lord, I ask
That thou bestow on me
The will and strength to do some task
For growth of love for thee;
Some task, not of my chosen will—
For wisdom is not mine—
But let my frailsome life fulfill
Some perfect thought of thine.

I WILL NOT SEEK

I cannot think but God must know
About the thing I long for so;
I know he is so good, so kind,
I cannot think but he will find
Some way to help, some way to show
Me to the thing I long for so.

I stretch my hand; it lies so near,
It looks so sweet, it looks so dear,
"Dear Lord," I pray, "O let me know
If it is wrong to want it so!"
He only smiles, he does not speak;
My heart grows weaker and more weak
With looking at the thing so dear,
Which lies so far, and yet so near.

Now, Lord, I leave at thy loved feet
This thing which looks so near, so sweet;
I will not seek, I will not long;
I almost fear I have been wrong;
I'll go, and work the harder, Lord,
And wait, till by some loud, clear word
Thou callest me to thy loved feet
To take this thing so dear, so sweet.
—Saxe Holm.

TRIUMPHING IN OTHERS

Others shall sing the song,
Others shall right the wrong,
Finish what I begin,
And all I fail of win.

What matter, I or they,
Mine or another's day,
So the right word be said,
And life the sweeter made?

Ring, bells in unreared steeples,
The joy of unborn peoples!
Sound, trumpets far-off blown,
Your triumph is my own.
—John Greenleaf Whittier.

Pitch thy behaviour low, thy projects high;
So shalt thou humble and magnanimous be;
Sink not in spirit; who aimeth at the sky
Shoots higher much than he that means a tree.
A grain of glory mixed with humbleness
Cures both a fever and lethargickness.
—George Herbert.

FOR DIVINE STRENGTH

Father, in thy mysterious presence kneeling,
Fain would our souls feel all thy kindling love;
For we are weak and need some deep revealing
Of trust, and strength, and calmness from above.

Lord, we have wandered far through doubt and sorrow,
And thou hast made each step an onward one;
And we will ever trust each unknown morrow—
Thou wilt sustain us till its work is done.

In the heart's depths a peace serene and holy
Abides; and when pain seems to have its will,
Or we despair, O may that peace rise slowly
Stronger than agony, and we be still!

Now, Father, now, in thy dear presence kneeling,
Our spirits yearn to feel thy kindling love;
Now make us strong, we need thy deep revealing,
Of trust, and strength, and calmness from above. —Samuel Johnson.

WHEN I AM WEAK THEN AM I STRONG

Half feeling our own weakness,
We place our hands in Thine—
Knowing but half our darkness
We ask for light divine.
Then, when Thy strong arm holds us,
Our weakness most we feel,
And thy love and light around us
Our darkness must reveal.

Too oft, when faithless doubtings
Around our spirits press,
We cry, "Can hands so feeble
Grasp such almightiness?"
While thus we doubt and tremble
Our hold still looser grows;
While on our darkness gazing
Vainly thy radiance glows.

Oh, cheer us with Thy brightness,
And guide us by thy hand,
In thy light teach us light to see,
In thy strength strong to stand.
Then though our hands be feeble,
If they but touch thine arm,
Thy light and power shall lead us,
And keep us strong and calm.

A HUMBLE HEART

I would not ask Thee that my days
Should flow quite smoothly on and on,
Lest I should learn to love the world
Too well, ere all my time was done.

I would not ask Thee that my work
Should never bring me pain nor fear;
Lest I should learn to work alone,
And never wish thy presence near.

I would not ask Thee that my friends
Should always kind and constant be;
Lest I should learn to lay my faith
In them alone, and not in thee.

But I would ask a humble heart,
A changeless will to work and wake,
A firm faith in Thy providence,
The rest—'tis thine to give or take.
—Alfred Norris.

Knowledge and wisdom, far from being one,
Have ofttimes no connection. Knowledge dwells
In heads replete with thoughts of other men;
Wisdom in minds attentive to their own.
Knowledge, a rude, unprofitable mass,
The mere material with which Wisdom builds,
Till smoothed, and squared, and fitted to its place,
Does but encumber whom it seems to enrich.
Knowledge is proud that he has learned so much,
Wisdom is humble that he knows no more. —William Cowper.

Humble we must be if to heaven we go;
High is the roof there; but the gate is low. —Robert Herrick.

NOT MINE

It is not mine to run, with eager feet,
Along life's crowded ways, my Lord to meet.

It is not mine to pour the oil and wine
Or bring the purple robe and linen fine.

It is not mine to break at his dear feet
The alabaster box of ointment sweet.

It is not mine to bear his heavy cross,
Or suffer, for his sake, all pain and loss.

It is not mine to walk through valleys dim,
Or climb far mountain heights alone with him.

He hath no need of me in grand affairs,
Where fields are lost or crowns won unawares.

Yet, Master, if I may make one pale flower
Bloom brighter, for thy sake, though one short hour;

If I in harvest fields where strong ones reap,
May bind one golden sheaf for love to keep;

May speak one quiet word when all is still,
Helping some fainting heart to bear thy will;

Or sing some high, clear song on which may soar
Some glad soul heavenward, I ask no more.
—Julia Caroline Ripley Dorr.

Christ wants the best. He in the far-off ages
Once claimed the firstling of the flock, the finest of the wheat;
And still he asks his own with gentlest pleading
To lay their highest hopes and brightest talents at his feet.
He'll not forget the feeblest service, humblest love;
He only asks that of our stores we give to him the best we have.

PRAISE DEPRECATED

My sins and follies, Lord, by thee
From others hidden are,
That such good words are spoke of me
As now and then I hear;
For sure if others know me such,
Such as myself I know,
I should have been dispraised as much
As I am praisèd now.

The praise, therefore, which I have heard,
Delights not so my mind,
As those things make my heart afeard
Which in myself I find;
And I had rather to be blamed,
So I were blameless made,
Than for much virtue to be famed
When I no virtues had.

Though slanders to an innocent
Sometimes do bitter grow,
Their bitterness procures content,
If clear himself he know.
And when a virtuous man hath erred
If praised himself he hear,
It makes him grieve and more afeard
Than if he slandered were.

Lord, therefore make my heart upright,
Whate'er my deeds do seem;
And righteous rather in thy sight,
Than in the world's esteem.
And if aught good appears to be
In any act of mine,
Let thankfulness be found in me,
And all the praise be thine.
—George Wither (1588–1667).

One part, one little part, we dimly scan,
Through the dark medium of life's feverish dream;
Yet dare arraign the whole stupendous plan,
If but that little part incongruous seem.
Nor is that part, perhaps, what mortals deem,
Oft from apparent ill our blessings rise.
O then renounce that impious self-esteem
That aims to trace the secrets of the skies;
For thou art but of dust, be humble and be wise.
—James Beattie.

HUMILITY

O humble me! I cannot bide the joy
That in my Saviour's presence ever flows;
May I be lowly, lest it may destroy
The peace his childlike spirit ever knows.
I would not speak thy word, but by thee stand
While thou dost to thine erring children speak;
O help me but to keep his own command,
And in my strength to feel me ever weak;
Then in thy presence shall I humbly stay,
Nor lose the life of love he came to give;
And find at last the life, the truth, the way
To where with him thy blessed servants live;
And walk forever in the path of truth—
A servant, yet a son; a sire and yet a youth.
—Jones Very.

TURN FROM SELF

This is the highest learning,
The hardest and the best—
From self to keep still turning,
And honor all the rest.

If one should break the letter,
Yea, spirit of command,
Think not that thou art better;
Thou may'st not always stand!

We all are weak—but weaker
Hold no one than thou art;
Then, as thou growest meeker,
Higher will go thy heart.
—George Macdonald.

In proud humility a pious man went through the field;
The ears of corn were bowing in the wind, as if they kneeled;
He struck them on the head, and modestly began to say,
"Unto the Lord, not unto me, such honors should you pay."
—From the Persian.

MEEKNESS OF MOSES

Moses, the patriot fierce, became
The meekest man on earth,
To show us how love's quickening flame
Can give our souls new birth.

Moses, the man of meekest heart,
Lost Canaan by self-will,
To show, where grace has done its part,
How sin defiles us still.

Thou who hast taught me in thy fear,
Yet seest me frail at best,
Oh, grant me loss with Moses here,
To gain his future rest.
—John Henry Newman.

LAUS DEO

Let praise devote thy work, and skill employ
Thy *whole mind, and thy heart be lost* in joy.
Well-doing bringeth pride; this constant thought
Humility, that thy best done is naught.
Man doeth nothing well, be it great or small,
Save to praise God; but that hath savèd all.
For God requires no more than thou hast done,
And takes thy work to bless it for his own. —Robert Bridges.

"A commonplace life," we say, and we sigh;
But why should we sigh as we say?
The commonplace sun in the commonplace sky
Makes up the commonplace day.
The moon and the stars are commonplace things,
And the flower that blooms and the bird that sings,
But dark were the world and sad our lot
If the flowers failed and the sun shone not;
And God, who studies each separate soul
Out of commonplace lives makes his beautiful whole.

Humility, that low, sweet root
From which all heavenly virtues shoot.
—Thomas Moore.

THE EVERLASTING MEMORIAL

Up and away, like the dew of the morning
That soars from the earth to its home in the sun,
So let me steal away, gently and lovingly,
Only remembered by what I have done.

My name, and my place, and my tomb all forgotten,
The brief race of time well and patiently run,
So let me pass away, peacefully, silently,
Only remembered by what I have done.

Gladly away from this toil would I hasten,
Up to the crown that for me has been won;
Unthought of by man in rewards or in praises,
Only remembered by what I have done.

Up and away, like the odors of sunset,
That sweeten the twilight as evening comes on,
So be my life—a thing felt but not noticed,—
And I but remembered by what I have done.

Yes, like the fragrance that wanders in freshness
When the flowers that it came from are closed up and gone,
So would I be to this world's weary dwellers
Only remembered by what I have done.

I need not be missed, if my life has been bearing
(As its summer and autumn move silently on)
The bloom, and the fruit, and the seed of its season;
I shall still be remembered by what I have done.

Needs there the praise of the love-written record,
The name and the epitaph graved on the stone?

The things we have lived for—let them
be our story—
We ourselves but remembered by
what we have done.

I need not be missed if another succeed
me,
To reap down the fields which in
spring I have sown;
He who plowed and who sowed is not
missed by the reaper,
He is only remembered by what he
has done.

Not myself, but the truth that in life I
have spoken,
Not myself, but the seed that in life
I have sown,
Shall pass on to ages—all about me forgotten,
Save the truth I have spoken, the
things I have done.

So let my living be, so be my dying;
So let my name lie, unblazoned, unknown;
Unpraised and unmissed, I shall still be
remembered;
Yes, but remembered for what I have
done. —Horatius Bonar.

SELF

O I could go through all life's troubles
singing,
Turning earth's night to day,
If self were not so fast around me clinging,
To all I do or say.

O Lord! that I could waste my life for
others,
With no ends of my own,
That I could pour myself into my
brothers
And live for them alone!

Such was the life thou livedst; self-abjuring,
Thine own pains never easing,
Our burdens bearing, our just doom
enduring;
A life without self-pleasing.
—Frederick William Faber.

BRINGING OUR SHEAVES WITH US

The time for toil is past, and night has
come—
The last and saddest of the harvest
eves;
Worn out with labor, long and wearisome,
Drooping and faint, the reapers hasten
home,
Each laden with his sheaves.

Last of the laborers, thy feet I gain,
Lord of the harvest! and my spirit
grieves
That I am burdened not so much with
grain
As with a heaviness of heart and brain;
Master, behold my sheaves.

Few, light, and worthless—yet their
trifling weight
Through all my frame a weary aching
leaves;
For long I struggled with my hapless
fate,
And stayed and toiled till it was dark
and late—
Yet these are all my sheaves.

Full well I know I have more tares than
wheat,
Brambles and flowers, dry stalks and
withered leaves;
Wherefore I blush and weep as at thy
feet
I kneel down reverently and repeat,
"Master, behold my sheaves!"

I know these blossoms clustering
heavily,
With evening dew upon their folded
leaves,
Can claim no value or utility—
Therefore shall fragrancy and beauty
be
The glory of my sheaves.

So do I gather strength and hope anew;
For well I know thy patient love perceives
Not what I did, but what I strove to do,
And though the full ripe ears be sadly
few
Thou wilt accept my sheaves.
—Elizabeth Akers.

I pray not that
Men tremble at
My power of place,
And lordly sway;
I only pray for simple grace
To look my neighbor in the face
Full honestly from day to day.
—James Whitcomb Riley.

If thou art blest,
Then let the sunshine of thy gladness rest
On the dark edges of each cloud that lies
Black in thy brother's skies.
If thou art sad,
Still be in thy brother's gladness glad.
—Hamilton.

Flower in the crannied wall,
I pluck you out of the crannies,
I hold you here, root and all, in my hand,
Little flower—but if I could understand
What you are, root and all, and all in all,
I should know what God and man is.
—Alfred Tennyson.

Praise not thy work, but let thy work praise thee;
For deeds, not words, make each man's memory stable.
If what thou dost is good, its good all men will see;
Musk by its smell is known, not by its label.

When thou art fain to trace a map of thine own heart,
An undiscovered land set down the largest part.
—Richard Chenevix Trench.

Patient, resigned and humble wills
Impregnably resist all ills.
—Thomas Ken.

He is one to whom
Long patience hath such mild composure given,
That patience now doth seem a thing of which
He hath no need.
—William Wordsworth.

Be not too ready to condemn
The wrong thy brothers may have done:
Ere ye too harshly censure them
For human faults, ask, "Have I none?"
—Eliza Cook.

Search thine own heart. What paineth thee
In others in thyself may be;
All dust is frail, all flesh is weak;
Be thou the true man thou dost seek.
—John Greenleaf Whittier.

Through wish, resolve, and act, our will
Is moved by undreamed forces still;
And no man measures in advance
His strength with untried circumstance.
—John Greenleaf Whittier.

Labor with what zeal we will,
Something still remains undone.
Something uncompleted still
Waits the rising of the sun.
—Henry Wadsworth Longfellow.

In the deed that no man knoweth,
Where no praiseful trumpet bloweth,
Where he may not reap who soweth,
There, Lord, let my heart serve thee.

O wad some power the giftie gie us
To see oursels as ithers see us!
It wad frae mony a blunder free us,
An' foolish notion.
—Robert Burns.

CONTENTMENT

RESIGNATION, PATIENCE, COMPENSATION

CONTENTMENT

Father, I know that all my life
Is portioned out for me,
And the changes that are sure to come
I do not fear to see;
I ask Thee for a patient mind,
Intent on pleasing thee.

I ask Thee for a thoughtful love,
Through constant watching wise,
To meet the glad with joyful smiles,
And wipe the weeping eyes,
And a heart, at leisure from itself,
To soothe and sympathize.

I would not have the restless will
That hurries to and fro,
Seeking for some great thing to do,
Or secret thing to know;
I would be treated as a child,
And *guided* where I go.

Wherever in this world I am,
In whatsoe'er estate,
I have a fellowship with hearts
To keep and cultivate,
And a work of lowly love to do
For the Lord on whom I wait.

So I ask Thee for the daily strength—
To none that ask denied—
And a mind to blend with outward life,
While keeping at thy side,
Content to fill a *little* space,
If thou be glorified.

And if some things I do not ask
In my cup of blessing be,
I would have my spirit filled the more
With grateful love to thee;
More careful not to serve thee much,
But to please thee perfectly.

There are briers besetting every path,
Which call for constant care;
There is a cross in every lot,
And an earnest need for prayer;
But a lowly heart, that leans on Thee,
Is happy everywhere.

In a service which Thy love appoints
There are no bonds for me,
For my secret heart has learned the truth
Which makes thy children free,
And a life of self-renouncing love
Is a life of liberty.

—Anna Letitia Waring.

TWO PICTURES

An old farm house with meadows wide,
And sweet with clover on each side;
A bright-eyed boy, who looks from out
The door with woodbine wreathed about,
And wishes his one thought all day:
"O if I could but fly away!
From this dull spot the world to see,
How happy, happy, happy,
How happy I should be!"

Amid the city's constant din,
A man who round the world has been,
Who, 'mid the tumult and the throng,
Is thinking, thinking all day long:
"O could I only tread once more
The field-path to the farm-house door,
The old green meadow could I see,
How happy, happy, happy,
How happy I should be!"

—Annie Douglas Robinson.

Happy the man, of mortals happiest he,
Whose quiet mind from vain desires is free;
Whom neither hopes deceive nor fears torment,
But lives in peace, within himself content;
In thought, or act, accountable to none
But to himself, and unto God alone.

—Henry P. F. Lansdowne.

CONTENT I LIVE

My mind to me a kingdom is;
  Such perfect joy therein I find
As far exceeds all earthly bliss
  That God or nature hath assigned:
Though much I want that most would
  have,
Yet still my mind forbids to crave.

Content I live; this is my stay—
  I seek no more than may suffice.
I press to bear no haughty sway;
  Look, what I lack my mind supplies.
Lo, thus I triumph like a king,
Content with what my mind doth bring.

I laugh not at another's loss,
  I grudge not at another's gain;
No worldly wave my mind can toss;
  I brook that as another's bane.
I fear no foe, nor fawn on friend.
I loathe not life, nor dread mine end.

My wealth is health and perfect ease;
My conscience clear my chief defense;
I never seek by bribes to please
  Nor by desert to give offense.
Thus do I live, thus will I die;
Would all did so, as well as I.
—Edward Dyer.
Alt. by William Byrd (1540–1625).

JUST AS GOD LEADS

Just as God leads me I would go;
  I would not ask to choose my way;
Content with what he will bestow,
  Assured he will not let me stray.
So, as he leads, my path I make,
And step by step I gladly take—
  A child, in him confiding.

Just as God leads I am content;
  I rest me calmly in his hands;
That which he has decreed and sent—
  That which his will for me commands—
I would that he should all fulfill,
That I should do his gracious will
  In living or in dying.

Just as God leads, I all resign;
  I trust me to my Father's will;
When reason's rays deceptive shine,
  His counsel would I yet fulfill;
That which his love ordained as right
Before he brought me to the right
  My all to him resigning.

Just as God leads me, I abide
  In faith, in hope, in suffering true;
His strength is ever by my side—
  Can aught my hold on him undo?
I hold me firm in patience, knowing
That God my life is still bestowing—
  The best in kindness sending.

Just as God leads I onward go,
  Out amid thorns and briers keen;
God does not yet his guidance show—
  But in the end it shall be seen.
How, by a loving Father's will,
Faithful and true, he leads me still.
  And so my heart is resting.
—From the German.

SWEET CONTENT

O Thou, by long experience tried,
Near whom no grief can long abide;
My Lord, how full of sweet content
I pass my years of banishment!

All scenes alike engaging prove
To souls impressed with sacred love!
Where'er they dwell they dwell in Thee
In heaven, in earth, or on the sea.

To me remains nor place nor time,
My country is in every clime;
I can be calm and free from care
On any shore, since God is there.

While place we seek, or place we shun,
The soul finds happiness in none;
But with a God to guide our way
'Tis equal joy to go or stay.

Could I be cast where Thou art not,
That were indeed a dreadful lot;
But regions none remote I call,
Secure of finding God in all.
—Madame Guyon.

CONTENT AND RICH

My conscience is my crown,
  Contented thoughts my rest;
My heart is happy in itself,
  My bliss is in my breast.

Enough I reckon wealth;
  A mean, the surest lot;
That lies too high for base contempt,
  Too low for envy's shot.

My wishes are but few,
  All easy to fulfill;
I make the limits of my power
  The bounds unto my will.

I feel no care of coin;
Well doing is my wealth;
My mind to me an empire is,
While grace affordeth health.

I clip high-climbing thoughts,
The wings of swelling pride;
Their fall is worst that from the height
Of greatest honor slide.

Since sails of largest size
The storm doth soonest tear,
I bear so low and small a sail
As freeth me from fear.

I wrestle not with rage
While fury's flame doth burn;
It is in vain to stop the stream
Until the tide doth turn.

But when the flame is out,
And ebbing wrath doth end,
I turn a late enragèd foe
Into a quiet friend.

And, taught with often proof,
A tempered calm I find
To be most solace to itself,
Best cure for angry mind.

No change of fortune's calms
Can cast my comforts down;
When Fortune smiles I smile to think
How quickly she will frown.

And when in froward mood
She proves an angry foe,
Small gain I found to let her come,
Less loss to let her go.
—Robert Southwell, 1561–95.
(One of the Jesuit Fathers who were cruelly executed by Queen Elizabeth.)

Don't lose Courage! Spirit brave
Carry with you to the grave.

Don't lose Time in vain distress!
Work, not worry, brings success.

Don't lose Hope! who lets her stray
Goes forlornly all the way.

Don't lose Patience, come what will!
Patience ofttimes outruns skill.

Don't lose Gladness! every hour
Blooms for you some happy flower.

Though be foiled your dearest plan,
Don't lose Faith in God and man!

A CONTRAST

Two men toiled side by side from sun to sun,
And both were poor;
Both sat with children, when the day was done,
About their door.
One saw the beautiful in crimson cloud
And shining moon;
The other, with his head in sadness bowed,
Made night of noon.
One loved each tree and flower and singing bird,
On mount or plain;
No music in the soul of one was stirred
By leaf or rain.
One saw the good in every fellow-man
And hoped the best;
The other marvelled at his Master's plan,
And doubt confessed.
One, having heaven above and heaven below,
Was satisfied;
The other, discontented, lived in woe,
And hopeless died.
—Sarah Knowles Bolton.

WHO BIDES HIS TIME

Who bides his time, and day by day
Faces defeat full patiently,
And lifts a mirthful roundelay
However poor his fortunes be—
He will not fail in any qualm
Of poverty; the paltry dime—
It will grow golden in his palm
Who bides his time.

Who bides his time—he tastes the sweet
Of honey in the saltest tear;
And though he fares with slowest feet
Joy runs to meet him drawing near;
The birds are heralds of his cause,
And like a never-ending rhyme
The roadsides bloom in his applause
Who bides his time.

Who bides his time, and fevers not
In a hot race that none achieves,
Shall wear cool wreathen laurel, wrought
With crimson berries in the leaves;
And he shall reign a goodly king
And sway his hand o'er every clime,
With peace writ on his signet ring,
Who bides his time.
—James Whitcomb Riley.

CARELESS CONTENT

I am content; I do not care;
  Wag as it will the world for me;
When Fuss and Fret was all my fare
  It got no ground, as I could see.
So when away my caring went
I counted cost and was content.

With more of thanks and less of thought
  I strive to make my matters meet;
To seek, what ancient sages sought,
  Physic and food in sour and sweet.
To take what passes in good part,
And keep the hiccups from the heart.

With good and gentle-humored hearts
  I choose to chat, whene'er I come,
Whate'er the subject be that starts;
  But if I get among the glum
I hold my tongue, to tell the truth,
And keep my breath to cool my broth.

For chance or change of peace or pain;
  For fortune's favor or her frown;
For luck or glut, for loss or gain,
  I never dodge, nor up nor down:
But swing what way the ship shall swim,
Or tack about with equal trim.

I suit not where I shall not speed,
  Nor trace the turn of every tide;
If simple sense will not succeed,
  I make no bustling, but abide;
For shining wealth, or scoring woe,
I force no friend, I fear no foe.

I love my neighbor as myself;
  Myself like him too, by his leave;
Nor to his pleasure, power, or pelf
  Came I to crouch, as I conceive;
Dame Nature doubtless has designed
A man the monarch of his mind.

Now taste and try this temper, sirs;
  Mood it and brood it in your breast;
Or if ye ween, for worldly stirs,
  That man does right to mar his rest,
Let me be left, and debonair;
I am content; I do not care.

—John Byrom (1692–1763).

Some of your hurts you have cured,
  And the sharpest you still have survived,
But what torments of grief you endured
  From the evils which never arrived.

—Ralph Waldo Emerson.

HAPPY ANY WAY

Lord, it belongs not to my care
  Whether I die or live;
To love and serve thee is my share,
  And this thy grace must give.

If life be long, I will be glad
  That I may long obey;
If short, yet why should I be sad
  To soar to endless day?

Christ leads me through no darker rooms
  Than he went through before;
He that into God's kingdom comes
  Must enter by his door.

Come, Lord, when grace hath made me meet
  Thy blessèd face to see;
For, if thy work on earth be sweet,
  What will thy glory be?

Then I shall end my sad complaints,
  And weary, sinful days,
And join with the triumphant saints
  Who sing Jehovah's praise.

My knowledge of that life is small;
  The eye of faith is dim;
But 'tis enough that Christ knows all,
  And I shall be with him.

—Richard Baxter.

THE THINGS I MISS

An easy thing, O Power Divine,
To thank thee for these gifts of thine!
For summer's sunshine, winter's snow,
For hearts that kindle, thoughts that glow;
But when shall I attain to this:
To thank thee for the things I miss?

For all young fancy's early gleams,
The dreamed-of joys that still are dreams,
Hopes unfulfilled, and pleasures known
Through others' fortunes, not my own,
And blessings seen that are not given,
And ne'er will be, this side of heaven.

Had I, too, shared the joys I see,
Would there have been a heaven for me?
Could I have felt thy presence near
Had I possessed what I held dear?
My deepest fortune, highest bliss,
Have grown, perchance, from things I miss.

Sometimes there comes an hour of calm;
Grief turns to blessing, pain to balm;
A Power that works above my will
Still leads me onward, upward still;
And then my heart attains to this:
To thank thee for the things I miss.
—Thomas Wentworth Higginson.

THE HERITAGE

The rich man's son inherits lands,
And piles of brick and stone and gold,
And he inherits soft, white hands,
And tender flesh that fears the cold,
Nor dares to wear a garment old;
A heritage, it seems to me,
One scarce would wish to hold in fee.

The rich man's son inherits cares;
The bank may break, the factory burn,
A breath may burst his bubble shares,
And soft white hands could hardly earn
A living that would serve his turn;
A heritage, it seems to me,
One scarce would wish to hold in fee.

The rich man's son inherits wants,
His stomach craves for dainty fare;
With sated heart he hears the pants
Of toiling hinds with brown arms bare,
And wearies in his easy-chair;
A heritage, it seems to me,
One scarce would wish to hold in fee.

What doth the poor man's son inherit?
Stout muscles and a sinewy heart;
A hardy frame, a hardier spirit,
King of two hands, he does his part
In every useful toil and art;
A heritage, it seems to me,
A king might wish to hold in fee.

What doth the poor man's son inherit?
Wishes o'erjoyed with humble things,
A rank adjudged by toil-won merit,
Content that from employment springs,
A heart that in his labor sings;
A heritage, it seems to me,
A king might wish to hold in fee.

What doth the poor man's son inherit?
A patience learned of being poor,
Courage, if sorrow come, to bear it,
A fellow-feeling that is sure
To make the outcast bless his door;
A heritage, it seems to me,
A king might wish to hold in fee.

O rich man's son! there is a toil
That with all others level stands;
Large charity doth never soil,
But only whiten soft, white hands;
This is the best crop from thy lands,
A heritage, it seems to me,
Worth being rich to hold in fee.

O poor man's son! scorn not thy state;
There is worse weariness than thine
In merely being rich and great;
Toil only gives the soul to shine,
And makes rest fragrant and benign;
A heritage, it seems to me,
Worth being poor to hold in fee.

Both, heirs to some six feet of sod,
Are equal in the earth at last;
Both, children of the same dear God,
Prove title to your heirship vast
By record of a well-filled past;
A heritage, it seems to me,
Well worth a life to hold in fee.
—James Russell Lowell.

I AM CONTENT

I am content. In trumpet tones
My song let people know;
And many a mighty man with thrones
And scepter is not so.
And if he is I joyful cry,
Why, then he's just the same as I.

My motto is—Content with this;
Gold—place—I prize not such.
That which I have my measure is:
Wise men desire not much.
Men wish and wish, and have their will,
And wish again as hungry still.

And gold and honor are besides
A very brittle glass;
And time, in his unresting tides
Makes all things change and pass:
Turns riches to a beggar's dole;
Sets glory's race an infant's goal.

Be noble—that is more than wealth;
Do right—that's more than place;
Then in the spirit there is health
And gladness in the face:
Then thou art with thyself at one
And, no man hating, fearest none.
—George Macdonald.

MADAME LOFTY

Mrs. Lofty keeps a carriage,
So do I;
She has dappled grays to draw it,
None have I.
She's no prouder of her coachman
Than am I
With my blue-eyed laughing baby
Trundling by.
I hide his face, lest she should see
The cherub boy and envy me.

Ier fine husband has white fingers,
Mine has not;
Ie can give his bride a palace,
Mine a cot.
Iers comes home beneath the starlight,
Ne'er cares she;
Iine comes in the purple twilight,
Kisses me,
And prays that He who turns life's sands
Will hold his loved ones in his hands.

Irs. Lofty has her jewels,
So have I;
She wears hers upon her bosom,
Inside I.
She will leave hers at Death's portals,
By and by;
shall bear the treasures with me
When I die—
For I have love, and she has gold;
She counts her wealth, mine can't be told.

She has those who love her station,
None have I,
But I've one true heart beside me;
Glad am I;
'd not change it for a kingdom,
No, not I;
God will weigh it in a balance,
By and by;
And then the difference he'll define
Twixt Mrs. Lofty's wealth and mine.

So long as life's hope-sparkle glows, 'tis good;
When death delivers from life's woes, 'tis good.
Oh praise the Lord who makes all good, and will;
Whether he life or death bestows, 'tis good.

THE WIND THAT BLOWS, THAT WIND IS BEST

Whichever way the wind doth blow,
Some heart is glad to have it so;
Then blow it east or blow it west,
The wind that blows, that wind is best.

My little craft sails not alone;
A thousand fleet from every zone
Are out upon a thousand seas;
And what for me were favoring breeze
Might dash another with the shock
Of doom upon some hidden rock.
And so I do not dare to pray
For winds to waft me on my way;
But leave it to a Higher Will
To stay or speed me, trusting still
That ill is well, and sure that He
Who launched my bark will sail with me
Through storm and calm, and will not fail,
Whatever breezes may prevail,
To land me, every peril past,
Within his sheltering heaven at last.

Then, whatsoever wind doth blow,
My heart is glad to have it so;
And, blow it east or blow it west,
The wind that blows, that wind is best.
—Caroline Atherton Mason.

THE DIFFERENCE

Some murmur, when their sky is clear
And wholly bright to view,
If one small speck of dark appear
In their great heaven of blue.
And some with thankful love are filled
If but one streak of light,
One ray of God's good mercy, gild
The darkness of their night.

In palaces are hearts that ask,
In discontent and pride,
Why life is such a dreary task
And all things good denied.
Yet hearts in poorest huts admire
How love has in their aid
(Love that not ever seems to tire)
Such rich provision made.
—Richard Chenevix Trench.

Give what Thou canst; without thee we are poor;
And with thee rich, take what thou wilt away. —William Cowper.

RICHES AND POWER

Cleon has a million acres,
 Ne'er a one have I;
Cleon dwelleth in a palace,
 In a cottage I.
Cleon hath a dozen fortunes,
 Not a penny I;
Yet the poorer of the twain is
 Cleon, and not I.

Cleon, true, possesseth acres,
 But the landscape I;
Half the charms to me it yieldeth,
 Money cannot buy.
Cleon harbors sloth and dullness,
 Freshening vigor I;
He in velvet, I in fustian,
 Richer man am I.

Cleon is a slave to grandeur,
 Free as thought am I;
Cleon fees a score of doctors,
 Need of none have I.
Wealth-surrounded, care-environed,
 Cleon fears to die.
Death may come. he'll find me ready.
 Happier man am I.

Cleon sees no charm in nature,
 In a daisy I;
Cleon hears no anthem ringing
 In the sea and sky;
Nature sings to me forever,
 Earnest listener I!
State for state, with all attendants,
 Who would change? Not I.
—Charles Mackay.

ENOUGH

I am so weak, dear Lord, I cannot stand
 One moment without thee;
But oh, the tenderness of thine enfolding,
And oh, the faithfulness of thine upholding,
And oh, the strength of thy right hand!
 That strength is enough for me.

I am so needy, Lord, and yet I know
 All fullness dwells in thee;
And hour by hour that never-failing treasure
Supplies and fills in overflowing measure,
My last, my greatest need. And so
 Thy grace is enough for me.

It is so sweet to trust THY WORD alone!
 I do not ask to see
The unveiling of thy purpose, or the shining
Of future light or mysteries untwining;
The promise-roll is all my own,
 Thy word is enough for me.

The human heart asks love. But now I know
 That my heart hath from Thee
All real, and full, and marvelous affection
So near, so human! yet Divine perfection
Thrills gloriously the mighty glow!
 Thy love is enough for me.

There were strange soul depths, restless, vast and broad
 Unfathomed as the sea.
An infinite craving for some infinite stilling;
But now Thy perfect love is perfect filling!
Lord Jesus Christ, my Lord, my God,
 Thou, thou art enough for me!
—Frances Ridley Havergal.

FULLY CONTENT

I know not, and I would not know,
 Content, I leave it all with Thee;
'Tis ever best it should be so;
 As thou wilt have it let it be.

But this I know: that every day
 And every step for me is planned;
I surely cannot lose the Way
 While He is holding fast my hand.

And surely, whatsoe'er betide,
 I never shall be left alone:
Thou standest ever by my side;
 To thee my future all is known.

And wheresoe'er my lot may fall
 The way before is marked by Thee;
The windings of my life are all
 Unfoldings of thy Love to me.

What matter will it be, O mortal man, when thou art dying,
Whether upon a throne or on the bare earth thou art lying?
—From the Persian.

CONTENT WITH ALL

Content that God's decree
Should order all for thee.
Content with sickness or with health—
Content with poverty or wealth—
Content to walk in humble guise,
And as He wills it sink or rise.

Content to live alone
And call no place thine own.
No sweet reunions day by day.
Thy kindred spirits far away.
And, since God wills to have it so,
Thou wouldst not change for weal or
woe.

Content that others rise
Before thy very eyes.
How bright their lot and portion here!
Wealth fills their coffers—friends are
near.
Behold their mansions tall and fair!
The timbrel and the dance are there.

Content to toil or rest—
God's peace within thy breast—
To feel thy times are in His hand
Who holds all worlds in his command—
Thy time to laugh—thy time to sigh—
Thy time to live—thy time to die.

And is it so indeed
Thou art with God agreed?
Content 'mid all the ills of life?
Farewell, then, sorrow, pain and strife!
Such high content is heaven begun.
The battle's fought, the victory won!
—Mary Ann W. Cook.

A BLESSED LESSON

Have I learned, in whatsoever
State to be content?
Have I learned this blessed lesson
By my Master sent—
And with joyous acquiescence
Do I greet His will
Even when my own is thwarted
And my hands lie still?

Surely it is best and sweetest
Thus to have Him choose,
Even though some work I've taken
By this choice I lose.
Folded hands need not be idle—
Fold them but in prayer;
Other souls may toil far better
For God's answer there.

They that "reap" receive their "wages,"
Those who "work" their "crown,"
Those who pray throughout the ages
Bring blest answers down;
In "whatever state" abiding
Till the Master call,
They at eventide will find Him
Glorified in all.

What though I can do so little
For my Lord and King,
At His feet I sit and listen,
At His feet I sing.
And, whatever my condition,
All in love is meant;
Sing, my soul, thy recognition,
Sing, and be content!

IT MIGHT HAVE BEEN

Led by kindlier hand than ours,
We journey through this earthly scene,
And should not, in our weary hours,
Turn to regret what might have been.

And yet these hearts, when torn by pain,
Or wrung by disappointment keen,
Will seek relief from present cares
In thoughts of joys that might have
been.

But let us still these wishes vain;
We know not that of which we dream.
Our lives might have been sadder yet
God only knows what might have
been.

Forgive us, Lord, our little faith;
And help us all, from morn to e'en,
Still to believe that lot were best
Which is—not that which might have
been.

And grant we may so pass the days
The cradle and the grave between,
That death's dark hour not darker be
For thoughts of what life might have
been. —George Z. Gray.

Hushing every muttered murmur,
Let your fortitude the firmer
Gird your soul with strength.
While, no treason near her lurking,
Patience in her perfect working,
Shall be Queen at length.

BE CONTENT

Be thou content; be still before
His face at whose right hand doth reign
Fullness of joy for evermore,
Without whom all thy toil is vain;
He is thy living spring, thy sun, whose rays
Make glad with life and light thy dreary days.
Be thou content.

In him is comfort, light, and grace,
And changeless love beyond our thought;
The sorest pang, the worst disgrace,
If he is there, shall harm thee not.
He can lift off thy cross and loose thy bands,
And calm thy fears; nay, death is in His hands.
Be thou content.

Or art thou friendless and alone—
Hast none in whom thou canst confide?
God careth for thee, lonely one—
Comfort and help he will provide.
He sees thy sorrows, and thy hidden grief,
He knoweth when to send thee quick relief;
Be thou content.

Thy heart's unspoken pain he knows,
Thy secret sighs he hears full well;
What to none else thou darest disclose
To him thou mayest with boldness tell.
He is not far away, but ever nigh,
And answereth willingly the poor man's cry:
Be thou content.

MANNA

'Twas in the night the manna fell
That fed the hosts of Israel.

Enough for each day's fullest store
And largest need; enough, no more.

For willful waste, for prideful show,
God sent not angels' food below.

Still in our nights of deep distress
The manna falls our heart to bless.

And, famished, as we cry for bread,
With heavenly food our lives are fed,

And each day's need finds each day's store
Enough. Dear Lord, what want we more!

—Margaret Elizabeth Sangster.

BLESSINGS NEAR AT HAND

We look too far for blessings;
We seek too far for joys;
We ought to be like children
Who find their chiefest toys

Ofttimes in nearest attic,
Or in some dingy lane—
Their aprons full of weeds or flowers
Gathered in sun or rain.

Within the plainest cottage
Unselfish love may grow;
The sweetest, the divinest gift,
Which mortals ever know.

We ought to count our joys, not woes;
Meet care with winsome grace;
For discontent plows furrows
Upon the loveliest face.

Hope, freedom, sunlight, knowledge,
Come not to wealth alone;
He who looks far for blessings
Will overlook his own.

—Sarah Knowles Bolton.

I WOULDN'T

A sprig of mint by the wayward brook,
A nibble of birch in the wood,
A summer day, and love, and a book,
And I wouldn't be a king if I could.

—John Vance Cheney.

The way to make thy son rich is to fill
His mind with rest before his trunk with riches:
For wealth without contentment climbs a hill
To feel those tempests which fly over ditches.

—George Herbert.

THE JEWEL

There is a jewel which no Indian mine
can buy,
No chemic art can counterfeit;
It makes men rich in greatest poverty,
Makes water wine, turns wooden cups to
gold,
The homely whistle to sweet music's
strain;
Seldom it comes, to few from heaven
sent,
That much in little, all in naught—
Content.

FINDING CONTENT

I could not find the little maid Content,
So out I rushed, and sought her far
and wide;
But not where Pleasure each new
fancy tried,
Heading the maze of rioting merriment,
Nor where, with restless eyes and bow
half bent,
Love in the brake of sweetbriar
smiled and sighed,
Nor yet where Fame towered,
crowned and glorified,
Found I her face, nor wheresoe'er I went.
So homeward back I crawled, like
wounded bird,
When lo! Content sate spinning at my
door;
And when I asked her where she was
before—
"Here all the time," she said; "I never
stirred;
Too eager in thy search, you passed
me o'er,
And, though I called you, neither saw
nor heard." —Alfred Austin.

DAILY STRENGTH

Day by day the manna fell;
O to learn this lesson well;
Still by constant mercy fed,
Give me, Lord, my daily bread.

"Day by day," the promise reads;
Daily strength for daily needs;
Cast foreboding fears away;
Take the manna of to-day.

Lord, my times are in thy hand.
All my sanguine hopes have planned
To thy wisdom I resign,
And would make thy purpose thine.

Thou my daily task shalt give;
Day by day to Thee I live;
So shall added years fulfill
Not my own—my Father's will.

Fond ambition, whisper not;
Happy is my humble lot;
Anxious, busy cares away;
I'm provided for to-day.

O to live exempt from care
By the energy of prayer;
Strong in faith, with mind subdued,
Yet elate with gratitude.
—Josiah Conder.

GOD IS ENOUGH

God is enough! thou, who in hope and
fear
Toilest through desert sands of life,
sore tried,
Climb, trustful, over death's black ridge,
for near
The bright wells shine; thou wilt be
satisfied.

God doth suffice! O thou, the patient
one,
Who puttest faith in him, and none
beside,
Bear yet thy load; under the setting sun
The glad tents gleam; thou wilt be
satisfied

By God's gold Afternoon! peace ye shall
have;
Man is in loss except he live aright,
And help his fellow to be firm and brave,
Faithful and patient; then the restful
night.
—Edwin Arnold, from the Arabian.

THE TRULY RICH

They're richer who diminish their de-
sires,
Though their possessions be not am-
plified,
Than monarchs, who in owning large
empires,
Have minds that never will be satis-
fied.
For he is poor who wants what he would
have,
And rich who, having naught, doth
nothing crave. —T. Urchard.

THY ALLOTMENT

Thou cam'st not to thy place by accident,
It is the very place God meant for thee;
And shouldst thou there small scope for action see
Do not for this give room to discontent,
Nor let the time thou owest God be spent
In idle dreaming how thou mightest be,
In what concerns thy spiritual life, more free
From outward hindrance or impediment.
For presently this hindrance thou shalt find
That without which all goodness were a task
So slight that virtue never could grow strong;
And wouldst thou do one duty to His mind—
The Imposer's—over-burdened thou shalt ask,
And own thy need of, grace to help ere long.
—Richard Chenevix Trench.

THE HAPPIEST HEART

Who drives the horses of the sun
Shall lord it but a day;
Better the lowly deed were done,
And kept the humble way.

The rust will find the sword of fame,
The dust will hide the crown;
Aye, none shall nail so high his name
Time will not tear it down.

The happiest heart that ever beat
Was in some quiet breast
That found the common daylight sweet,
And left to Heaven the rest.
—John Vance Cheney.

WELCOME THE SHADOWS

Welcome the shadows; where they blackest are
Burns through the bright supernal hour;
From blindness of wide dark looks out the star,
From all death's night the April flower.

For beauty and for gladness of the days
Bring but the meed of trust;
The April grass looks up from barren ways,
The daisy from the dust.

When of this flurry thou shalt have thy fill,
The thing thou seekest, it will seek thee then:
The heavens repeat themselves in waters still
And in the faces of contented men.
—John Vance Cheney.

THE DAILY COURSE

New every morning is the love
Our wakening and uprising prove;
Through sleep and darkness safely brought,
Restored to life, and power, and thought.

New mercies each returning day
Hover around us while we pray;
New perils past, new sins forgiven,
New thoughts of God, new hopes of heaven.

If on our daily course our mind
Be set to hallow all we find,
New treasures still, of countless price,
God will provide for sacrifice.

Old friends, old scenes, will lovelier be
As more of heaven in each we see;
Some softening gleam of love and prayer
Shall dawn on every cross and care.

We need not bid, for cloistered cell,
Our neighbor and our work farewell,
Nor strive to wind ourselves too high
For sinful man beneath the sky.

The trivial round, the common task,
Will furnish all we ought to ask:
Room to deny ourselves a road
To bring us daily nearer God.

Seek we no more; content with these,
Let present rapture, comfort, ease,
As Heaven shall bid them, come and go;
The secret, this, of rest below.

Only, O Lord, in thy dear love
Fit us for perfect rest above;
And help us this and every day,
To live more nearly as we pray.
—John Keble.

GOD ENOUGH

Let nothing disturb thee,
Nothing affright thee;
All things are passing;
God never changeth;
Patient endurance
Attaineth to all things;
Who God possesseth
In nothing is wanting;
Alone God sufficeth.

—St. Teresa, tr. by Henry Wadsworth Longfellow.

THE GOLDEN MEAN

He that holds fast the golden mean
And lives contentedly between
The little and the great,
Feels not the wants that pinch the poor,
Nor plagues that haunt the rich man's door,
Embittering all his state.

WITHOUT AND WITHIN

If every man's internal care
Were written on his brow,
How many would our pity share
Who raise our envy now?

The fatal secret, when revealed,
Of every aching breast,
Would prove that only while concealed
Their lot appeared the best.

—Pietro Metastasio.

Let us be content in work
To do the thing we can, and not presume
To fret because it's little.

—Elizabeth Barrett Browning.

If none were sick and none were sad,
What service could we render?
I think if *we* were always glad,
We scarcely could be tender.
If sorrow never claimed our heart,
And every wish were granted,
Patience would die and hope depart—
Life would be disenchanted.

A pilgrim, bound to Mecca, quite away his sandals wore,
And on the desert's blistering sand his feet grew very sore.
"To let me suffer thus, great Allah, is not kind nor just,
While in thine service I confront the painful heat and dust."
He murmured in complaining tone; and in this temper came
To where, around the Kaaba, pilgrims knelt of every name;
And there he saw, while pity and remorse his bosom beat,
A pilgrim who not only wanted shoes, but *feet*.

—From the Persian, tr. by William Rounseville Alger.

Be still, sad heart! and cease repining;
Behind the clouds is the sun still shining;
Thy fate is the common fate of all,
Into each life some rain must fall,
Some days must be dark and dreary.

—Henry Wadsworth Longfellow.

Strength for to-day is all that we need,
As there never will be a to-morrow;
For to-morrow will prove but another to-day
With its measure of joy or of sorrow.

Don't think your lot the worst because
Some griefs your joy assail;
There aren't so very many saws
That never strike a nail.

—Nixon Waterman.

When it drizzles and drizzles,
If we cheerfully smile,
We can make the weather,
By working together,
As fair as we choose in a little while.
For who will notice that clouds are drear
If pleasant faces are always near,
And who will remember that skies are gray
If he carries a happy heart all day?

ASPIRATION

DESIRE, SUPPLICATION, GROWTH

GRADATIM

Heaven is not reached by a single bound;
But we build the ladder by which we rise
From the lowly earth to the vaulted skies,
And we mount to its summit round by round.

I count this thing to be grandly true:
That the noble deed is a step toward God,
Lifting the soul from the common clod
To a purer air and a broader view.

We rise by the things that are under feet;
By what we have mastered of good and gain,
By the pride deposed and the passion slain,
And the vanquished ills that we hourly meet.

We hope, we aspire, we resolve, we trust,
When the morning calls us to life and light;
But our hearts grow weary, and ere the night
Our lives are treading the sordid dust.

We hope, we resolve, we aspire, we pray,
And we think that we mount the air on wings,
Beyond the recall of sensual things,
While our feet still cling to the heavy clay.

Wings for the angels, but feet for men!
We may borrow the wings to find the way;
We may hope, and resolve, and aspire, and pray;
But our feet must rise, or we fall again.

Only in dreams is a ladder thrown
From the weary earth to the sapphire walls,
But the dreams depart, and the vision falls,
And the sleeper wakes on his pillow of stone.

Heaven is not reached at a single bound;
But we build the ladder by which we rise
From the lowly earth to the vaulted skies,
And we mount to its summit round by round.

—Josiah Gilbert Holland.

MORE AND MORE

Purer yet and purer
I would be in mind,
Dearer yet and dearer
Every duty find;
Hoping still and trusting
God without a fear,
Patiently believing
He will make it clear.

Calmer yet and calmer
Trials bear and pain,
Surer yet and surer
Peace at last to gain;
Suffering still and doing,
To his will resigned,
And to God subduing
Heart and will and mind.

Higher yet and higher
Out of clouds and night,
Nearer yet and nearer
Rising to the light—
Light serene and holy—
Where my soul may rest,
Purified and lowly,
Sanctified and blest.

—Johann W. von Goethe.

THE CHAMBERED NAUTILUS

This is the ship of pearl which, poets feign,
Sails the unshadowed main,—
The venturous bark that flings
On the sweet summer wind its purpled wings
In gulfs enchanted, where the Siren sings
And coral reefs lie bare,
Where the cold sea maids rise to sun their streaming hair.

Its webs of living gauze no more unfurl;
Wrecked is the ship of pearl!
And every chambered cell,
Where its dim dreaming life was wont to dwell,
As the frail tenant shaped his growing shell,
Before thee lies revealed—
Its irised ceiling rent, its sunless crypt unsealed.

Year after year beheld the silent toil
That spread his lustrous coil;
Still, as the spiral grew,
He left the last year's dwelling for the new,
Stole with soft step its shining archway through,
Built up its idle door,
Stretched in its last-found home, and knew the old no more.

Thanks for the heavenly message brought by thee,
Child of the wandering sea,
Cast from her lap, forlorn!
From thy dead lips a clearer note is born
Than ever Triton blew from wreathed horn;
While on my ear it rings,
Through the deep caves of thought I hear a voice that sings:

Build thee more stately mansions, O my soul!
As the swift seasons roll!
Leave thy low-vaulted past!
Let each new temple, nobler than the last,
Shut thee from heaven with a dome more vast
Till thou at length art free,
Leaving thine outgrown shell by life's unresting sea!

—Oliver Wendell Holmes.

WALKING WITH JESUS

My Saviour, on the Word of Truth
In earnest hope I live,
I ask for all the precious things
Thy boundless love can give.
I look for many a lesser light
About my path to shine;
But chiefly long to walk with thee,
And only trust in thine.

Thou knowest that I am not blest
As Thou would'st have me be
Till all the peace and joy of faith
Possess my soul in thee;
And still I seek 'mid many fears,
With yearnings unexpressed,
The comfort of thy strengthening love,
Thy soothing, settling rest.

It is not as Thou wilt with me
Till, humbled in the dust,
I know no place in all my heart
Wherein to put my trust:
Until I find, O Lord! in thee—
The lowly and the meek—
That fullness which thy own redeemed
Go nowhere else to seek.

Then, O my Saviour! on my soul,
Cast down but not dismayed,
Still be thy chastening healing hand
In tender mercy laid:
And while I wait for all thy joys
My yearning heart to fill,
Teach me to walk and work with thee,
And at thy feet sit still.

—Anna Letitia Waring.

A PRAYER TO THE GOD OF NATURE

God of the roadside weed,
Grant I may humbly serve the humblest need.

God of the scarlet rose,
Give me the beauty that Thy love bestows.

God of the hairy bee,
Help me to suck deep joys from all I see.

God of the spider's lace,
Let me, from mine own heart, unwind such grace.

God of the lily's cup,
Fill me! I hold this empty chalice up.

God of the sea-gull's wing,
Bear me above each dark and turbulent
thing.

God of the watchful owl,
Help me to see at midnight, like this
fowl.

God of the antelope,
Teach me to scale the highest crags of
Hope.

God of the eagle's nest,
Oh, let me make my eyrie near thy
breast!

God of the burrowing mole,
Let cold earth have no terrors for my soul.

God of the chrysalis,
Grant that my grave may be a cell of
bliss.

God of the butterfly,
Help me to vanquish Death, although
I die.

—Frederic Lawrence Knowles.

O JESUS CHRIST, GROW THOU IN ME

O Jesus Christ, grow thou in me,
And all things else recede!
My heart be daily nearer thee,
From sin be daily freed.

Each day let Thy supporting might
My weakness still embrace;
My darkness vanish in thy light,
Thy life my death efface.

In thy bright beams which on me fall
Fade every evil thought;
That I am nothing, Thou art all,
I would be daily taught.

More of thy glory let me see,
Thou holy, wise and true,
I would thy living image be,
In joy and sorrow too.

Fill me with gladness from above,
Hold me by strength divine;
Lord, let the glow of thy great love
Through my whole being shine.

Make this poor self grow less and less;
Be Thou my life and aim;
Oh, make me daily through thy grace
More meet to bear thy name!

Let faith in Thee and in thy might
My every motive move;
Be thou alone my soul's delight,
My passion and my love.

—Henry B. Smith.

DAY BY DAY

Looking upward every day,
Sunshine on our faces,
Pressing onward every day
Toward the heavenly places;
Growing every day in awe,
For thy name is holy;
Learning every day to love
With a love more lowly.

Walking every day more close
To our Elder Brother;
Growing every day more true
Unto one another;
Every day more gratefully
Kindnesses receiving,
Every day more readily
Injuries forgiving.

Leaving every day behind
Something which might hinder;
Running swifter every day,
Growing purer, kinder—
Lord, so pray we every day;
Hear us in thy pity,
That we enter in at last
To the holy city. —Mary Butler.

Better to have the poet's heart than
brain,
Feeling than song; but, better far than
both,
To be a song, a music of God's making.
Or but a table on which God's finger of
flame,
In words harmonious of triumphant
verse,
That mingles joy and sorrow, sets down
clear
That out of darkness he hath called the
light.
It may be voice to such is after given
To tell the mighty tale to other worlds.

—George Macdonald.

FREE FROM SIN

The bird let loose in eastern skies,
  When hastening fondly home,
Ne'er stoops to earth her wing, nor flies
  Where idle warblers roam;
But high she shoots through air and light
  Above all low delay,
Where nothing earthly bounds her flight,
  Nor shadow dims her way.

So grant me, God, from every care
  And stain of passion free,
Aloft, through Virtue's purer air,
  To hold my course to thee!
No sin to cloud, no lure to stay
  My soul, as home she springs;
Thy sunshine on her joyful way,
  Thy freedom in her wings!
—Thomas Moore.

A PRAYER

O that mine eyes might closèd be
To what concerns me not to see;
That deafness might possess mine ear
To what concerns me not to hear;
That truth my tongue might always tie
From ever speaking foolishly;
That no vain thought might ever rest
Or be conceived within my breast;
That by each deed and word and thought
Glory may to my God be brought.
But what are wishes! Lord, mine eye
On Thee is fixed; to Thee I cry!
Wash, Lord, and purify my heart,
And make it clean in every part;
And when 'tis clean, Lord, keep it, too,
For that is more than I can do.
—Thomas Elwood, A.D. 1639.

THE ALTERED MOTTO

O the bitter shame and sorrow,
  That a time could ever be
When I let the Saviour's pity
Plead in vain, and proudly answered,
  "All of self, and none of Thee!"

Yet He found me; I beheld him
  Bleeding on the accursèd tree,
Heard him pray, "Forgive them, Father!"
And my wistful heart said faintly,
  "Some of self and some of Thee."

Day by day his tender mercy,
  Healing, helping, full and free,
Sweet and strong, and, ah! so patient,
Brought me lower, while I whispered,
  "Less of self, and more of Thee."

Higher than the highest heaven,
  Deeper than the deepest sea,
Lord, thy love at last hath conquered;
Grant me now my supplication—
  "None of self, and all of Thee."
—Theodore Monod.

INDWELLING

O dwell in me, my Lord,
  That I in thee may dwell;
Fulfill thy tender word,
  That thy evangels tell;
In me Thou, I in thee,
By thy sweet courtesy.

But wilt thou my guest be,
  In this poor heart of mine?
Thy guest? Is this for me
  In that pure heart of thine?
In me thou, I in thee,
By thy sweet courtesy.

My chamber, Lord, prepare
  Whither thou deignest come;
I may not seek to share
  The making of thy home;
In me thou, I in thee,
By thy sweet courtesy.

Thy gracious gifts bestow,
  Humility and love;
O cause my heart to glow
  By fire sent from above.
In me thou, I in thee,
By thy sweet courtesy.
—Alexander B. Grosart.

Thy name to me, thy nature grant;
  This, only this be given;
Nothing besides my God I want,
  Nothing in earth or heaven.

Come, Father, Son, and Holy Ghost,
  And seal me thine abode;
Let all I am in thee be lost,
  Let all I am be God.
—Charles Wesley.

PERFECTION

O how the thought of God attracts,
 And draws the heart from earth,
And sickens it of passing shows
 And dissipating mirth!

'Tis not enough to save our souls,
 To shun the eternal fires;
The thought of God will rouse the heart
 To more sublime desires.

God only is the creature's home,
 Though rough and strait the road;
Yet nothing less can satisfy
 The love that longs for God.

Oh, utter but the name of God
 Down in your heart of hearts,
And see how from the world at once
 All tempting light departs.

A trusting heart, a yearning eye
 Can win their way above;
If mountains can be moved by faith
 Is there less power in love?

How little of that road, my soul,
 How little hast thou gone!
Take heart, and let the thought of God
 Allure thee further on.

Dole not thy duties out to God,
 But let thy hand be free;
Look long at Jesus; his sweet blood—
 How was it dealt to thee?

The perfect way is hard to flesh;
 It is not hard to love;
If thou wert sick for want of God
 How swiftly wouldst thou move.

Be docile to thine unseen Guide;
 Love him as he loves thee;
Time and obedience are enough,
 And thou a saint shalt be.
 —Frederick William Faber.

Thou broadenest out with every year
 Each breadth of life to meet;
I scarce can think thou art the same,
 Thou art so much more sweet.
With gentle swiftness lead me on,
 Dear God, to see thy face;
And meanwhile in my narrow heart
 O make thyself more space!
 —Frederick William Faber.

LONGING

Of all the myriad moods of mind
 That through the soul come thronging,
Which one was e'er so dear, so kind,
 So beautiful, as Longing?
The thing we long for, *that* we are
 For one transcendent moment,
Before the Present poor and bare
 Can make its sneering comment.

Still, through our paltry stir and strife,
 Glows down the wished ideal,
And longing molds in clay what life
 Carves on the marble real;
To let the new life in, we know,
Desire must ope the portal;
Perhaps the longing to be so
 Helps make the soul immortal.

Longing is God's fresh heavenward will
 With our poor earthward striving;
We quench it that we may be still
 Content with merely living;
But, would we learn that heart's full
 scope
 Which we are hourly wronging,
Our lives must climb from hope to hope,
 And realize our longing.

Ah! let us hope that to our praise
 Good God not only reckons
The moments when we tread his ways,
 But when the spirit beckons;
That some slight good is also wrought,
 Beyond self-satisfaction,
When we are simply good in thought
 Howe'er we fail in action.
 —James Russell Lowell.

MORE HOLINESS

More holiness give me;
 More strivings within.
More patience in suffering,
 More sorrow for sin.
More faith in my Saviour,
 More sense of his care,
More joy in his service,
 More purpose in prayer.

More gratitude give me,
 More trust in the Lord,
More pride in his glory,
 More hope in his word.
More tears for his sorrows,
 More pain at his grief,
More meekness in trial,
 More praise for relief.

More purity give me,
More strength to o'ercome,
More freedom from earth-stains,
More longings for home;
More fit for the kingdom,
More used I would be,
More blessed and holy—
More, Saviour, like thee.
—Philip Paul Bliss.

"MY SOUL DOTH MAGNIFY THE LORD"

My soul shall be a telescope,
Searching the distant bounds of time and space,
That somehow I may image, as I grope,
Jehovah's power and grace.

My soul a microscope shall be,
In all minutest providences keen
Jehovah's patient thoughtfulness to see,
And read his love between.

My soul shall be a burning-glass
That diligence to worship may succeed,
That I may catch God's glories as they pass,
And focus to a deed.

So, even so,
A mote in his creation, even I
Seeking alone to do, to feel, to know,
The Lord must magnify.
—Amos R. Wells.

Lord, let me not be too content
With life in trifling service spent—
Make me aspire!
When days with petty cares are filled
Let me with fleeting thoughts be thrilled
Of something higher!

Help me to long for mental grace
To struggle with the commonplace
I daily find.
May little deeds not bring to fruit
A crop of little thought to suit
A shriveled mind.

I know this earth is not my sphere,
For I cannot so narrow me but that
I still exceed it.
—Robert Browning.

A SHRINKING PRAYER

Give me, O Lord, a heart of grace,
A voice of joy, a smiling face,
That I may show, where'er I turn,
Thy love within my soul doth burn!

Then life be sweet, and joy be dear,
Be in my mind a quiet fear;
A patient love of pain and care,
An enmity to dark despair.

A tenderness for all that stray,
With strength to help them on their way;
A cheerfulness, a heavenly mirth,
Brightening my steps along the earth.

I ask and shrink, yet shrink and ask;
I know thou wilt not set a task
Too hard for hands that thou hast made,
Too hard for hands that thou canst aid.

So let me dwell all peacefully,
Content to live, content to die;
Rejoicing now, rejoicing then,
Rejoicing evermore. Amen.
—Rosa Mulholland.

THAT I MAY SOAR

Great God, I ask thee for no meaner pelf
Than that I may not disappoint myself;
That in my action I may soar as high
As I can now discern with this clear eye.

And next in value which thy kindness lends,
That I may greatly disappoint my friends,
Howe'er they think or hope that it may be,
They may not dream how thou'st distinguished me.

That my weak hand may equal my firm faith,
And my life practise more than my tongue saith;
That my low conduct may not show,
Nor my relenting lines,
That I thy purpose did not know,
Or overrated thy designs.
—Henry David Thoreau.

A CRY OF THE SOUL

O God of truth, for whom alone I sigh,
  Knit thou my heart by strong, sweet cords to thee.
I tire of hearing; books my patience try;
Untired to thee I cry;
  Thyself my all shalt be.

Lord, be thou near and cheer my lonely way;
  With thy sweet peace my aching bosom fill;
Scatter my cares and fears; my griefs allay;
And be it mine each day
  To love and please thee still.

My God! Thou hearest me; but clouds obscure
  Even yet thy perfect radiance, truth divine!
O for the stainless skies, the splendors pure,
The joys that aye endure.
  When thine own glories shine!

—Pierre Corneille.

A PURPOSE TRUE

Lord, make me quick to see
Each task awaiting me,
  And quick to do;
Oh, grant me strength, I pray,
With lowly love each day
  And purpose true.

To go as Jesus went,
Spending and being spent,
  Myself forgot;
Supplying human needs
By loving words and deeds,
  Oh, happy lot!

—Robert M. Offord.

There are deep things of God. Push out from shore;
Hast thou found much? Give thanks, and look for more.
Dost fear the generous Giver to offend?
Then know his store of bounty hath no end.
He doth not need to be implored or teased;
The more we take the better he is pleased.

—Charles Gordon Ames.

BREATHE ON ME

Breathe on me, Breath of God,
  Fill me with life anew,
That I may love what thou dost love,
  And do what thou wouldst do.

Breathe on me, Breath of God,
  Until my heart is pure,
Until with thee I will one will,
  To do or to endure.

Breathe on me, Breath of God,
  Till I am wholly thine;
Till all this earthly part of me
  Glows with thy fire divine.

Breathe on me, Breath of God,
  So shall I never die,
But live with thee the perfect life
  Of thine eternity.

—Edwin Hatch.

THE COMPARATIVE DEGREE

What weight of woe we owe to thee,
Accurst comparative degree!
Thy paltry step can never give
Access to the superlative;
For he who would the wisest be,
Strives to make others wise as he,
And never yet was man judged best
Who would be better than the rest;
So does comparison unkind
Dwarf and debase the haughty mind.

Make not a man your measuring-rod
If you would span the way to God;
Heed not our petty "worse" or "less,'
But fix your eyes on perfectness.
Make for the loftiest point in view,
And draw your friends along with you.

—Amos R. Wells.

Thy nature be my law,
  Thy spotless sanctity,
And sweetly every moment draw
  My happy soul to thee.

Soul of my soul remain;
  Who didst for me fulfill,
In me, O Lord, fulfill again
  Thy heavenly Father's will.

—Charles Wesley.

LEAD ON, O LORD

Jesus still lead on
Till our rest be won;
And although the way be cheerless,
We will follow, calm and fearless;
Guide us by thy hand
To our Fatherland.

If the way be drear,
If the foe be near,
Let not faithless fears o'ertake us,
Let not faith and hope forsake us;
For, through many a foe
To our home we go.

When we seek relief
From a long-felt grief:
When oppressed by new temptations,
Lord, increase and perfect patience;
Show us that bright shore
Where we weep no more.

Jesus, still lead on
Till our rest be won;
Heavenly Leader, still direct us,
Still support, control, protect us,
Till we safely stand
In our Fatherland.
—Nicolaus Ludwig Zinzendorf.

Give me this day
A little work to occupy my mind;
A little suffering to sanctify
My spirit; and, dear Lord, if thou canst find
Some little good that I may do for thee,
I shall be glad, for that will comfort me.
Mind, spirit, hand—I lift them all to thee.

O make me patient, Lord,
Patient in daily cares;
Keep me from thoughtless words,
That slip out unawares.
And help me, Lord, I pray,
Still nearer thee to live,
And as I journey on,
More of thy presence give.

O square thyself for use. A stone that may
Fit in the wall is not left in the way.
—From the Persian.

Think, and be careful what thou art within,
For there is sin in the desire of sin:
Think and be thankful in a different case;
For there is grace in the desire of grace.
—George Gordon Byron.

A man's higher being is knowing and seeing;
Not having or toiling for more;
In the senses and soul is the joy of control,
Not in pride and luxurious store.
—John Boyle O'Reilly.

Be with me, Lord, where'er my path may lead;
Fulfill thy word, supply my every need;
Help me to live each day more close to thee.
And O, dear Lord, I pray abide with me.

In all I think or speak or do,
Whatever way my steps are bent,
God shape and keep me strong and true,
Courageous, cheerful, and content.
—W. D. Russell.

Make my mortal dreams come true
With the work I fain would do:
Clothe with life the weak intent,
Let me be the thing I meant.
—John Greenleaf Whittier.

This be my prayer, from dawn to eve,
Working between the suns;
Lord, make my arm as firm as a knight's
My soul as white as a nun's.

Every hour that fleets so slowly has its task to do or bear;
Luminous the crown and holy, if we set each gem with care.

O for a man to rise in me,
That the man that I am
May cease to be.
—Alfred Tennyson.

PRAYER

WORSHIP, COMMUNION, DEVOTION

THE UNIVERSAL PRAYER

Father of all! in every age,
In ev'ry clime adored,
By saint, by savage, and by sage,
Jehovah, Jove, or Lord!

Thou great First Cause, least understood,
Who all my sense confined
To know but this, that thou art good,
And that myself am blind:

Yet gave me, in this dark estate,
To see the good from ill;
And binding nature fast in fate,
Left free the human will.

What conscience dictates to be done,
Or warns me not to do,
This, teach me more than hell to shun,
That, more than heaven pursue.

What blessings thy free bounty gives
Let me not cast away;
For God is paid when man receives—
T' enjoy is to obey.

Yet not to earth's contracted span
Thy goodness let me bound;
Or think thee Lord alone of man
When thousand worlds are round;

Let not this weak, unknowing hand
Presume thy bolts to throw,
And deal damnation round the land
On each I judge thy foe.

If I am right, thy grace impart
Still in the right to stay;
If I am wrong, O teach my heart
To find that better way.

Save me alike from foolish pride
Or impious discontent,
At aught thy wisdom has denied
Or aught thy wisdom lent.

Teach me to feel another's woe;
To hide the fault I see;
That mercy I to others show,
That mercy show to me.

Mean though I am, not wholly so
Since quicken'd by thy breath;
O lead me wheresoe'er I go,
Through this day's life or death.

This day be bread and peace my lot:
All else beneath the sun
Thou know'st if best bestowed or not;
And let thy will be done.

To Thee, whose temple is all space,
Whose altar earth, sea, skies!
One chorus let all Being raise,
All Nature's incense rise!

—Alexander Pope.

THE HOUR OF PRAYER

My God, is any hour so sweet,
From blush of morn to evening star,
As that which calls me to thy feet:
The hour of prayer?

Blest is that tranquil hour of morn,
And blest that solemn hour of eve,
When, on the wings of prayer upborne,
The world I leave.

Then is my strength by thee renewed;
Then are my sins by thee forgiven;
Then dost thou cheer my solitude
With hopes of heaven.

No words can tell what sweet relief
Here for my every want I find;
What strength for warfare, balm for grief,
What peace of mind.

Hushed is each doubt, gone every fear;
My spirit seems in heaven to stay;
And e'en the penitential tear
Is wiped away.

Lord, till I reach that blissful shore,
No privilege so dear shall be
As thus my inmost soul to pour
In prayer to thee.
—Charlotte Elliott.

PETITION

Be not afraid to pray—to pray is right.
Pray, if thou canst, with hope; but ever pray,
Though hope be weak or sick with long delay;
Pray in the darkness if there be no light.

Far is the time, remote from human sight,
When war and discord on the earth shall cease;
Yet every prayer for universal peace
Avails the blessed time to expedite.

Whate'er is good to wish, ask that of heaven,
Though it be what thou canst not hope to see.
Pray to be perfect, though material leaven
Forbid the spirit so on earth to be;
But if for any wish thou darest not pray,
Then pray to God to cast that wish away. —Hartley Coleridge.

SOMETIME, SOMEWHERE

Unanswered yet the prayer your lips have pleaded
In agony of heart these many years?
Does faith begin to fail? Is hope departing?
And think you all in vain those falling tears?
Say not the Father hath not heard your prayer;
You shall have your desire sometime, somewhere.

Unanswered yet?--though when you first presented
This one petition at the Father's throne
It seemed you could not wait the time of asking,
So urgent was your heart to make it known!
Though years have passed since then, do not despair;
The Lord will answer you sometime, somewhere.

Unanswered yet? Nay, do not say ungranted;
Perhaps your work is not yet wholly done.
The work began when first your prayer was uttered,
And God will finish what he has begun.
If you will keep the incense burning there
His glory you shall see sometime, somewhere.

Unanswered yet? Faith cannot be unanswered,
Her feet were firmly planted on the Rock;
Amid the wildest storms she stands undaunted,
Nor quails before the loudest thunder shock.
She knows Omnipotence has heard her prayer,
And cries, "It shall be done"—sometime, somewhere.
—Frederick G. Browning.

SECRET PRAYER

Lord, I have shut my door—
Shut out life's busy cares and fretting noise,
Here in this silence they intrude no more.
Speak thou, and heavenly joys
Shall fill my heart with music sweet and calm—
A holy psalm.

Yes, I have shut my door,
Even on all the beauty of thine earth—
To its blue ceiling, from its emerald floor,
Filled with spring's bloom and mirth;
From these, thy works, I turn; thyself I seek;
To thee I speak.

And I have shut my door
On earthly passion—all its yearning love,
Its tender friendships, all the priceless store
Of human ties. Above
All these my heart aspires, O Heart divine!
Stoop thou to mine.

Lord, I have shut my door!
Come thou and visit me: I am alone!
Come as when doors were shut thou cam'st of yore
And visited thine own.
My Lord, I kneel with reverence, love, and fear,
For thou art here.
—Mary Ellen Atkinson.

WHAT MAN IS THERE OF YOU?

The homely words—how often read!
How seldom fully known:
"Which father of you, asked for bread,
Would give his son a stone?"

How oft has bitter tear been shed,
And heaved how many a groan,
Because thou wouldst not give for bread
The thing that was a stone!

How oft the child thou wouldst have fed
Thy gift away has thrown;
He prayed, thou heardst, and gavest bread—
He cried, "It is a stone!"

Lord, if I ask in doubt and dread,
Lest I be left to moan,
Am I not he, who, asked for bread,
Would give his son a stone?
—George Macdonald.

DENIAL

I want so many, many things,
My wishes on my prayers take wings,
And heavenward fly to sue for grace
Before the loving Father's face.

But He, well knowing all my need,
Kindly rebukes my foolish greed,
And, granting not the gift I ask,
Sets me instead to do some task—

Some lowly task—for love of him,
So lowly, and in light so dim,
My sorrowing soul must cease to sing,
And only sigh, " 'Tis for the King."

And scarcely can my faith repeat
Her sad petition at his feet:
"These daily tasks Thou giv'st to me,
Help, Lord, to do as unto thee!"

Yet while his bidding thus I do—
I know not how, or why, 'tis true—
My thoughts to sweet contentment glide,
And I forget the wish denied.

And so my prayers he hears and heeds,
Mindful of all my daily needs;
Gracious, most gracious, too, in this—
Denying, when I ask amiss.
—Luella Clark.

A BLESSING IN PRAYER

If when I kneel to pray,
With eager lips I say:
"Lord, give me all the things that I desire—
Health, wealth, fame, friends, brave heart, religious fire,
The power to sway my fellow men at will,
And strength for mighty works to banish ill"—
In such a prayer as this
The blessing I must miss.

Or if I only dare
To raise this fainting prayer:
"Thou seest, Lord, that I am poor and weak,
And cannot tell what things I ought to seek;
I therefore do not ask at all, but still
I trust thy bounty all my wants to fill"—
My lips shall thus grow dumb,
The blessing shall not come.

But if I lowly fall,
And thus in faith I call:
"Through Christ, O Lord, I pray thee give to me
Not what I would, but what seems best to thee
Of life, of health, of service, and of strength,
Until to thy full joy I come at length"—
My prayer shall then avail;
The blessing shall not fail.
—Charles F. Richardson.

Teach me, dear Lord, what thou wouldst have me know;
Guide me, dear Lord, where thou wouldst have me go;
Help me, dear Lord, the precious seed to sow;
Bless thou the seed that it may surely grow.

THE TIME FOR PRAYER

When is the time for prayer?
With the first beams that light the morning sky,
Ere for the toils of day thou dost prepare,
Lift up thy thoughts on high;
Commend thy loved ones to his watchful care:
Morn is the time for prayer!

And in the noontide hour,
If worn by toil or by sad care oppressed,
Then unto God thy spirit's sorrows pour,
And he will give thee rest:
Thy voice shall reach him through the fields of air:
Noon is the time for prayer!

When the bright sun hath set,
Whilst yet eve's glowing colors deck the skies,
When with the loved, at home, again thou'st met,
Then let thy prayers arise
For those who in thy joys and sorrows share:
Eve is the time for prayer!

And when the stars come forth—
When to the trusting heart sweet hopes are given
And the deep stillness of the hour gives birth
To pure bright dreams of heaven—
Kneel to thy God; ask strength life's ills to bear:
Night is the time for prayer.

When is the time for prayer?
In every hour, while life is spared to thee—
In crowds or solitude—in joy or care—
Thy thoughts should heavenward flee.
At home—at morn and eve—with loved ones there,
Bend thou the knee in prayer!

NOT A SOUND INVADES THE STILLNESS

Not a sound invades the stillness,
Not a form invades the scene,
Save the voice of my Belovèd,
And the person of my King.

And within those heavenly places,
Calmly hushed in sweet repose,
There I drink, with joy absorbing,
All the love thou wouldst disclose.

Wrapt in deep adoring silence,
Jesus, Lord, I dare not move,
Lest I lose the smallest saying
Meant to catch the ear of love.

Rest, then, O my soul, contented:
Thou hast reached thy happy place
In the bosom of thy Saviour,
Gazing up in his dear face.

FORMAL PRAYER

I often say my prayers,
But do I ever pray;
And do the wishes of my heart
Go with the words I say?

I may as well kneel down
And worship gods of stone,
As offer to the living God
A prayer of words alone.

For words without the heart
The Lord will never hear:
Nor will he to those lips attend
Whose prayers are not sincere.
—John Burton.

BLESSINGS OF PRAYER

What various hindrances we meet
In coming to a mercy-seat!
Yet who that knows the worth of prayer
But wishes to be often there!

Prayer makes the darkened cloud withdraw;
Prayer climbs the ladder Jacob saw;
Gives exercise to faith and love;
Brings every blessing from above.

Restraining prayer, we cease to fight;
Prayer keeps the Christian's armor bright;
And Satan trembles when he sees
The weakest saint upon his knees.

Were half the breath that's vainly spent
To heaven in supplication sent,
Our cheerful song would oftener be
"Hear what the Lord has done for me."
—William Cowper.

WHAT IS PRAYER?

Prayer is the soul's sincere desire,
Uttered or unexpressed;
The motion of a hidden fire
That trembles in the breast.

Prayer is the burden of a sigh,
The falling of a tear,
The upward glancing of an eye,
When none but God is near.

Prayer is the simplest form of speech
That infant lips can try;
Prayer the sublimest strains that reach
The Majesty on high.

Prayer is the contrite sinner's voice,
Returning from his ways;
While angels in their songs rejoice
And cry, "Behold, he prays!"

Prayer is the Christian's vital breath,
The Christian's native air,
His watchword at the gates of death;
He enters heaven with prayer.

O Thou, by whom we come to God,
The Life, the Truth, the Way;
The path of prayer thyself hast trod:
Lord, teach us how to pray!

—James Montgomery.

SPIRITUAL DEVOTION

The woman singeth at her spinning wheel
A pleasant chant, ballad, or baracolle;
She thinketh of her song, upon the whole,
Far more than of her flax; and yet the reel
Is full, and artfully her fingers feel,
With quick adjustment, provident control,
The lines, too subtly twisted to unroll,
Out to a perfect thread. I hence appeal
To the dear Christian Church, that we may do
Our Father's business in these temples mirk
Thus, swift and steadfast; thus, intent and strong;
While, thus, apart from toil, our souls pursue
Some high, calm, spheric tune and prove our work
The better for the sweetness of our song.

—Elizabeth Barrett Browning.

PRAYER OF DEEDS

The deed ye do is the prayer ye pray;
"Lead us into temptation, Lord;
Withhold the bread from our babes this day;
To evil we turn us, give evil's reward!"

Over to-day the to-morrow bends
With an answer for each acted prayer;
And woe to him who makes not friends
With the pale hereafter hovering there.

—George S. Burleigh.

SUNDAY

Not a dread cavern, hoar with damp and mould,
Where I must creep and in the dark and cold
Offer some awful incense at a shrine
That hath no more divine
Than that 'tis far from life, and stern, and old;

But a bright hilltop, in the breezy air
Full of the morning freshness, high and clear,
Where I may climb and drink the pure new day
And see where winds away
The path that God would send me, shining fair.

—Edward Rowland Sill.

PRAYER

When prayer delights thee least, then learn to say,
Soul, now is greatest need that thou should'st pray:

Crooked and warped I am, and I would fain
Straighten myself by thy right line again.

Oh, come, warm sun, and ripen my late fruits;
Pierce, genial showers, down to my parchèd roots.

My well is bitter, cast therein the tree,
That sweet henceforth its brackish waves may be.

Say, what is prayer, when it is prayer indeed?
The mighty utterance of a mighty need.

The man is praying who doth press with might
Out of his darkness into God's own light.

White heat the iron in the furnace won,
Withdrawn from thence 'twas cold and hard anon.

Flowers, from their stalk divided, presently
Droop, fall, and wither in the gazer's eye.

The greenest leaf, divided from its stem,
To speedy withering doth itself condemn.

The largest river, from its fountain-head
Cut off, leaves soon a parched and dusty bed.

All things that live from God their sustenance wait,
And sun and moon are beggars at his gate.

All skirts extended of thy mantle hold
When angel hands from heaven are scattering gold.

—Richard Chenevix Trench.

MEANING OF PRAYER

One thing, alone, dear Lord, I dread—
To have a secret spot
That separates my soul from thee,
And yet to know it not.

Prayer was not meant for luxury,
Or selfish pastime sweet;
It is the prostrate creature's place
At his Creator's feet.

But if this waiting long hath come
A present from on high,
Teach me to find the hidden wealth
That in its depths may lie.

So in the darkness I can learn
To tremble and adore;
To sound my own vile nothingness,
And thus to love thee more.

—Frederick William Faber.

TALKING WITH GOD

To stretch my hand and touch Him
Though he be far away;
To raise my eyes and see him
Through darkness as through day;
To lift my voice and call him—
This is to pray!

To feel a hand extended
By One who standeth near;
To view the love that shineth
In eyes serene and clear;
To know that he is calling—
This is to hear!

—Samuel W. Duffield.

MY PRAYER

Being perplexed, I say,
"Lord, make it right!
Night is as day to thee,
Darkness is light.
I am afraid to touch
Things that involve so much;
My trembling hand may shake—
My skillful hand may break;
Thine can make no mistake."

Being in doubt, I say,
"Lord, make it plain!
Which is the true, safe way?
Which would be vain?
I am not wise to know,
Nor sure of foot to go;
My blind eyes cannot see
What is so clear to thee.
Lord, make it clear to me."

THE SOURCE OF POWER

There is an eye that never sleeps
Beneath the wing of night;
There is an ear that never shuts
When sink the beams of light.

There is an arm that never tires
When human strength gives way;
There is a love that never fails
When earthly loves decay.

That eye is fixed on seraph throngs;
That arm upholds the sky;
That ear is filled with angel songs,
That love is throned on high.

But there's a power which man can wield
 When mortal aid is vain,
That eye, that arm, that love to reach,
 That listening ear to gain.

That power is prayer, which soars on high,
 Through Jesus, to the throne,
And moves the hand which moves the world,
 To bring salvation down.
—James Cowden Wallace.

DIFFERENT PRAYERS

Three doors there are in the temple
 Where men go up to pray,
And they that wait at the outer gate
 May enter by either way.

There are some that pray by asking;
 They lie on the Master's breast,
And, shunning the strife of the lower life,
 They utter their cry for rest.

There are some that pray by seeking;
 They doubt where their reason fails;
But their mind's despair is the ancient prayer
 To touch the print of the nails.

There are some that pray by knocking;
 They put their strength to the wheel
For they have not time for thoughts sublime;
 They can only act what they feel.

Father, give each his answer,
 Each in his kindred way;
Adapt thy light to his form of night
 And grant him his needed day.
—William Watson.

TRUE PRAYER

I.

It is not prayer,
This clamor of our eager wants
That fills the air
With wearying, selfish plaints.

It is not faith
To boldly count all gifts as ours—
The pride that saith,
"For me his wealth he ever showers."

It is not praise
To call to mind our happier lot,
And boast bright days,
God-favored, with all else forgot.

II.

It is true prayer
To seek the giver more than gift
God's life to share
And love—for this our cry to lift.

It is true faith
To simply trust his loving will,
Whiche'er he saith—
"Thy lot be glad" or "ill."

It is true praise
To bless alike the bright and dark;
To sing, all days
Alike, with nightingale and lark.
—James W. White.

THE POWER OF PRAYER

Lord, what a change within us one short hour
Spent in thy presence will prevail to make;
What heavy burdens from our bosoms take;
What parchèd grounds refresh as with a shower!
We kneel—and all about us seems to lower;
We rise—and all, the distant and the near,
Stands forth in sunny outline, brave and clear.
We kneel, how weak! we rise, how full of power!
Why, therefore, should we do ourselves this wrong,
Or others, that we are not always strong;
That we are ever overborne with care,
Anxious and troubled, when with us is prayer,
And joy and strength and courage are with thee?
—Richard Chenevix Trench.

Asked and unasked, thy heavenly gifts unfold,
And evil, though we ask it, Lord, withhold.
—Homer, tr. by Frederic Rowland Marvin.

MARY OF BETHANY

Her eyes are homes of silent prayer,
  Nor other thought her mind admits
  But, he was dead, and there he sits.
And he that brought him back is there.

Then one deep love doth supersede
  All other, when her ardent gaze
  Roves from the living brother's face
And rests upon the Life indeed.

All subtle thought, all curious fears.
  Borne down by gladness so complete,
  She bows, she bathes the Saviour's feet
With costly spikenard and with tears.

Thrice blest whose lives are faithful prayers,
  Whose loves in higher love endure;
  What souls possess themselves so pure,
Or is there blessedness like theirs?
—Alfred Tennyson.

PRAYER ITS OWN ANSWER

'Allah, Allah!" cried the sick man, racked with pain the long night through;
Till with prayer his heart was tender, till his lips like honey grew.

But at morning came the Tempter; said, "Call louder, child of pain!
See if Allah ever hear, or answer 'Here am I' again."

Like a stab the cruel cavil through his brain and pulses went;
To his heart an icy coldness, to his brain a darkness, sent.

Then before him stands Elias; says "My child! why thus dismayed?
Dost repent thy former fervor? Is thy soul of prayer afraid?"

'Ah!" he cried, "I've called so often; never heard the 'Here am I';
And I thought, God will not pity, will not turn on me his eye."

Then the grave Elias answered, "God said, 'Rise, Elias, go,
Speak to him, the sorely tempted; lift him from his gulf of woe.

"'Tell him that his very longing is itself an answering cry;
That his prayer, "Come, gracious Allah," is my answer, "Here am I'".

"Every inmost aspiration is God's angel undefiled;
And in every 'O my Father!' slumbers deep a 'Here, my child!'"
—Jelal-ed-Deen, tr. by James Freeman Clarke.

THE CONTENTS OF PIETY

"Allah!" was all night long the cry of one oppressed with care,
Till softened was his heart, and sweet became his lips with prayer.
Then near the subtle tempter stole, and spake:
  "Fond babbler, cease!
For not one 'Here am I' has God e'er sent to give thee peace."
With sorrow sank the suppliant's soul, and all his senses fled.
But lo! at midnight, the good angel, Chiser, came, and said:
"What ails thee now, my child, and why art thou afraid to pray?
And why thy former love dost thou repent? declare and say."
"Ah!" cries he, "never once spake God to me, 'Here am I, son.'
Cast off methinks I am, and warned far from his gracious throne."
To whom the angel answered, "Hear the word from God I bear:
'Go tell,' he said, 'yon mourner, sunk in sorrow and despair,
Each "Lord, appear!" thy lips pronounce contains my "Here am I";
A special messenger I send beneath thine every sigh;
Thy love is but a guerdon of the love I bear to thee.
And sleeping in thy "Come, O Lord!" there lies "Here, son!" from me.'"
—Oriental, tr. by William Rounseville Alger.

He prayeth well who loveth well
Both man and bird and beast.
He prayeth best who loveth best
All things, both great and small;
For the dear God who loveth us
He made and loveth all.
—Samuel Taylor Coleridge.

ADORATION

I love my God, but with no love of mine,
  For I have none to give;
I love thee, Lord, but all the love is thine
  For by thy love I live.
I am as nothing, and rejoice to be
Emptied and lost and swallowed up in
    thee.

Thou, Lord, alone art all thy children
    need,
  And there is none beside;
From thee the streams of blessedness
    proceed,
  In thee the blest abide—
Fountain of life and all-abounding grace,
Our source, our center, and our dwelling
    place. —Madame Guyon.

WALKING WITH GOD

O Master, let me walk with thee
In lowly paths of service free;
Tell me thy secret; help me bear
The strain of toil, the fret of care.

Help me the slow of heart to move
By some clear, winning word of love;
Teach me the wayward feet to stay,
And guide them in the homeward way.

Teach me thy patience! still with Thee
In closer, dearer company:
In work that keeps faith sweet and
    strong,
In trust that triumphs over wrong.

In hope that sends a shining ray
Far down the future's broadening way;
In peace that only thou canst give,
With thee, O Master, let me live.
—Washington Gladden.

There was a man who prayed
  For wisdom that he might
Sway men from sinful ways
  And lead them into light.
Each night he knelt and asked the Lord
To let him guide the sinful horde.
And every day he rose again,
  To idly drift along,
One of the many common men
  Who form the common throng.

GRANTED OR DENIED

To long with all our longing powers,
  And have the wish denied;
To urge and strain our force in vain
  Against the unresting tide
Of fate and circumstance, which still
Baffles and beats and thwarts our will;

To reach the goal toward which we
    strove
  All the long way and hard;
To win the prize which, to our eyes,
  Seemed life's one best reward—
Love's rose, Fame's laurel, olived Peace,
The gold-fruit of Hesperides—

And then to find the prize all vain,
  The joys all empty made—
To taste the sting in each sweet thing,
  To watch Love's roses fade,
The fruit to ashes turn, the gold
To worthless dross within our hold!

Now which has most of grief and pain,
  Which is the worse to bear:
The joy we crave and never have,
  Or the curse of the granted prayer?
The baffled wish or the bitter rue—
Could our hearts choose between the
    two?

O will of God, thou blessèd will!
  Which, like a balmèd air,
The breath of souls about us rolls,
  Touching us everywhere,
Imparting, like a soft caress,
Healing, and help, and tenderness,

O will of God, be thou our will!
  Then, come or joy or pain,
Made one with thee it cannot be
  That we shall wish in vain,
And, whether granted or denied,
Our hearts shall be all satisfied.
—Susan Coolidge.

OUT OF TOUCH

  Only a smile, yes, only a smile
That a woman o'erburdened with grief
Expected from you; 'twould have given
    relief,
  For her heart ached sore the while;
But weary and cheerless she went away,
Because, as it happened, that very day
  You were "out of touch" with your
    Lord.

Only a word, yes, only a word,
That the Spirit's small voice whispered "Speak";
But the worker passed onward unblessed and weak
Whom you were meant to have stirred
To courage, devotion, and love anew,
Because when the message came to you
You were "out of touch" with your Lord.

Only a note, yes, only a note
To a friend in a distant land.
The Spirit said "Write," but then you had planned
Some different work, and you thought
It mattered little. You did not know
'Twould have saved a soul from sin and woe;
You were "out of touch" with your Lord.

Only a song, yes, only a song
That the Spirit said "Sing to-night;
Thy voice is thy Master's by purchased right";
But you thought, "'Mid this motley throng
I care not to sing of the city of gold"—
And the heart that your words might have reached grew cold;
You were "out of touch" with your Lord.

Only a day, yes, only a day!
But oh, can you guess, my friend,
Where the influence reaches, and where it will end
Of the hours that you frittered away?
The Master's command is "Abide in me"
And fruitless and vain will your service be
If "out of touch" with your Lord.
—Jean H. Watson.

Prayer is Innocence's friend; and willingly flieth incessant
'Twixt the earth and the sky, the carrier-pigeon of heaven.
—Henry Wadsworth Longfellow.

We may question with wand of science,
Explain, decide, and discuss;
But only in meditation
The Mystery speaks to us.
—John Boyle O'Reilly.

THE VALLEY OF SILENCE

I walk down the Valley of Silence,
Down the dim, voiceless valley alone!
And I hear not the fall of a footstep
Around me—save God's and my own!
And the hush of my heart is as holy
As hovers where angels have flown.

Long ago was I weary of voices
Whose music my heart could not win;
Long ago was I weary of noises
That fretted my soul with their din;
Long ago was I weary of places
Where I met but the human and sin.

And still did I pine for the perfect,
And still found the false with the true;
I sought 'mid the human for heaven,
But caught a mere glimpse of the blue;
And I wept when the clouds of the world veiled
Even *that* glimpse from my view.

And I toiled on, heart-tired of the human,
And I moaned 'mid the mazes of men,
Till I knelt, long ago, at an altar,
And heard a Voice call me. Since then
I walk down the Valley of Silence
That lies far beyond mortal ken.

Do you ask what I found in the Valley?
'Tis my trysting place with the Divine.
When I fell at the feet of the Holy,
And about me a voice said, "Be mine,"
There arose from the depths of my spirit
An echo: "My heart shall be thine."

Do you ask how I live in the Valley?
I weep, and I dream, and I pray;
But my tears are as sweet as the dew-drops
That fall on the roses in May;
And my prayer, like a perfume from censer,
Ascendeth to God night and day.

In the hush of the Valley of Silence,
I dream all the songs that I sing;
And the music floats down the dim valley
Till each finds a word for a wing,
That to men, like the doves of the deluge
The message of peace they may bring.

But far out on the deep there are billows
  That never shall break on the beach;
And I have heard songs in the silence
  That never shall float into speech;
And I have had dreams in the valley
  Too lofty for language to reach.

And I have seen thoughts in the valley—
  Ah, me! how my spirit was stirred!
And they wear holy veils on their faces—
  Their footsteps can scarcely be heard;
They pass through the valley like virgins
  Too pure for the touch of a word.

Do you ask me the place of the Valley,
  Ye hearts that are harrowed by care?
It lieth afar, between mountains,
  And God and his angels are there;
And one is the dark Mount of Sorrow,
  The other, the bright Mount of Prayer.
—Abram Joseph Ryan.

HELP THOU MY UNBELIEF

Because I seek thee not O seek thou me!
  Because my lips are dumb O hear the cry
  I do not utter as thou passest by,
And from my lifelong bondage set me free!
Because, content, I perish far from thee,
  O seize me, snatch me from my fate and try
  My soul in thy consuming fire! Draw nigh
And let me, blinded, thy salvation see.

If I were pouring at thy feet my tears,
  If I were clamoring to see thy face,
  I should not need thee, Lord, as now I need,
Whose dumb, dead soul knows neither hopes nor fears,
  Nor dreads the outer darkness of this place.
Because I seek not, pray not, give thou heed.

PHARISEE AND PUBLICAN

Two went to pray? O, rather say
One went to brag, the other to pray;
One stands up close and treads on high,
Where the other dares not lend his eye;
One nearer to God's altar trod,
The other to the altar's God.
—Richard Crashaw.

A MOMENT IN THE MORNING

A moment in the morning, ere the cares of the day begin,
Ere the heart's wide door is open for the world to enter in,
Ah, then, alone with Jesus, in the silence of the morn,
In heavenly sweet communion, let your duty-day be born.
In the quietude that blesses with a prelude of repose
Let your soul be smoothed and softened, as the dew revives the rose.

A moment in the morning take your Bible in your hand,
And catch a glimpse of glory from the peaceful promised land:
It will linger still before you when you seek the busy mart,
And like flowers of hope will blossom into beauty in your heart.
The precious words, like jewels, will glisten all the day
With a rare effulgent glory that will brighten all the way;
When comes a sore temptation, and your feet are near a snare,
You may count them like a rosary and make each one a prayer.

A moment in the morning—a moment, if no more—
Is better than an hour when the trying day is o'er.
'Tis the gentle dew from heaven, the manna for the day;
If you fail to gather early—alas! it melts away.
So, in the blush of morning, take the offered hand of love,
And walk in heaven's pathway and the peacefulness thereof.
—Arthur Lewis Tubbs.

AN INVITATION TO PRAYER

Come to the morning prayer,
  Come, let us kneel and pray;
Prayer is the Christian pilgrim's staff
  To walk with God all day.

At noon, beneath the Rock
  Of Ages rest and pray;
Sweet is the shadow from the heat
  When the sun smites by day.

At eve, shut to the door,
Round the home altar pray;
And finding there "the house of God"
At "heaven's gate" close the day.

When midnight seals our eyes,
Let each in spirit say,
"I sleep, but my heart waketh, Lord,
With thee to watch and pray."
—James Montgomery.

SELFISH PRAYER

How we, poor players on life's little stage,
Thrust blindly at each other in our rage,
Quarrel and fret, yet rashly dare to pray
To God to keep us on our selfish way.

We think to move him with our prayer and praise
To serve our needs, as in the old Greek days
Their gods came down and mingled in the fight
With mightier arms the flying foe to smite.

The laughter of those gods pealed down to man;
For heaven was but earth's upper story then,
Where goddesses about an apple strove
And the high gods fell humanly in love.

We own a God whose presence fills the sky;
Whose sleepless eyes behold the worlds roll by;
Whose faithful memory numbers, one by one,
The sons of man, and calls them each his son.
—Louise Chandler Moulton.

To make rough places plain, and crooked straight;
To help the weak; to envy not the strong;
To make the earth a sweeter dwelling place,
In little ways, or if we may, in great,
And in the world to help the heavenly song,
We pray, Lord Jesus, grant to us thy grace!

THE TWO RELIGIONS

A woman sat by a hearthside place
Reading a book, with a pleasant face,
Till a child came up, with a childish frown,
And pushed the book, saying, "Put it down."
Then the mother, slapping his curly head,
Said, "Troublesome child, go off to bed;
A great deal of Christ's life I must know
To train you up as a child should go."
And the child went off to bed to cry,
And denounce religion—by and by.

Another woman bent over a book
With a smile of joy and an intent look,
Till a child came up and jogged her knee,
And said of the book, "Put it down—take me."
Then the mother sighed as she stroked his head,
Saying softly, "I never shall get it read:
But I'll try by loving to learn His will,
And his love into my child instill."
That child went to bed without a sigh,
And will love religion—by and by.

A LIFE HID WITH CHRIST

I have a life with Christ to live;
But ere I live it must I wait
Till learning can clear answer give
Of this or that book's date?

I have a life in Christ to live,
I have a death in Christ to die;
And must I wait till science give
All doubts a full reply?

Nay, rather, while the sea of doubt
Is raging wildly round about,
Questioning of life and death and sin,
Let me but creep within
Thy fold, O Christ, and at thy feet
Take but the lowest seat,
And hear thine awful voice repeat
In gentlest accents, heavenly sweet,
"Come unto me and rest;
Believe me, and be blest."
—John Campbell Shairp.

Still raise for good the supplicating voice,
But leave to Heaven the measure and the choice. —Dr. Samuel Johnson.

PRAY ALWAYS

Go when the morning shineth,
 Go when the noon is bright,
Go when the eve declineth,
 Go in the hush of night;
Go with pure mind and feeling,
 Fling earthly thoughts away,
And, in thy chamber kneeling,
 Do thou in secret pray.

Remember all who love thee,
 All who are loved by thee;
Pray, too, for those who hate thee,
 If any such there be.
Then for thyself in meekness
 A blessing humbly claim,
And link with thy petition
 The great Redeemer's name.

Or, if 'tis e'er denied thee
 In solitude to pray,
Should holy thoughts come o'er thee
 When friends are round thy way,
E'en then the silent breathing
 Of thy spirit, raised above,
May reach His throne of glory
 Who is mercy, truth and love.

Oh! not a joy or blessing
 With this can we compare:
The power that he hath given us
 To pour our hearts in prayer.
Whene'er thou pin'st in sadness
 Before His footstool fall,
And remember in thy gladness
 His grace who gave thee all.
—Jane C. Simpson.

More things are wrought by prayer
Than this world dreams of. Wherefore let thy voice
Rise like a fountain for me night and day.
For what are men better than sheep or goats,
That nourish a blind life within the brain,
If, knowing God, they lift not hands of prayer,
Both for themselves and those who call them friend.
For so the whole round earth is every way
Bound by gold chains about the feet of God. —Alfred Tennyson.

ENOCH

He walked with God, by faith, in solitude,
 At early dawn or tranquil eventide;
 In some lone leafy place he would abide
Till his whole being was with God imbued.
He walked with God amid the multitude;
 No threats or smiles could his firm soul divide
 From that beloved presence at his side
Whose still small voice silenced earth's noises rude.
Boldly abroad to men he testified
How "the Lord cometh" and the judgment brings;
Gently at home he trained his "sons and daughters";
Till, praying, a bright chariot he espied
Sent to translate him, as on angels' wings,
To walk with God beside heaven's "living waters." —R. Wilton.

A WORKER'S PRAYER

Lord, speak to me, that I may speak
 In living echoes of thy tone;
As thou hast sought, so let me seek
 Thy erring children, lost and lone.

Oh, teach me, Lord, that I may teach
 The precious things thou dost impart;
And wing my words that they may reach
 The hidden depths of many a heart.

Oh, give thine own sweet rest to me,
 That I may speak with soothing power
A word in season, as from thee,
 To weary ones in needful hour.

Oh, use me, Lord, use even me,
 Just as thou wilt, and when and where;
Until thy blessed face I see,
 Thy rest, thy joy, thy glory share.

God answers prayer—
Answers always, everywhere,
I may cast my anxious care,
Burdens I could never bear,
On the God who heareth prayer.

SUBMISSION AND REST

The camel, at the close of day
Kneels down upon the sandy plain
To have his burden lifted off
And rest again.

My soul, thou too should to thy knees
When daylight draweth to a close,
And let thy Master lift the load
And grant repose.

Else how couldst thou to-morrow meet,
With all to-morrow's work to do,
If thou thy burden all the night
Dost carry through?

The camel kneels at break of day
To have his guide replace his load;
Then rises up anew to take
The desert road.

So thou shouldst kneel at morning's dawn
That God may give thee daily care;
Assured that he no load too great
Will make thee bear.

TAKE TIME TO BE HOLY

Take time to be holy;
Speak oft with thy Lord;
Abide in him always,
And feed on his word;
Make friends of God's children,
Help those who are weak,
Forgetting in nothing
His blessing to seek.

Take time to be holy;
The world rushes on;
Spend much time in secret
With Jesus alone;
By looking at Jesus
Like him thou shalt be;
Thy friends in thy conduct
His likeness shall see.

Take time to be holy;
Let him be thy Guide,
And run not before him
Whatever betide;
In joy or in sorrow
Still follow thy Lord,
And, looking to Jesus,
Still trust in his word.

Take time to be holy;
Be calm in thy soul;
Each thought and each motive
Beneath his control;
Thus led by his Spirit
To fountains of love,
Thou soon shalt be fitted
For service above.

—W. D. Longstaff.

PRAYER FOR STRENGTH

Father, before thy footstool kneeling,
Once more my heart goes up to thee,
For aid, for strength, to thee appealing,
Thou who alone canst succor me.

Hear me! for heart and flesh are failing,
My spirit yielding in the strife;
And anguish wild as unavailing
Sweeps in a flood across my life.

Help me to stem the tide of sorrow;
Help me to bear thy chastening rod;
Give me endurance; let me borrow
Strength from thy promise, O my God!

Not mine the grief which words may lighten;
Not mine the tears of common woes;
The pang with which my heart-strings tighten
Only the All-seeing One may know.

And I am weak, my feeble spirit
Shrinks from life's task in wild dismay;
Yet not that thou that task wouldst spare it,
My Father, do I dare to pray.

Into my soul thy might infusing,
Strengthening my spirit by thine own;
Help me, all other aid refusing,
To cling to thee, and thee alone.

And O in my exceeding weakness
Make thy strength perfect; thou art strong:
Aid me to do thy will with meekness,
Thou to whom all my powers belong.

O let me feel that thou art near me;
Close to thy side, I shall not fear;
Hear me, O Strength of Israel, hear me,
Sustain and aid! in mercy hear.

LIGHT

Lord, send thy light,
Not only in the darkest night,
But in the shadowy, dim twilight,
Wherein my strained and aching sight
Can scarce distinguish wrong from right,
Then send thy light.

Teach me to pray.
Not only in the morning gray,
Or when the moonbeam's silver ray
Falls on me, but at high noonday,
When pleasure beckons me away,
Teach me to pray.
—Constance Milman.

OUR BURDEN BEARER

The little sharp vexations
And the briars that cut the feet,
Why not take all to the Helper
Who has never failed us yet?
Tell him about the heartache,
And tell him the longings too,
Tell him the baffled purpose
When we scarce know what to do.
Then, leaving all our weakness
With the One divinely strong,
Forget that we bore the burden
And carry away the song.
—Phillips Brooks.

My proud foe at my hands to take no boon will choose.
Thy prayers are that one gift which he cannot refuse.
—Richard Chenevix Trench.

ANSWER TO PRAYER

Man's plea to man is, that he nevermore
Will beg, and that he never begged before;
Man's plea to God is, that he did obtain
A former suit, and therefore sues again.
How good a God we serve, that, when we sue,
Makes his old gifts examples of his new.
—Francis Quarles.

TALHAIRN'S PRAYER

Grant me, O God, thy merciful protection;
And, in protection, give me strength, I pray;
And, in my strength, O grant me wise discretion;
And, in discretion, make me ever just;
And, with my justice, may I mingle love,
And, with my love, O God, the love of thee;
And, with the love of thee, the love of all.
—From the Welsh.

O sad estate
Of human wretchedness! so weak is man,
So ignorant and blind, that did not God
Sometimes withhold in mercy what we ask,
We should be ruined at our own request.
—Hannah More.

Why win we not at once what we in prayer require?
That we may learn great things as greatly to desire.
—Richard Chenevix Trench.

JOY

PRAISE, CHEERFULNESS, HAPPINESS

THE SECRET OF A HAPPY DAY

Just to let thy Father do
What he will;
Just to know that he is true
And be still.
Just to follow hour by hour
As He leadeth;
Just to draw the moment's power
As it needeth.
Just to trust Him, this is all!
Then the day will surely be
Peaceful, whatsoe'er befall,
Bright and blessèd, calm and free.

Just to let Him speak to thee
Through his word,
Watching that his voice may be
Clearly heard.
Just to tell Him every thing
As it rises,
And at once to him to bring
All surprises.
Just to listen, and to stay
Where you cannot miss His voice,
This is all! and thus to-day,
Communing, you shall rejoice.

Just to ask Him what to do
All the day,
And to make you quick and true
To obey.
Just to know the needed grace
He bestoweth,
Every bar of time and place
Overfloweth.
Just to take thy orders straight
From the Master's own command.
Blessèd day! when thus we wait
Always at our Sovereign's hand.

Just to recollect his love,
Always true;
Always shining from above,
Always new.
Just to recognize its light,
All-enfolding;
Just to claim its present might,
All-upholding.
Just to know it as thine own,
That no power can take away;
Is not this enough alone
For the gladness of the day?

Just to trust, and yet to ask
Guidance still;
Take the training or the task
As He will.
Just to take the joy or pain
As He lends it;
Just to take the loss or gain
As he sends it
He who formed thee for his praise
Will not miss the gracious aim;
So to-day, and all thy days,
Shall be molded for the same.

Just to leave in His dear hand
Little things;
All we cannot understand,
All that stings.
Just to let Him take the care
Sorely pressing,
Finding all we let him bear
Changed to blessing.
This is all! and yet the way
Marked by Him who loves thee best;
Secret of a happy day,
Secret of his promised rest.

—Frances Ridley Havergal.

GOD MEANS US TO BE HAPPY

God means us to be happy;
He fills the short-lived years
With loving, tender mercies—
With smiles as well as tears.
Flowers blossom by the pathway,
Or, withering, they shed
Their sweetest fragrance over
The bosoms of our dead.

God filled the earth with beauty;
He touched the hills with light;
He crowned the waving forest
With living verdure bright;
He taught the bird its carol,
He gave the wind its voice,
And to the smallest insect
Its moment to rejoice.

What life hath not its blessing?
Who hath not songs to sing,
Or grateful words to utter,
Or wealth of love to bring?
Tried in affliction's furnace
The gold becomes more pure—
So strong doth sorrow make us,
So patient to endure.

No way is dark and dreary
If God be with us there;
No danger can befall us
When sheltered by his care.
Why should our eyes be blinded
To all earth's glorious bloom?
Why sit we in the shadow
That falls upon the tomb?

Look up and catch the sunbeams!
See how the day doth dawn!
Gather the scented roses
That grow beside the thorn!
God's pitying love doth seek us;
He leads us to his rest;
And from a thousand pathways
He chooses what is best.

THE PICTURE OF A HAPPY MAN

How blest is he, though ever crossed,
That can all crosses blessings make;
That finds himself ere he be lost,
And lose that found for virtue's sake.

Yea, blest is he, in life and death,
That fears not death nor loves this life;
That sets his will his wit beneath;
And hath continual peace in strife.

That naught observes but what preserves
His mind and body from offense;
That neither courts nor seasons serves,
And learns without experience.

That loves his body for his soul,
Soul for his mind, his mind for God,
God for himself, and doth control
Content, if it with him be odd.

That rests in action, acting naught
But what is good in deed and show;
That seeks but God within his thought,
And thinks but God to love and know.

That lives too low for envy's looks,
And yet too high for loathed contempt;
That makes his friends good men and books
And naught without them doth attempt.

That ever lives a light to all,
Though oft obscurèd like the sun;
And, though his fortunes be but small,
Yet Fortune doth not seek nor shun.

That never looks but grace to find,
Nor seeks for knowledge to be known;
That makes a kingdom of his mind,
Wherein, with God, he reigns alone.

This man is great with little state,
Lord of the world epitomized,
Who with staid front outfaceth Fate
And, being empty, is sufficed—
Or is sufficed with little, since (at least)
He makes his conscience a continual feast.—John Davies, of Hereford.

THANKS FOR PAIN

My God, I thank thee who hast made
The earth so bright;
So full of splendor and of joy,
Beauty and light;
So many glorious things are here,
Noble and right.

I thank thee, too, that thou hast made
Joy to abound;
So many gentle thoughts and deeds
Circling us round;
That in the darkest spot of earth
Some love is found.

I thank thee more that all our joy
Is touched with pain;
That shadows fall on brightest hours;
That thorns remain;
So that earth's bliss may be our guide
And not our chain.

I thank thee, Lord, that thou hast kept
The best in store;
We have enough, yet not too much,
To long for more;
A yearning for a deeper peace
Not known before.

thank thee, Lord, that here our souls
  Though amply blest,
:an never find, although they seek,
  A perfect rest;
Nor ever shall until they lean
  On Jesus' breast.
—Adelaide Anne Procter.

THE RIDICULOUS OPTIMIST

There was once a man who smiled
  Because the day was bright,
  Because he slept at night,
  Because God gave him sight
To gaze upon his child;
  Because his little one,
  Could leap and laugh and run;
  Because the distant sun
Smiled on the earth he smiled.

He smiled because the sky
  Was high above his head,
  Because the rose was red,
  Because the past was dead!
He never wondered why
  The Lord had blundered so
  That all things have to go
  The wrong way, here below
The overarching sky.

He toiled, and still was glad
  Because the air was free,
  Because he loved, and she
  That claimed his love and he
Shared all the joys they had!
  Because the grasses grew,
  Because the sweet winds blew,
  Because that he could hew
And hammer, he was glad.

Because he lived he smiled,
  And did not look ahead
  With bitterness or dread,
  But nightly sought his bed
As calmly as a child.
  And people called him mad
  For being always glad
  With such things as he had,
And shook their heads and smiled.
—Samuel Ellsworth Kiser.

The soul contains a window where
It may receive the sun and air,
But some with self the window cloy,
And shut out all the light and joy.
—Nixon Waterman.

PRAISE

O Thou, whose bounty fills my cup
  With every blessing meet!
I give thee thanks for every drop—
  The bitter and the sweet.

I praise Thee for the desert road,
  And for the riverside;
For all thy goodness hath bestowed,
  And all thy grace denied.

I thank Thee for both smile and frown,
  And for the gain and loss;
I praise thee for the future crown
  And for the present cross.

I thank Thee for the wing of love
  Which stirred my worldly nest;
And for the stormy clouds which drove
  Me, trembling, to thy breast.

I bless Thee for the glad increase,
  And for the waning joy;
And for this strange, this settled peace,
  Which nothing can destroy.
—Jane Crewdson.

THANKSGIVING

Lord, for the erring thought
Not into evil wrought,
Lord, for the wicked will,
Betrayed and baffled still,
For the heart from itself kept,
Our thanksgiving accept.

For the ignorant hopes that were
Broken to our blind prayer;
For pain, death, sorrow, sent
Unto our chastisement;
For all loss of seeming good,
Quicken our gratitude.
—William Dean Howells.

RING, HAPPY BELLS

Ring out the grief that saps the mind,
  For those that here we see no more;
  Ring out the feud of rich and poor,
Ring in redress to all mankind.

Ring out a slowly-dying cause,
  And ancient forms of party strife;
  Ring in the nobler modes of life,
With sweeter manners, purer laws.

Ring out the want, the care, the sin,
The faithless coldness of the times;
Ring out, ring out my mournful rhymes,
But ring the fuller minstrel in.

Ring out false pride in place and blood,
The civic slander and the spite;
Ring in the love of truth and right
Ring in the common love of good.

Ring out old shapes of foul disease;
Ring out the narrowing lust of gold;
Ring out the thousand wars of old,
Ring in the thousand years of peace.

Ring in the valiant man and free,
The larger heart, the kindlier hand;
Ring out the darkness of the land,
Ring in the Christ that is to be.
—Alfred Tennyson.

THE CLEAR VISION

Break forth, my lips, in praise, and own
The wiser love severely kind;
Since, richer for its chastening grown,
I see, whereas I once was blind.
The world, O Father, hath not wronged
With loss the life by thee prolonged;
But still, with every added year,
More beautiful thy works appear.

As thou hast made thy world without,
Make thou more fair my world within;
Shine through its lingering clouds of doubt;
Rebuke its haunting shapes of sin;
Fill, brief or long, my granted span
Of life with love to thee and man;
Strike when thou wilt the hour of rest.
But let my last days be my best.
—John Greenleaf Whittier.

Then let us smile when skies are gray,
And laugh at stormy weather!
And sing life's lonesome times away;
So—worry and the dreariest day
Will find an end together!

Paul and Silas in their prison
Sang of Christ the Lord arisen;
And an earthquake's arm of might
Broke their dungeon gates at night.
—Henry Wadsworth Longfellow.

SCATTER SUNSHINE

In a world where sorrow ever will be known,
Where are found the needy, and the sad and lone;
How much joy and comfort we can all bestow
If we scatter sunshine everywhere we go.

Slightest actions often meet the sorest needs,
For the world wants daily little kindly deeds;
Oh, what care and sorrow we may help remove,
With our songs and courage, sympathy and love.

When the days are gloomy, sing some happy song,
Meet the world's repining with a courage strong;
Go, with faith undaunted, through the ills of life,
Scatter smiles and sunshine o'er its toil and strife.
—Lanta Wilson Smith.

SOWING JOY

I met a child, and kissed it; who shall say
I stole a joy in which I had no part?
The happy creature from that very day
Hath felt the more his little human heart.
Now when I pass he runs away and smiles,
And tries to seem afraid with pretty wiles.
I am a happier and a richer man,
Since I have sown this new joy in the earth;
'Tis no small thing for us to reap stray mirth
In every sunny wayside where we can.
It is a joy to me to be a joy
Which may in the most lowly heart take root;
And it is gladness to that little boy
To look out for me at the mountain foot.
—Frederick William Faber.

Sow thou sorrow and thou shalt reap it;
Sow thou joy and thou shalt keep it.
—Richard Watson Gilder.

A LANCASHIRE DOXOLOGY

(Written in May, 1863, when cotton came to Lancashire, enabling the mills to open after being long closed. The suffering, grateful women sang the Doxology.)

"Praise God from whom all blessings flow."
Praise Him who sendeth joy and woe.
The Lord who takes—the Lord who gives—
O praise him, all that dies, and lives.

He opens and he shuts his hand,
But why, we cannot understand.
Pours and dries up his mercies' flood,
And yet is still All-perfect Good.

We fathom not the mighty plan,
The mystery of God and man;
We women, when afflictions come,
We only suffer and are dumb.

And when, the tempest passing by,
He gleams out, sun-like, through our sky,
We look up and, through black clouds riven,
We recognize the smile of Heaven.

Ours is no wisdom of the wise.
We have no deep philosophies;
Childlike we take both kiss and rod,
For he who loveth knoweth God.

—Dinah Maria Mulock Craik.

VIA CRUCIS, VIA LUCIS

Through night to light! And though to mortal eyes
  Creation's face a pall of horror wear,
Good cheer! good cheer! the gloom of midnight flies;
  Then shall a sunrise follow, mild and fair.

Through storm to calm! And though his thunder car
  The rumbling tempest drive through earth and sky,
Good cheer! good cheer! The elemental war
  Tells that the blessèd healing hour is nigh.

Through frost to spring! And though the biting blast
  Of Eurus stiffen nature's juicy veins,
Good cheer! good cheer! When winter's wrath is past,
  Soft-murmuring spring breathes sweetly o'er the plains.

Through strife to peace! And though with bristling front
  A thousand frightful deaths encompass thee,
Good cheer! good cheer! brave thou the battle's brunt,
  For the peace-march and song of victory.

Through toil to sleep! And though the sultry noon
  With heavy drooping wing oppress thee now,
Good cheer! good cheer! the cool of evening soon
  Shall lull to sweet repose thy weary brow.

Through cross to crown! And though thy spirit's life
  Trials untold assail with giant strength,
Good cheer! good cheer! soon ends the bitter strife,
  And thou shalt reign in peace with Christ at length.

Through woe to joy! And though at morn thou weep,
  And though the midnight find thee weeping still,
Good cheer! good cheer! the Shepherd loves his sheep;
  Resign thee to the watchful Father's will.

—Rosegarten, tr. by Charles Timothy Brooks.

Talk Happiness. The world is sad enough
Without your woes. No path is wholly rough;
Look for the places that are smooth and clear,
And speak of those to rest the weary ear
Of earth, so hurt by one continuous strain
Of human discontent and grief and pain.

SERVE GOD AND BE CHEERFUL

Serve God and be cheerful. Make brighter
The brightness that falls to thy lot;
The rare, or the daily sent, blessing
Profane not with gloom or with doubt.

Serve God and be cheerful. Each sorrow
Is—with thy will in God's—for the best.
O'er the cloud hangs the rainbow. Tomorrow
Will see the blue sky in the west.

Serve God and be cheerful. Look upward!
God's countenance scatters the gloom;
And the soft summer light of his heaven
Shines over the cross and the tomb.

Serve God and be cheerful. The wrinkles
Of age we may take with a smile;
But the wrinkles of faithless foreboding
Are the crow's-feet of Beelzebub's guile.

Serve God and be cheerful. The winter
Rolls round to the beautiful spring.
And o'er the green grave of the snowdrift
The nest-building robins will sing.

Serve God and be cheerful. Live nobly,
Do right, and do good. Make the best
Of the gifts and the work put before you,
And to God without fear leave the rest.
—William Newell.

BRING EVERY BURDEN

Be trustful, be steadfast, whatever betide thee,
Only one thing do thou ask of the Lord—
Grace to go forward wherever he guide thee,
Simply believing the truth of his word.

Earthliness, coldness, unthankful behavior—
Ah! thou mayst sorrow, but do not despair.
Even this grief thou mayst bring to thy Saviour,
Cast upon him this burden of care!

Bring all thy hardness—His power can subdue it,
How full is the promise! The blessing how free:
"Whatsoever ye ask in my name, I will do it;
Abide in my love and be joyful in me."

THY LOVING KINDNESS

Not always the path is easy;
There are thickets hung with gloom,
There are rough and stony places
Where never the roses bloom.
But oft, when the way is hardest,
I am conscious of One at my side
Whose hands and whose feet are wounded,
And I'm happy and safe with my Guide.

Better than friends and kindred,
Better than love and rest,
Dearer than hope and triumph,
Is the name I wear on my breast.
I feel my way through the shadows
With a confident heart and brave;
I shall live in the light beyond them;
I shall conquer death and the grave.

Often when tried and tempted,
Often, ashamed of sin—
That, strong as an armed invader,
Has made wreck of the peace within—
That wonderful loving-kindness,
Patient and full and free,
Has stooped for my consolation;
Has brought a blessing to me.

Therefore my lips shall praise thee,
Therefore, let come what may,
To the height of a solemn gladness
My song shall arise to-day.
Not on the drooping willow
Shall I hang my harp in the land,
When the Lord himself has cheered me
By the touch of his pierced hand.
—Margaret Elizabeth Sangster.

To try each day his will to know;
To tread the way his will may show;
To live for him who gave me life;
To strive for him who suffered strife
And sacrifice through death for me—
Let this my joy, my portion be.

THANKS

I thank thee, Lord, for mine unanswered prayers,
Unanswered save thy quiet, kindly "Nay";
Yet it seemed hard among my heavy cares—
That bitter day.

I wanted joy; but Thou didst know for me
That sorrow was the gift I needed most,
And in its mystic depths I learned to see
The Holy Ghost.

I wanted health; but thou didst bid me sound
The secret treasuries of pain,
And in the moans and groans my heart oft found
Thy Christ again.

I wanted wealth; 'twas not the better part;
There is a wealth with poverty oft given.
And thou didst teach me of the gold of heart—
Best gift of heaven.

I thank thee, Lord, for these unanswered prayers,
And for thy word, the quiet, kindly "Nay."
'Twas thy withholding lightened all my cares
That blessed day.

—Oliver Huckel.

THE GLORIOUS MORN

Open the shutters free and wide.
And "glorify the room";
That no dark shadows here may bide—
That there be naught of gloom.

What joy to breathe the morning air,
And see the sun again;
With living things God's love to share,
In recompense for pain.

—Henry Coyle.

For all the evils under the sun
There is some remedy or none;
If there is one be sure to find it;
If there is none, why, never mind it.

EVENING PRAISE

Again, O God, the night shuts down,
Again I kneel to praise!
Thy wisdom, love, and truth and power
Have long made glad my days.
And, now, with added gratitude,
An evening hymn I raise.

I take the attitude of prayer,
But not for gifts to plead;
Thy bounty, far beyond desert,
Has more than met my need;
So, well content, I worship Thee
In thought and word and deed.

Thou bidst me ask, if I'd receive,
And seek, if I would find;
But surely Thou wilt not condemn
A heart to trust inclined.
Give what is best; Thou knowest all.
How blest the quiet mind!

I praise thee that in all the hours
And moments, as they glide,
Thy providence enfoldeth close;
Thy blessings rich abide;
And Thou dost keep in perfect peace
Those who in thee confide.

I praise thee for what seemeth good,
And for what seemeth ill.
Appearances are vain deceits;
Above them stands thy will;
By faith, not sight, thy children walk,
In hottest fire hold still.

Accept the off'ring that I lay
In gladness at thy feet;
My heart o'erflows with keenest joy,
With ecstacy complete.
Because, in all vicissitudes,
Thy constancy I greet.

Thou wilt not cease to love me well,
Nor fail to hold me fast:
Though pain may come, it cannot harm;
My care on thee is cast,
For future good he'll surely send
Who sent so sweet a past.

Praise waits in Zion, Lord, for thee,
Praise runs the world around;
And so this little heart of mine
Shall ne'er in gloom be found,
Rejoicing that all days and nights
May with thy praise resound.

—James Mudge.

GO TELL JESUS

Bury thy sorrow,
The world has its share;
Bury it deeply,
Hide it with care.

Think of it calmly
When curtained by night;
Tell it to Jesus,
And all will be right.

Tell it to Jesus,
He knoweth thy grief;
Tell it to Jesus,
He'll send thee relief.

Gather the sunlight
Aglow on thy way;
Gather the moonbeams,
Each soft silver ray.

Hearts grown aweary
With heavier woe,
Droop 'mid the darkness—
Go comfort them, go!

Bury thy sorrow,
Let others be blest;
Give them the sunshine,
Tell Jesus the rest.

WE WILL PRAISE THEE

Great Jehovah! we will praise thee,
Earth and heaven thy will obey;
Suns and systems move obedient
To thy universal sway.

Deep and awful are thy counsels;
High and glorious is thy throne;
Reigning o'er thy vast dominion,
Thou art God and thou alone.

In thy wondrous condescension
Thou hast stooped to raise our race;
Thou hast given to us a Saviour,
Full of goodness and of grace.

By his blood we are forgiven,
By his intercession free,
By his love we rise to glory
There to reign eternally.

God of Power—we bow before thee;
God of Wisdom—thee we praise;
God of Love—so kind and tender,
We would praise thee all our days.

Praise to thee—our loving Father;
Praise to thee—redeeming Son;
Praise to thee—Almighty Spirit;
Praise to thee—Thou Holy One.
—John White.

AFTER ALL

We take our share of fretting,
Of grieving and forgetting;
The paths are often rough and steep, and heedless feet may fall;
But yet the days are cheery,
And night brings rest when weary
And somehow this old planet is a good world after all.

Though sharp may be our trouble,
The joys are more than double,
The brave surpass the cowards and the leal are like a wall
To guard their dearest ever,
To fail the feeblest never;
And somehow this old earth remains a bright world after all.

There's always love that's caring,
And shielding and forbearing,
Dear woman's love to hold us close and keep our hearts in thrall.
There's home to share together
In calm or stormy weather,
And while the hearth-flame burns it is a good world after all.

The lisp of children's voices,
The chance of happy choices,
The bugle sounds of hope and faith, through fogs and mists that call;
The heaven that stretches o'er us,
The better days before us,
They all combine to make this earth a good world after all.
—Margaret Elizabeth Sangster.

Sound an anthem in your sorrows,
Build a fortress of your fears;
Throw a halo round your trials,
Weave a rainbow of your tears.

Never mind if shadows darken,
Never fear though foes be strong;
Lift your heads and shout hosannah!
Praise the Lord, it won't be long.

BE OF GOOD CHEER

God is near thee, Christian; cheer thee,
Rest in him, sad soul;
He will keep thee when around thee
Billows roll.

Calm thy sadness, look in gladness
To thy Friend on high;
Faint and weary pilgrim, cheer thee;
Help is nigh.

Mark the sea-bird wildly wheeling
Through the stormy skies;
God defends him, God attends him
When he cries.

Fare thee onward through the sunshine
Or through wintry blast;
Fear forsake thee; God will take thee
Home at last.

PESSIMIST AND OPTIMIST

This one sits shivering in Fortune's smile,
Taking his joy with bated, doubtful breath.
This one, gnawed by hunger, all the while
Laughs in the teeth of death.
—Thomas Bailey Aldrich.

PRAISE WAITETH FOR THEE

They stand, the regal mountains, with crowns of spotless snow,
Forever changeless, grand, sublime, while ages come and go!
Each day the morning cometh in through the eastern gate,
With trailing robes of pink and gold; yet still they watch and wait
For that more glorious morning, till that glad message sounds—
"Lift up your heads, ye gates of God! the King of glory comes!"

And so they stand o'erlooking earth's trouble, pain and sin,
And wait the call to lift their gates and let the King come in.
O calm, majestic mountains! O everlasting hills!
Beside your patient watch how small seem all life's joys and ills!

Beyond, the restless ocean, mysterious, vast, and dim,
Whose changeful waves forever chant their grand triumphal hymn.
Now tempest-lashed and raging, with deep and hungry roar,
The foam-capped billows dash themselves in anger on the shore,

Now wavelets ripple gently along the quiet strand,
While summer's sunshine broodeth soft o'er all the sea and land.
O mighty waves! as chainless, as free, as birds that skim!
There's One who rules the stormy sea—thy song is all of him.

And so in the shadowy forest the birds sing loud and sweet
From swaying boughs where breezes rock their little broods to sleep.
The golden cups of the cowslip spring from the mossy sod,
And the sweet blue violet blooms alone—just for itself and God.

It is aye the same old lesson, from mountain, wood, and sea,
The old, old story, ever new, and wondrous grand to me—
Of One who holds the waters in the hollow of his hand;
Whose presence shone from mountain top in that far eastern land.

"The groves are God's own temples"; the wild birds sing his praise;
And every flower in the forest dim its humble tribute pays;
For God loves all his creatures, however weak and small;
His grandest works give praise to him, for he is Lord of all.

We cannot make bargains for blisses,
Nor catch them like fishes in nets;
And sometimes the thing our life misses
Helps more than the thing which it gets.
For good lieth not in pursuing,
Nor gaining of great nor of small,
But just in the doing, and doing
As we would be done by is all.
—Alice Cary.

DON'T TAKE IT TO HEART

There's many a trouble
Would break like a bubble,
And into the waters of Lethe depart,
Did we not rehearse it,
And tenderly nurse it,
And give it a permanent place in the heart.

There's many a sorrow
Would vanish to-morrow
Were we but willing to furnish the wings;
So sadly intruding,
And quietly brooding,
It hatches out all sorts of horrible things.

How welcome the seeming
Of looks that are beaming
Whether one's wealthy or whether one's poor;
Eyes bright as a berry,
Cheeks red as a cherry,
The groan and the curse and the heart-ache can cure.

Resolve to be merry,
All worry to ferry
Across the famed waters which bid us forget,
And no longer fearful,
But happy and cheerful,
We feel life has much that's worth living for yet.

ALTHOUGH—YET

Away! my unbelieving fear!
Fear shall in me no more have place;
My Saviour doth not yet appear,
He hides the brightness of his face,
But shall I therefore let him go,
And basely to the tempter yield?
No, in the strength of Jesus, no;
I never will give up my shield.

Although the vine its fruit deny,
Although the olive yield no oil,
The withering fig-trees droop and die,
The fields elude the tiller's toil.
The empty stall no herd afford,
And perish all the bleating race,
Yet will I triumph in the Lord—
The God of my salvation praise.
—Charles Wesley.

'Tis impious in a good man to be sad.
—Edward Young.

AS A BIRD IN MEADOWS FAIR

As a bird in meadows fair
Or in lovely forest sings,
Till it fills the summer air
And the green wood sweetly rings,
So my heart to thee would raise,
O my God, its song of praise
That the gloom of night is o'er
And I see the sun once more.

If thou, Sun of love, arise,
All my heart with joy is stirred,
And to greet thee upward flies,
Gladsome as yon tiny bird.
Shine thou in me, clear and bright,
Till I learn to praise thee right;
Guide me in the narrow way,
Let me ne'er in darkness stray.

Bless to-day whate'er I do;
Bless whate'er I have and love;
From the paths of virtue true
Let me never, never rove;
By thy spirit strengthen me
In the faith that leads to Thee,
Then, an heir of life on high,
Fearless I may live and die.

"HE DOETH ALL THINGS WELL!"

Pleased in the sunshine, pleased in the blast,
Pleased when the heavens are all over-cast,
Pleased when I can or cannot see
God's loving hand is dealing with me.

Pleased, for Christ's promises never can fail;
Pleased in the calm and also the gale;
Knowing Omniscience at midnight can see,
Since he was Pilot on dark Galilee.

Pleased when in health or when I am ill,
Pleased, since I know I'm in the Lord's will,
Pleased with whatever my lot may be
Knowing Omnipotence careth for me.

Beneath the tiger's jaw I heard a victim cry,
"Thanks, God, that, though in pain, yet not in guilt I die."
—From the Persian.

THE ROBIN'S SONG

I'll sing you a lay ere I wing on my way,
Cheer up! Cheer up! Cheer up!
Whenever you're blue find something to do
For somebody else who is sadder than you.
Cheer up! Cheer up! Cheer up!

He growled at morning, noon, and night,
And trouble sought to borrow;
Although to-day the sky were bright
He knew 'twould storm to-morrow;
A thought of joy he could not stand,
And struggled to resist it;
Though sunshine dappled all the land
This sorry pessi*mist* it.

—Nixon Waterman.

Oh, be in God's clear world no dark and troubled sprite!
To Christ, thy Master mild, do no such foul despite;
But show in look, word, mien, that thou belongst to him,
Who says, "My yoke is easy, and my burden light."

—Friedrich Rückert.

Let us gather up the sunbeams
Lying all around our path;
Let us keep the wheat and roses,
Casting out the thorns and chaff;
Let us find our sweetest comfort
In the blessings of to-day,
With a patient hand removing
All the briars from our way.

O give me the joy of living
And some glorious work to do!
A spirit of thanksgiving,
With loyal heart and true;
Some pathway to make brighter,
Where tired feet now stray;
Some burden to make lighter,
While 'tis day.

True happiness (if understood)
Consists alone in doing good.

Talk happiness each chance you get—and talk it good and strong!
Look for it in the byways as you grimly pass along;
Perhaps it is a stranger now whose visit never comes,
But talk it! Soon you'll find that you and happiness are chums.

'Tis Being and Doing and Having that make
All the pleasures and pains of which mortals partake.
To Be what God pleases, to Do a man's best,
And to Have a good heart, is the way to be blest.

If the weather is cold don't scold,
If the weather is wet don't fret,
If the weather is warm don't storm,
If the weather is dry don't cry;
But be cheerful together, whatever the weather.

The inner side of every cloud
Is bright and shining;
Therefore I turn my clouds about,
And always wear them inside out,
To show the lining.

—Ellen Thornycroft Fowler Felkin.

Let him that loves his ease, his ease,
Keep close and house him fair;
He'll still be a stranger to the merry thrill of danger
And the joy of the open air.

—Richard Hovey.

There is no human being
With so wholly dark a lot,
But the heart, by turning the picture,
May find some sunny spot.

Let us cry, All good things
Are ours, nor soul helps flesh more now
Than flesh helps soul.

—Robert Browning.

AFFLICTION

CONSOLATION, TRIAL, ENDURANCE

RESIGNATION

There is no flock, however watched and
tended,
But one dead lamb is there!
There is no fireside, howsoe'er defended,
But has one vacant chair.

The air is full of farewells to the dying
And mourning for the dead;
The heart of Rachel, for her children
crying,
Will not be comforted!

Let us be patient! These severe afflictions
Not from the ground arise,
But oftentimes celestial benedictions
Assume this dark disguise.

We see but dimly through the mists and
vapors;
Amid these earthly damps
What seem to us but sad, funereal
tapers
May be heaven's distant lamps.

There is no Death! What seems so is
transition;
This life of mortal breath
Is but a suburb of the life elysian,
Whose portal we call death.

She is not dead—the child of our affection—
But gone unto that school
Where she no longer needs our poor protection,
And Christ himself doth rule.

In that great cloister's stillness and
seclusion,
By guardian angels led,
Safe from temptation, safe from sin's
pollution,
She lives, whom we call dead.

Day after day we think what she is
doing
In those bright realms of air;
Year after year, her tender steps pursuing,
Behold her grown more fair.

Thus do we walk with her and keep unbroken
The bond which nature gives,
Thinking that our remembrance, though
unspoken,
May reach her where she lives.

* * * * *

We will be patient, and assuage the
feeling
We may not wholly stay;
By silence sanctifying, not concealing,
The grief that must have way.

—Henry Wadsworth Longfellow.

MADE PERFECT THROUGH SUFFERING

I bless thee, Lord, for sorrows sent
To break my dream of human power;
For now, my shallow cistern spent,
I find thy founts, and thirst no more.

I take Thy hand, and fears grow still;
Behold thy face, and doubts remove;
Who would not yield his wavering will
To perfect Truth and boundless Love?

That Love this restless soul doth teach
The strength of thine eternal calm;
And tune its sad but broken speech
To join on earth the angel's psalm.

Oh, be it patient in thy hands,
And drawn, through each mysterious
hour,
To service of thy pure commands,
The narrow way of Love and Power.

—Samuel Johnson.

GO NOT FAR FROM ME

Go not far from me, O my strength,
 Whom all my times obey:
Take from me any thing Thou wilt,
 But go not thou away—
And let the storm that does thy work
 Deal with me as it may.

On thy compassion I repose,
 In weakness and distress;
I will not ask for greater ease,
 Lest I should love Thee less.
Oh 'tis a blessed thing for me
 To need thy tenderness.

While many sympathizing hearts
 For my deliverance care,
Thou, in thy wiser, stronger love,
 Art teaching me to bear—
By the sweet voice of thankful song,
 And calm, confiding prayer.

Thy love has many a lighted path,
 No outward eye can trace,
And my heart sees thee in the deep,
 With darkness on its face.
And communes with thee, 'mid the storm,
 As in a secret place.

O Comforter of God's redeemed,
 Whom the world does not see,
What hand should pluck me from the flood
 That casts my soul on thee?
Who would not suffer pain like mine
 To be consoled like me?

When I am feeble as a child,
 And flesh and heart give way,
Then on thy everlasting strength
 With passive trust I stay.
And the rough wind becomes a song,
 The darkness shines like day.

O blessed are the eyes that see—
 Though silent anguish show—
The love that in their hours of sleep
 Unthanked may come and go.
And blessed are the ears that hear,
 Though kept awake by woe.

Happy are they that learn, in thee—
 Though patient suffering teach—
The secret of enduring strength
 And praise too deep for speech:
Peace that no pressure from without,
 No strife within, can reach.

There is no death for me to fear,
 For Christ, my Lord, hath died;
There is no curse in this my pain,
 For he was crucified.
And it is fellowship with him
 That keeps me near his side.

My heart is fixed—O God, my strength—
 My heart is strong to bear;
I will be joyful in thy love,
 And peaceful in thy care.
Deal with me, for my Saviour's sake,
 According to his prayer.

No suffering while it lasts is joy,
 How blest soe'er it be,
Yet may the chastened child be glad
 His Father's face to see;
And oh, it is not hard to bear
 What must be borne in thee.

It is not hard to bear by faith,
 In thine own bosom laid,
The trial of a soul redeemed,
 For thy rejoicing made.
Well may the heart in patience rest
 That none can make afraid.

Safe in thy sanctifying grace—
 Almighty to restore—
Borne onward, sin and death behind,
 And love and life before,
O let my soul abound in hope,
 And praise thee more and more.

Deep unto deep may call, but I
 With peaceful heart will say—
Thy loving-kindness hath a charge
 No waves can take away;
And let the storm that speeds me home
 Deal with me as it may.

—Anna Letitia Waring.

Walking along the shore one morn,
 A holy man by chance I found
Who by a tiger had been torn
 And had no salve to heal his wound.
Long time he suffered grievous pain,
 But not the less to the Most High
 He offered thanks. They asked him, Why?
For answer he thanked God again;
And then to them: "That I am in
 No greater peril than you see:
 That what has overtaken me
Is but misfortune—and not sin."

—Richard Henry Stoddard.

THE CELESTIAL SURGEON

If I have faltered more or less
In my great task of happiness;
If I have moved among my race
And shown no glorious morning face;
If beams from happy human eyes
Have moved me not; if morning skies,
Books, and my food, and summer rain
Knocked on my sullen heart in vain;
Lord, thy most pointed pleasure take
And stab my spirit broad awake;
Or, Lord, if too obdurate I,
Choose thou, before that spirit die,
A piercing pain, a killing sin,
And to my dead heart run them in.
—Robert Louis Stevenson.

I ASKED THE LORD THAT I MIGHT GROW

I asked the Lord that I might grow
In faith and love and every grace;
Might more of his salvation know,
And seek more earnestly his face.

'Twas He who taught me thus to pray,
And he, I trust, has answer'd prayer;
But it has been in such a way
As almost drove me to despair.

I hop'd that in some favor'd hour
At once he'd answer my request,
And by his love's constraining power
Subdue my sins and give me rest.

Instead of this he made me feel
The hidden evils of my heart,
And let the angry powers of hell
Assault my soul in ev'ry part.

Yes, more: with his own hand he seem'd
Intent to aggravate my woe,
Cross'd all the fair designs I schemed,
Blasted my gourds and laid them low.

"Lord, why is this?" I trembling cried;
"Wilt thou pursue thy worm to death?"
" 'Tis in this way," the Lord replied,
"I answer prayer for grace and faith.

"These inward trials I employ
From self and pride to set thee free,
And break thy schemes of earthly joy
That thou mayest set thine all in me!"
—John Newton.

"THOU MAINTAINEST MY LOT"

Source of my life's refreshing springs,
Whose presence in my heart sustains me,
Thy love appoints me pleasant things,
Thy mercy orders all that pains me.

If loving hearts were never lonely,
If all they wished might always be,
Accepting what they look for only,
They might be glad—but not in thee.

Well may thy own beloved, who see
In all their lot their Father's pleasure,
Bear loss of all they love save thee,
Their living, everlasting treasure.

Well may thy happy children cease
From restless wishes, prone to sin,
And, in thine own exceeding peace,
Yield to thy daily discipline.

We need as much the cross we bear
As air we breathe, as light we see!
It draws us to thy side in prayer,
It binds us to our strength in thee.
—Anna Letitia Waring.

THE MASTER'S TOUCH

In the still air the music lies unheard;
In the rough marble beauty hides unseen;
To make the music and the beauty needs
The master's touch, the sculptor's chisel keen.

Great Master, touch us with thy skillful hand;
Let not the music that is in us die.
Great Sculptor, hew and polish us; nor let
Hidden and lost thy form within us lie!

Spare not the stroke! Do with us as thou wilt!
Let there be naught unfinished, broken, marred;
Complete thy purpose that we may become
Thy perfect image, thou our God and Lord!
—Horatius Bonar.

The childish smile is fair, but lovelier far
The smiles which tell of griefs that now no longer are.
—John Sterling.

A BLESSING IN TEARS

Home they brought her warrior dead;
She nor swoon'd nor uttered cry.
All her maidens, watching, said,
"She must weep or she will die."

Then they praised him, soft and low,
Call'd him worthy to be loved,
Truest friend, and noblest foe;
Yet she neither spoke nor moved.

Stole a maiden from her place,
Lightly to the warrior stept,
Took the face-cloth from the face;
Yet she neither moved nor wept.

Rose a nurse of ninety years,
Set his child upon her knee;
Like summer tempest came her tears:
"Sweet my child, I live for thee."
—Alfred Tennyson.

EVERY DAY

O trifling task so often done,
Yet ever to be done anew!
O cares which come with every sun,
Morn after morn, the long years through!
We sink beneath their paltry sway—
The irksome calls of every day.

The restless sense of wasted power,
The tiresome round of little things,
Are hard to bear, as hour by hour
Its tedious iteration brings;
Who shall evade or who delay
The small demands of every day?

The bowlder, in the torrent's course
By tide and tempest lashed in vain,
Obeys the wave-whirled pebble's force
And yields its substance grain by grain;
So crumble strongest lives away
Beneath the wear of every day.

Who finds the lion in his lair,
Who tracks the tiger for his life
May wound them ere they are aware,
Or conquer them in desperate strife,
Yet powerless he to scathe or slay
The vexing gnats of every day.

The steady strain that never stops
Is mightier than the fiercest shock;
The constant fall of water drops
Will groove the adamantine rock;
We feel our noblest powers decay
In feeble wars with every day.

We rise to meet a heavy blow—
Our souls a sudden bravery fills—
But we endure not always so
The drop by drop of little ills;
We still deplore, and still obey,
The hard behests of every day.

The heart which boldly faces death
Upon the battle-field, and dares
Cannon and bayonet, faints beneath
The needle-points of frets and cares;
The stoutest spirits they dismay—
The tiny stings of every day.

And even saints of holy fame,
Whose souls by faith have overcome,
Who won amid the cruel flame
The molten crown of martyrdom,
Bore not without complaint alway
The petty pains of every day.

Ah, more than martyr's aureole,
And more than hero's heart of fire,
We need the humble strength of soul
Which daily toils and ills require;
Sweet Patience! grant us, if you may,
An added grace for every day.

PEACEABLE FRUIT

(Heb. 12. 11.)

What shall thine "afterward" be, O Lord,
For this dark and suffering night?
Father, *what* shall thine "afterward" be?
Hast thou a morning of joy for me,
And a new and joyous light?

What shall thine "afterward" be, O Lord,
For the moan that I cannot stay?
Shall it issue in some new song of praise,
Sweeter than sorrowless heart could raise,
When the night hath passed away?

What shall thine "afterward" be, O Lord,
For this helplessness of pain?
A clearer view of my home above,
Of my Father's strength and my Father's love—
Shall *this* be my lasting gain?

What shall thine "afterward" be, O Lord?
How long must thy child endure?
Thou knowest! 'Tis well that I know it not!
Thine "afterward" cometh—I cannot tell what,
But I know that thy word is sure.

What shall thine "afterward" be, O Lord,
I wonder—and wait to see
(While to thy chastening hand I bow)
What "peaceable fruit" may be ripening now—
Ripening fast for me!
—Frances Ridley Havergal.

HOW WE LEARN

Great truths are dearly bought. The common truth,
Such as men give and take from day to day,
Comes in the common walk of easy life,
Blown by the careless wind across our way.

Great truths are greatly won, not found by chance,
Nor wafted on the breath of summer dream;
But grasped in the great struggle of the soul
Hard buffeting with adverse wind and stream.

But in the day of conflict, fear and grief,
When the strong hand of God, put forth in might,
Plows up the subsoil of the stagnant heart
And brings the imprisoned truth-seed to the light,

Wrung from the troubled spirit in hard hours
Of weakness, solitude, perchance of pain,
Truth springs like harvest from the well-plowed field,
And the soul feels it has not wept in vain. —Horatius Bonar.

Though trouble-tossed and torture-torn
The kingliest kings are crowned with thorn. —Gerald Massey.

HEAVIER THE CROSS

Heavier the cross the stronger faith:
The loaded palm strikes deeper root;
The vine-juice sweetly issueth
When men have pressed the clustered fruit;
And courage grows where dangers come
Like pearls beneath the salt sea foam.

Heavier the cross the heartier prayer;
The bruisèd herbs most fragrant are;
If sky and wind were always fair
The sailor would not watch the star;
And David's psalms had ne'er been sung
If grief his heart had never wrung.

Heavier the cross the more aspiring;
From vales we climb to mountain's crest;
The pilgrim, of the desert tiring,
Longs for the Canaan of his rest.
The dove has here no rest in sight,
And to the ark she wings her flight.

Heavier the cross the easier dying;
Death is a friendlier face to see;
To life's decay one bids defying,
From life's distress one then is free;
The cross sublimely lifts our faith
To him who triumphed over death.

Thou Crucified! the cross I carry—
The longer may it dearer be;
And, lest I faint while here I tarry,
Implant thou such a heart in me
That faith, hope, love, may flourish there
Till for the cross my crown I wear.
—Benjamin Schmolke.

LA ROCHELLE

A worthy man of Paris town
Came to the bishop there:
His face, o'erclouded with dismay,
Betrayed a fixed despair.

"Father," said he, "a sinner vile
Am I, against my will:
Each hour I humbly pray for faith,
But am a doubter still.

"Sure were I not despised of God,
He would not leave me so
To struggle thus in constant strife
Against the deadly foe."

The bishop to his sorrowing son
 Thus spoke a kind relief:
"The King of France has castles twain;
 To each he sends a chief.

"There's Montelhéry, far inland,
 That stands in place secure;
While La Rochelle, upon the coast,
 Doth sieges oft endure.

"Now for these castles—both preserved—
 First in his prince's love
Shall Montelhéry's chief be placed,
 Or La Rochelle's above?"

"Oh! doubtless, sire," the sinner said,
 "That king will love the most
The man whose task was hard to keep
 His castle on the coast!"

"Son," said the bishop, "thou art right;
 Apply this reasoning well:
My heart is Montelhéry fort,
 And thine is La Rochelle!"

IF THOU COULD'ST KNOW

I think, if thou could'st know,
 O soul, that will complain,
What lies concealed below
 Our burden and our pain—
How just our anguish brings
Nearer those longed-for things
We seek for now in vain—
I think thou would'st rejoice and not complain.

I think, if thou could'st see,
 With thy dim mortal sight,
How meanings, dark to thee,
 Are shadows hiding light;
Truth's efforts crossed and vexed,
Life's purpose all perplexed—
If thou could'st see them right,
I think that they would seem all clear, and wise, and bright.

And yet thou can'st not know;
 And yet thou can'st not see;
Wisdom and sight are slow
 In poor humanity.
If thou could'st *trust*, poor soul,
In him who rules the whole,
Thou would'st find peace and rest:
Wisdom and sight are well, but trust is best.

MY CROSS

"O Lord, my God!" I oft have said,
"Had I some other cross instead
Of this I bear from day to day,
'Twere easier to go on my way.

"I do not murmur at its weight;
That Thou hast made proportionate
To my scant strength; but oh! full sore
It presses where it pressed before.

"Change for a space, however brief,
The wonted burden, that relief
May o'er my aching shoulders steal,
And the deep bruise have room to heal!"

While thus I sadly sighed to-day
I heard my gracious Father say,
"Can'st thou not trust my love, my child,
And to thy cross be reconciled?

"I fashioned it thy needs to meet;
Nor were thy discipline complete
Without that very pain and bruise
Which thy weak heart would fain refuse."

Ashamed, I answered, "As Thou wilt!
I own my faithlessness and guilt;
Welcome the weary pain shall be,
Since only that is best for me."

GOD KNOWETH BEST

He took them from me, one by one,
The things I set my heart upon;
They looked so harmless, fair, and blest;
Would they have hurt me? God knows best.
He loves me so, he would not wrest
Them from me if it were not best.

He took them from me, one by one,
The friends I set my heart upon.
O did they come, they and their love,
Between me and my Lord above?
Were they as idols in my breast?
It may be. God in heaven knows best.

I will not say I did not weep,
As doth a child that wants to keep
The pleasant things in hurtful play
His wiser parent takes away;
But in this comfort I will rest:
He who hath taken knoweth best.

THE ONLY SOLACE

O Thou who driest the mourner's tear,
How dark this world would be
If, when deceived and wounded here,
We could not fly to thee!

The friends who in our sunshine live
When winter comes are flown;
And he who has but tears to give
Must weep those tears alone.

But Thou wilt heal that broken heart
Which, like the plants that throw
Their fragrance from the wounded part,
Breathes sweetness out of woe.

O who could bear life's stormy doom
Did not Thy wing of love
Come brightly wafting through the gloom
Our peace-branch from above!

Then sorrow, touched by Thee, grows bright
With more than rapture's ray;
As darkness shows us worlds of light
We never saw by day.
—Thomas Moore.

CONSOLATION

If none were sick and none were sad
What service could we render?
I think if we were always glad
We scarcely could be tender.
Did our beloved never need
Our patient ministration
Earth would grow cold, and miss indeed
Its sweetest consolation.
If sorrow never claimed our heart,
And every wish were granted,
Patience would die and hope depart—
Life would be disenchanted.

Banish far from me all I love,
The smiles of friends, the old fireside,
And drive me to that home of homes,
The heart of Jesus crucified.

Take all the light away from earth,
Take all that men can love from me;
Let all I lean upon give way,
That I may lean on naught but Thee.
—Frederick William Faber.

PERFECT THROUGH SUFFERING

God never would send you the darkness
If he felt you could bear the light;
But you would not cling to his guiding hand
If the way were always bright;
And you would not care to walk by faith
Could you always walk by sight.

'Tis true he has many an anguish
For your sorrowful heart to bear,
And many a cruel thorn-crown
For your tired head to wear:
He knows how few would reach heaven at all
If pain did not guide them there.

So he sends you the blinding darkness,
And the furnace of seven-fold heat.
'Tis the only way, believe me,
To keep you close to his feet,
For 'tis always so easy to wander
When our lives are glad and sweet.

Then nestle your hand in your Father's
And sing, if you can, as you go;
Your song may cheer some one behind you
Whose courage is sinking low.
And—well—if your lips do quiver—
God will love you better so.

A LITTLE PARABLE

I made the cross myself whose weight
Was later laid on me.
This thought is torture as I toil
Up life's steep Calvary.

To think mine own hands drove the nails!
I sang a merry song,
And chose the heaviest wood I had
To build it firm and strong.

If I had guessed—if I had dreamed—
Its weight was meant for me,
I should have made a lighter cross
To bear up Calvary.
—Anne Reeve Aldrich.

The unpolished pearl can never shine—
'Tis sorrow makes the soul divine.
—From the Japanese, tr. by Frederic Rowland Marvin.

THE SOWER

I

A Sower went forth to sow;
His eyes were dark with woe;
He crushed the flowers beneath his feet,
Nor smelt the perfume, warm and sweet,
That prayed for pity everywhere.
He came to a field that was harried
By iron, and to heaven laid bare;
He shook the seed that he carried
O'er that brown and bladeless place.
He shook it, as God shakes hail
Over a doomèd land.
When lightnings interlace
The sky and the earth, and his wand
Of love is a thunder-flail.
Thus did that Sower sow;
His seed was human blood,
And tears of women and men.
And I, who near him stood,
Said: When the crop comes, then
There will be sobbing and sighing,
Weeping and wailing and crying,
Flame, and ashes, and woe.

II

It was an autumn day
When next I went that way.
And what, think you, did I say,
What was it that I heard,
What music was in the air?
The song of a sweet-voiced bird?
Nay—but the songs of many
Thrilled through with praise and prayer.
Of all those voices not any
Were sad of memory;
But a sea of sunlight flowed,
A golden harvest glowed,
And I said, Thou only art wise,
God of the earth and skies!
And I praise thee, again and again,
For the Sower whose name is Pain.
—Richard Watson Gilder.

Not disabled in the combat,
  No, nor absent from your post;
You are doing gallant service
  Where the Master needs you most.

It was noble to give battle
  While the world stood cheering on;
It is nobler to lie patient,
  Leaving half one's work undone.

And the King counts up his heroes
  Where the desperate charge was led,
But he writes, "My Best Belovèd,"
  Over many a sick man's bed.

I DO NOT ASK, O LORD

I do not ask, O Lord, that life may be
    A pleasant road;
I do not ask that thou wouldst take from me
    Aught of its load.

I do not ask that flowers should always spring
    Beneath my feet;
I know too well the poison and the sting
    Of things too sweet.

For one thing only, Lord, dear Lord, I plead:
    Lead me aright,
Though strength should falter and though heart should bleed,
    Through peace to light.

I do not ask, O Lord, that thou shouldst shed
    Full radiance here;
Give but a ray of peace, that I may tread
    Without a fear.

I do not ask my cross to understand,
    My way to see;
Better in darkness just to feel thy hand,
    And follow Thee.

Joy is like restless day; but peace divine
    Like quiet night.
Lead me, O Lord, till perfect day shall shine
    Through peace to light.
—Adelaide Anne Procter.

ANGELS OF GRIEF

With silence only as their benediction
    God's angels come,
Where, in the shadow of a great affliction,
    The soul sits dumb.

Yet would we say, what every heart approveth,
    Our Father's will,
Calling to him the dear ones whom he loveth,
    Is mercy still.

Not upon us or ours the solemn angel
    Hath evil wrought;
The funeral anthem is a glad evangel—
    The good die not!

God calls our loved ones, but we lose not wholly
What he has given;
They live on earth in thought and deed as truly
As in his heaven.
—John Greenleaf Whittier.

FURNACE AND HAMMER

Pain's furnace-heat within me quivers,
God's breath upon the flame doth blow;
And all my heart in anguish shivers
And trembles at the fiery glow;
And yet I whisper—"*As God will!*"
And in his hottest fire stand still.

He comes, and lays my heart, all heated,
On the hard anvil, minded so
Into his own fair shape to beat it
With his great hammer, blow on blow;
And yet I whisper—"*As God will!*"
And at his heaviest blows hold still.

He takes my softened heart and beats it;
The sparks fly off at every blow;
He turns it o'er and o'er and heats it,
And lets it cool, and makes it glow;
And yet I whisper—"*As God will!*"
And in his mighty hand hold still.

Why should I murmur? for the sorrow
Thus only longer-lived would be;
Its end may come, and will to-morrow,
When God has done his work in me;
So I say trusting—"*As God will!*"
And, trusting to the end, hold still.
—Julius Sturm.

WITH SELF DISSATISFIED

Not when with self dissatisfied,
O Lord, I lowly lie,
So much I need thy grace to guide,
And thy reproving eye,

As when the sound of human praise
Grows pleasant to my ear,
And in its light my broken ways
Fair and complete appear.

By failure and defeat made wise,
We come to know, at length,
What strength within our weakness lies,
What weakness in our strength;

What inward peace is born of strife
What power of being spent;
What wings unto our upward life
Is noble discontent.

O Lord, we need thy shaming look
That burns all low desire;
The discipline of thy rebuke
Shall be refining fire!
—Frederick Lucian Hosmer.

TOO MUCH SELF

Some evil upon Rabia fell;
And one who loved and knew her well
Murmured that God with pain undue
Should strike a child so fond and true.
But she replied, "Believe and trust
That all I suffer is most just.
I had, in contemplation, striven
To realize the joys of heaven;
I had extended fancy's flights
Through all that region of delights,
Had counted, till the numbers failed,
The pleasures on the blest entailed,
Had sounded the ecstatic rest
I should enjoy on Allah's breast—
And for these thoughts I now atone;
They were of something of my own,
And were not thoughts of him alone."
—From the Arabian.

THE GAIN OF LOSS

O thou so weary of thy self-denials,
And so impatient of thy little cross,
Is it so hard to bear thy daily trials,
And count all earthly things a gainful loss?

Canst thou forget thy Christian superscription,
"Behold, we count them happy which endure"?
What treasure wouldst thou, in the land Egyptian,
Repass the stormy water to secure?

And wilt thou yield thy sure and glorious promise
For the poor, fleeting joys earth can afford?
No hand can take away the treasure from us
That rests within the keeping of the Lord.

A STRANGE BOON

Oft when of God we ask
  For fuller, happier life,
He sets us some new task
  Involving care and strife;
Is this the boon for which we sought?
Has prayer new trouble on us brought?

This is indeed the boon,
  Though strange to us it seems;
We pierce the rock, and soon
  The blessing on us streams;
For when we are the most athirst,
Then the clear waters on us burst.

We toil as in the field
  Wherein, to us unknown,
A treasure lies concealed
  Which may be all our own.
And shall we of the toil complain
That speedily will bring such gain?

We dig the wells of life,
  And God the waters gives;
We win our way by strife,
  Then he within us lives;
And only war could make us meet
For peace so sacred and so sweet.

—Thomas Toke Lynch.

STILL HOPE! STILL ACT!

Still hope! still act! Be sure that life
  The source and strength of every good,
Wastes down in feeling's empty strife,
  And dies in dreaming's sickly mood.

To toil in tasks however mean
  For all we know of right and true—
In this alone our worth is seen,
  'Tis this we were ordained to do.

So shalt thou find, in work and thought:
  The peace that sorrow cannot give;
Though grief's worst pangs to thee be taught,
  By thee let others nobler live.

Oh, wait not in the darksome forest,
  Where thou must needs be left alone,
But e'en when memory is sorest,
  Seek out a path and journey on!

Thou wilt have angels near above
  By whom invisible aid is given;
They journey still on tasks of love,
  And never rest except in heaven.

—John Sterling.

THEY SHALL NOT OVERFLOW

In the floods of tribulation,
  While the billows o'er me roll,
Jesus whispers consolation
  And supports my fainting soul;
    Sweet affliction
  That brings Jesus to my soul.

Thus the lion yields me honey,
  From the eater food is given;
Strengthened thus I still press forward,
  Singing on my way to heaven.
    Sweet affliction,
  Helping speed me on to heaven.

So in darkest dispensations
  Doth my faithful Lord appear,
With his richest consolations
  To reanimate and cheer;
    Sweet affliction,
  Thus to bring my Saviour near.

Floods of tribulation heighten,
  Billows still around me roar;
Those who know not Christ they frighten;
  But my soul defies their power:
    Sweet affliction,
  Thus to bring my Saviour near.

In the sacred page recorded,
  Thus His word securely stands;
"Fear not; I'm, in trouble, near thee,
  Naught shall pluck thee from my hands."
    Sweet affliction,
  Every word my love demands.

All I meet, I find, assists me
  In my path to heavenly joy,
Where, though trials now attend me,
  Trials never more annoy.
    Sweet affliction,
  Every promise gives me joy.

Wearing there a weight of glory,
  Still the path I'll ne'er forget,
But, exulting, cry it led me
  To my blessed Saviour's seat;
    Sweet affliction,
  Which hath brought me to his feet.

—Pearce.

Glory to God—to God! he saith,
Knowledge by suffering entereth,
And life is perfected by death.

—Elizabeth Barrett Browning.

HIS WAYS

I asked for grace to lift me high,
  Above the world's depressing cares.
God sent me sorrows,—with a sigh
  I said, He has not heard my prayers.

I asked for light, that I might see
  My path along life's thorny road;
But clouds and darkness shadowed me
  When I expected light from God.

I asked for peace, that I might rest
  To think my sacred duties o'er,
When lo! such horrors filled my breast
  As I had never felt before.

And O, I cried, can this be prayer
  Whose plaints the steadfast mountains move?
Can this be heaven's prevailing care?
  And, O my God, is this thy love?

But soon I found that sorrow, worn
  As duty's garment, strength supplies,
And out of darkness meekly borne
  Unto the righteous light doth rise.

And soon I found that fears which stirred
  My startled soul God's will to do,
On me more real peace conferred
  Than in life's calm I ever knew.

Then, Lord, in thy mysterious ways
  Lead my dependent spirit on,
And whensoe'er it kneels and prays,
  Teach it to say, "Thy will be done!"

Let its one thought, one hope, one prayer,
  Thine image seek, thy glory see;
Let every other wish and care
  Be left confidingly to thee.

—John Samuel Bewley Monsell.

COMPENSATION

Not in each shell the diver brings to air
Is found the priceless pearl, but only where
Mangled, and torn, and bruised well-nigh to death,
The wounded oyster draws its laboring breath.
O tired and suffering soul! gauge here your gain;
The pearl of patience is the fruit of pain.

—Caroline Atherton Mason.

THE DARK ANGEL

Count each affliction, whether light or grave,
  God's messenger sent down to thee. Do thou
  With courtesy receive him, rise and bow,
And, ere his shadow pass thy threshold, crave
Permission first his heavenly feet to lave,
  Then lay before him all thou hast. Allow
  No cloud of passion to usurp thy brow
Or mar thy hospitality; no wave
Of mortal tumult to obliterate
  Thy soul's marmoreal calmness. Grief should be,
Like joy, majestic, equable, sedate;
  Confirming, cleansing, raising, making free;
Strong to consume small troubles, to commend
Great thoughts, grave thoughts, thoughts lasting to the end.

—Aubrey Thomas De Vere.

SONG—SERMON

Lord, what is man,
That thou art mindful of him?
Though in creation's van,
Lord, what is man?
He wills less than he can,
Lets his ideal scoff him!
Lord, what is man,
That thou art mindful of him?

—George Macdonald.

Lord, shall we grumble when thy flames do scourge us?
Our sins breathe fire; thy fire returns to purge us.
Lord, what an alchemist art thou, whose skill
Transmutes to perfect good from perfect ill!

—Francis Quarles.

The path of sorrow, and that path alone,
Leads to the land where sorrow is unknown;
No traveler e'er reached that blest abode
Who found not thorns and briers in his road.

—William Cowper.

TAKE AWAY PAIN

The cry of man's anguish went up unto God:
"Lord, take away pain—
The shadow that darkens the world thou hast made,
The close-coiling chain
That strangles the heart, the burden that weighs
On the wings that would soar—
Lord, take away pain from the world thou hast made,
That it love thee the more!"

Then answered the Lord to the cry of his world:
"Shall I take away pain
And with it the power of the soul to endure,
Made strong by the strain?
Shall I take away pity, that knits heart to heart,
And sacrifice high?
Will ye lose all your heroes that lift from the fire
White brows to the sky?
Shall I take away love, that redeems with a price
And smiles at its loss?
Can ye spare from your lives, that would climb unto mine,
The Christ on his cross?"

'Tis not alone in the sunshine
Our lives grow pure and true;
There is growth as well in the shadow,
And pain has a work to do.

So it comes to me more and more
As I enter upon each new day:
The love of the Father eternal
Is over us all the way.

"In pastures green"? Not always; sometimes he
Who knoweth best in kindness leadeth me
In weary ways where heavy shadows be.

But where He leads me I can safely go,
And in the blest hereafter I shall know
Why in his wisdom he hath led me so.

A SONG OF SOLACE

Thou sweet hand of God, that so woundest my heart,
Thou makest me smile while thou mak'st me to smart;
It seems as if God were at ball-play; and I,
The harder he strikes me the higher I fly.

I own it, he bruises, he pierces me sore;
But the hammer and chisel afflict me no more.
Shall I tell you the reason? It is that I see
The Sculptor will carve out an angel for me.

I shrink from no suffering, how painful soe'er,
When once I can feel that my God's hand is there;
For soft on the anvil the iron shall glow
When the Smith with his hammer deals blow upon blow.

God presses me hard, but he gives patience, too!
And I say to myself, " 'Tis no more than my due,"
And no tone from the organ can swell on the breeze
Till the organist's fingers press down on the keys.

So come, then, and welcome the blow and the pain!
Without them no mortal to heaven can attain;
For what can the sheaves on the barn floor avail
Till the thresher shall beat out the chaff with his flail?

'Tis only a moment God chastens with pain;
Joy follows on sorrow like sunshine on rain.
Then bear thou what God on thy spirit shall lay;
Be dumb; but, when tempted to murmur, then pray.

—From the German.

When thou hast thanked thy God for every blessing sent,
What time will then remain for murmurs or lament?

We must live through the weary winter
If we would value the spring;
And the woods must be cold and silent
Before the robins sing.
The flowers must lie buried in darkness
Before they can bud and bloom;
And the sweetest and warmest sunshine
Comes after the storm and gloom.
—Agnes L. Pratt.

We look along the shining ways,
To see the angel faces;
They come to us in darkest days
And in the blackest places.
The strongest hearts have strongest need,
To them the fiery trial;
Who walks a saint in word and deed
Is saint by self-denial.

Is it true, O Christ in heaven,
That the strongest suffer most,
That the wisest wander farthest,
And most hopelessly are lost?
That the mark of rank in nature
Is capacity for pain,
That the anguish of the singer
Makes the sweetness of the strain?

O, block by block, with sore and sharp endeavor,
Lifelong we build these human natures up
Into a temple fit for freedom's shrine.
And trial ever consecrates the cup.
Wherefrom we pour her sacrificial wine. —James Russell Lowell.

But all God's angels come to us disguised;
Sorrow and sickness, poverty and death,
One after other lift their frowning masks,
And we behold the seraph's face beneath
All radiant with the glory and the calm
Of having looked upon the front of God.
—James Russell Lowell.

The man whom God delights to bless
He never curses with success.
Thrice happy loss which makes me see
My happiness is all in thee.
—Charles Wesley.

Who ne'er has suffered, he has lived but half.
Who never failed, he never strove or sought.
Who never wept is stranger to a laugh
And he who never doubted never thought. —J. B. Goode.

I thank thee, Lord, that all my joy
Is touched with pain;
That shadows fall on brightest hours;
That thorns remain;
So that earth's bliss may be my guide,
And not my chain.

Would'st thou from sorrow find a sweet relief?
Or is thy heart oppressed with woes untold?
Balm would'st thou gather for corroding grief?
Pour blessings round thee like a shower of gold.

Art thou weary, tender heart?
Be glad of pain;
In sorrow sweetest things will grow
As flowers in rain.
God watches; and thou wilt have sun
When clouds their perfect work have done. —Lucy Larcom.

'Tis sorrow builds the shining ladder up,
Whose golden rounds are our calamities
Whereon our firm feet planting nearer God
The spirit climbs, and hath its eyes unsealed. —James Russell Lowell.

In the pleasant orchard closes,
"God bless all our gains," say we;
But "May God bless all our losses,"
Better suits with our degree.
—Elizabeth Barrett Browning.

Our toil is sweet with thankfulness,
Our burden is our boon;
The curse of earth's gray morning is
The blessing of its noon.
—John Greenleaf Whittier.

I hold it true, whate'er befall,
I feel it, when I sorrow most;
'Tis better to have loved and lost
Than never to have loved at all.
—Alfred Tennyson.

The fountain of joy is fed by tears,
And love is lit by the breath of sighs;
The deepest griefs and the wildest fears
Have holiest ministries.
—Josiah Gilbert Holland.

I held it truth, with him who sings
To one clear harp in divers tones
That men may rise on stepping stones
Of their dead selves to higher things.
—Alfred Tennyson.

When God afflicts thee, think he hews a rugged stone,
Which must be shaped or else aside as useless thrown.
—Richard Chenevix Trench.

My sorrows have not been so light
Thy chastening hand I could not trace,
Nor have my blessings been so great
That they have hid my Father's face.

Put pain from out the world, what room were left
For thanks to God, for love to man?
—Robert Browning.

Heaven is not always angry when he strikes,
But most chastises those whom most he likes.
—John Pomfret.

The good are better made by ill,
As odors crushed are sweeter still.
—Samuel Rogers.

Only those are crowned and sainted
Who with grief have been acquainted.
—Henry Wadsworth Longfellow.

LOVE

DIVINE GOODNESS, UNSELFISHNESS

LOVE'S FULFILLING

O Love is weak
Which counts the answers and the gains,
Weighs all the losses and the pains,
And eagerly each fond word drains
A joy to seek.

When Love is strong
It never tarries to take heed,
Or know if its return exceed
Its gifts; in its sweet haste no greed,
No strifes belong.

It hardly asks
If it be loved at all; to take
So barren seems, when it can make
Such bliss, for the belovèd's sake,
Of bitter tasks.

Its ecstacy
Could find hard death so beauteous,
It sees through tears how Christ loved us,
And speaks, in saying "I love thus,"
No blasphemy.

So much we miss
If love is weak, so much we gain
If love is strong, God thinks no pain
Too sharp or lasting to ordain
To teach us this.
—Helen Hunt Jackson.

LOVE

If suddenly upon the street
My gracious Saviour I should meet,
And he should say, "As I love thee,
What love hast thou to offer me?"
Then what could this poor heart of mine
Dare offer to that heart divine?

His eye would pierce my outward show,
His thought my inmost thought would know;
And if I said, "I love thee, Lord,"
He would not heed my spoken word,
Because my daily life would tell
If verily I loved him well.

If on the day or in the place
Wherein he met me face to face
My life could show some kindness done,
Some purpose formed, some work begun,
For his dear sake, then, it were meet
Love's gift to lay at Jesus' feet.
—Charles Francis Richardson.

THE COMMON OFFERING

It is not the deed we do—
Tho' the deed be never so fair—
But the *love* that the dear Lord looketh for
Hidden with holy care
In the heart of the deed so fair.

The love is the priceless thing,
The treasure our treasure must hold
Or ever our Lord will take the gift,
Or tell the worth of the gold
By the love that cannot be told.

Behold us—the rich and the poor—
Dear Lord, in thy service draw near;
One consecrateth a precious coin,
One droppeth only a tear;
Look, Master, the love is here!
—Harriet McEwen Kimball.

True love shall trust, but selfish love must die,
For trust is peace, and self is full of pain;
Arise and heal thy brother's grief; his tears
Shall wash thy love, and it will live again. —John Boyle O'Reilly.

EXPECTING AND KNOWING

Faith, Hope and Love were questioned
 what they thought
Of future glory which religion taught;
Now Faith *believed* it to be firmly true,
And Hope *expected* so to find it too;
Love answered, smiling with uncon-
 scious glow,
"Believe? expect? I *know* it to be so."
—John Wesley.

THE LOVE OF GOD

Could we with ink the ocean fill,
 Were the whole world of parchment
 made,
Were every single stick a quill,
 Were every man a scribe by trade;
To write the love of God alone
 Would drain the ocean dry;
Nor could the scroll contain the whole
 Though stretched from sky to sky.

THE KINGDOM OF GOD

I say to thee—do thou repeat
 To the first man thou mayest meet
In lane, highway, or open street—

That he, and we, and all men move
 Under a canopy of love
As broad as the blue sky above;

That doubt and trouble, fear and pain
 And anguish, all are shadows vain;
That death itself shall not remain;

That weary deserts we may tread,
 A dreary labyrinth may thread,
Through dark ways under ground be led,

Yet, if we will our Guide obey,
 The dreariest path, the darkest way,
Shall issue out in heavenly day,

And we, on divers shores now cast,
 Shall meet, our perilous voyage past,
All in our Father's house at last.

And, ere thou leave him, say thou this
 Yet one word more: They only miss
The winning of that final bliss

Who will not count it true that love,
 Blessing, not cursing, rules above,
And that in it we live and move.

And one thing further make him know:
 That to believe these things are so,
This firm faith never to forego,

Despite of all that seems at strife
 With blessing, all with curses rife,
That *this* is blessing, *this* is life.
—Richard Chenevix Trench.

GOD'S ALL-EMBRACING LOVE

Thou grace divine, encircling all,
 A soundless, shoreless sea
Wherein at last our souls shall fall;
 O love of God most free,

When over dizzy steeps we go
 One soft hand blinds our eyes,
The other leads us, safe and slow,
 O love of God, most wise!

And though we turn us from thy face,
 And wander wide and long,
Thou hold'st us still in thine embrace,
 O love of God most strong!

The saddened heart, the restless soul,
 The toil-worn frame and mind,
Alike confess thy sweet control,
 O love of God most kind!

But not alone thy care we claim
 Our wayward steps to win;
We know thee by a dearer name,
 O love of God, within!

And filled and quickened by thy breath
 Our souls are strong and free
To rise o'er sin, and fear, and death,
 O love of God, to thee!
—Eliza Scudder.

Ah, how skillful grows the hand
That obeyeth Love's command!
It is the heart, and not the brain,
That to the highest doth attain,
And he who followeth Love's behest
Far excelleth all the rest.
—Henry Wadsworth Longfellow.

If I truly love the One
 All the loves are mine;
Alien to my heart is none
 And life grows divine.

GOD'S MERCY

There's a wideness in God's mercy
  Like the wideness of the sea;
There's a kindness in his justice
  Which is more than liberty.
There is welcome for the sinner,
  And more graces for the good;
There is mercy with the Saviour;
  There is healing in his blood.

There is no place where earth's sorrows
  Are more felt than up in heaven;
There is no place where earth's failings
  Have such kindly judgment given.
There is plentiful redemption
  In the blood that has been shed;
There is joy for all the members
  In the sorrows of the Head.

For the love of God is broader
  Than the measure of man's mind,
And the heart of the Eternal
  Is most wonderfully kind.
If our love were but more simple,
  We should take him at his word,
And our lives would be all sunshine
  In the sweetness of our Lord.
—Frederick William Faber.

THE LOVE THAT PASSETH KNOWLEDGE

Not what I am, O Lord, but what thou art,
  That, that alone, can be my soul's true rest;
Thy love, not mine, bids fear and doubt depart,
  And stills the tempest of my tossing breast.

It is thy perfect love that casts out fear;
  I know the voice that speaks the "It is I."
And in these well-known words of heavenly cheer
  I hear the joy that bids each sorrow fly.

Thy name is Love! I hear it from the Cross;
  Thy name is Love! I read it in yon tomb;
All meaner love is perishable dross,
  But this shall light me through time's thickest gloom.

It blesses now, and shall forever bless;
  It saves me now, and shall forever save;
It holds me up in days of helplessness,
  It bears me safely o'er each swelling wave.

Girt with the love of God on every side,
  Breathing that love as heaven's own healing air,
I work or wait, still following my Guide,
  Braving each foe, escaping every snare.

'Tis what I know of thee my Lord and God,
  That fills my soul with peace, my lips with song;
Thou art my health, my joy, my staff, my rod,
  Leaning on thee, in weakness I am strong.

I am all want and hunger; this faint heart
  Pines for a fullness which it finds not here,
Dear ones are leaving, and as they depart,
  Make room within for something yet more dear.

More of thyself, oh, show me hour by hour
  More of thy glory, O my God and Lord!
More of thyself in all thy grace and power
  More of thy love and truth, Incarnate Word.

Love that asketh love again
Finds the barter naught but pain;
Love that giveth in full store,
Aye receives as much, and more.

Love, exacting nothing back,
Never knoweth any lack;
Love, compelling love to pay,
Sees him bankrupt every day.
—Dinah Maria Mulock Craik.

Such power there is in clear-eyed self-restraint
And purpose clean as light from every selfish taint.
—James Russell Lowell.

HIS BANNER OVER ME

Surrounded by unnumbered foes,
Against my soul the battle goes!
Yet, though I weary, sore distrest,
I know that I shall reach my rest.
I lift my tearful eyes above;
His banner over me is love.

Its sword my spirit will not yield,
Though flesh may faint upon the field;
He waves before my fading sight
The branch of palm—the crown of light;
I lift my brightening eyes above,
His banner over me is love.

My cloud of battle-dust may dim,
His veil of splendor curtain him,
And in the midnight of my fear
I may not feel him standing near;
But, as I lift mine eyes above,
His banner over me is love.
—Gerald Massey.

THE SPILT PEARLS

His courtiers of the caliph crave:
"O say how this may be,
That of thy slaves this Ethiop slave
Is best beloved by thee?

"For he is hideous as the night:
Yet when has ever chose
A nightingale for its delight
A hueless, scentless rose?"

The caliph then: "No features fair,
No comely mien are his;
Love is the beauty he doth wear;
And love his glory is.

"Once when a camel of my train
There fell, in narrow street,
From broken casket rolled amain
Rich pearls before my feet.

"I nodding to my slaves that I
Would freely give them these,
At once upon the spoil they fly
The costly boon to seize.

"One only at my side remained—
Beside this Ethiop none;
He, moveless as the steed he reined,
Behind me sat alone.

"'What will thy gain, good fellow, be,
Thus lingering at my side?'
'My king, that I shall faithfully
Have guarded thee,' he cried.

"True servant's title he may wear,
He only, who has not,
For his lord's gifts, how rich soe'er,
His lord himself forgot!"

So thou alone dost walk before
Thy God with perfect aim,
From him desiring nothing more
Beside himself to claim.

For if thou not to him aspire,
But to his gifts alone,
Not love, but covetous desire,
Has brought thee to his throne.

While such thy prayer; it climbs above
In vain—the golden key
Of God's rich treasure-house of love
Thine own will never be.
—Saadi, tr. by Richard Chenevix Trench.

THE HIGHER PRIVILEGE

For some the narrow lane of "must,"
Be mine the big, broad "may";
Better to love—be happy—trust,
Than simply to obey.

O troubled over many things,
Choose thou the better part:
Service unconscious of itself,
And childlikeness of heart.

Why cast your burden on the Lord
And strive to drag it, too?
Call work an opportunity
Till it grows joy to you.

"Ought" is a servant's work, not mine;
I sign no grudging pledge;
I am a child and son; my toil
Is only privilege.

Who'd be a thrall to vain debates
Of "were this right or wrong,"
When he might toss these cares to God
And catch instead a song!

Why breathe earth's heavy atmosphere,
Forgetful we can fly,
When the high zenith, "God is Love,"
Allures us to the sky?

The virtues hide their vanquished fires
Within that whiter flame,
Till conscience grows irrelevant,
And duty but a name!
—Frederic Lawrence Knowles.

THE WIDOW'S OIL

2 Kings 4. 1–6

Pour forth the oil, pour boldly forth,
It will not fail until
Thou failest vessels to provide
Which it may freely fill.

But then, when such are found no more,
Though flowing broad and free
Till then, and nourished from on high,
It straightway stanched will be.

Dig channels for the streams of love,
Where they may broadly run;
And love has overflowing streams
To fill them every one.

But if at any time thou cease
Such channels to provide,
The very founts of love for thee
Will soon be parched and dried.

For we must share, if we would keep,
That good thing from above;
Ceasing to give, we cease to have;
Such is the law of love.
—Richard Chenevix Trench.

ONLY LOVE

Lord and Father, great and holy!
Fearing naught, we come to thee;
Fearing naught, though weak and lowly,
For thy love has made us free.
By the blue sky bending o'er us,
By the green earth's flowery zone,
Teach us, Lord, the angel chorus,
"Thou art Love, and Love alone!"

Though the worlds in flame should perish,
Suns and stars in ruin fall,
Trust in thee our hearts should cherish,
Thou to us be all in all.
And though heavens thy name are praising,
Seraphs hymn no sweeter tone
Than the strains our hearts are raising,
"Thou art Love, and Love alone!"
—Frederic William Farrar.

That love for one from which there doth not spring
Wide love for all is but a worthless thing.
—James Russell Lowell.

JOHN AND JESUS

A voice by Jordan's shore!
A summons stern and clear:
Reform! be just! and sin no more!
God's judgment draweth near!

A voice by Galilee,
A holier voice I hear;
Love God! thy neighbor love! for, see,
God's mercy draweth near!

O voice of Duty, still
Speak forth; I hear with awe.
In thee I own the sovereign will,
Obey the sovereign law.

Thou higher voice of Love!
Yet speak thy word in me;
Through Duty let me upward move
To thy pure liberty!
—Samuel Longfellow.

WHAT REDRESS?

I pray you, do not use this thing
For vengeance; but if questioning
What wound, when dealt your humankind,
Goes deepest—surely he shall find
Who wrongs you, loving *him* no less—
There's nothing hurts like tenderness.
—James Whitcomb Riley.

FORGIVENESS

When on the fragrant sandal-tree
The woodman's axe descends,
And she who bloomed so beauteously
Beneath the keen stroke bends,
E'en on the edge that wrought her death
Dying she breathed her sweetest breath,
As if to token, in her fall,
Peace to her foes, and love to all.

How hardly man this lesson learns,
To smile, and bless the hand that spurns;
To see the blow, to feel the pain,
But render only love again!
This spirit not to earth is given—
ONE had it, but he came from heaven.
Reviled, rejected, and betrayed,
No curse he breathed, no plaint he made,
But when in death's deep pang he sighed
Prayed for his murderers, and died.

LOVE COUNTETH NOT THE COST

There is an ancient story, simply told,
As ever were the holy things of old,
Of one who served through many a toiling year
To earn at last the joy he held most dear;
A weary term, to others strangely lost.
What mattered it? Love counteth not the cost.

Yet not alone beneath far Eastern skies
The faithful life hath, patient, won its prize;
Whenever hearts beat high and brave hopes swell
The soul, some Rachel waits beside the well;
For her the load is borne, the desert crossed.
What matters it? Love counteth not the cost.

This then of man—and what, dear Lord, of thee,
Bowed in the midnight of Gethsemane—
Come from those regions infinite with peace,
To buy with such a price the world's release?
Thy voice descends, through ages tempest-tossed,
"What matters it? Love counteth not the cost."

O Christ, Redeemer, Master! I who stand
Beneath the pressure of thy gracious hand—
What is the service thou wouldst have from me?
What is the burden to be borne for thee?
I, too, would say, though care and fear exhaust,
"What matters it? Love counteth not the cost."

LOVE OF HOME

Thy voice is heard through rolling drums
That beat to battle where he stands;
Thy face across his fancy comes,
And gives the battle to his hands.
A moment, while the trumpets blow,
He sees his brood about thy knee;
The next, like fire he meets the foe,
And strikes him dead for thine and thee.

—Alfred Tennyson.

BE KIND TO THYSELF

Comes a message from above—
"As thyself thy neighbor love."
With myself so vexed I grow—
Of my weakness weary so;
Easier may I tolerate
My neighbor than myself not hate.

Take not part of thee for whole;
Thou art neighbor to thy soul;
The ray from heaven that gilds the clod
Love thou, for it comes from God.
Bear thou with thy human clay,
Lest thou miss the heaven-sent ray.

—Edward Sandford Martin.

LOVE AND LIGHT

Through love to light! oh wonderful the way
That leads from darkness to the perfect day!
From darkness and from sorrow of the night
To morning that comes singing o'er the sea,
Through love to light! Through light, O God, to thee,
Who art the love of love, the eternal light of light.

—Richard Watson Gilder.

SYMPATHETIC LOVE

O Love divine, that stooped to share
Our sharpest pang, our bitterest tear!
On thee we cast each earthborn care;
We smile at pain while thou art near.

Though long the weary way we tread,
And sorrow crown each lingering year,
No path we shun, no darkness dread,
Our hearts still whispering, "Thou art near!"

When drooping pleasure turns to grief
And trembling faith is changed to fear,
The murmuring wind, the quivering leaf,
Shall softly tell us, "Thou art near!"

On thee we fling our burdening woe,
O Love divine, forever dear;
Content to suffer while we know,
Living and dying, thou art near!

—Oliver Wendell Holmes.

Love took up the glass of Time, and turned it in his glowing hands;
Every moment, lightly shaken, ran itself in golden sands.
Love took up the harp of Life, and smote on all the chords with might;
Smote the chord of Self, that, trembling, passed in music out of sight.
—Alfred Tennyson.

For, lo! in hidden deep accord
The servant may be like his Lord.
And thy love, our love shining through,
May tell the world that thou art true,
Till those who see us see thee too.
—Anna Letitia Waring.

Who loves, no law can ever bind;
He'd cleave to God as well
Were there no golden heaven's reward,
And no dark cave of hell.
—Scheffler, tr. by Frederic Rowland Marvin.

To halls of heavenly truth admission wouldst thou win?
Oft knowledge stands without, while Love may enter in.
—Richard Chenevix Trench.

For others' sake to make life sweet
Though thorns may pierce your weary feet;
For others' sake to walk each day
As if joy helped you all the way.
While in the heart may be a grave
That makes it hard to be so brave.
Herein, I think, is love.

Talk not of wasted affection, affection never was wasted;
If it enrich not the heart of another, its waters, returning
Back to their springs, like the rain, shall fill them full of refreshment.
—Henry Wadsworth Longfellow.

Ah, yes! I would a phœnix be,
And burn my heart in Deity!
Then I should dwell by his dear side,
And in the self of God abide.
—Scheffler, tr. by Frederic Rowland Marvin.

The man is happy, Lord, who love like this doth owe:
Loves thee, his friend in thee, and, for thy sake, his foe.
—Richard Chenevix Trench.

HOPE

PROGRESS, OPTIMISM, ENTHUSIASM

THE PROMISED LAND—TO-MORROW

High hopes that burned like stars sublime
  Go down the heavens of freedom,
And true hearts perish in the time
  We bitterliest need them;
But never sit we down and say,
  There's nothing left but sorrow—
We walk the wilderness to-day,
  The Promised Land to-morrow.

Our birds of song are silent now,
  There are no flowers blooming,
But life beats in the frozen bough
  And freedom's spring is coming.
And freedom's tide comes up alway
  Though we may stand in sorrow;
And our good bark, aground to-day,
  Shall float again to-morrow.

Though hearts brood o'er the past, our eyes
  With shining futures glisten;
Lo! now the dawn bursts up the skies:
  Lean out your souls and listen!
The earth rolls freedom's radiant way,
  And ripens with her sorrow;
And 'tis the martyrdom to-day
  Brings victory to-morrow.

Through all the long night of the years
  The people's cry ascended;
The earth was wet with blood and tears
  Ere their meek sufferings ended.
The few shall not forever sway,
  The many toil in sorrow,
The bars of hell are strong to-day
  But Christ shall rise to-morrow.

'Tis weary watching wave on wave,
  But still the tide heaves onward;
We climb like corals, grave on grave,
  But build a pathway sunward;
We're beaten back in many a fray,
  But strength divine will borrow—
And where our vanguard rests to-day
  Our rear shall march to-morrow.

Then, Youth! flame-earnest, still aspire,
  With energies immortal,
To many a haven of desire
  Your yearning opes a portal.
And though age wearies by the way,
  And hearts break in the furrow,
We sow the golden grain to-day—
  The harvest comes to-morrow.

—Gerald Massey.

THE RIGHT MUST WIN

O it is hard to work for God,
  To rise and take his part
Upon this battle-field of earth,
  And not sometimes lose heart!

He hides himself so wondrously,
  As though there were no God;
He is least seen when all the powers
  Of ill are most abroad.

Or He deserts us at the hour
  The fight is all but lost;
And seems to leave us to ourselves
  Just when we need him most.

Yes, there is less to try our faith,
  In our mysterious creed,
Than in the godless look of earth
  In these our hours of need.

Ill masters good, good seems to change
  To ill with greatest ease;
And, worst of all, the good with good
  Is at cross purposes.

It is not so, but so it looks,
  And we lose courage then;
And doubts will come if God hath kept
  His promises to men.

Ah! God is other than we think;
  His ways are far above;
Far beyond reason's height, and reached
  Only by childlike love.

The look, the fashion, of God's ways
  Love's lifelong study are;
She can be bold, and guess, and act
  When reason would not dare.

She has a prudence of her own;
Her step is firm and free.
Yet there is cautious science, too
In her simplicity.

Workman of God! oh, lose not heart,
But learn what God is like,
And in the darkest battle-field,
Thou shalt know where to strike.

Thrice blest is he to whom is given
The instinct that can tell
That God is on the field when he
Is most invisible.

Blest, too, is he who can divine
Where real right doth lie,
And dares to take the side that seems
Wrong to man's blindfold eye.

Then learn to scorn the praise of men
And learn to lose with God;
For Jesus won the world through shame
And beckons thee his road.

God's glory is a wondrous thing,
Most strange in all its ways,
And, of all things on earth, least like
What men agree to praise.

God's justice is a bed where we
Our anxious hearts may lay,
And, weary with ourselves, may sleep
Our discontent away.

For right is right, since God is God,
And right the day must win;
To doubt would be disloyalty,
To falter would be sin.
—Frederick William Faber.

Let us believe
That there is hope for all the hearts that grieve;
That somewhere night
Drifts to a morning beautiful with light,
And that the wrong
Though now it triumphs, wields no scepter long.
But right will reign
Throned where the waves of error beat in vain.
—Frank L. Stanton.

To change and change is life; to move and never rest;
Not what we are, but what we hope, is best.
—James Russell Lowell.

HAVE HOPE

Have Hope! it is the brightest star
That lights life's pathway down:
A richer, purer gem than decks
An Eastern monarch's crown.
The Midas that may turn to joy
The grief-fount of the soul;
That paints the prize and bids thee press
With fervor to the goal.

Have Hope! as the tossed mariner
Upon the wild sea driven
With rapture hails the polar star—
His guiding light to haven—
So Hope shall gladden thee, and guide
Along life's stormy road,
And as a sacred beacon stand
To point thee to thy God.
—B. A. G. Fuller.

WAITING

Serene, I fold my hands and wait,
Nor care for wind or tide or sea;
I rave no more 'gainst time or fate,
For, lo! my own shall come to me.

I stay my haste, I make delays,
For what avails this eager pace?
I stand amid the eternal ways,
And what is mine shall know my face.

Asleep, awake, by night or day,
The friends I seek are seeking me;
No wind can drive my bark astray,
Nor change the tide of destiny.

What matter if I stand alone?
I wait with joy the coming years;
My heart shall reap where it has sown
And garner up its fruit of tears.

The waters know their own, and draw
The brook that springs in yonder height;
So flows the good, with equal law,
Unto the soul of pure delight.

The stars come nightly to the sky;
The tidal wave unto the sea;
Nor time nor space, nor deep nor high,
Can keep my own away from me.
—John Burroughs.

THE LARGER HOPE

O, yet we trust that somehow good
 Will be the final goal of ill,
 To pangs of nature, sins of will,
Defects of doubt and taints of blood;

That nothing walks with aimless feet;
 That not one life shall be destroyed,
 Or cast as rubbish to the void
When God hath made the pile complete;

That not a worm is cloven in vain;
 That not a moth with vain desire
 Is shriveled in a fruitless fire,
Or but subserves another's gain.

Behold, we know not anything;
 I can but trust that good shall fall
 At last—far off—at last, to all,
And every winter change to spring.

So runs my dream; but what am I?
 An infant crying in the night;
 An infant crying for the light,
And with no language but a cry.

. . . .

I falter where I firmly trod,
 And falling with my weight of cares
 Upon the great world's altar-stairs
That slope through darkness up to God,

I stretch lame hands of faith and grope,
 And gather dust and chaff, and call
 To what I feel is Lord of all,
And faintly trust the larger hope.
—Alfred Tennyson.

DESPONDENCY REBUKED

Say not, the struggle naught availeth;
 The labor and the wounds are vain;
The enemy faints not, nor faileth;
 And as things have been they remain.

If hopes were dupes, fears may be liars;
 It may be—in yon smoke concealed—
Your comrades chase e'en now the fliers,
 And, but for you, possess the field.

For while the tired waves, vainly breaking,
 Seem here no painful inch to gain,
Far back, through creeks and inlets making,
 Comes, silent, flooding in, the main.

And not by eastern windows only,
 When daylight comes, comes in the light;
In front the sun climbs slow—how slowly!
 But westward, look, the land is bright!
—Arthur Hugh Clough.

COMMIT THY WAY

Commit thy way to God,
 The weight which makes thee faint;
Worlds are to him no load,
 To him breathe thy complaint.
He who for winds and clouds
 Maketh a pathway free,
Through wastes or hostile crowds,
 Can make a way for thee.

Thou must in him be blest
 Ere bliss can be secure;
On his works must thou rest
 If thy work shall endure.
To anxious, prying thought,
 And weary, fretting care,
The highest yieldeth naught:
 He giveth all to prayer.

Father, thy faithful love,
 Thy mercy, wise and mild,
Sees what will blessing prove,
 Or what will hurt thy child;
And what thy wise foreseeing
 Doth for thy children choose
Thou bringest into being,
 Nor sufferest them to lose.

Hope, then, though woes be doubled;
 Hope and be undismayed;
Let not thy heart be troubled,
 Nor let it be afraid.
This prison where thou art—
 Thy God will break it soon,
And flood with light thy heart
 In his own blessed noon.

Up! up! the day is breaking;
 Say to thy cares, Good night!
Thy troubles from thee shaking
 Like dreams in day's fresh light.
Thou wearest not the crown,
 Nor the best course can tell;
God sitteth on the throne
 And guideth all things well.
—Paul Gerhardt, tr. by Elizabeth Rundle Charles.

THE SILVER LINING

There's never a day so sunny
  But a little cloud appears,
There's never a life so happy
  But has its time of tears;
Yet the sun shines out the brighter
  Whenever the tempest clears.

There's never a garden growing
  With roses in every plot;
There's never a heart so hardened
  But has one tender spot;
We have only to prune the border
  To find the forget-me-not.

There's never a sun that rises
  But we know 'twill set at night;
The tints that gleam in the morning
  At evening are just as bright;
And the hour that is the sweetest
  Is between the dark and light.

There is never a cup so pleasant
  But has bitter with the sweet;
There is never a path so rugged,
  Bearing not the print of feet,
But we have a helper furnished
  For the trials we may meet.

There is never a way so narrow
  But the entrance is made straight,
There is always a guide to point us
  To the "little wicket gate."
And the angels will be nearest
  To a soul that's desolate.

There is never a heart so haughty
  But will some day bow and kneel;
  There is never a heart so wounded
  That the Saviour cannot heal;
There is many a lowly forehead
  Bearing now the hidden seal.

There's never a dream so happy
  But the waking makes us sad;
There's never a dream of sorrow
  But the waking makes us glad;
We shall look some day with wonder
  At the troubles we have had.

Yet sometimes glimmers on my sight,
Through present wrong, the eternal right;
And, step by step, since time began,
I see the steady gain of man.
—John Greenleaf Whittier.

FARTHER ON

I hear it singing, singing sweetly,
  Softly in an undertone,
Singing as if God had taught it,
  "It is better farther on!"

Night and day it sings the song,
  Sings it while I sit alone,
Sings so that the heart may hear it,
  "It is better farther on!"

Sits upon the grave and sings it,
  Sings it when the heart would groan,
Sings it when the shadows darken,
  "It is better farther on!"

Farther on? How much farther?
  Count the milestones one by one?
No! no counting—only trusting,
  "It is better farther on!"

NEW EVERY MORNING

Every day is a fresh beginning,
  Every morn is the world made new;
You who are weary of sorrow and sinning,
  Here is a beautiful hope for you—
  A hope for me and a hope for you.

All the past things are past and over,
  The tasks are done and the tears are shed;
Yesterday's errors let yesterday cover;
  Yesterday's wounds, which smarted and bled,
  Are healed with the healing which night has shed.

Yesterday is a part of forever,
Bound up in a sheaf which God holds tight;
With glad days, and sad days, and bad days, which never
  Shall visit us more with their bloom and their blight,
  Their fullness of sunshine or sorrowful night.

Let them go, since we cannot relieve them;
  Cannot undo, and cannot atone;
God in his mercy, receive, forgive them!
  Only the new days are our own.
  To-day is ours, and to-day alone.

Here are the skies all burnished brightly,
Here is the spent earth all reborn;
Here are the tired limbs springing lightly
To face the sun, and to share with the morn
In the chrism of dew and the cool of dawn.

Every day is a fresh beginning;
Listen, my soul, to the glad refrain,
And, spite of all sorrow and old sinning,
And puzzle forecasted, and possible pain,
Take heart with the day, and begin again. —Susan Coolidge.

CHEER UP

Never go gloomily, man with a mind;
Hope is a better companion than fear;
Providence, ever benignant and kind,
Gives with a smile what you take with a tear.
All will be right; look to the light;
Morning is ever the daughter of night;
All that was black will be all that is bright;
Cheerily, cheerily, then, cheer up.

Many a foe is a friend in disguise,
Many a sorrow a blessing most true,
Helping the heart to be happy and wise,
Bringing true love and joys ever new.
Stand in the van; strive like a man;
This is the bravest and cleverest plan—
Trusting in God while you do what you can,
Cheerily, cheerily, then, cheer up.

PROGRESS

Idly as thou, in that old day
Thou mournest, did thy sire repine;
So, in his time, thy child grown gray
Shall sigh for thine.

But life shall on and upward go;
Th' eternal step of Progress beats
To that great anthem, calm and slow,
Which God repeats.

Take heart! The Waster builds again;
A charmèd life old Goodness hath;
The tares may perish, but the grain
Is not for death.
—John Greenleaf Whittier.

THE VEILED FUTURE

Veiled the future comes, refusing,
To be seen, like Isaac's bride
Whom the lonely man met musing
In the fields at eventide.

Round him o'er the darkening waste
Deeper shades of evening fall,
And behind him in the past
Mother Sarah's funeral.

Mother Sarah being dead,
There comes his veilèd destiny;
The veiled Rebecca he must wed
Whatsoe'er her features be.

On he walks in silent prayer,
Bids the veiled Rebecca hail,
Doubting not she will prove fair
When at length she drops the veil.

When the veil is dropped aside,
Dropped in Mother Sarah's tent,
Oh! she is right fair, this bride
Whom his loving God has sent.

To those walking 'twixt the two—
'Twixt the past with pleasures dead
And the future veiled from view—
The veiled future thou must wed;

Walk like Isaac, praying God;
Walk by faith and not by sight;
And though darker grows the road
Doubt not all will yet come right.

Things behind forgetting, hail
Every future from above.
Doubt not when it drops the veil
'Twill be such as thou wouldst love.

Till at death-eve, when the past
Rings dear Mother Earth's own knells,
Bridal heaven unveils at last
With a peal of marriage bells.
—William Robertson.

The night is mother of the day,
The winter of the spring;
And ever upon old decay
The greenest mosses cling.
Behind the cloud the starlight lurks,
Through showers the sunbeams fall;
For God, who loveth all his works,
Has left his hope with all.
—John Greenleaf Whittier.

IMAGINARY EVILS

Let to-morrow take care of to-morrow;
Leave things of the future to fate;
What's the use to anticipate sorrow?
Life's troubles come never too late!
If to hope overmuch be an error,
'Tis one that the wise have preferred;
And how often have hearts been in terror
Of evils that never occurred.

Have faith, and thy faith shall sustain thee;
Permit not suspicion and care
With invisible bonds to acclaim thee,
But bear what God gives thee to bear.
By his spirit supported and gladdened,
Be ne'er by forebodings deterred;
But think how oft hearts have been saddened
By fear of what never occurred.

Let to-morrow take care of to-morrow;
Short and dark as our life may appear
We may make it still darker by sorrow,
Still shorter by folly and fear!
Half our troubles are half our invention,
And often from blessings conferred
Have we shrunk, in the wild apprehension
Of evils that never occurred.
—Charles Swain.

THE MORNING STAR

There is a morning star, my soul!
There is a morning star;
'Twill soon be near and bright, my soul,
Though now it seem so dim and far.
And when time's stars have come and gone,
And every mist of earth has flown,
That better star shall rise
On this world's clouded skies
To shine forever!

The night is well-nigh spent, my soul!
The night is well-nigh spent;
And soon above our heads shall rise
A glorious firmament.
A sky all clear and glad and bright,
The Lamb once slain its perfect light,
A star without a cloud,
Whose light no mists enshroud,
Descending never!

THREE LESSONS

There are three lessons I would write—
Three words as with a burning pen,
In tracings of eternal light,
Upon the hearts of men.

Have Hope. Though clouds environ now,
And gladness hides her face in scorn,
Put thou the shadow from thy brow—
No night but hath its morn.

Have Faith. Where'er thy bark is driven—
The calm's disport, the tempest's mirth—
Know this: God rules the host of heaven,
The inhabitants of earth.

Have Love. Not love alone for one,
But man as man thy brother call;
And scatter like the circling sun
Thy charities on all.

Thus grave these lessons on thy soul—
Faith, Hope, and Love—and thou shalt find
Strength when life's surges rudest roll,
Light when thou else wert blind.
—Johann Christopher Friedrich von Schiller.

Knowing this, that never yet
Share of truth was vainly set
In the world's wide fallow;
After hands shall sow the seed,
After hands from hill and mead
Reap the harvests yellow.
—John Greenleaf Whittier.

Yet I argue not
Against Thy hand or will, nor bate a jot
Of heart or hope, but still bear up and steer
Right onward. —John Milton.

The world is growing better,
No matter what they say;
The light is shining brighter
In one refulgent ray;
And though deceivers murmur,
And turn another way,
Yet still the world grows better
And better every day.

Never give up! it is wiser and better
Always to hope than once to despair;
Fling off the load of Doubt's cankering fetter,
And break the dark spell of tyrannical care;
Never give up, or the burden may sink you—
Providence kindly has mingled the cup;
And in all trials and troubles bethink you
The watchword of life must be—
Never give up.

It's wiser being good than bad;
It's safer being meek than fierce;
It's fitter being sane than mad.
My own hope is a sun will pierce
The thickest cloud earth ever stretched;
That, after Last, returns the First,
Though a wide compass round be fetched;
That what began best, can't end worst,
Nor what God blest once, prove accurst.
—Robert Browning.

Hope, Christian soul! in every stage
Of this thine earthly pilgrimage,
Let heavenly joy thy thoughts engage;
Abound in hope.
Hope through the watches of the night;
Hope till the morrow brings the light;
Hope till thy faith be lost in sight;
Abound in hope.

God works in all things; all obey
His first propulsion from the night;
Wake thou and watch! the world is gray
With morning light.
—John Greenleaf Whittier.

When the sun of joy is hidden,
And the sky is overcast,
Just remember—light is coming,
And the storm won't always last.

The mist denies the mountains;
The wind forbids the sea;
But, mist or wind, I go to find
The day that calls to me.

For there are mornings yonder
And noons that call and call;
And there's a day with arms outheld,
That waits beyond them all.
—Josephine Preston Peabody.

Open the door of your hearts, my lads,
To the angel of Love and Truth
When the world is full of unnumbered joys,
In the beautiful dawn of youth.
Casting aside all things that mar,
Saying to wrong, Depart!
To the voices of hope that are calling you
Open the door of your heart.
—Edward Everett Hale.

A little bit of hope
Makes a rainy day look gay;
A little bit of charity
Makes glad a weary way!

Hope, child, to-morrow, and to-morrow still,
And every morrow hope; trust while you live.
Hope! each time the dawn doth heaven fill,
Be there to ask as God is there to give.
—Victor Hugo.

FAITH

ASSURANCE, DOUBT, UNBELIEF

THE ETERNAL GOODNESS

I bow my forehead to the dust,
  I veil mine eyes for shame,
And urge, in trembling self-distrust,
  A prayer without a claim.
No offering of mine own I have,
  Nor works my faith to prove;
I can but give the gifts he gave,
  And plead his love for love.

I dimly guess, from blessings known,
  Of greater out of sight;
And, with the chastened psalmist, own
  His judgments too are right.
And if my heart and flesh are weak
  To bear an untried pain,
The bruisèd reed he will not break,
  But strengthen and sustain.

I know not what the future hath
  Of marvel or surprise,
Assured alone that life and death
  His mercy underlies.
And so beside the silent sea
  I wait the muffled oar;
No harm from him can come to me
  On ocean or on shore.

I know not where his islands lift
  Their fronded palms in air;
I only know I cannot drift
  Beyond his love and care.
And thou, O Lord, by whom are seen
  Thy creatures as they be,
Forgive me if too close I lean
  My human heart on thee.
—John Greenleaf Whittier.

Forgive us, Lord, our little faith;
  And help us all, from morn till e'en,
Still to believe that lot the best
  Which is, not that which might have been.

And grant we may so pass the days
  The cradle and the grave between,
That death's dark hour not darker be
  For thoughts of what life might have been.

THE ONE THING NEEDFUL

My prayer to the promise shall cling—
  I will not give heed to a doubt;
For I ask for the one needful thing
  Which I cannot be happy without:

A spirit of lowly repose
  In the love of the Lamb that was slain;
A heart to be touched with his woes,
  And a care not to grieve him again;

The peace that my Saviour has bought,
  The cheerfulness nothing can dim,
The love that can bring every thought
  Into perfect obedience to him;

The wisdom his mercy to own
  In the way he directs me to take—
To glory in Jesus alone,
  And to love and do good for his sake.

All this thou hast offered to me
  In the promise whereon I will rest;
For faith, O my Saviour! in thee,
  Is the substance of all my request.

Thy word has commanded my prayer,
  Thy Spirit has taught me to pray;
And all my unholy despair
  Is ready to vanish away.

Thou wilt not be weary of me;
  Thy promise my faith shall sustain;
And soon, very soon, shall I see
  I have not been asking in vain.
—Anna Letitia Waring.

Ah, God! I have not had thee day and night
In thought, nor magnified thy name aright,
Nor lauded thee, nor glorified, nor laid
Upon thine altars one poor kusa-blade!
Yet now, when I seek refuge, Lord! with thee,
I ask, and thou wilt give, all good to me.
—Edwin Arnold, from the Sanskrit.

ABOVE ALL, THE SHIELD

Faith fails;
Then in the dust
Lie failing rest and light and trust.
So doth the troubled soul itself distress,
And choke the fountain in the wilderness.
I care not what your peace assails!
The deep root is, faith fails.

Faith fails
When in the breast
The Lord's sweet presence doth not rest;
For who believes, clouds cannot make afraid;
He knows the sun doth shine behind the shade;
He rides at anchor through the gales.
Do you not so? Faith fails.

Faith fails;
Its foes alarm,
And persecution's threats disarm;
False friends can scarcely wish it a good day,
Before it taketh fright and shrinks away.
When God doth guard, what foe prevails?
Why then the fear? Faith fails.

Faith fails;
Else cares would die,
And we should on God's care rely.
Man for the coming day doth grieve and fret,
And all past days doth sinfully forget.
For every beast God's care avails;
Why not for us? Faith fails.

Faith fails;
Then cometh fear,
If sickness comes, if death is near.
O man, why is it, when the times are bad
And the days evil, that thy face is sad?
How is it that thy courage quails?
It must be this: Faith fails.

My God!
Let my faith be
Living, and working actively
With hope and joy, that death may not surprise.
So let them sweetly close my eyes;
The Christian's life to death may yield—
Hope stands; faith has the field.

—S. C. Schœner.

LOOKING UNTO GOD

I look to Thee in every need,
And never look in vain;
I feel thy strong and tender love,
And all is well again:
The thought of thee is mightier far
Than sin and pain and sorrow are.

Discouraged in the work of life,
Disheartened by its load,
Shamed by its failures or its fears,
I sink beside the road;
But let me only think of Thee,
And then new heart springs up in me.

Thy calmness bends serene above
My restlessness to still;
Around me flows thy quickening life,
To nerve my faltering will;
Thy presence fills my solitude;
Thy providence turns all to good.

Embosomed deep in Thy dear love,
Held in thy law, I stand;
Thy hand in all things I behold,
And all things in thy hand;
Thou leadest me by unsought ways,
And turn'st my mourning into praise.

—Samuel Longfellow.

FAITH

If I could feel my hand, dear Lord, in thine,
And surely know
That I was walking in the light divine
Through weal or woe;

If I could hear thy voice in accents sweet
But plainly say,
To guide my groping, wandering feet,
"This is the way;"

I would so gladly walk therein; but now
I cannot see.
Oh, give me, Lord, the faith to humbly bow
And trust in thee!

There is no *faith* in seeing. Were we led
Like children here,
And lifted over rock and river-bed,
No care, no fear,

We should be useless in the busy throng;
Life's work undone;
Lord, make us brave and earnest, true and strong,
Till heaven is won.

—Sarah Knowles Bolton.

DOUBTING NOTHING

Acts 10. 9–20.

Not to thy saints of old alone dost Thou
In heavenly trance make known thy perfect will,
But to each hungry soul thy love would fill—
Descending out of heaven, we wist not how—
Comes by thy grace the holy vision now;
While we whose hearts should with the message thrill
Cry "Common and unholy!" to thee still,
And, uninspired, in grief before thee bow.

O Thou, whose Own the way we fare hath trod,
Give to thy children quick, discerning eyes
To see in life upspringing from the sod
All the divineness that within it lies,
Till humble service lift us to the skies
Who, "doubting nothing," seek thy will, O God!

—Louise Manning Hodgkins.

THE EYE OF FAITH

I do not ask for earthly store
Beyond a day's supply;
I only covet more and more
The clear and single eye.
To see my duty face to face
And trust the Lord for daily grace.

I care not for the empty show
That thoughtless worldlings see;
I crave to do the best I know,
And leave the rest with thee;
Well satisfied that sweet reward
Is sure to those who trust the Lord.

Whate'er the crosses mine shall be,
I will not dare to shun;
I only ask to live for thee,
And that thy will be done;
Thy will, O Lord, be mine each day,
While passing on my homeward way.

And when at last, my labor o'er,
I cross the narrow sea,
Grant, Lord, that on the other shore
My soul may dwell with thee,
And learn what here I cannot know:
Why thou hast ever loved me so.

—J. J. Maxfield.

HAVE FAITH IN GOD

Have faith in God! for he who reigns on high
Hath borne thy grief and hears the suppliant's sigh,
Still to his arms, thine only refuge, fly.
Have faith in God!

Fear not to call on him, O soul distressed!
Thy sorrow's whisper wooes thee to his breast;
He who is oftenest there is oftenest blest.
Have faith in God!

Lean not on Egypt's reeds; slake not thy thirst
At earthly cisterns. Seek the kingdom first.
Though man and Satan fight thee with their worst,
Have faith in God!

Go tell him all! The sigh thy bosom heaves
Is heard in heaven. Strength and grace he gives
Who gave himself for thee. Our Jesus lives;
Have faith in God!

FAITH IN GOD

Though time may dig the grave of creeds,
And dogmas wither in the sod,
My soul will keep the thought it needs—
Its swerveless faith in God.

No matter how the world began,
Nor where the march of science goes,
My trust in something more than man
Shall help me bear life's woes.

Let progress take the props away,
And moldering superstitions fall;
Still God retains his regal sway—
The Maker of us all.

Why cavil over that or this?
One thought is vast enough for me—
The great Creator was, and is,
And evermore will be.

A STRONGER FAITH

Perplext in faith, but pure in deeds,
At last he beat his music out.
There lives more faith in honest doubt,
Believe me, than in half the creeds.

He fought his doubts and gathered strength,
He would not make his judgment blind,
He faced the specters of the mind
And laid them; thus he came at length

To find a stronger faith his own,
And Power was with him in the night,
Which makes the darkness and the light,
And dwells not in the light alone.

—Alfred Tennyson.

A PERFECT FAITH

O for a faith that will not shrink
Though pressed by every foe,
That will not tremble on the brink
Of any earthly woe!

That will not murmur nor complain
Beneath the chastening rod,
But in the hour of grief or pain
Will lean upon its God;

A faith that shines more bright and clear
When tempests rage without;
That when in danger knows no fear.
In darkness feels no doubt;

That bears, unmoved, the world's dread frown,
Nor heeds its scornful smile;
That seas of trouble cannot drown,
Nor Satan's arts beguile.

Lord, give us such a faith as this,
And then, whate'er may come,
We'll taste, e'en here, the hallowed bliss
Of an eternal home.

—William H. Bathurst.

Who liveth best? Not he whose sail,
Swept on by favoring tide and gale,
Swift wins the haven fair;
But he whose spirit strong doth still
A victory wrest from every ill;
Whose faith sublime
On every cloud a rainbow paints—
'Tis he redeems the time.

BELIEVE GOOD THINGS OF GOD

When in the storm it seems to thee
That he who rules the raging sea
Is sleeping—still, with bended knee,
Believe good things of God.

When thou hast sought in vain to find
The silver thread of love entwined
With life's oft-tangled web—resigned,
Believe good things of God.

And should he smite thee till thy heart
Is crushed beneath the bruising smart,
Still, while the bitter tear-drops start,
Believe good things of God.

'Tis true, thou canst not understand
The dealings of thy Father's hand;
But, trusting what his love has planned,
Believe good things of God.

He loves thee! In that love confide—
Unchanging, faithful, true, and tried;
And let or joy or grief betide,
Believe good things of God.

Thou canst not raise thy thoughts too high;
As spreads above the earth the sky,
So do his thoughts thy thoughts outvie:
Believe good things of God.

In spite of what thine eyes behold;
In spite of what thy fears have told;
Still to his gracious promise hold—
Believe good things of God.

For know that what thou canst believe
Thou shalt in his good time receive;
Thou canst not half his love conceive—
Believe good things of God.

—William Luff.

BE NOT WEARY

Then, fainting soul, arise and sing;
Mount, but be sober on the wing;
Mount up, for heaven is won by prayer,
Be sober, for thou art not there.
Till death the weary spirit free,
Thy God hath said 'tis good for thee
To walk by faith, and not by sight,
Take it on trust a little while;
Soon thou shalt read the mystery right
In the full sunshine of his smile.

—John Keble.

ALL'S FOR THE BEST

All's for the best; be sanguine and cheerful;
Trouble and sorrow are friends in disguise;
Nothing but folly goes faithless and fearful,
Courage forever is happy and wise.

All's for the best, if a man would but know it;
Providence wishes us all to be blest;
This is no dream of the pundit or poet,
Heaven is gracious and all's for the best.

All's for the best; then fling away terrors;
Meet all your fears and your foes in the van;
And in the midst of your dangers or errors,
Trust like a child, while you strive like a man.

All's for the best; unbiased, unbounded,
Providence reigns from the east to the west;
And, by both wisdom and mercy surrounded,
Hope, and be happy, that all's for the best.

—Martin Farquhar Tupper.

BLEST IS THE FAITH DIVINE AND STRONG

Blest is the faith divine and strong,
Of thanks and praise an endless fountain,
Whose life is one perpetual song
High up the Saviour's holy mountain.

Blest is the hope that holds to God,
In doubt and darkness still unshaken;
And sings along the heavenly road,
Sweetest when most it seems forsaken.

Blest is the love that cannot love
Aught that earth gives of best and brightest;
Whose raptures thrill, like saints above,
Most when its earthly gifts are lightest.

Blest is the time that in the eye
Of God its hopeful watch is keeping,
And grows into eternity
Like noiseless trees when men are sleeping.

—Frederick William Faber.

GOD'S VOICE

Around my path life's mysteries
Their deepening shadows throw;
And as I gaze and ponder,
They dark and darker grow;
Yet still amid the darkness
I feel the light is near,
And in the awful stillness
God's voice I seem to hear.

Thy voice I hear above me,
Which says, "Wait, trust, and pray;
The night will soon be over,
And light will come with day."
Amen! the light and darkness
Are both alike to thee;
Then to thy waiting servant
Alike they both shall be.

That great unending future,
I cannot pierce its shroud,
But nothing doubt nor tremble,
God's bow is on the cloud;
To him I yield my spirit,
On him I lay my load;
Fear ends with death; beyond it
I nothing see but God.

—Samuel Greg.

FLOWERS WITHOUT FRUIT

Prune thou thy words; the thoughts control
That o'er thee swell and throng;—
They will condense within thy soul,
And change to purpose strong.

But he who lets his feelings run
In soft luxurious flow
Shrinks when hard service must be done,
And faints at every woe.

Faith's meanest deed more favor bears,
Where hearts and wills are weighed,
Than brightest transports, choicest prayers,
Which bloom this hour, and fade.

—John Henry Newman.

Fair is the soul, rare is the soul
Who has kept, after youth is past,
All the art of the child, all the heart of the child,
Holding his faith at last.

—Frank Gelett Burgess.

GOD KNOWS

God knows—not I—the devious way
  Wherein my faltering feet may tread,
Before into the light of day,
  My steps from out this gloom are led,
And, since my Lord the path doth see,
What matter if 'tis hid from me?

God knows—not I—how sweet accord
  Shall grow at length from out this clash
Of earthly discords which have jarred
  On soul and sense; I hear the crash,
Yet feel and know that on his ear
Breaks harmony—full, deep, and clear.

God knows—not I—why, when I'd fain
  Have walked in pastures green and fair,
The path he pointed me hath lain
  Through rocky deserts, bleak and bare.
I blindly trust—since 'tis his will—
This way lies safety, that way ill.

He knoweth, too, despite my will
  I'm weak when I should be most strong.
And after earnest wrestling still
  I see the right yet do the wrong.
Is it that I may learn at length
Not mine, but his, the saving strength?

His perfect plan I may not grasp,
  Yet I can trust Love Infinite,
And with my feeble fingers clasp
  The hand which leads me into light.
My soul upon his errands goes,
The end I know not—but God knows.

THE LORD'S LEADING

Thus far the Lord hath led us, in darkness and in day,
Through all the varied stages of the narrow homeward way;
Long since he took that journey—he trod that path alone;
Its trials and its dangers full well himself hath known.

Thus far the Lord hath led us; the promise hath not failed.
The enemy, encountered oft, has never quite prevailed:
The shield of faith has turned aside, or quenched each fiery dart,
The Spirit's sword in weakest hands has forced him to depart.

Thus far the Lord hath led us; the waters have been high,
But yet in passing through them we felt that he was nigh.
A very present helper in trouble we have found,
His comforts most abounded when our sorrows did abound.

Thus far the Lord hath led us; our need hath been supplied,
And mercy hath encompassed us about on every side;
Still falls the daily manna; the pure rock-fountains flow;
And many flowers of love and hope along the wayside grow.

Thus far the Lord hath led us; and will he now forsake
The feeble ones whom for his own it pleases him to take?
Oh, never, never! earthly friends may cold and faithless prove,
But his is changeless pity and everlasting love.

Calmly we look behind us, our joys and sorrows past,
We know that all is mercy now, and shall be well at last;
Calmly we look before us; we fear no future ill,
Enough for safety and for peace, if *Thou* art with us still.

Yes, they that know thy name, Lord, shall put their trust in thee,
While nothing in themselves but sin and helplessness they see.
The race thou hast appointed us with patience we can run,
Thou wilt perform unto the end the work thou hast begun.

Have you found your life distasteful?
  My life did and does smack sweet.
Was your youth of pleasure wasteful?
  Mine I saved, and hold complete.
Do your joys with age diminish?
  When mine fail me I'll complain.
Must in death your daylight finish?
  My sun sets to rise again.
I find earth not gray, but rosy;
  Heaven not grim, but fair of hue.
Do I stoop? I pluck a posy;
  Do I stand and stare? All's blue.
—Robert Browning.

WE SHALL KNOW

In wise proportion does a fond hand mingle
The sweet and bitter in our life-cup here;
Each drop of either is by love eternal
Poured forth in wisdom for his children dear.

The loving Father, as a wise physician,
Knows what the wants of all those children are;
Knows which is needed most—the joy or sorrow,
The peace of comfort, or affliction's war.

Then, should the bitter be our daily portion,
So that we cannot any sweet discern,
Let us, in childlike faith, receive with meekness
The needed tonic, and its lessons learn.

And if we cannot even that decipher,
Let us be still, nay, thank him for his care,
Contented that we soon shall know—hereafter—
When we the fullness of his presence share.
—Charlotte Murray.

THE STEPS OF FAITH

Know well, my soul, God's hand controls
Whate'er thou fearest;
Round him in calmest music rolls
Whate'er thou hearest.

Nothing before, nothing behind;
The steps of faith
Fall on the seeming void, and find
The rock beneath.

The Present, the Present is all thou hast
For thy sure possessing;
Like the patriarch's angel, hold it fast
Till it gives its blessing.
—John Greenleaf Whittier.

I am of sinfulness and sorrows full!
Thou art the Mighty, Great, and Merciful!
How should we not be friends, or thou not save
Me who bring naught to thee who all things gave?
—Edwin Arnold, from the Sanskrit.

MY GUIDE

I know not the way I am going,
But well do I know my Guide!
With a childlike trust do I give my hand
To the mighty Friend by my side;
And the only thing that I say to him,
As he takes it, is, "Hold it fast!
Suffer me not to lose the way,
And lead me home at last."

As when some helpless wanderer
Alone in some unknown land,
Tells the guide his destined place of rest,
And leaves all else in his hand;
'Tis home—'tis home that I wish to reach,
He who guides me may choose the way;
And little I care what path I take
When nearer home each day.

THE LORD'S PROVISION

In some way or other the Lord will provide;
It may not be *my* way, it may not be *thy* way;
And yet in his *own* way, "The Lord will provide."

At some time or other the Lord will provide;
It may not be *my* time, it may not be *thy* time;
And yet in his *own* time, "The Lord will provide."

Despond, then, no longer, the Lord will provide.
And this be the token—no word he hath spoken
Was ever yet broken: "The Lord will provide."

March on, then, right boldly; the sea shall divide;
The pathway made glorious, with shoutings victorious
We'll join in the chorus, "The Lord will provide."
—Mary Ann W. Cook.

It is faith,
The feeling that there's God. He reigns and rules
Out of this low world.
—Robert Browning.

FAITH IS THE VICTORY

Encamped along the hills of light,
  Ye Christian soldiers, rise,
And press the battle ere the night
  Shall veil the glowing skies;
Against the foe in vales below
  Let all our strength be hurled;
Faith is the victory, we know,
  That overcomes the world.

His banner over us is love,
  Our sword the word of God;
We tread the road the saints above
  With shouts of triumph trod;
By faith they, like a whirlwind's breath,
  Swept on o'er every field;
The faith by which they conquered death
  Is still our shining shield.

On every hand the foe we find
  Drawn up in dread array;
Let tents of ease be left behind,
  And—onward to the fray;
Salvation's helmet on each head,
  With truth all girt about,
The earth shall tremble 'neath our tread,
  And echo with our shout.

To him that overcomes the foe
  White raiment shall be given;
Before the angels he shall know
  His name confessed in heaven;
Then onward from the hills of light,
  Our hearts with love aflame,
We'll vanquish all the hosts of night
  In Jesus' conquering name.

—John H. Yates.

RELIGIOUS DIFFERENCES

Yes, we do differ when we most agree,
For words are not the same to you and me,
And it may be our several spiritual needs
Are best supplied by seeming different creeds.
  And, differing, we agree in one
  Inseparable communion,
If the true life be in our hearts; the faith
  Which not to want is death;
  To want is penance; to desire
  Is purgatorial fire;
To hope is paradise; and to believe
Is all of heaven that earth can e'er receive.

—Hartley Coleridge.

THE LORD WILL PROVIDE

Though troubles assail, and dangers affright,
Though friends should all fail, and foes all unite,
Yet one thing secures us, whatever betide,
The promise assures us, "The Lord will provide."

The birds, without barn or store-house, are fed;
From them let us learn to trust for our bread:
His saints what is fitting shall ne'er be denied,
So long as 'tis written, "The Lord will provide."

When Satan appears to stop up our path,
And fills us with fears, we triumph by faith;
He can not take from us, though oft he has tried,
The heart-cheering promise, "The Lord will provide."

He tells us we're weak, our hope is in vain;
The good that we seek we ne'er shall obtain:
But when such suggestions our graces have tried,
This answers all questions, "The Lord will provide."

No strength of our own nor goodness we claim;
Our trust is all thrown on Jesus's name:
In this our strong tower for safety we hide:
The Lord is our power, "The Lord will provide."

When life sinks apace, and death is in view,
The word of his grace shall comfort us through;
Not fearing or doubting, with Christ on our side,
We hope to die shouting, "The Lord will provide."

—John Newton.

Art thou afraid his power will fail
  When comes thy evil day?
And can an all-creating arm
  Grow weary, or decay!

IF WE BELIEVED

If we believed we should arise and sing,
Dropping our burdens at his piercèd feet.
Sorrow would flee and weariness take wing,
Hard things grow fair, and bitter waters sweet.

If we believed, what room for fear or care
Within his arms, safe sheltered on his breast?
Peace for our pain, and hope for our despair,
Is what he meant who said, "I give thee rest."

Why linger, turn away, or idly grieve?
Where else is rest—the soul's supremest need?
Grandly he offers; meanly we receive.
Yet love that gives us rest is love indeed.

The love that rests—say, shall it not do more?
Make haste, sad soul, thy heritage to claim.
It calms; it heals; it bears what erst ye bore,
And marks thy burdens with his own dear name.

Carried in him and for him, can they harm
Or press thee sore, or prove a weary weight?
Nay, nay; into thy life his blessed calm
Shall drop, and thou no more be desolate.

TO FAITH

Beside thy gracious hearth content I stay,
Or with thee fate's appointed journey go;
I lean upon thee when my step is slow,
I wrap me with thee in the naked day.

With thee no loneliness, no pathless way;
The wind is heaven's, to take as it shall blow;
More than thy voice, thy hand, I need not know;
I may not murmur, for I shall not stray.

WAIT ON GOD

Not so in haste, my heart!
Have faith in God, and wait;
Although he seems to linger long
He never comes too late.

He never comes too late;
He knoweth what is best;
Vex not thyself, it is in vain;
Until he cometh, rest.

Until he cometh, rest;
Nor grudge the hours that roll;
The feet that wait for God, 'tis they
Are soonest at the goal.

Are soonest at the goal
That is not gained by speed;
Then hold thee still, O restless heart,
For I shall wait his lead.
—Bradford Torrey.

BEGONE, UNBELIEF

Begone, unbelief, my Saviour is near,
And for my relief will surely appear.
His love in time past forbids me to think
He'll leave me at last in trouble to sink.

Since all that I meet shall work for my good,
The bitter is sweet, the medicine food;
Though painful at present, 'twill cease before long,
And then, oh, how pleasant the conqueror's song! —John Newton.

As yonder tower outstretches to the earth
The dark triangle of its shade alone
When the clear day is shining on its top,
So, darkness in the pathway of man's life
Is but the shadow of God's providence,
By the great Sun of Wisdom cast therein;
And what is dark below is light in Heaven.
—John Greenleaf Whittier.

Faith is a grasping of Almighty power;
The hand of man laid on the arm of God;
The grand and blessèd hour
In which the things impossible to me
Become the possible, O Lord, through thee. —Anna E. Hamilton.

There is no faith in seeing. Were we led
Like children here,
And lifted over rock and river bed,
No care, no fear,
We should be useless in the busy throng,
Life's work undone;
Lord, make us brave and earnest, in faith strong,
Till heaven is won.

The cross on Golgotha can never save
Thy soul from deepest hell;
Unless with loving faith thou setts't it up
Within thy heart as well.
—Scheffler, tr. by Frederic Rowland Marvin.

In vain they smite me. Men but do
What God permits with different view.
To outward sight they hold the rod,
But faith proclaims it all of God.
—Madame Guyon.

Talk Faith. The world is better off without
Your uttered ignorance and morbid doubt.
If you have faith in God, or man, or self,
Say so; if not, push back upon the shelf
Of silence lower thoughts till faith shall come.

The body sins not, 'tis the will
That makes the action good or ill.
—Robert Herrick.

Who never doubted, never half believed;
Where doubt, there truth is—'tis her shadow.
—Philip James Bailey.

'Tis not the grapes of Canaan that repay,
But the high faith that failed not by the way.
—James Russell Lowell.

No more with downcast eyes go faltering on,
Alone and sick at heart, and closely pressed.
Thy chains shall break, thy heavy heart is gone,
For he who calls thee, he will "give thee rest."
—Mary Lowe Dickinson.

My God, I would not live
Save that I think this gross hard-seeming world
Is our misshaping vision of the Powers
Behind the world that make our griefs our gains.
—Alfred Tennyson.

And all is well, though faith and form
Be sundered in the night of fear.
Well roars the storm to those that hear
A deeper voice across the storm.
—Alfred Tennyson.

The crowd of cares, the weightiest cross,
Seem trifles less than light;
Earth looks so little and so low,
When faith shines full and bright.
—Frederick William Faber.

A faith that shines by night and day
Will lighten every earthly load.

Grant us, O God, in love to thee—
Clear eyes to measure things below,
Faith the invisible to see,
And wisdom thee in all to know.

Our doubts are traitors,
And make us lose the good we oft might win,
By fearing to attempt.
—William Shakespeare.

TRUST

GUIDANCE, SAFETY, GLADNESS

RESTING IN GOD

Since thy Father's arm sustains thee,
Peaceful be;
When a chastening hand restrains thee,
It is he.
Know his love in full completeness
Fills the measure of thy weakness;
If He wound the spirit sore,
Trust him more.

Without murmur, uncomplaining,
In His hand.
Lay whatever things thou canst not
Understand.
Though the world thy folly spurneth,
From thy faith in pity turneth,
Peace thy inmost soul shall fill,
Lying still.

Like an infant, if thou thinkest
Thou canst stand,
Childlike, proudly pushing back
The offered hand,
Courage soon is changed to fear,
Strength doth feebleness appear;
In his love if thou abide,
He will guide.

Fearest sometimes that thy Father
Hath forgot?
When the clouds around thee gather,
Doubt him not.
Always hath the daylight broken;
Always hath He comfort spoken;
Better hath he been for years
Than thy fears.

Therefore, whatsoe'er betideth,
Night or day,
Know His love for thee provideth
Good alway.
Crown of sorrow gladly take;
Grateful wear it for His sake;
Sweetly bending to his will,
Lying still.

To his own thy Saviour giveth
Daily strength.
To each troubled soul that liveth,
Peace at length.
Weakest lambs have largest share
Of the tender Shepherd's care;
Ask him not the "When," or "How";
Only bow.

—Charles Rudolf Hagenbach.

I WILL TRUST

I am glad to think
I am not bound to make the world go right,
But only to discover and to do
With cheerful heart the work that God appoints.

I will trust in him
That he can hold his own; and I will take
His will, above the work he sendeth me,
To be my chiefest good.

—Jean Ingelow.

I KNOW NOT IF THE DARK OR BRIGHT

I know not if the dark or bright
Shall be my lot;
If that wherein my hopes delight
Be best or not.

It may be mine to drag for years
Toil's heavy chain;
Or day and night my meat be tears,
On bed of pain.

Dear faces may surround my hearth
With smiles and glee;
Or I may dwell alone, and mirth
Be strange to me.

My bark is wafted to the strand
By breath divine;
And on the helm there rests a hand
Other than mine.

One who has known in storms to sail
I have on board;
Above the raging of the gale
I hear my Lord.

He holds me when the billows smite;
I shall not fall;
If sharp, 'tis short; if long, 'tis light,
He tempers all.

Safe to the land, safe to the land!
The end is this:
And then with him go, hand in hand,
Far into bliss.

—Dean Alford.

I CAN TRUST

I cannot see, with my small human sight,
Why God should lead this way or that for me;
I only know he saith, "Child, follow me."
But I can trust.

I know not why my path should be at times
So straitly hedged, so strongly barred before;
I only know God could keep wide the door;
But I can trust.

I find no answer, often, when beset
With questions fierce and subtle on my way,
And often have but strength to faintly pray;
But I can trust.

I often wonder, as with trembling hand
I cast the seed along the furrowed ground,
If ripened fruit will in my life be found;
But I can trust.

I cannot know why suddenly the storm
Should rage so fiercely round me in its wrath;
But this I know—God watches all my path,
And I can trust.

I may not draw aside the mystic veil
That hides the unknown future from my sight;
Nor know if for me waits the dark or light;
But I can trust.

I have no power to look across the tide,
To see, while here, the land beyond the river;
But this I know, I shall be God's forever;
So I can trust.

The world is wide
In time and tide,
And God is guide;
Then do not hurry.
That man is blest
Who does his best
And leaves the rest;
Then do not worry.
—Charles F. Deems.

WISDOM OF DISCIPLINE

Whate'er my God ordains is right;
His will is ever just;
Howe'er he orders now my cause
I will be still, and trust.
He is my God,
Though dark my road,
He holds me that I shall not fall,
Wherefore to him I leave it all.

Whate'er my God ordains is right;
He never will deceive;
He leads me by the proper path,
And so to him I cleave,
And take, content,
What he hath sent;
His hand can turn my grief away,
And patiently I wait his day.

Whate'er my God ordains is right;
He taketh thought for me;
The cup that my Physician gives
No poisoned draught can be,
But medicine due;
For God is true;
And on that changeless truth I build,
And all my heart with hope is filled.

Whate'er my God ordains is right;
Though I the cup must drink
That bitter seems to my faint heart,
I will not fear nor shrink;
Tears pass away
With dawn of day;
Sweet comfort yet shall fill my heart,
And pain and sorrow all depart.

Whate'er my God ordains is right;
My Light, my Life, is he,
Who cannot will me aught but good;
I trust him utterly;
For well I know,
In joy or woe,
We soon shall see, as sunlight clear,
How faithful was our Guardian here.

Whate'er my God ordains is right;
Here will I take my stand;
Though sorrow, need, or death, make earth
For me a desert land.
My Father's care
Is round me there;
He holds me that I shall not fall,
And so to him I leave it all.
—S. Rodigast.

MY TIMES ARE IN THY HAND

"My times are in thy hand";
My God, I wish them there;
My life, my friends, my soul, I leave
Entirely to thy care.

"My times are in thy hand,"
Whatever they may be;
Pleasing or painful, dark or bright,
As best may seem to thee.

"My times are in thy hand";
Why should I doubt or fear?
My Father's hand will never cause
His child a needless tear.

"My times are in thy hand,"
Jesus, the crucified!
The hand my cruel sins had pierced
Is now my guard and guide.

"My times are in thy hand";
I'll always trust in thee;
And, after death, at thy right hand
I shall forever be.

—William F. Lloyd.

ALL FOR THE BEST

Away, my needless fears,
And doubts no longer mine;
A ray of heavenly light appears,
A messenger divine.

Thrice comfortable hope,
That calms my troubled breast;
My Father's hand prepares the cup
And what he wills is best.

If what I wish is good,
And suits the will divine,
By earth and hell in vain withstood,
I know it shall be mine.

Still let them counsel take
To frustrate his decree;
They cannot keep a blessing back,
By heaven designed for me.

Here, then, I doubt no more;
But in his pleasure rest
Whose wisdom, love, and truth, and power,
Engage to make me blest.

—Charles Wesley.

GOD NEVER FORSAKES

Leave God to order all thy ways,
And hope in him, whate'er betide,
Thou'lt find in him, in evil days,
Thy all-sufficient strength and guide.
Who trusts in God's unchanging love
Builds on the rock that naught can move.

What can these anxious cares avail,
The never-ceasing moans and sighs?
What can it help us to bewail
Each painful moment as it flies?
Our cross and trials do but press
The heavier for our bitterness.

Only thy restless heart keep still,
And wait in cheerful hope, content
To take whate'er his gracious will,
His all-discerning love, hath sent.
Nor doubt our inmost wants are known
To him who chose us for his own.

He knows when joyful hours are best;
He sends them as he sees it meet;
When thou hast borne the fiery test,
And now art freed from all deceit,
He comes to thee all unaware
And makes thee own his loving care.

Nor in the heat of pain and strife
Think God has cast thee off unheard,
And that the man whose prosperous life
Thou enviest is of him preferred.
Time passes, and much change doth bring
And sets a bound to everything.

All are alike before his face;
'Tis easy to our God most high
To make the rich man poor and base,
To give the poor man wealth and joy;
True wonders still by him are wrought
Who setteth up and brings to naught.

Sing, pray, and swerve not from his ways,
But do thine own part faithfully;
Trust his rich promises of grace,
So shall they be fulfilled in thee.
God never yet forsook at need
The soul that trusted him indeed.

—George Neumarck.

Bear up, bear on, the end shall tell
The dear Lord ordereth all things well.

—John Greenleaf Whittier.

THE SECRET PLACE

There is a safe and secret place,
Beneath the wings divine,
Reserved for all the heirs of grace:
O be that refuge mine!

The least and feeblest there may bide,
Uninjured and unawed;
While thousands fall on every side,
He rests secure in God.

He feeds in pastures large and fair
Of love and trust divine;
O child of God, O glory's heir,
How rich a lot is thine!

A hand almighty to defend,
An ear for every call,
An honored life, a peaceful end,
And heaven to crown it all!
—Henry F. Lyte.

GOD KNOWS

Our Father! through the coming year
We know not what shall be;
But we would leave without a fear
Its ordering all to thee.

It may be we shall toil in vain
For what the world holds fair;
And all the good we thought to gain
Deceive, and prove but care.

It may be it shall darkly blend
Our love with anxious fears,
And snatch away the valued friend,
The tried of many years.

It may be it shall bring us days
And nights of lingering pain;
And bid us take a farewell gaze
Of these loved haunts of men.

But calmly, Lord, on thee we rest;
No fears our trust shall move;
Thou knowest what for each is best,
And thou art Perfect Love.
—Eliza Cleghorn Gaskell.

Forever in their Lord abiding
Who can their gladness tell;
Within his love forever hiding,
They feel that all is well.

NO FEAR

I know no life divided,
O Lord of life, from thee;
In thee is life provided
For all mankind and me:
I know no death, O Jesus,
Because I live in thee;
Thy death it is which frees us
From death eternally.

I fear no tribulation,
Since, whatsoe'er it be,
It makes no separation
Between my Lord and me.
If thou, my God and Teacher,
Vouchsafe to be my own,
Though poor, I shall be richer
Than monarch on his throne.

If while on earth I wander
My heart is light and blest,
Ah, what shall I be yonder,
In perfect peace and rest?
O blessed thought! in dying
We go to meet the Lord,
Where there shall be no sighing,
A kingdom our reward.
—Carl J. P. Spitta.

THE LORD'S APPOINTMENT

I say it over and over, and yet again to-day,
It rests my heart as surely as it did yesterday:
It is the Lord's appointment;
Whatever my work may be,
I am sure in my heart of hearts
He has offered it to me.

I must say it over and over, and again to-day
For my work is different from that of yesterday:
It is the Lord's appointment;
It quiets my restless will
Like the voice of a tender mother,
And my heart and will are still.

I will say it over and over, this and every day,
Whatsoever the Master orders, come what may:
It is the Lord's appointment;
For only his love can see
What is wisest, best and right—
What is truly good for me.

TRUST

I know not what the future holds,
  Of good or ill for me and mine;
I only know that God enfolds
  Me in his loving arms divine.

So I shall walk the earth in trust
  That He who notes the sparrow's fall
Will help me bear whate'er I must
  And lend an ear whene'er I call.

It matters not if dreams dissolve
  Like mists beneath the morning sun,
For swiftly as the worlds revolve
  So swiftly will life's race be run.

It matters not if hopes depart,
  Or life be pressed with toil and care,
If love divine shall fill my heart
  And all be sanctified with prayer.

Then let me learn submission sweet
  In every thought, in each desire,
And humbly lay at his dear feet
  A heart aglow with heavenly fire.

"SOMETIME"

Sometime, when all life's lessons have been learned,
  And sun and stars forevermore have set,
The things which our weak judgment here had spurned,
  The things o'er which we grieve with lashes wet,
Will flash before us out of life's dark night,
  As stars shine most in deeper tints of blue,
And we shall see how all God's plans were right,
  And how what seemed reproof was love most true.

And we shall see how, while we frown and sigh,
  God's plans go on as best for you and me;
How when we called he heeded not our cry,
  Because his wisdom to the end could see;
And even as prudent parents disallow
  Too much of sweet to crooning baby's best,
So God perhaps is keeping from us now
  Life's sweetest things because it seemeth best.

And if sometimes commingled with life's wine
  We find the wormwood, and rebel and shrink,
Be sure a wiser hand than yours or mine
  Poured out the potion for our lips to drink;
And if some one we love is lying low,
  Where human kisses can not reach the face,
O do not blame the loving Father so,
  But wear your sorrow with obedient grace,

And you will shortly know that lengthened breath
  Is not the sweetest gift God gives his friend;
And that sometimes the sable pall of death
  Conceals the fairest boon his love can send.
If we could push ajar the gates of life,
  And stand within, and all God's workings see,
We could interpret all this doubt and strife,
  And for each mystery could find a key.

But not to-day. Then be content, poor heart,
  God's plans, like lilies pure and white, unfold;
We must not tear the close-shut leaves apart,
  Time will reveal the calyxes of gold.
And if through patient toil we reach the land
  Where tired feet with sandals loosed may rest,
When we shall clearly know and understand,
  I think that we will say: "God knew the best."

—May Louise Riley Smith.

O why and whither? God knows all;
  I only know that he is good,
And that whatever may befall,
  Or here or there, must be the best that could.
For He is merciful as just;
  And so, by faith correcting sight,
I bow before his will, and trust
Howe'er they seem he doeth all things right.

—John Greenleaf Whittier.

NOT KNOWING

I know not what shall befall me;
God hangs a mist o'er my eyes,
And thus each step of my onward path
He makes new scenes to rise,
And every joy he sends me comes
As a sweet and glad surprise.

I see not a step before me
As I tread on another year;
But the past is in God's keeping,
The future his mercy shall clear,
And what looks dark in the distance
May brighten as I draw near.

For perhaps the dreaded future
Is less bitter than I think;
The Lord may sweeten the waters
Before I stoop to drink,
Or, if Marah must be Marah,
He will stand beside its brink.

It may be he keeps waiting
Till the coming of my feet
Some gift of such rare blessedness,
Some joy so strangely sweet,
That my lips shall only tremble
With the thanks they cannot speak.

O restful, blissful ignorance!
'Tis blessed not to know,
It stills me in those mighty arms
Which will not let me go,
And hushes my soul to rest
On the bosom which loves me so!

So I go on not knowing;
I would not if I might;
I would rather walk in the dark with God
Than go alone in the light;
I would rather walk with him by faith,
Than walk alone by sight.

My heart shrinks back from trials
Which the future may disclose,
Yet I never had a sorrow
But what the dear Lord chose;
So I send the coming tears back
With the whispered word, "He knows."

—Mary Gardner Brainard.

"Trust is truer than our fears,"
Runs the legend through the moss;
"Gain is not in added years,
Nor in death is loss."

—John Greenleaf Whittier.

CONFIDO ET CONQUIESCO

Fret not, poor soul; while doubt and fear
Disturb thy breast,
The pitying angels, who can see
How vain thy wild regret must be,
Say, "Trust and Rest."

Plan not, nor scheme, but calmly wait;
His choice is best;
While blind and erring is thy sight
His wisdom sees and judges right;
So Trust and Rest.

Strive not, nor struggle; thy poor might
Can never wrest
The meanest thing to serve thy will;
All power is his alone. Be still,
And Trust and Rest.

Desire thou not; self-love is strong
Within thy breast,
And yet he loves thee better still:
So let him do his loving will,
And Trust and Rest.

What dost thou fear? His wisdom reigns
Supreme confessed;
His power is infinite; his love
Thy deepest, fondest dreams above!
So Trust and Rest.

—Adelaide Anne Procter.

BE CAREFUL FOR NOTHING

My spirit on thy care,
Blest Saviour, I recline;
Thou wilt not leave me to despair,
For thou art Love divine.

In Thee I place my trust,
On thee I calmly rest;
I know thee good, I know thee just,
And count thy choice the best.

Whate'er events betide,
Thy will they all perform;
Safe in thy breast my head I hide,
Nor fear the coming storm.

Let good or ill befall,
It must be good for me;
Secure of having thee in all,
Of having all in thee.

—Henry F. Lyte.

IN HIM CONFIDING

Sometimes a light surprises
  The Christian while he sings;
It is the Lord who rises
  With healing on his wings.
When comforts are declining
  He grants the soul again
A season of clear shining,
  To cheer it after rain.

In holy contemplation
  We sweetly then pursue
The theme of God's salvation,
  And find it ever new.
Set free from present sorrow,
  We cheerfully can say,
Let the unknown to-morrow
  Bring with it what it may.

It can bring with it nothing
  But He will bear us through;
Who gives the lilies clothing,
  Will clothe his people too.
Beneath the spreading heavens
  No creature but is fed;
And He who feeds the ravens
  Will give his children bread.

Though vine nor fig tree neither
  Their wonted fruit should bear,
Though all the fields should wither,
  Nor flocks nor herds be there;
Yet God the same abiding,
  His praise shall tune my voice;
For while in him confiding,
  I cannot but rejoice.

—William Cowper.

TRUSTING GOD

Whoever plants a leaf beneath the sod,
And waits to see it push away the clod,
    He trusts in God.

Whoever says, when clouds are in the sky,
"Be patient, heart; light breaketh by and by,"
    He trusts in God.

Whoever sees 'neath winter's field of snow
The silent harvest of the future grow,
    God's power must know.

Whoever lies down on his couch to sleep,
Content to lock each sense in slumber deep,
    Knows God will keep.

TRUST IN GOD

The child leans on its parent's breast,
Leaves there its cares and is at rest;
The bird sits singing by his nest,
    And tells aloud
His trust in God, and so is blest
    'Neath every cloud.

He has no store, he sows no seed;
Yet sings aloud, and doth not heed;
By flowing stream or grassy mead,
    He sings to shame
Men, who forget, in fear of need,
    A Father's name.

The heart that trusts for ever sings,
And feels as light as it had wings;
A well of peace within it springs;
    Come good or ill.
Whate'er to-day, to-morrow, brings,
    It is his will.

—Isaac Williams.

NO FEARS

Give to the winds thy fears;
  Hope, and be undismayed;
God hears thy sighs and counts thy tears;
  God shall lift up thy head.

Through waves, and clouds, and storms,
  He gently clears thy way;
Wait thou his time, so shall this night
  Soon end in joyous day.

Still heavy is thy heart?
  Still sink thy spirits down?
Cast off the weight, let fear depart,
  And every care be gone.

What though thou rulest not?
  Yet heaven, and earth, and hell
Proclaim, "God sitteth on the throne,
  And ruleth all things well."

Leave to his sovereign sway
  To choose and to command:
So shalt thou, wondering, own his way,
  How wise, how strong his hand!

Far, far above thy thought,
  His counsel shall appear,
When fully he the work hath wrought
  That caused thy needless fear.

—Paul Gerhardt.

SIMPLE TRUST

I do not know why sin abounds
Within this world so fair,
Why numerous discordant sounds
Destroy the heavenly air—
I can't explain this thing, I must
Rely on God in simple trust.

I do not know why pain and loss
Oft fall unto my lot.
Why I must bear the heavy cross
When I desire it not—
I do not know, unless 'tis just
To teach my soul in God to trust.

I know not why the evil seems
Supreme on every hand:
Why suffering flows in endless streams
I do not understand—
Solution comes not to adjust
These mysteries. I can but trust.

I do not know why grief's dark cloud
Bedims my sunny sky,
The tear of bitterness allowed
To swell within my eye—
But, sorrow-stricken to the dust,
I will look up to God and trust.

—R. F. Mayer.

ALL IS YOURS

O foolish heart, be still!
And vex thyself no more!
Wait thou for God, until
He open pleasure's door.
Thou knowest not what is good for thee,
But God doth know—
Let him thy strong reliance be,
And rest thee so.

He counted all my days,
And every joy and tear,
Ere I knew how to praise,
Or even had learned to fear.
Before I him my Father knew
He called me child;
His help has guarded me all through
This weary wild.

The least of all my cares
Is not to him unknown—
He sees and he prepares
The pathway for his own;
And what his hand assigns to me,
That serves my peace;
The greatest burden it might be,
Yet joys increase.

I live no more for earth;
Nor seek my full joy here;
The world seems little worth
When heaven is shining clear.
Yet joyfully I go my way
So free, so blest!
Sweetening my toil from day to day
With thoughts of rest.

Give me, my Lord, whate'er
Will bind my heart to thee;
For that I make my prayer,
And know thou hearest me!
But all that might keep back my soul—
Make thee forgot—
Though of earth-good it were the whole,
O give it not!

When sickness, pains, distress,
And want doth follow fear,
And men their hate express,
My sky shall still be clear.
Then wait I, Lord, and wait for thee;
And I am still,
Though mine should unaccomplished be,
Do thou thy will!

Thou art the strength and stay
Of every weary soul;
Thy wisdom rules the way
Thy pity does control.
What ill can happen unto me
When thou art near?
Thou wilt, O God, my keeper be;
I will not fear.

—Christian F. Gellert (1715-1769).

I SHALL NOT WANT

I shall not want: in desert wilds
Thou spreadst thy table for thy child;
While grace in streams, for thirsting souls,
Through earth and heaven forever rolls.

I shall not want: my darkest night
Thy lovely smile shall fill with light;
While promises around me bloom,
And cheer me with divine perfume.

I shall not want: thy righteousness
My soul shall clothe with glorious dress;
My blood-washed robe shall be more fair
Than garments kings or angels wear.

I shall not want: whate'er is good
Of daily bread or angels' food
Shall to my Father's child be sure,
So long as earth and heaven endure.

—Charles F. Deems.

NO CARES

O Lord! how happy should we be
If we could leave our cares to thee;
  If we from self could rest,
And feel at heart that One above,
In perfect wisdom, perfect love,
  Is working for the best.

For when we kneel and cast our care
Upon our God, in humble prayer,
  With strengthened souls we rise;
Sure that our Father, who is nigh
To hear the ravens when they cry,
  Will hear his children's cries.

How far from this our daily life;
How oft disturbed by anxious strife,
  By sudden wild alarm!
O could we but relinquish all
Our earthly props and simply fall
  On thine Almighty arms!

We cannot trust him as we should,
So chafes weak nature's restless mood
  To cast its peace away;
But birds and flowers around us preach
All, all, the present evil teach,
  Sufficient for the day.

O may these anxious hearts of ours
The lesson learn from birds and flowers,
  And learn from self to cease,
Leave all things to our Father's will,
And, in his mercy trusting, still
  Find in each trial peace.

—Joseph Anstice.

CARE CAST ON GOD

Lord, I delight in thee,
  And on thy care depend;
To thee in every trouble flee,
  My best, my only Friend.

When nature's streams are dried
  Thy fullness is the same;
With this will I be satisfied,
  And glory in thy name.

Who made my heaven secure
  Will here all good provide;
While Christ is rich can I be poor?
  What can I want beside?

I cast my care on thee;
  I triumph and adore;
Henceforth my great concern shall be
  To love and please thee more.

—John Ryland.

GOD KNOWS ALL

Nay, all by Thee is ordered, chosen, planned;
Each drop that fills my daily cup; thy hand
Prescribes for ills none else can understand.
  All, all is known to thee.

Be trustful, be steadfast, whatever betide thee,
  Only one thing do thou ask of the Lord—
Grace to go forward wherever he guide thee,
  Simply believing the truth of his word.

Whatsoe'er our lot may be,
  Calmly in this thought we'll rest
Could we see as thou dost see
  We should choose it as the best.

—Eliza Cleghorn Gaskell.

O FOR A PERFECT TRUST

O for the peace of a perfect trust,
  My loving God, in thee;
Unwavering faith, that never doubts,
  Thou choosest best for me.

Best, though my plans be all upset;
  Best, though the way be rough;
Best, though my earthly store be scant;
  In thee I have enough.

Best, though my health and strength be gone,
  Though weary days be mine,
Shut out from much that others have;
  Not my will, Lord, but thine!

And even though disappointments come,
  They, too, are best for me—
To wean me from this changing world
  And lead me nearer thee.

O for the peace of a perfect trust
  That looks away from all;
That sees thy hand in everything,
  In great events or small;

That hears thy voice—a Father's voice—
  Directing for the best;
O for the peace of a perfect trust,
  A heart with thee at rest!

A SONG OF TRUST

I cannot always see the way that leads
To heights above;
I sometimes quite forget that he leads on
With hands of love;
But yet I know the path must lead me to
Immanuel's land,
And when I reach life's summit I shall know
And understand.

I cannot always trace the onward course
My ship must take,
But, looking backward, I behold afar
Its shining wake
Illumined with God's light of love; and so
I onward go,
In perfect trust that he who holds the helm
The course must know.

I cannot always see the plan on which
He builds my life;
For oft the sound of hammers, blow on blow,
The noise of strife,
Confuse me till I quite forget he knows
And oversees,
And that in all details with his good plan
My life agrees.

I cannot always know and understand
The Master's rule;
I cannot always do the tasks he gives
In life's hard school;
But I am learning, with his help, to solve
Them one by one,
And, when I cannot understand, to say,
"Thy will be done."
—Gertrude Benedict Custis.

ALL IS WELL

The clouds which rise with thunder slake
Our thirsty souls with rain;
The blow most dreaded falls to break
From off our limbs a chain;
And wrongs of man to man but make
The love of God more plain.
As through the shadowy lens of even
The eye looks farthest into heaven—
On gleams of star and depths of blue
The glaring sunshine never knew.
—Johh Greenleaf Whittier.

CHOOSE FOR US, GOD

Still will we trust, though earth seem dark and dreary,
And the heart faint beneath his chastening rod;
Though rough and steep our pathway, worn and weary,
Still will we trust in God.

Our eyes see dimly till by faith anointed,
And our blind choosing brings us grief and pain;
Through him alone who hath our way appointed,
We find our peace again.

Choose for us, God! nor let our weak preferring
Cheat our poor souls of good thou hast designed;
Choose for us, God! thy wisdom is unerring,
And we are fools and blind.

Let us press on in patient self-denial,
Accept the hardship, shrink not from the loss;
Our portion lies beyond the hour of trial,
Our crown beyond the cross.
—William H. Burleigh.

ALL THINGS WORK GOOD

With strength of righteous purpose in the heart
What cause to fear for consequence of deed?
God guideth then, not we; nor do we need
To care for aught but that we play our part.
Most simple trust is often highest art.
The issue we would fly may be a seed
Ordained by God to bear our souls a meed
Of peace that no self-judging could impart.
"All things work good for him who trusteth God!"
Doth God not love us with a longing love
To make us happy, and hath he not sight
From end to end of our short earthly road?
This, Lord, I hold—aye, *know* that thou wouldst move
The world to lead one trusting soul aright.
—Edward Harding.

RELIGIOUS INFIDELS

How many chatterers of a creed
  Think doubt the gravest sin,
Jnmindful of her double birth—
  For worry is her twin.

\h! Christian atheism seems
  The most insulting kind,
'or, though the tongue says, God is love,
  The heart is deaf and blind.

Iow he who marks the sparrow's fall
  Must be aggrieved to see
These loud lip-champions manifest
  Such infidelity!

Each fretful line upon their brow,
  Dug by the plow of care,
s treason to their pledge of faith
  And satire on their prayer.

) just to hold, without one fear,
  The strong, warm Hand above,
Vith orthodoxy of the heart—
  The childlike creed of love!

None such can be a heretic;
  Nay, only he forsooth
Who lives the falsity of doubt,
  But prates the cant of truth.
    —Frederic Lawrence Knowles.

Vorry and Fret were two little men
That knocked at my door again and
    again.
'O pray let us in, but to tarry a night,
\nd we will be off with the dawning of
    light."
\t last, moved to pity, I opened the door
To shelter these travelers, hungry and
    poor;
But when on the morrow I bade them
    "Adieu,"
They said, quite unmoved, "We'll tarry
    with you."
\nd, deaf to entreaty and callous to
    threat,
These troublesome guests abide with me
    yet.

Yet, in the maddening maze of things,
  And tossed by storm and flood,
To one fixed trust my spirit clings:
  I know that God is good!
    —John Greenleaf Whittier.

MAKE THY WAY MINE

Father, hold thou my hand;
  The way is steep;
I cannot see the path my feet must keep,
I cannot tell, so dark the tangled way,
  Where next to step. O stay;
Come close; take both my hands in thine;
  Make thy way mine!

Lead me. I may not stay;
I must move on; but oh, the way!
  I must be brave and go,
Step forward in the dark, nor know
If I shall reach the goal at all—
  If I shall fall.
  Take thou my hand.
Take it! Thou knowest best
How I should go, and all the rest
  I cannot, cannot see:
Lead me: I hold my hands to thee;
  I own no will but thine;
  Make thy way mine!

MY PSALM

All as God wills, who wisely heeds
  To give or to withhold;
And knoweth more of all my needs
  Than all my prayers have told!

Enough that blessings undeserved
  Have marked my erring track;
That wheresoe'er my feet have swerved,
  His chastening turned me back;

That more and more a Providence
  Of love is understood,
Making the springs of time and sense
  Sweet with eternal good;

That death seems but a covered way
  Which opens into light,
Wherein no blinded child can stray
  Beyond the Father's sight.
    —John Greenleaf Whittier.

What most you wish and long for
  Might only bring you pain;
You cannot see the future,
  God's purpose to explain.

So trust, faint heart, thy Master!
  He doeth all things well,
He loveth more than heart can guess,
  And more than tongue can tell.

BETTER TRUST

Better trust all and be deceived,
And weep that trust and that deceiving,
Than doubt one heart that, if believed,
Had blest one's life with true believing.

Oh, in this mocking world too fast
The doubting fiend o'ertakes our youth;
Better be cheated to the last
Than lose the blessed hope of truth.
—Frances Anne Kemble.

Be patient; keep thy lifework
Well in hand;
Be trustful where thou canst not
Understand;
Thy lot, whate'er it be, is
Wisely planned;
Whate'er its mysteries, God holds the key;
Thou well canst trust him, and bide patiently.

There is never a day so dreary
But God can make it bright;
And unto the soul that trusts him
He giveth songs in the night.
There is never a path so hidden
But God will show the way,
If we seek the Spirit's guidance
And patiently watch and pray.

Build a little fence of trust
Around to-day;
Fill the space with loving deeds,
And therein stay.
Look not through the sheltering bars
Upon to-morrow;
God will help thee bear what comes
Of joy or sorrow.
—Mary Frances Butts.

On God for all events depend;
You cannot want when God's your friend.
Weigh well your part and do your best;
Leave to your Maker all the rest.
—Cotton.

OUR STRONG STAY

Then, O my soul, be ne'er afraid;
On him who thee and all things made
With calm reliance rest;
Whate'er may come, where'er we go,
Our Father in the heavens must know
In all things what is best.
—Paul Fleming.

If the wren can cling
To a spray a-swing
In the mad May wind, and sing and sing
As if she'd burst for joy—

Why cannot I
Contented lie
In his quiet arms, beneath his sky,
Unmoved by life's annoy.
—Robert Haven Schauffler.

Be like the bird that, halting in her flight
Awhile on boughs too slight,
Feels them give way beneath her and yet sings—
Knowing that she hath wings.
—Victor Hugo.

Let not your heart be troubled, Jesus said;
Let not your heart be troubled or afraid.
My peace into your hands I freely give;
Trust in your God, and in his precepts live.

Thunder, lightning, fire and rain,
Poverty, sorrow, loss and gain,
Death and heaven, and earth and hell,
For us must work together well.

With patient course thy path of duty run
God nothing does, or suffers to be done,
But thou wouldst do the same if thou couldst see
The end of all events as well as he.

I welcome all thy sovereign will,
For all that will is love;
And when I know not what thou dost,
I wait the light above.

GOD'S CARE

PROVIDENCE, GOD'S KNOWLEDGE AND BENEFICENCE

CONSIDER THE RAVENS

Lord, according to thy words,
I have considered thy birds;
And I find their life good,
And better, the better understood;
Sowing neither corn nor wheat
They have all that they can eat;
Reaping no more than they sow
They have more than they could stow;
Having neither barn nor store,
Hungry again they eat more.

Considering, I see too that they
Have a busy life, but plenty of play;
In the earth they dig their bills deep,
And work well, though they do not heap;
Then to play in the way they are not loth,
And their nests between are better than both.

But this is when there blow no storms,
When berries are plenty in winter, and worms,
When feathers are rife, with oil enough
To keep the cold out and send the rain off;
If there come, indeed, a long, hard frost,
Then it looks as though thy birds were lost.

But I consider further and find
A hungry bird has a free mind;
He is hungry to-day, but not to-morrow,
Steals no comfort, no grief doth borrow;
This moment is his, thy will hath said it,
The next is nothing till Thou hast made it.

The bird has pain, but has no fear—
Which is the worst of any gear;
When cold and hunger and harm betide him,
He does not take them and stuff inside him;
Content with the day's ill he has got,
He waits just, nor haggles with his lot;
Neither jumbles God's will
With driblets from his own still.

But next I see, in my endeavor,
The birds here do not live forever;
That cold or hunger, sickness or age,
Finishes their earthly stage;
The rooks drop in cold nights,
Leaving all their wrongs and rights;
Birds lie here and birds lie there
With their feathers all astare;
And in thine own sermon, thou
That the sparrow falls dost allow.

It shall not cause me any alarm,
For neither so comes the bird to harm,
Seeing our Father, thou hast said,
Is by the sparrow's dying bed;
Therefore it is a blessèd place,
And a sharer in high grace.

It cometh therefore to this, Lord:
I have considered thy word;
And henceforth will be thy bird.
—George Macdonald.

GOD KEEPS HIS OWN

I do not know whether my future lies
Through calm or storm;
Whether the way is strewn with broken ties,
Or friendships warm.

This much I know: Whate'er the pathway trod,
All else unknown,
I shall be guided safely on, for God
Will keep his own.

Clouds may obscure the sky, and drenching rain
Wear channels deep;
And haggard want, with all her bitter train,
Make angels weep.

And those I love the best, beneath the sod
May sleep alone;
But through it all I shall be led, for God
Will keep his own.
—Sarah Knowles Bolton.

CARE THOU FOR ME

Care Thou for me! Let me not care!
Too weak am I, dear Lord, to bear
The heavy burdens of the day;
And oft I walk with craven feet
Upon life's rough and toilsome way;
How sweet to feel, how passing sweet,
Thy watchful presence everywhere!
Care Thou for me! Let me not care!

Care Thou for me! Why should I care,
And looks of gloomy sadness wear,
And fret because I cannot see
(Thy wisdom doth ordain it so)
The path thou hast marked out for me?
My Father's plan is best, I know,
It will be light, sometime—somewhere—
Care thou for me! Why should I care?

Care Thou for me! Let me not care!
This, each new day, shall be my prayer;
Thou, who canst read my inmost heart,
Dost know I am exceeding frail;
Both just and merciful thou art,
Whose loving kindness ne'er shall fail;
My human nature thou wilt spare;
Care Thou for me! I will not care!

THE SPARROW

I am only a little sparrow,
A bird of low degree;
My life is of little value,
But the dear Lord cares for me.

He gave me a coat of feathers;
It is very plain, I know,
With never a speck of crimson,
For it was not made for show,

But it keeps me warm in winter,
And it shields me from the rain;
Were it bordered with gold or purple
Perhaps it would make me vain.

I have no barn or storehouse,
I neither sow nor reap;
God gives me a sparrow's portion,
But never a seed to keep.

If my meal is sometimes scanty,
Close picking makes it sweet;
I have always enough to feed me,
And "life is more than meat."

I know there are many sparrows,
All over the world we are found;
But our heavenly Father knoweth
When one of us falls to the ground.

Though small, we are not forgotten;
Though weak we are never afraid;
For we know that the dear Lord keepeth
The life of the creatures he made.

HE KNOWETH ALL

The twilight falls, the night is near,
I fold my work away
And kneel to One who bends to hear
The story of the day.

The old, old story, yet I kneel
To tell it at thy call;
And cares grow lighter as I feel
That Jesus knows them all.

Yes, all! The morning and the night,
The joy, the grief, the loss,
The roughened path, the sunbeam bright,
The hourly thorn and cross—

Thou knowest all; I lean my head,
My weary eyelids close,
Content and glad awhile to tread
This path, since Jesus knows!

And he has loved me! All my heart
With answering love is stirred,
And every anguished pain and smart
Finds healing in the Word.

So here I lay me down to rest,
As nightly shadows fall,
And lean, confiding, on his breast,
Who knows and pities all!

If to Jesus for relief
My soul has fled by prayer,
Why should I give way to grief
Or heart-consuming care?
While I know his providence
Disposes each event
Shall I judge by feeble sense,
And yield to discontent?
Sparrows if he kindly feed,
And verdure clothe in rich array,
Can he see a child in need,
And turn his eyes away?

HE NEVER FORGETS

Nay, nay, do not tell me that God will not hear me.
I know he is high over all,
Yet I know just as well that he always is near me
And never forgets me at all.

He shows not his face, for its glory would blind me,
Yet I walk on my way unafraid;
Though lost in the desert He surely would find me
His angels would come to my aid.

He sits on his throne in the wonderful city,
And I—I am ashes and dust!
Yet I am at rest in His wonderful pity,
And I in his promises trust.

He lighteth the stars, and they shine in their places;
He maketh his sun like a flame;
But better and brighter to Him are the faces
Of mortals that call on his name.

Nay, nay! do not tell me that, wrapped in his glory,
He hears not my voice when I cry;
He made me! He loves me! He knows all my story!
I shall look on his face by and by!

THE SURE REFUGE

O I know the Hand that is guiding me
Through the shadow to the light;
And I know that all betiding me
Is meted out aright.
I know that the thorny path I tread
Is ruled with a golden line;
And I know that the darker life's tangled thread
The brighter the rich design.

When faints and fails each wilderness hope,
And the lamp of faith burns dim,
O! I know where to find the honey drop
On the bitter chalice brim.
For I see, though veiled from my mortal sight,
God's plan is all complete;
Though the darkness at present be not light,
And the bitter be not sweet.

I can wait till the dayspring shall overflow
The night of pain and care;
For I know there's a blessing for every woe,
A promise for every prayer.
Yes, I feel that the Hand which is holding me
Will ever hold me fast;
And the strength of the arms that are folding me
Will keep me to the last.

FOLLOWING

As God leads me will I go,
Nor choose my way.
Let him choose the joy or woe
Of every day;
They cannot hurt my soul,
Because in his control;
I leave to him the whole—
His children may.

As God leads me I am still
Within his hand;
Though his purpose my self-will
Doth oft withstand;
Yet I wish that none
But his will be done
Till the end be won
That he hath planned.

As God leads I am content;
He will take care!
All things by his will are sent
That I must bear;
To him I take my fear.
My wishes, while I'm here;
The way will all seem clear,
When I am there!

As God leads me it is mine
To follow him;
Soon all shall wonderfully shine
Which now seems dim.
Fulfilled be his decree!
What he shall choose for me
That shall my portion be,
Up to the brim!

As God leads me so my heart
In faith shall rest.
No grief nor fear my soul shall part
From Jesus' breast.
In sweet belief I know
What way my life doth go—
Since God permitteth so—
That must be best.

—L. Gedicke.

"YOUR HEAVENLY FATHER KNOWETH"

There are two words of light divine
That fall upon this heart of mine,
That thrill me in the hour of gain,
That still me in the hour of pain:
Two words endued with magic power,
Sufficient unto any hour—
He knows.

As summer breezes, cool and sweet,
Bring rest, relief from toil and heat;
As showers, needed as they fall,
Renew, refresh and comfort all;
So to my feverish heart is given
This loving message, fresh from heaven:
He knows.

My fainting heart finds strength in this,
My hungry heart here seeks its bliss;
Here angry billows never surge,
Here death can never sing its dirge;
My rising fears, with murmuring fraught,
Find sudden calm beneath this thought:
He knows.

O lullaby for children grown!
O nectar sweet for lips that moan!
O balm to stricken hearts oppressed!
O pillow where worn heads may rest!
All joy, all comfort in thee meet,
O blessed words, surpassing sweet,
He knows.

FEAR NOT

Don't you trouble trouble
Till trouble troubles you.
Don't you look for trouble;
Let trouble look for you.

Don't you borrow sorrow;
You'll surely have your share.
He who dreams of sorrow
Will find that sorrow's there.

Don't you hurry worry
By worrying lest it come.
To flurry is to worry,
'Twill miss you if you're mum.

If care you've got to carry
Wait till 'tis at the door;
For he who runs to meet it
Takes up the load before.

If minding will not mend it,
Then better not to mind;
The best thing is to end it—
Just leave it all behind.

Who feareth hath forsaken
The Heavenly Father's side;
What he hath undertaken
He surely will provide.

The very birds reprove thee
With all their happy song;
The very flowers teach thee
That fretting is a wrong.

"Cheer up," the sparrow chirpeth,
"Thy Father feedeth me;
Think how much more he careth,
O lonely child, for thee!"

"Fear not," the flowers whisper;
"Since thus he hath arrayed
The buttercup and daisy,
How canst thou be afraid?"

Then don't you trouble trouble,
Till trouble troubles you;
You'll only double trouble,
And trouble others too.

HE LEADS US ON

He leads us on
By paths we did not know;
Upward he leads us, though our steps be slow,
Though oft we faint and falter on the way,
Though storms and darkness oft obscure the day,
Yet when the clouds are gone
We know he leads us on.

He leads us on.
Through all the unquiet years;
Past all our dreamland hopes, and doubts, and fears,
He guides our steps. Through all the tangled maze
Of sin, of sorrow, and o'erclouded days
We know his will is done;
And still he leads us on.

And he, at last,
After the weary strife—
After the restless fever we call life—
After the dreariness, the aching pain,
The wayward struggles which have proved in vain,
After our toils are past,
Will give us rest at last.

THE DEVIL IS A FOOL

Saint Dominic, the glory of the schools,
Writing, one day, "The Inquisition's" rules,
Stopt, when the evening came, for want of light.
The devils, who below from morn till night,
Well pleased, had seen his work, exclaimed with sorrow,
"Something he will forget before tomorrow!"
One zealous imp flew upward from the place,
And stood before him, with an angel face.
"I come," said he, "sent from God's Realm of Peace,
To light you, lest your holy labors cease."
Well pleased, the saint wrote on with careful pen.
The candle was consumed; the devil then
Lighted his *thumb;* the saint, quite undisturbed,
Finished his treatise to the final word.
Then he looked up, and started with affright;
For lo! the thumb blazed with a lurid light.
"Your thumb is burned!" said he. The child of sin
Changed to his proper form, and with a grin
Said, "I will quench it in the martyrs' blood
Your book will cause to flow—a crimson flood!"

Triumphantly the fiend returned to hell
And told his story. Satan said, "'Tis well!
Your aim was good, but foolish was the deed;
For blood of martyrs is the Church's seed."

—Herder, tr. by James Freeman Clarke.

PROVIDENCE

We all acknowledge both thy power and love
To be exact, transcendent, and divine;
Who dost so strongly and so sweetly move,
While all things have their will, yet none but thine.

For either thy *command* or thy *permission*
Lay hands on all: they are thy right and left:
The first puts on with speed and expedition;
The other curbs sin's stealing pace and theft.

Nothing escapes them both; all must appear
And be disposed and dressed and tuned by thee,
Who sweetly temperest all. If we could hear
Thy skill and art what music would it be!

Thou art in small things great, nor small in any;
Thy even praise can neither rise nor fall.
Thou art in all things one, in each thing many;
For thou art infinite in one and all.

—George Herbert.

THE MYSTERIOUS WAY

God moves in a mysterious way
His wonders to perform;
He plants his footsteps in the sea
And rides upon the storm.

Deep in unfathomable mines
Of never-failing skill,
He treasures up his bright designs
And works his sovereign will.

Ye fearful saints, fresh courage take:
The clouds ye so much dread
Are big with mercy, and shall break
In blessings on your head.

Judge not the Lord by feeble sense,
But trust him for his grace;
Behind a frowning providence
He hides a smiling face.

His purposes will ripen fast,
Unfolding every hour;
The bud may have a bitter taste,
But sweet will be the flower.

Blind unbelief is sure to err,
And scan his work in vain;
God is his own interpreter,
And he will make it plain.

—William Cowper.

DISAPPOINTMENT

Our yet unfinished story
  Is tending all to this:
To God the greatest glory,
  To us the greatest bliss.

If all things work together
  For ends so grand and blest,
What need to wonder whether
  Each in itself is best!

If some things were omitted,
  Or altered as we would,
The whole might be unfitted
  To work for perfect good.

Our plans may be disjointed,
  But we may calmly rest;
What God has once appointed,
  Is better than our best.

We cannot see before us,
  But our all-seeing Friend
Is always watching o'er us,
  And knows the very end.

What though we seem to stumble?
  He will not let us fall;
And learning to be humble
  Is not lost time at all.

What though we fondly reckoned
  A smoother way to go
Than where his hand hath beckoned?
  It will be better so.

What only seemed a barrier
  A stepping-stone shall be;
Our God is no long tarrier,
  A present help is he.

And when amid our blindness
  His disappointments fall,
We trust his loving-kindness
  Whose wisdom sends them all;

The discord that involveth
  Some startling change of key,
The Master's hand revolveth
  In richest harmony.

Then tremble not, and shrink not,
  When disappointment nears;
Be trustful still, and think not
  To realize all fears.

While we are meekly kneeling
  We shall behold her rise,
Our Father's love revealing,
  An angel in disguise.

—Frances Ridley Havergal.

GOD'S CARE

Not a brooklet floweth
  Onward to the sea,
Not a sunbeam gloweth
  On its bosom free,
Not a seed unfoldeth
  To the glorious air,
But our Father holdeth
  It within his care.

Not a floweret fadeth,
  Not a star grows dim,
Not a cloud o'ershadeth,
  But 'tis marked by him.
Dream not that thy gladness
  God doth fail to see;
Think not in thy sadness
  He forgetteth thee.

Not a tie is broken,
  Not a hope laid low,
Not a farewell spoken,
  But our God doth know.
Every hair is numbered,
  Every tear is weighed
In the changeless balance
  Wisest Love has made.

Power eternal resteth
  In his changeless hand;
Love immortal hasteth
  Swift at his command,
Faith can firmly trust him
  In the darkest hour,
For the keys she holdeth
  To his love and power.

"I WILL ABIDE IN THINE HOUSE"

Among so many can he care?
Can special love be everywhere?
A myriad homes—a myriad ways—
And God's eye over every place?

Over; but *in?* The world is full;
A grand omnipotence must rule;
But is there life that doth abide
With mine own, loving, side by side?

So many, and so wide abroad;
Can any heart have all of God?
From the great spaces vague and dim,
May one small household gather him?

I asked; my soul bethought of this:
In just that very place of his
Where he hath put and keepeth you,
God hath no other thing to do.

—Adeline Dutton Train Whitney.

CONSTANT CARE

How gentle God's commands!
  How kind his precepts are!
Come, cast your burdens on the Lord,
  And trust his constant care.

Beneath his watchful eye
  His saints securely dwell;
That hand which bears all nature up
  Shall guard his children well.

Why should this anxious load
  Press down your weary mind?
Haste to your heavenly Father's throne
  And sweet refreshment find.

His goodness stands approved,
  Unchanged from day to day;
I'll drop my burden at his feet,
  And bear a song away.

—Philip Doddridge.

THOU KNOWEST

Thou knowest, Lord, the weariness and sorrow
  Of the sad heart that comes to thee for rest.
Cares of to-day and burdens for to-morrow,
  Blessings implored, and sins to be confest,
I come before thee, at thy gracious word,
And lay them at thy feet. *Thou knowest, Lord!*

Thou knowest all the past—how long and blindly
  On the dark mountains the lost wanderer strayed,
How the good Shepherd followed, and how kindly
  He bore it home upon his shoulders laid,
And healed the bleeding wounds, and soothed the pain,
And brought back life, and hope, and strength again.

Thou knowest all the present—each temptation,
  Each toilsome duty, each foreboding fear;
All to myself assigned of tribulation,
  Or to belovèd ones than self more dear!
All pensive memories, as I journey on,
Longings for sunshine and for music gone!

Thou knowest all the future—gleams of gladness
  By stormy clouds too quickly overcast—
Hours of sweet fellowship and parting sadness,
  And the dark river to be crossed at last:
Oh, what could confidence and hope afford
To tread this path, but this—*Thou knowest, Lord!*

Thou knowest not alone as God—all-knowing—
  As *man* our mortal weakness thou hast proved
On earth; with purest sympathies o'erflowing,
  O Saviour, thou hast wept, and thou hast loved.
And love and sorrow still to thee may come
And find a hiding-place, a rest, a home.

Therefore I come, thy gentle call obeying,
  And lay my sins and sorrows at thy feet;
On everlasting strength my weakness staying,
  Clothed in thy robe of righteousness complete.
Then rising, and refreshed, I leave thy throne,
And follow on to know as I am known!

A GREAT DIFFERENCE

Men lose their ships, the eager things
  To try their luck at sea,
But none can tell, by note or count,
  How many there may be.

One turneth east, another south—
  They never come again,
And then we know they must have sunk,
  But neither how nor when.

God sends his happy birds abroad—
  "They're less than ships," say we;
No moment passes but he knows
  How many there should be.

One buildeth high, another low,
  With just a bird's light care—
If only one, perchance, doth fall,
  God knoweth when and where.

HE CARETH FOR YOU

If I could only surely know
That all these things that tire me so
Were noticed by my Lord.
The pang that cuts me like a knife,
The lesser pains of daily life,
The noise, the weariness, the strife,
What peace it would afford!

I wonder if he really shares
In all my little human cares,
This mighty King of kings.
If he who guides each blazing star
Through realms of boundless space afar
Without confusion, sound or jar,
Stoops to these petty things.

It seems to me, if sure of this,
Blent with each ill would come such bliss
That I might covet pain,
And deem whatever brought to me
The loving thought of Deity,
And sense of Christ's sweet sympathy,
No loss, but richest gain.

Dear Lord, my heart hath not a doubt
That thou dost compass me about
With sympathy divine.
The love for me once crucified
Is not a love to leave my side,
But waiteth ever to divide
Each smallest care of mine.

MOMENT BY MOMENT

Never a trial that He is not there;
Never a burden that He doth not bear;
Never a sorrow that He doth not share.
Moment by moment I'm under his care.

Never a heart-ache, and never a groan,
Never a tear-drop, and never a moan,
Never a danger but there, on the throne,
Moment by moment, He thinks of his own.

Never a weakness that He doth not feel;
Never a sickness that He cannot heal.
Moment by moment, in woe or in weal,
Jesus, my Saviour, abides with me still.
—Daniel W. Whittle.

There's a divinity that shapes our ends
Rough-hew them how we will.
—William Shakespeare.

EVENING HYMN

It is the evening hour,
And thankfully,
Father, thy weary child
Has come to thee.

I lean my aching head
Upon thy breast,
And there, and only there,
I am at rest.

Thou knowest all my life,
Each petty sin,
Nothing is hid from thee
Without, within.

All that I have or am
Is wholly thine,
So is my soul at peace,
For thou art mine.

To-morrow's dawn may find
Me here, or there;
It matters little, since thy love
Is everywhere!

THE BELIEVER'S HERITAGE

No care can come where God doth guard;
No ill befall whom he doth keep;
In safety hid, of trouble rid,
I lay me down in peace and sleep.

I wholly love thy holy name;
I hail with glee thy glorious will;
Where'er I go, 'tis joy to know
That thou, my King, art near me still.

Thy power immense, consummate, grand,
Thy wisdom, known to thee alone,
Thy perfect love, all thought above,
Make me a sharer in thy throne.

With thee abiding none can fear,
Nor lack, of every good possessed;
Thy grace avails, whate'er assails,
And I in thee am fully blest.

Then leap, my heart, exultant, strong,
Cast every doubt and weight away;
Give thanks and praise to God always,
For he will guide to perfect day!
—James Mudge.

"HE CARETH FOR THEE"

What can it mean? Is it aught to him
That the nights are long and the days
are dim?
Can he be touched by griefs I bear
Which sadden the heart and whiten the
hair?
Around his throne are eternal calms,
And strong, glad music of happy psalms,
And bliss unruffled by any strife.
How can he care for my poor life?

And yet I want him to care for me
While I live in this world where the sor-
rows be;
When the lights die down on the path I
take,
When strength is feeble, and friends for-
sake,
When love and music, that once did
bless,
Have left me to silence and loneliness,
And life's song changes to sobbing
prayers—
Then my heart cries out for God who
cares.

When shadows hang o'er me the whole
day long,
And my spirit is bowed with shame and
wrong;
When I am not good, and the deeper
shade
Of conscious sin makes my heart afraid;
And the busy world has too much to do
To stay in its course to help me through,
And I long for a Saviour—can it be
That the God of the Universe cares for
me?

Oh, wonderful story of deathless love!
Each child is dear to that heart above;
He fights for me when I cannot fight;
He comforts me in the gloom of night;
He lifts the burden, for he is strong;
He stills the sigh and awakes the song;
The sorrow that bowed me down he
bears,
And loves and pardons because he cares.

Let all who are sad take heart again;
We are not alone in hours of pain;
Our Father stoops from his throne above
To soothe and quiet us with his love.
He leaves us not when the storm is high,
And we have safety, for he is nigh.
Can it be trouble which he doth share?
O rest in peace, for the Lord does care.

CAST THY BURDEN ON THE LORD

Thou who art touched with feeling of our
woes,
Let me on thee my heavy burden cast!
My aching, anguished heart on thee re-
pose.
Leaving with thee the sad mysterious
past;
Let me submissive bow and kiss the rod;
Let me "be still, and know that thou
art God."

Why should my harassed agitated mind
Go round and round this terrible
event?
Striving in vain some brighter side to
find,
Some cause why all this anguish has
been sent?
Do I indeed that sacred truth believe—
Thou dost not willingly afflict and
grieve?

My lovely gourd is withered in an hour!
I droop, I faint beneath the scorching
sun;
My Shepherd, lead me to some sheltering
bower;
There where thy little flock "lie down
at noon";
Though of my dearest earthly joy bereft
Thou art my portion still; thou, thou,
my God, art left.

—Charlotte Elliott.

Says God: "Who comes towards me an
inch through doubtings dim,
In blazing light I do approach a yard
towards him."

—Oriental, tr. by William Rounse-
ville Alger.

The light of love is round His feet,
His paths are never dim;
And He comes nigh to us, when we
Dare not come nigh to Him.

—Frederick William Faber.

Not in our waking hours alone
His constancy and care are known,
But locked in slumber fast and deep
He giveth to us while we sleep.

—Frederick Lucian Hosmer.

HIS CARE

God holds the key of all unknown,
And I am glad.
If other hands should hold the key,
Or if he trusted it to me,
I might be sad.

What if to-morrow's cares were here
Without its rest?
I'd rather he unlock the day,
And as the hours swing open say,
"Thy will be best."

The very dimness of my sight
Makes me secure;
For groping in my misty way,
I feel his hand; I hear him say,
"My help is sure."

I cannot read his future plan,
But this I know:
I have the smiling of his face,
And all the refuge of his grace,
While here below.

Enough; this covers all my want,
And so I rest;
For what I cannot he can see,
And in his care I sure shall be
Forever blest. —John Parker.

Forever, from the hand that takes
One blessing from us, others fall;
And soon or late our Father makes
His perfect recompense to all.
—John Greenleaf Whittier.

Nothing pays but God,
Served—in work obscure done honestly,
Or vote for truth unpopular, or faith maintained
To ruinous convictions.
—James Russell Lowell.

He did God's will, to him all one,
If on the earth or in the sun.
—Robert Browning.

I am
Part of that Power, not understood,
Which always wills the bad
And always works the good.
(Mephistopheles, in Faust.)
—Johann Wolfgang von Goethe.

I have no answer, for myself or thee,
Save that I learned beside my mother's knee:
"All is of God that is, and is to be;
And God is good." Let this suffice us still,
Resting in childlike trust upon his will
Who moves to his great ends unthwarted by the ill.
—John Greenleaf Whittier.

He knows, he loves, he cares,
Nothing his truth can dim;
He gives his very best to those
Who leave the choice to him.

No help! nay, it is not so!
Though human help be far, thy God is nigh.
Who feeds the ravens hears his children's cry;
He's near thee wheresoe'er thy footsteps roam,
And he will guide thee, light thee, help thee home.

God sees me though I see him not;
I know I shall not be forgot;
For though I be the smallest dot,
It is his mercy shapes my lot.
—From the Scandinavian, tr. by
Frederic Rowland Marvin.

Teach me to answer still,
Whate'er my lot may be,
To all thou sendest me, of good or ill,
"All goeth as God will."

Dance, O my soul! 'tis God doth play;
His will makes music all the day;
That song which rings the world around
This heart of mine shall ever sound.
—James Mudge.

Let one more attest:
I have seen God's hand through a life time,
And all was for best.
—Robert Browning.

GOD'S WILL

OBEDIENCE, DIVINE UNION

THE WILL OF GOD

I worship thee, sweet will of God!
  And all thy ways adore.
And every day I live I seem
  To love thee more and more.

Thou wert the end, the blessed rule
  Of our Saviour's toils and tears;
Thou wert the passion of his heart
  Those three and thirty years.

And he hath breathed into my soul
  A special love of thee,
A love to lose my will in his,
  And by that loss be free.

I love to kiss each print where thou
  Hast set thine unseen feet;
I cannot fear thee, blessed will!
  Thine empire is so sweet.

When obstacles and trials seem
  Like prison walls to be,
I do the little I can do,
  And leave the rest to thee.

I know not what it is to doubt;
  My heart is ever gay;
I run no risk, for come what will
  Thou always hast thy way.

I have no cares, O blessed will!
  For all my cares are thine;
I live in triumph, Lord, for thou
  Hast made thy triumphs mine.

And when it seems no chance or change
  From grief can set me free,
Hope finds its strength in helplessness,
  And gayly waits on thee.

Man's weakness waiting upon God
  Its end can never miss,
For man on earth no work can do
  More angel-like than this.

Ride on, ride on triumphantly,
  Thou glorious Will! ride on;
Faith's pilgrim sons behind thee take
  The road that thou hast gone.

He always wins who sides with God,
  To him no chance is lost;
God's will is sweetest to him when
  It triumphs at his cost.

Ill that he blesses is our good,
  And unblest good is ill;
And all is right that seems most wrong,
  If it be his sweet will!

—Frederick William Faber.

THE WILL DIVINE

Thy will, O God, is joy to me,
  A gladsome thing;
For in it naught but love I see,
  Whate'er it bring.

No bed of pain, no rack of woe—
  Thy will is good;
A glory wheresoe'er I go,
  My daily food.

Within the circle of thy will
  All things abide;
So I, exulting, find no ill
  Where thou dost guide.

In that resplendent will of thine
  I calmly rest;
Triumphantly I make it mine,
  And count it best.

To doubt and gloom and care and fear
  I yield no jot;
Thy choice I choose, with soul sincere,
  Thrice happy lot!

In all the small events that fall
  From day to day
I mark thy hand, I hear thy call,
  And swift obey.

I walk by faith, not sense or sight;
  Calm faith in thee;
My peace endures, my way is bright,
  My heart is free.

Unfaltering trust, complete content,
  The days ensphere,
Each meal becomes a sacrament,
  And heaven is here.

—James Mudge.

THE TREE GOD PLANTS

The wind that blows can never kill
The tree God plants;
It bloweth east, it bloweth west,
The tender leaves have little rest,
But any wind that blows is best;
The tree God plants
Strikes deeper root, grows higher still,
Spreads wider boughs, for God's good will
Meets all its wants.

There is no frost hath power to blight
The tree God shields;
The roots are warm beneath soft snows,
And when Spring comes it surely knows,
And every bud to blossom grows.
The tree God shields
Grows on apace by day and night,
Till sweet to taste and fair to sight
Its fruit it yields.

There is no storm hath power to blast
The tree God knows;
No thunderbolt, nor beating rain,
Nor lightning flash, nor hurricane—
When they are spent it doth remain.
The tree God knows
Through every tempest standeth fast,
And from its first day to its last
Still fairer grows.

If in the soul's still garden-place
A seed God sows—
A little seed—it soon will grow,
And far and near all men will know
For heavenly lands he bids it blow.
A seed God sows,
And up it springs by day and night;
Through life, through death, it groweth right;
Forever grows.

—Lillian E. Barr.

GOD'S WILL

Take thine own way with me, dear Lord,
Thou canst not otherwise than bless.
I launch me forth upon a sea
Of boundless love and tenderness.

I could not choose a larger bliss
Than to be wholly thine; and mine
A will whose highest joy is this,
To ceaselessly unclasp in thine.

I will not fear thee, O my God!
The days to come can only bring
Their perfect sequences of love,
Thy larger, deeper comforting.

Within the shadow of this love,
Loss doth transmute itself to gain;
Faith veils earth's sorrow in its light,
And straightway lives above her pain.

We are not losers thus; we share
The perfect gladness of the Son,
Not conquered—for, behold, we reign;
Conquered and Conqueror are one.

Thy wonderful, grand will, my God,
Triumphantly I make it mine;
And faith shall breathe her glad "Amen"
To every dear command of thine.

Beneath the splendor of thy choice,
Thy perfect choice for me, I rest;
Outside it now I dare not live,
Within it I must needs be blest.

Meanwhile my spirit anchors calm
In grander regions still than this;
The fair, far-shining latitudes
Of that yet unexplorèd bliss.

Then may thy perfect glorious will
Be evermore fulfilled in me,
And make my life an answering chord
Of glad, responsive harmony.

Oh! it is life indeed to live
Within this kingdom strangely sweet;
And yet we fear to enter in,
And linger with unwilling feet.

We fear this wondrous will of thine
Because we have not reached thy heart.
Not venturing our all on thee
We may not know how good thou art.

—Jean Sophia Pigott.

Deep at the heart of all our pain,
In loss as surely as in gain,
His love abideth still.
Let come what will my heart shall stand
On this firm rock at his right hand,
" Father, it is thy will."

—John White Chadwick.

THE CARPENTER

O Lord! at Joseph's humble bench
  Thy hands did handle saw and plane,
Thy hammer nails did drive and clench,
  Avoiding knot, and humoring grain.

That thou didst seem thou *wast* indeed,
  In sport thy tools thou didst not use,
Nor, helping hind's or fisher's need,
  The laborer's *hire* too nice refuse.

Lord! might I be but as a saw,
  A plane, a chisel in thy hand!
No, Lord! I take it back in awe,
  Such prayer for me is far too grand.

I pray, O Master! let me lie,
  As on thy bench the favored wood;
Thy saw, thy plane, thy chisel ply,
  And work me into something good.

No! no! Ambition holy, high,
  Urges for more than both to pray;
Come in, O gracious force, I cry,
  O Workman! share my shed of clay.

Then I at bench, or desk, or oar,
  With last, or needle, net, or pen,
As thou in Nazareth of yore,
  Shall do the Father's will again.
—George Macdonald.

THE DIVINE MAJESTY

The Lord our God is clothed with might,
  The winds obey his will;
He speaks, and in his heavenly height
  The rolling sun stands still.

Rebel, ye waves, and o'er the land
  With threatening aspect roar;
The Lord uplifts his awful hand,
  And chains you to the shore.

Ye winds of night, your force combine;
  Without his high behest,
Ye shall not, in the mountain pine,
  Disturb the sparrow's nest.

His voice sublime is heard afar;
  In distant peals it dies;
He yokes the whirlwind to his car
  And sweeps the howling skies.

Ye sons of earth, in reverence bend;
  Ye nations, wait his nod;
And bid the choral song ascend
  To celebrate our God.
—H. Kirke White.

THOU SWEET, BELOVED WILL OF GOD

Thou sweet, beloved will of God,
  My anchor ground, my fortress hill,
My spirit's silent, fair abode,
  In thee I hide me and am still.

O Will, that willest good alone,
  Lead thou the way, thou guidest best;
A little child, I follow on,
  And, trusting, lean upon thy breast.

Thy beautiful sweet will, my God,
  Holds fast in its sublime embrace
My captive will, a gladsome bird,
  Prisoned in such a realm of grace.

Within this place of certain good
  Love evermore expands her wings,
Or, nestling in thy perfect choice,
  Abides content with what it brings.

Oh lightest burden, sweetest yoke!
  It lifts, it bears my happy soul,
It giveth wings to this poor heart;
  My freedom is thy grand control.

Upon God's will I lay me down,
  As child upon its mother's breast;
No silken couch, nor softest bed,
  Could ever give me such deep rest.

Thy wonderful grand will, my God,
  With triumph now I make it mine;
And faith shall cry a joyous Yes!
  To every dear command of thine.

AS IT WAS TO BE

The sky is clouded, the rocks are bare!
The spray of the tempest is white in air;
The winds are out with the waves at
    play,
And I shall not tempt the sea to-day.

The trail is narrow, the wood is dim,
The panther clings to the arching limb;
And the lion's whelps are abroad at play,
And I shall not join in the chase to-day.

But the ship sailed safely over the sea,
And the hunters came from the chase in
    glee;
And the town that was builded upon a
    rock
Was swallowed up in the earthquake's
    shock. —Francis Bret Harte.

USEFUL ACCORDING TO GOD'S WILL

Let me not die before I've done for thee
My earthly work, whatever it may be;
Call me not hence with mission unfulfilled;
Let me not leave my space of ground untilled;
Impress this truth upon me, that not one
Can do my portion that I leave undone.

Then give me strength all faithfully to toil,
Converting barren earth to fruitful soil.
I long to be an instrument of thine
For gathering worshipers into thy shrine:
To be the means one human soul to save
From the dark terrors of a hopeless grave.

Yet most I want a spirit of content
To work where'er thou'lt wish my labor spent,
Whether at home or in a stranger's clime,
In days of joy or sorrow's sterner time;
I want a spirit passive to be still,
And by thy power to do thy holy will.

And when the prayer unto my lips doth rise,
"Before a new home doth my soul surprise,
Let me accomplish *some great work* for thee,"
Subdue it, Lord; let my petition be,
"O make me useful in this world of thine,
In ways according to thy will, not mine."

AS THOU WILT

My Jesus, as thou wilt:
O may thy will be mine;
Into thy hand of love
I would my all resign.
Through sorrow or through joy
Conduct me as thine own,
And help me still to say,
"My Lord, thy will be done."

My Jesus, as thou wilt:
If needy here, and poor,
Give me thy people's bread,
Their portion rich and sure.
The manna of thy word
Let my soul feed upon;
And if all else should fail—
My Lord, thy will be done.

My Jesus, as thou wilt:
If among thorns I go,
Still sometimes here and there
Let a few roses blow.
But thou on earth along
The thorny path hast gone;
Then lead me after thee.
My Lord, thy will be done!

My Jesus, as thou wilt:
Though seen through many a tear,
Let not my star of hope
Grow dim or disappear.
Since thou on earth hast wept
And sorrowed oft alone,
If I must weep with thee,
My Lord, thy will be done.

My Jesus, as thou wilt:
If loved ones must depart
Suffer not sorrow's flood
To overwhelm my heart.
For they are blest with thee,
Their race and conflict won;
Let me but follow them.
My Lord, thy will be done!

My Jesus, as thou wilt:
When death itself draws nigh,
To thy dear wounded side
I would for refuge fly.
Leaning on thee, to go
Where thou before hast gone;
The rest as thou shalt please.
My Lord, thy will be done!

My Jesus, as thou wilt:
All shall be well for me;
Each changing future scene
I gladly trust with thee.
Straight to my home above,
I travel calmly on,
And sing in life or death,
"My Lord, thy will be done."

—Benjamin Schmolke, tr. by J. Borthwick.

GREAT AND SMALL

There is no great nor small in Nature's plan,
Bulk is but fancy in the mind of man;
A raindrop is as wondrous as a star,
Near is not nearest, farthest is not far;
And suns and planets in the vast serene
Are lost as midges in the summer sheen,
Born in their season; and we live and die
Creatures of Time, lost in Eternity.

—Charles Mackay.

GOD'S WILL BE DONE

My God, my Father, while I stray
Far from my home, on life's rough way,
O teach me from my heart to say,
"Thy will be done!"

Though dark my path, and sad my lot,
Let me "be still," and murmur not;
O breathe the prayer divinely taught,
"Thy will be done!"

What though in lonely grief I sigh
For friends beloved, no longer nigh,
Submissive still would I reply,
"Thy will be done!"

Though thou hast called me to resign
What most I prized, it ne'er was mine;
I have but yielded what was thine;
"Thy will be done!"

Should grief or sickness waste away
My life in premature decay;
My Father! still I strive to say,
"Thy will be done!"

Let but my fainting heart be blest
With thy sweet Spirit for its guest;
My God! to thee I leave the rest:
"Thy will be done!"

Renew my will from day to day!
Blend it with thine; and take away
All that now makes it hard to say,
"Thy will be done!"

Then, when on earth I breathe no more
The prayer oft mixed with tears before,
I'll sing upon a happier shore:
"Thy will be done!"

—Charlotte Elliott.

THE TWO ANGELS

All is of God! If he but wave his hand,
The mists collect, the rain falls thick and loud,
Till, with a smile of light on sea and land,
Lo! he looks back from the departing cloud.

Angels of Life and Death alike are his;
Without his leave they pass no threshold o'er;
Who, then, would wish or dare, believing this,
Against his messengers to shut the door?

—Henry Wadsworth Longfellow.

AMEN!

I cannot say,
Beneath the pressure of life's cares to-day,
I joy in these;
But I can say
That I had rather walk this rugged way,
If *Him* it please.

I cannot feel
That all is well when darkening clouds conceal
The shining sun;
But then I know
God lives and loves, and say, since it is so,
Thy will be done.

I cannot speak
In happy tones; the tear-drops on my cheek
Show I am sad:
But I can speak
Of *grace* to suffer with submission meek
Until made glad.

I do not see
Why God should e'en permit some things to be,
When *He is love;*
But I can see,
Though often dimly, through the mystery
His hand above!

I do not know
Where falls the seed that I have tried to sow
With greatest care;
But I *shall know*
The meaning of each waiting hour below
Sometime, somewhere!

I do not look
Upon the present, nor in Nature's book,
To read my fate;
But I *do look*
For *promised blessings* in God's holy Book;
And *I can wait.*

I may not try
To keep the hot tears back—but hush that sigh,
"It might have been";
And try to still
Each rising murmur, and to *God's sweet will*
Respond "*Amen!*"

—Frederick G. Browning.

AS HE WILLS

He sendeth sun, he sendeth shower,
Alike they're needful for the flower;
And joys and tears alike are sent
To give the soul fit nourishment.
As comes to me or cloud or sun,
Father! thy will, not mine, be done.

Can loving children e'er reprove,
With murmurs, whom they trust and love?
Creator! I would ever be
A trusting, loving child to thee:
As comes to me or cloud or sun,
Father! thy will, not mine, be done.

O ne'er will I at life repine—
Enough that thou hast made it mine;
When falls the shadow cold of death
I yet will sing with parting breath,
As comes to me or cloud or sun,
Father! thy will, not mine, be done.

—Sarah Flower Adams.

ACCORDING TO THY WILL

If I were told that I must die to-morrow,
That the next sun
Which sinks should bear me past all fear and sorrow
For any one,
All the fight fought, all the short journey through,
What should I do?

I do not think that I should shrink or falter,
But just go on
Doing my work, nor change nor seek to alter
Aught that is gone;
But rise, and move, and love, and smile, and pray
For one more day.

And lying down at night, for a last sleeping,
Say in that ear
Which harkens ever, "Lord, within thy keeping,
How should I fear?
And when to-morrow brings thee nearer still,
Do thou thy will."

I might not sleep for awe; but peaceful, tender,
My soul would lie
All night long; and when the morning splendor
Flashed o'er the sky,
I think that I could smile—could calmly say,
"It is his day."

But if a wondrous hand from the blue yonder
Held out a scroll
On which my life was writ, and I with wonder
Beheld unroll
To a long century's end its mystic clew—
What should I do?

What could I do, O blessed Guide and Master!
Other than this,
Still to go on as now, not slower, faster,
Nor fear to miss
The road, although so very long it be,
While led by thee?

Step by step, feeling thee close beside me,
Although unseen;
Through thorns, through flowers, whether the tempest hide thee
Or heavens serene,
Assured thy faithfulness cannot betray,
Thy love decay.

I may not know, my God; no hand revealeth
Thy counsels wise;
Along the path no deepening shadow stealeth;
No voice replies
To all my questioning thought the time to tell,
And it is well.

Let me keep on, abiding and unfearing
Thy will always;
Through a long century's ripe fruition
Or a short day's;
Thou canst not come too soon; and I can wait
If thou come late!

—Susan Coolidge.

God's in his heaven,
All's right with the world.
—Robert Browning.

WHAT PLEASETH GOD

What pleaseth God with joy receive;
Though storm-winds rage and billows heave
And earth's foundations all be rent,
Be comforted; to thee is sent
What pleaseth God.

God's will is best; to this resigned,
How sweetly rests the weary mind!
Seek, then, this blessed conformity,
Desiring but to do and be
What pleaseth God.

God's thoughts are wisest; human schemes
Are vain delusions, idle dreams;
Our purposes are frail and weak;
With earthly mind we seldom seek
What pleaseth God.

God is the holiest; and his ways
Are full of kindness, truth, and grace;
His blessing crowns our earnest prayer,
While worldlings scorn, and little care
What pleaseth God.

God's is the truest heart; his love
Nor time, nor life, nor death, can move;
To those his mercies daily flow,
Whose chief concern it is to know
What pleaseth God.

Omnipotent he reigns on high
And watcheth o'er thy destiny;
While sea, and earth, and air produce
For daily pleasure, daily use,
What pleaseth God.

He loves his sheep, and when they stray
He leads them back to wisdom's way;
Their faithless, wandering hearts to turn,
Gently chastising, till they learn
What pleaseth God.

He knows our every need, and grants
A rich supply to all our wants;
No good withholds from those whose mind
Is bent with earnest zeal to find
What pleaseth God.

Then let the world, with stubborn will,
Its earth-born pleasures follow still;
Be this, my soul, thy constant aim,
Thy riches, honor, glory, fame,
What pleaseth God.

Should care and grief thy portion be,
To thy strong refuge ever flee;
For all his creatures but perform,
In peace and tumult, calm and storm,
What pleaseth God.

Faith lays her hand on God's rich grace,
And hope gives patience for the race;
These virtues in thy heart enshrined,
Thy portion thou wilt surely find,
What pleaseth God.

In heaven thy glorious portion is;
There is thy throne, thy crown, thy bliss;
There shalt thou taste, and hear, and see,
There shalt thou ever do and be,
What pleaseth God.

—Paul Gerhardt.

"THE SPLENDOR OF GOD'S WILL"

O words of golden music
Caught from the harps on high,
Which find a glorious anthem
Where we have found a sigh,
And peal their grandest praises
Just where ours faint and die.

O words of holy radiance
Shining on every tear
Till it becomes a rainbow,
Reflecting, bright and clear,
Our Father's love and glory
So wonderful, so dear!

O words of sparkling power,
Of insight full and deep!
Shall they not enter other hearts
In a grand and gladsome sweep,
And lift the lives to songs of joy
That only droop and weep?

And O, it is a splendor,
A glow of majesty,
A mystery of beauty,
If we will only see;
A very cloud of glory
Enfolding you and me.

A splendor that is lighted
At one transcendent flame,
The wondrous love, the perfect love,
Our Father's sweetest name;
For his very name and essence
And his will are all the same.

—Frances Ridley Havergal.

NOT BY CHANCE

No chance has brought this ill to me;
'Tis God's sweet will, so let it be;
He seeth what I cannot see.

There is a need-be for each pain,
And he will make it one day plain
That earthly loss is heavenly gain.

Like as a piece of tapestry,
Viewed from the back, appears to be
Naught but threads tangled hopelessly,

But in the front a picture fair
Rewards the worker for his care,
Proving his skill and patience rare.

Thou art the workman, I the frame;
Lord, for the glory of thy name,
Perfect thine image on the same!

SUBMISSION TO GOD

Whate'er God wills let that be done;
His will is ever wisest;
His grace will all thy hope outrun
Who to that faith arisest.
The gracious Lord
Will help afford;
He chastens with forbearing;
Who God believes,
And to him cleaves,
Shall not be left despairing.

My God is my sure confidence,
My light, and my existence;
His counsel is beyond my sense,
But stirs no weak resistance;
His word declares
The very hairs
Upon my head are numbered;
His mercy large
Holds me in charge
With care that never slumbered.

There comes a day when at his will
The pulse of nature ceases.
I think upon it, and am still,
Let come whate'er he pleases.
To him I trust
My soul, my dust,
When flesh and spirit sever;
The Christ we sing
Has plucked the sting
Away from death forever.
—Albert of Brandenburg, 1586.

THY WILL BE DONE

We see not, know not; all our way
Is night; with thee alone is day.
From out the torrent's troubled drift,
Above the storm our prayers we lift:
Thy will be done!

The flesh may fail, the heart may faint,
But who are we to make complaint
Or dare to plead, in times like these,
The weakness of our love of ease?
Thy will be done!

We take, with solemn thankfulness,
Our burden up, nor ask it less,
And count it joy that even we
May suffer, serve, or wait for thee,
Whose will be done!

Though dim as yet in tint and line,
We trace thy picture's wise design,
And thank thee that our age supplies
Its dark relief of sacrifice.
Thy will be done!

And if, in our unworthiness,
Thy sacrificial wine we press;
If from thy ordeal's heated bars
Our feet are seamed with crimson scars,
Thy will be done!

If, for the age to come, this hour
Of trial hath vicarious power,
And, blest by thee, our present pain
Be liberty's eternal gain,
Thy will be done.

Strike, thou the Master, we thy keys,
The anthem of the destinies!
The minor of thy loftier strain,
Our hearts shall breathe the old refrain,
Thy will be done!
—John Greenleaf Whittier.

There is no sense, as I can see,
In mortals such as you and me
A-faulting nature's wise intents
And locking horns with Providence.

It is no use to grumble and complain;
It's just as cheap and easy to rejoice;
When God sorts out the weather and sends rain—
Why, rain's my choice.
—James Whitcomb Riley.

THY WILL

Not in dumb resignation
We lift our hands on high;
Not like the nerveless fatalist,
Content to do and die.
Our faith springs like the eagle
Who soars to meet the sun,
And cries, exulting, unto thee,
"O Lord, thy will be done!"

Thy will! It bids the weak be strong;
It bids the strong be just;
No lip to fawn, no hand to beg,
No brow to seek the dust.
Wherever man oppresses man,
Beneath the liberal sun,
O Lord, be there! Thine arm make bare!
Thy righteous will be done!

—John Hay.

AS GOD WILL

All goeth but God's will!
The fairest garden flower
Fades after its brief hour
Of brightness. Still,
This is but God's good will.

All goeth but God's will!
The brightest, dearest day
Doth swiftly pass away,
And darkest night
Succeeds the vision bright.

But still strong-hearted be,
Yea, though the night be drear;
How sad and long soe'er
Its gloom may be,
This darkness, too, shall flee.

Weep not yon grave beside!
Dear friend, he is not gone;
God's angel soon this stone
Shall roll aside.
Yea, death shall not abide!

Earth's anguish, too, shall go,
O then be strong, my soul!
When sorrows o'er thee roll
Be still, and know
'Tis God's will worketh so.

Dear Lord and God, incline
Thine ear unto my call!
O grant me that in all,
This will of mine
May still be one with thine!

Teach me to answer still,
Whate'er my lot may be,
To all thou sendest me,
Of good or ill;
"All goeth as God will."

—Alice Williams.

THE SHADOW OF THE GREAT ROCK

Sweet is the solace of thy love,
My heavenly Friend, to me,
While through the hidden way of faith
I journey home with thee,
Learning by quiet thankfulness
As a dear child to be.

Though from the shadow of thy peace
My feet would often stray,
Thy mercy follows all my steps,
And will not turn away;
Yea, thou wilt comfort me at last
As none beneath thee may.

No other comforter I need
If thou, O Lord, be mine;
Thy rod will bring my spirit low,
Thy fire my heart refine,
And cause me pain that none may feel
By other love than thine.

Then in the secret of my soul,
Though hosts my peace invade,
Though through a waste and weary land
My lonely way be made,
Thou, even thou, wilt comfort me;
I need not be afraid.

O there is nothing in the world
To weigh against thy will;
Even the dark times I dread the most
Thy covenant fulfill;
And when the pleasant morning dawns
I find thee with me still.

Still in the solitary place
I would awhile abide,
Till with the solace of thy love
My soul is satisfied,
And all my hopes of happiness
Stay calmly at thy side.

On thy compassion I repose
In weakness and distress;
I will not ask for greater ease
Lest I should love thee less,
It is a blessed thing for me
To need thy tenderness.

—Anna Letitia Waring.

RABIA

There was of old a Moslem saint
 Named Rabia. On her bed she lay
Pale, sick, but uttered no complaint.
 "Send for the holy men to pray."
And two were sent. The first drew near:
"The prayers of no man are sincere
Who does not bow beneath the rod,
And bear the chastening strokes of God."
Whereto the second, more severe:
"The prayers of no man are sincere
Who does not in the rod rejoice
And make the strokes he bears his choice."
Then she, who felt that in such pain
The love of self did still remain,
Answered, "No prayers can be sincere
 When they from whose wrung hearts they fall
Are not as I am, lying here,
 Who long since have forgotten all.
Dear Lord of love! There is no pain."
So Rabia, and was well again.

—Edmund Clarence Stedman.

THREE STAGES OF PIETY

Rabia, sick upon her bed,
By two saints was visited:

Holy Malik, Hassan wise,
Men of mark in Moslem eyes.

Hassan said: "Whose prayer is pure
Will God's chastisement *endure*."

Malik, from a deeper sense,
Uttered his experience:

"He who loves his Master's choice
Will in chastisement *rejoice*."

Rabia saw some selfish will
In their maxims lingering still,

And replied: "O men of grace!
He who sees his Master's face

"Will not in his prayer recall
That he is chastised at all."

—Arabian, tr. by James Freeman Clarke, from the German of Tholuck.

(Rabia was a very holy Arabian woman who lived in the second century of the Hegira, or the eighth century of our era.)

PRAYER'S GRACE

Round holy Rabia's suffering bed
 The wise men gathered, gazing gravely.
"Daughter of God!" the youngest said,
 "Endure thy Father's chastening bravely;
They who have steeped their souls in prayer
 Can any anguish calmly bear."

She answered not, and turned aside,
Though not reproachfully nor sadly.
"Daughter of God!" the eldest cried,
"Sustain thy Father's chastening gladly;
They who have learned to pray aright
From pain's dark well draw up delight."

Then spake she out: "Your words are fair;
But, oh, the truth lies deeper still.
I know not, when absorbed in prayer,
Pleasure or pain, or good or ill.
They who God's face can understand
Feel not the workings of his hand."

—Monckton Milnes.

I LOVE THY WILL

I love thy will, O God!
 Thy blessèd, perfect will,
In which this once rebellious heart
 Lies satisfied and still.

I love thy will, O God!
 It is my joy, my rest;
It glorifies my common task,
 It makes each trial blest.

I love thy will, O God!
 The sunshine or the rain;
Some days are bright with praise, and some
 Sweet with accepted pain.

I love thy will, O God!
 O hear my earnest plea,
That as thy will is done in heaven
 It may be done in me!

—Bessie Pegg MacLaughlin.

Though the mills of God grind slowly, yet they grind exceeding small;
Though with patience he stands waiting, with exactness grinds he all.

—Tr. by Henry Wadsworth Longfellow.

DAILY BREAD

I pray, with meek hands on my breast,
"Thy will be done, thy kingdom come,"
But shouldst thou call my dear ones home
Should I still say, "'Tis best;
Thy will be done"?

I cannot tell. I probe my heart
With sharpest instruments of pain,
And listen if the sweet refrain
Still wells up through the smart—
"Thy will be done!"

I cannot tell. I yield the quest,
Content if only day by day
My God shall give me grace to say,
"Father, thou knowest best;
Thy will be done!"

He gives no strength for coming ill,
Until its advent. Then he rolls
His love in on his waiting souls,
Sure of their sweet "Thy will,
Thy will be done!"

"Give us this day our daily bread"—
So prayed the Christ, and so will I;
Father, my daily bread supply,
Or, if I go unfed,
"Thy will be done!"
—Caroline Atherton Mason.

APPROACHES

When thou turnest away from ill
Christ is this side of thy hill.

When thou turnest towards good
Christ is walking in thy wood.

When thy heart says, "Father, pardon!"
Then the Lord is in thy garden.

When stern duty wakes to watch
Then his hand is on the latch.

But when hope thy song doth rouse
Then the Lord is in the house.

When to love is all thy wit
Christ doth at thy table sit.

When God's will is thy heart's pole
Then is Christ thy very soul.
—George Macdonald.

SUBMISSION

But that thou art my wisdom, Lord,
And both mine eyes are thine,
My mind would be extremely stirred
For missing my design.

Were it not better to bestow
Some place and power on me?
Then should thy praises with me grow,
And share in my degree.

But when I thus dispute and grieve
I do resume my sight;
And, pilfering what I once did give,
Disseize thee of thy right.

How know I, if thou shouldst me raise,
That I should then raise thee?
Perhaps great places and thy praise
Do not so well agree.

Wherefore unto my gift I stand;
I will no more advise;
Only do thou lend me a hand,
Since thou hast both mine eyes.
—George Herbert.

YOUTH'S WARNING

Beware, exulting youth, beware,
When life's young pleasures woo,
That ere you yield yon shrine your heart,
And keep your conscience true!
For sake of silver spent to-day
Why pledge to-morrow's gold?
Or in hot blood implant remorse,
To grow when blood is cold?
If wrong you do, if false you play,
In summer among the flowers,
You must atone, you must repay,
In winter among the showers.

To turn the balances of heaven
Surpasses mortal power;
For every white there is a black,
For every sweet a sour.
For every up there is a down,
For every folly shame,
And retribution follows guilt
As burning follows flame.
If wrong you do, if false you play,
In summer among the flowers,
You must atone, you must repay
In winter among the showers.
—George Macdonald.

THE BEAUTY OF HOLINESS

I love thy skies, thy sunny mists,
Thy fields, thy mountains hoar,
Thy wind that bloweth where it lists;
Thy will, I love it more.

I love thy hidden truth to seek
All round, in sea, on shore;
The arts whereby like gods we speak;
Thy will to me is more.

I love thy men and women, Lord,
The children round thy door,
Calm thoughts that inward strength afford;
Thy will, O Lord, is more.

But when thy will my life shall hold,
Thine to the very core,
The world which that same will did mold
I shall love ten times more.
—George Macdonald.

No child of man may perish ere his time arrives;
A thousand arrows pierce him and he still survives;
But when the moment fixed in heaven's eternal will
Comes round, a single blade of yielding grass may kill.
—From the Mahabharata, tr. by Frederic Rowland Marvin.

God gives to man the power to strike or miss you;
It is not thy foe who did the thing.
The arrow from the bow may seem to issue,
But we know an archer drew the string.
—Saadi, tr. by James Freeman Clarke.

On two days it steads not to run from thy grave:
The appointed and the unappointed day;
On the first neither balm nor physician can save,
Nor thee on the second the universe slay.
—Ralph Waldo Emerson.

ROUNDEL

I do not know thy final will,
It is too good for me to know.
Thou willest that I mercy show,
That I take heed and do no ill,
That I the needy warm and fill,
Nor stones at any sinner throw;
But I know not thy final will,
It is too good for me to know.

I know thy love unspeakable—
For love's sake able to send woe!
To find thine own thou lost didst go,
And wouldst for men thy blood yet spill!
How should I know thy final will,
Godwise too good for me to know!
—George Macdonald.

One prayer I have—all prayers in one—
When I am wholly thine:
Thy will, my God, thy will be done,
And let that will be mine;
All-wise, almighty, and all-good,
In thee I firmly trust,
Thy ways, unknown or understood,
Are merciful and just.

Fear him, ye saints, and you will then
Have nothing else to fear;
Make you his service your delight,
He'll make your wants his care.

The best will is our Father's will,
And we may rest there calm and still;
O make it hour by hour thine own,
And wish for naught but that alone
Which pleases God.
—Paul Gerhardt.

It is Lucifer,
The son of mystery;
And since God suffers him to be
He, too, is God's minister,
And labors for some good
By us not understood!
—Henry Wadsworth Longfellow.

Rabbi Jehosha had the skill
To know that heaven is in God's will.
—James Russell Lowell.

GOD'S PRESENCE

POSSESSION, SATISFACTION, REFLECTION

THE SECRET OF HIS PRESENCE

In the secret of his presence
  I am kept from strife of tongues;
His pavilion is around me,
  And within are ceaseless songs!
Stormy winds, his word fulfilling,
  Beat without, but cannot harm,
For the Master's voice is stilling
  Storm and tempest to a calm.

In the secret of his presence
  All the darkness disappears;
For a sun that knows no setting,
  Throws a rainbow on my tears.
So the day grows ever lighter,
  Broadening to the perfect noon;
So the day grows ever brighter,
  Heaven is coming, near and soon.

In the secret of his presence
  Never more can foes alarm;
In the shadow of the Highest,
  I can meet them with a psalm;
For the strong pavilion hides me,
  Turns their fiery darts aside,
And I know, whate'er betides me,
  I shall live because he died!

In the secret of his presence
  Is a sweet, unbroken rest;
Pleasures, joys, in glorious fullness,
  Making earth like Eden blest;
So my peace grows deep and deeper,
  Widening as it nears the sea,
For my Saviour is my keeper,
  Keeping mine and keeping me!

—Henry Burton.

EYESERVICE

Eyeservice let me give
  The while I live;
  In shadow or in light,
  By day or night,
  With all my heart and skill—
  Eyeservice still!

Yes, for the eyes I'll serve—
  Nor faint nor swerve—
  Are not the eyes of man,
  That lightly scan,
  But God's, that pierce and see
  The whole of me!

Beneath the farthest skies,
  Where morning flies,
  In heaven or in hell,
  If I should dwell,
  In dark or daylight fair,
  The Eyes are there!

No trembling fugitive,
  Boldly I live
  If, as in that pure sight,
  I live aright,
  Yielding with hand and will
  Eyeservice still!

—Amos R. Wells.

OMNIPRESENCE

Lord of all being, throned afar,
Thy glory flames from sun and star;
Center and soul of every sphere,
Yet to each loving heart how near!

Sun of our life, thy quickening ray
Sheds on our path the glow of day;
Star of our hope, thy softened light
Cheers the long watches of the night.

Our midnight is thy smile withdrawn;
Our noontide is thy gracious dawn;
Our rainbow arch thy mercy's sign;
All, save the clouds of sin, are thine!

Lord of all life, below, above,
Whose light is truth, whose warmth is
  love,
Before thy ever-blazing throne
We ask no luster of our own.

Grant us thy truth to make us free,
And kindling hearts that burn for thee,
Till all thy living altars claim
One holy light, one heavenly flame.

—Oliver Wendell Holmes.

THE CHERUBIC PILGRIM

God's spirit falls on me as dew drops on a rose,
If I but like a rose my heart to him unclose.

The soul wherein God dwells—what Church can holier be?
Becomes a walking tent of heavenly majesty.

Lo! in the silent night a child to God is born,
And all is brought again that ere was lost or lorn.

Could but thy soul, O man, become a silent night
God would be born in thee and set all things aright.

Ye know God but as Lord, hence Lord his name with ye,
I feel him but as love, and Love his name with me.

Though Christ a thousand times in Bethlehem be born,
If he's not born in thee thy soul is all forlorn.

The cross on Golgotha will never save thy soul,
The cross in thine own heart alone can make thee whole.

Christ rose not from the dead, Christ still is in the grave
If thou for whom he died art still of sin the slave.

In all eternity no tone can be so sweet
As where man's heart with God in unison doth beat.

Whate'er thou lovest, man, that, too, become thou must;
God, if thou lovest God, dust, if thou lovest dust.

Ah, would thy heart but be a manger for the birth,
God would once more become a child on earth.

Immeasurable is the highest; who but knows it?
And yet a human heart can perfectly enclose it.

—Johannes Scheffler.

THE LARGER VIEW

In buds upon some Aaron's rod
The childlike ancient saw his God;
Less credulous, more believing, we
Read in the grass—Divinity.

From Horeb's bush the Presence spoke
To earlier faiths and simpler folk;
But now each bush that sweeps our fence
Flames with the Awful Immanence!

To old Zacchæus in his tree
What mattered leaves and botany?
His sycamore was but a seat
Whence he could watch that hallowed street.

But now to us each elm and pine
Is vibrant with the Voice divine,
Not only from but in the bough
Our larger creed beholds him now.

To the true faith, bark, sap, and stem
Are wonderful as Bethlehem;
No hill nor brook nor field nor herd
But mangers the Incarnate Word!

Far be it from our lips to cast
Contempt upon the holy past—
Whate'er the Finger writes we scan
In manger, prophecy, or man.

Again we touch the healing hem
In Nazareth or Jerusalem;
We trace again those faultless years;
The cross commands our wondering tears.

Yet if to us the Spirit writes
On Morning's manuscript and Night's,
In gospels of the growing grain,
Epistles of the pond and plain,

In stars, in atoms, as they roll,
Each tireless round its occult pole,
In wing and worm and fin and fleece,
In the wise soil's surpassing peace—

Thrice ingrate he whose only look
Is backward focussed on the Book,
Neglectful what the Presence saith,
Though he be near as blood and breath!

The only atheist is one
Who hears no Voice in wind or sun,
Believer in some primal curse,
Deaf in God's loving universe!

—Frederic Lawrence Knowles.

STILL WITH THEE

Still, still with thee, when purple morning breaketh,
When the bird waketh, and the shadows flee;
Fairer than morning, lovelier than daylight,
Dawns the sweet consciousness, I am with thee.

Alone with thee amid the mystic shadows,
The solemn hush of nature newly born;
Alone with thee in breathless adoration,
In the calm dew and freshness of the morn.

As in the dawning o'er the waveless ocean
The image of the morning-star doth rest,
So in this stillness thou beholdest only
Thine image in the waters of my breast.

Still, still with thee! as to each new born morning
A fresh and solemn splendor still is given,
So does this blessèd consciousness awaking
Breathe each day nearness unto thee and heaven.

When sinks the soul, subdued by toil, to slumber,
Its closing eyes look up to thee in prayer;
Sweet the repose beneath thy wings o'ershading,
But sweeter still, to wake and find thee there.

So shall it be at last, in that bright morning,
When the soul waketh, and life's shadows flee;
O in that hour, fairer than daylight dawning,
Shall rise the glorious thought—I am with thee.

—Harriet Beecher Stowe.

There lives and works a soul in all things,
And that soul is God.

—William Cowper.

THE ELIXIR

Teach me, my God and King,
In all things thee to see,
And what I do, in anything,
To do it as for thee.

A man that looks on glass
On it may stay his eye,
Or, if he pleaseth, through it pass
And then to heaven espy.

All may of thee partake.
Nothing can be so mean
Which with this tincture (*for thy sake*)
Will not grow bright and clean.

A servant with this clause
Makes drudgery divine.
Who sweeps a room as for thy laws
Makes that and th' action fine.

This is the famous stone
That turneth all to gold;
For that which God doth touch and own
Cannot for less be told.

—George Herbert.

GOD'S PRESENCE

But God is never so far off
As even to be near.
He is within; our spirit is
The home he holds most dear.

To think of him as by our side
Is almost as untrue
As to remove his throne beyond
Those skies of starry blue.

So all the while I thought myself
Homeless, forlorn, and weary,
Missing my joy, I walked the earth,
Myself God's sanctuary.

I come to thee once more, my God!
No longer will I roam;
For I have sought the wide world through
And never found a home.

Though bright and many are the spots
Where I have built a nest—
Yet in the brightest still I pined
For more abiding rest.

For thou hast made this wondrous soul
All for thyself alone;
Ah! send thy sweet transforming grace
To make it more thine own.

—Frederick William Faber.

GOD IS MINE

If God is mine then present things
  And things to come are mine;
Yea, Christ, his word, and Spirit, too,
  And glory all divine.

If he is mine then from his love
  He every trouble sends;
All things are working for my good,
  And bliss his rod attends.

If he is mine I need not fear
  The rage of earth and hell;
He will support my feeble power,
  Their utmost force repel.

If he is mine let friends forsake,
  Let wealth and honor flee;
Sure he who giveth me himself
  Is more than these to me.

If he is mine I'll boldly pass
  Through death's tremendous vale;
He is a solid comfort when
  All other comforts fail.

Oh! tell me, Lord, that thou art mine;
  What can I wish beside?
My soul shall at the fountain live,
  When all the streams are dried.

A PRESENT SAVIOUR

I have thee every hour,
  Most gracious Lord,
That tender voice of thine
  Doth peace afford.

I have thee every hour,
  Thou stay'st near by;
Temptations lose their power
  Since thou art nigh.

I have thee every hour,
  In joy and pain;
With me thou dost abide,
  And life is gain.

I have thee every hour,
  Teach me thy will;
All thy rich promises
  Thou dost fulfill.

I have thee every hour,
  Most Holy One,
And I am thine indeed,
  Thou blessed Son.
—Annie S. Hawks, altered by J. M.

THE THOUGHT OF GOD

The thought of God, the thought of thee,
  Who liest near my heart,
And yet beyond imagined space
  Outstretched and present art—

The thought of thee, above, below,
  Around me and within,
Is more to me than health and wealth,
  Or love of kith and kin.

The thought of God is like the tree
  Beneath whose shade I lie
And watch the fleet of snowy clouds
  Sail o'er the silent sky.

'Tis like that soft invading light
  Which in all darkness shines,
The thread that through life's somber web
  In golden pattern twines.

It is a thought which ever makes
  Life's sweetest smiles from tears,
It is a daybreak to our hopes,
  A sunset to our fears.

Within a thought so great, our souls
  Little and modest grow,
And, by its vastness awed, we learn
  The art of walking slow.

The wild flower on the grassy mound
  Scarce bends its pliant form
When overhead the autumnal wood
  Is thundering like a storm.

So is it with our humbled souls,
  Down in the thought of God,
Scarce conscious in their sober peace
  Of the wild storms abroad.

To think of thee is almost prayer,
  And is outspoken praise;
And pain can even passive thoughts
  To actual worship raise.

All murmurs lie inside thy will
  Which are to thee addressed;
To suffer for thee is our work,
  To think of thee, our rest.
—Frederick William Faber.

Let thy sweet presence light my way,
  And hallow every cross I bear;
  Transmuting duty, conflict, care,
Into love's service day by day.

OUR HEAVENLY FATHER

My God, how wonderful thou art,
Thy majesty how bright,
How beautiful thy mercy seat
In depths of burning light!

How dread are thine eternal years,
O everlasting Lord,
By prostrate spirits, day and night,
Incessantly adored.

How beautiful, how beautiful
The sight of thee must be,
Thine endless wisdom, boundless power,
And awful purity!

O how I fear thee, living God!
With deepest, tenderest fears,
And worship thee with trembling hope
And penitential tears.

Yet I may love thee too, O Lord!
Almighty as thou art,
For thou hast stooped to ask of me
The love of this poor heart.

Oh, then, this worse than worthless heart
In pity deign to take,
And make it love thee for thyself,
And for thy glory's sake.

No earthly father loves like thee,
No mother half so mild
Bears and forbears, as thou hast done
With me, thy sinful child.

Only to sit and think of God,
O what a joy it is!
To think the thought, to breathe the name—
Earth has no higher bliss.

Father of Jesus, love's Reward!
What rapture will it be,
Prostrate before thy throne to lie
And gaze, and gaze on thee!
—Frederick William Faber.

RULES FOR DAILY LIFE

Begin the day with God:
Kneel down to him in prayer;
Lift up thy heart to his abode
And seek his love to share.

Open the Book of God,
And read a portion there;
That it may hallow all thy thoughts
And sweeten all thy care.

Go through the day with God,
Whate'er thy work may be;
Where'er thou art—at home, abroad,
He still is near to thee.

Converse in mind with God;
Thy spirit heavenward raise;
Acknowledge every good bestowed,
And offer grateful praise.

Conclude the day with God:
Thy sins to him confess;
Trust in the Lord's atoning blood,
And plead his righteousness.

Lie down at night with God,
Who gives his servants sleep;
And when thou tread'st the vale of death
He will thee guard and keep.

HE FILLS ALL

All are but parts of one stupendous whole;
Whose body nature is, and God the soul;
That, changed through all, and yet in all the same;
Great in the earth as in th' ethereal frame;
Warms in the sun, refreshes in the breeze,
Glows in the stars and blossoms in the trees;
Lives through all life, extends through all extent,
Spreads undivided, operates unspent;
Breathes in our souls, informs our mortal part,
As full, as perfect, in a hair as heart;
As full, as perfect, in vile man that mourns,
As the rapt seraph that adores and burns.
To him no high, no low, no great, no small,
He fills, he bounds, connects, and equals all.

* * * * *

All nature is but art, unknown to thee;
All chance, direction which thou canst not see;
All discord, harmony not understood;
All partial evil, universal good;
And, spite of pride, in erring reason's spite,
One truth is clear—whatever is, is right.
—Alexander Pope.

THE PRESENCE

I sit within my room and joy to find
That thou who always lov'st art with me here;
That I am never left by thee behind,
But by thyself thou keep'st me ever near.
The fire burns brighter when with thee I look,
And seems a kindlier servant sent to me;
With gladder heart I read thy holy book,
Because thou art the eyes with which I see;
This aged chair, that table, watch, and door
Around in ready service ever wait;
Nor can I ask of thee a menial more
To fill the measure of my large estate;
For thou thyself, with all a Father's care,
Where'er I turn art ever with me there.

—Jones Very.

BLESSED THOUGHT OF GOD

One thought I have—my ample creed,
So deep it is and broad,
And equal to my every need—
It is the thought of God.

Each morn unfolds some fresh surprise,
I feast at life's full board;
And rising in my inner skies,
Shines forth the thought of God.

At night my gladness is my prayer;
I drop my daily load,
And every care is pillowed there
Upon the thought of God.

I ask not far before to see,
But take in trust my road;
Life, death, and immortality,
Are in my thought of God.

To this their secret strength they owed
The martyr's path who trod;
The fountains of their patience flowed
From out their thought of God.

Be still the light upon my way,
My pilgrim staff and rod,
My rest by night, my strength by day,
O blessèd thought of God.

—Frederick Lucian Hosmer.

EVENTIDE

At cool of day with God I walk
My garden's grateful shade;
I hear his voice among the trees,
And I am not afraid.

I see his presence in the night—
And though my heart is awed
I do not quail before the sight
Or nearness of my God.

He speaks to me in every wind,
He smiles from every star;
He is not deaf to me, nor blind,
Nor absent, nor afar.

His hand, that shuts the flowers to sleep,
Each in its dewy fold,
Is strong my feeble life to keep,
And competent to hold.

I cannot walk in darkness long,
My light is by my side;
I cannot stumble or go wrong
While following such a guide.

He is my stay and my defense;
How shall I fail or fall?
My helper is Omnipotence!
My ruler ruleth all!

The powers below and powers above
Are subject to his care;
I cannot wander from his love
Who loves me everywhere.

Thus dowered, and guarded thus, with him
I walk this peaceful shade,
I hear his voice among the trees,
And I am not afraid.

—Caroline Atherton Mason.

From cellar unto attic all is clean:
Nothing there is that need evade the eye;
All the dark places, by the world unseen,
Are as well ordered as what open lie.

Ah! souls are houses; and to keep them well,
Nor, spring and autumn, mourn their wretched plight,
To daily toil must vigilance compel,
Right underneath God's scrutinizing light.

SAINTSHIP

To heaven approached a Sufi saint,
  From groping in the darkness late,
And, tapping timidly and faint,
  Besought admission at God's gate.

Said God, "Who seeks to enter here?"
  "'Tis I, dear Friend," the saint replied,
And trembling much with hope and fear.
  "If it be *thou*, without abide."

Sadly to earth the poor saint turned,
  To bear the scourging of life's rods;
But aye his heart within him yearned
  To mix and lose its love in God's.

He roamed alone through weary years,
  By cruel men still scorned and mocked,
Until from faith's pure fires and tears
  Again he rose, and modest knocked.

Asked God: "Who now is at the door?"
  "It is thyself, beloved Lord,"
Answered the saint, in doubt no more,
  But clasped and rapt in his reward.
    —From the Persian, tr. by William Rounseville Alger.

OPEN THOU OUR EYES

(Luke 24. 15)

And he drew near and talked with them,
  But they perceived him not,
And mourned, unconscious of that light,
The gloom, the darkness, and the night
  That wrapt his burial spot.

Wearied with doubt, perplexed and sad,
  They knew nor help nor guide;
While he who bore the secret key
To open every mystery,
  Unknown was by their side.

Thus often when we feel alone,
  Nor help nor comfort near,
'Tis only that our eyes are dim,
Doubting and sad we see not him
  Who waiteth still to hear.

"The darkness gathers overhead,
  The morn will never come."
Did we but raise our downcast eyes,
In the white-flushing eastern skies
  Appears the glowing sun.

In all our daily joys and griefs
  In daily work and rest,
To those who seek him Christ is near,
Our bliss to calm, to soothe our care,
  In leaning on his breast.

Open our eyes, O Lord, we pray,
  To see our way, our Guide:
That by the path that here we tread,
We, following on, may still be led
  In thy light to abide.

MAN

My God, I heard this day
That none doth build a stately habitation
  But he that means to dwell therein.
  What house more stately hath there been,
Or can be, than is man? to whose creation
    All things are in decay.

More servants wait on man
Than he'll take notice of: in every path
  He treads down that which doth befriend him,
  When sickness makes him pale and wan.
O mighty love! man is one world, and hath
    Another to attend him.

For us the winds do blow,
The earth doth rest, heaven move, and fountains flow;
  Nothing we see but means our good,
  As our delight or as our treasure;
The whole is either cupboard of our food,
    Or cabinet of pleasure.

The stars have us to bed;
Night draws the curtain, which the sun withdraws;
  Music and light attend our head;
  All things unto our flesh are kind
In their descent and being; to our mind,
    In their ascent and cause.

Since then, my God, thou hast
So brave a palace built, O dwell in it
  That it may dwell with thee at last.
  Till then, afford us so much wit
That, as the world serves us, we may serve thee,
    And both thy servants be.
      —George Herbert.

EVER WITH THEE

I am with thee, my God—
Where I desire to be:
By day, by night, at home, abroad,
I always am with thee.

With thee when dawn comes on
And calls me back to care,
Each day returning to begin
With thee, my God, in prayer.

With thee amid the crowd
That throngs the busy mart;
I hear thy voice, when time's is loud,
Speak softly to my heart.

With thee when day is done
And evening calms the mind;
The setting as the rising sun
With thee my heart shall find.

With thee when darkness brings
The signal of repose;
Calm in the shadow of thy wings
Mine eyelids gently close.

With thee, in thee, by faith
Abiding I shall be;
By day, by night, in life, in death,
I always am with thee.
—James D. Burns, altered by J. M.

SELF-EXAMINATION

By all means use sometime to be alone.
Salute thyself: see what thy soul doth wear.
Dare to look in thy chest; for 'tis thine own;
And tumble up and down what thou findst there.
Who cannot rest till he good fellows find,
He breaks up homes, turns out of doors his mind.

Sum up by night what thou hast done by day;
And in the morning, what thou hast to do.
Dress and undress thy soul; mark the decay
And growth of it; if, with thy watch, that too
Be down, then wind up both; since we shall be
Most surely judged, make thy accounts agree. —George Herbert.

"SHOW ME THY FACE"

Show me thy face—
One transient gleam
Of loveliness divine
And I shall never think or dream
Of other love save thine.
All lesser light will darken quite,
All lower glories wane;
The beautiful of earth will scarce
Seem beautiful again!

Show me thy face—
My faith and love
Shall henceforth fixèd be,
And nothing here have power to move
My soul's serenity.
My life shall seem a trance, a dream,
And all I feel and see
Illusive, visionary—thou
The one reality.

Show me thy face—
I shall forget
The weary days of yore;
The fretting ghosts of vain regret
Shall haunt my soul no more;
All doubts and fears for future years
In quiet rest subside,
And naught but blest content and calm
Within my breast reside.

Show me thy face—
The heaviest cross
Will then seem light to bear;
There will be gain in every loss,
And peace with every care.
With such light feet
The years will fleet,
Life seem as brief as blest,
Till I have laid my burden down
And entered into rest.

Show me thy face—
And I shall be
In heart and mind renewed;
With wisdom, grace, and energy
To work thy work endued.
Shine clear, though pale,
Behind the veil
Until, the veil removed,
In perfect glory I behold
The Face that I have loved!

I stand in the great Forever,
All things to me are divine;
I eat of the heavenly manna,
I drink of the heavenly wine.

LISTENING FOR GOD

I hear it often in the dark,
  I hear it in the light:
Where *is* the voice that calls to me
  With such a quiet might?
It seems but echo to my thought,
  And yet beyond the stars;
It seems a heart-beat in a hush,
  And yet the planet jars.

O may it be that, far within
  My inmost soul, there lies
A spirit-sky that opens with
  Those voices of surprise?
And can it be, by night and day,
  That firmament serene
Is just the heaven where God himself,
  The Father, dwells unseen?

O God within, so close to me
  That every thought is plain,
Be judge, be friend, be Father still,
  And in thy heaven reign!
Thy heaven is mine, my very soul!
  Thy words are sweet and strong;
They fill my inward silences
  With music and with song.

They send me challenges to right,
  And loud rebuke my ill;
They ring my bells of victory,
  They breathe my "Peace, be still!"
They even seem to say: "My child,
  Why seek me so all day?
Now journey inward to thyself,
  And listen by the way."

—William C. Gannett.

ALLAH'S HOUSE

Nanac the faithful, pausing once to pray,
From holy Mecca turned his face away;
A Moslem priest who chanced to see him
  there,
Forgetful of the attitude in prayer,
Cried "Infidel, how durst thou turn thy
  feet
Toward Allah's house—the sacred tem-
  ple seat?"
To whom the pious Nanac thus replied:
"Knowest thou God's house is, as the
  world is, wide?
Then, turn thee, if thou canst, toward
  any spot
Where mighty Allah's awful house is
  not."

—Frank Dempster Sherman.

IF THE LORD SHOULD COME

If the Lord should come in the morning,
  As I went about my work—
The little things and the quiet things
  That a servant cannot shirk,
Though nobody ever sees them,
  And only the dear Lord cares
That they always are done in the light of
  the sun—
  Would he take me unawares?

If my Lord should come at noonday—
  The time of the dust and heat,
When the glare is white and the air is
  still
  And the hoof-beats sound in the
  street;
If my dear Lord came at noonday,
  And smiled in my tired eyes,
Would it not be sweet his look to meet?
  Would he take me by surprise?

If my Lord came hither at evening,
  In the fragrant dew and dusk,
When the world drops off its mantle
  Of daylight, like a husk,
And flowers, in wonderful beauty,
  And we fold our hands in rest,
Would his touch of my hand, his low
  command,
  Bring me unhoped-for zest?

Why do I ask and question?
  He is ever coming to me,
Morning and noon and evening,
  If I have but eyes to see.
And the daily load grows lighter,
  The daily cares grow sweet,
For the Master is near, the Master is
  here,
  I have only to sit at his feet.

—Margaret Elizabeth Sangster.

The day is long and the day is hard;
We are tired of the march and of keeping
  guard;
Tired of the sense of a fight to be won,
Of days to live through, and of work to
  be done;
Tired of ourselves and of being alone.

And all the while, did we only see,
We walk in the Lord's own company;
We fight, but 'tis he who nerves our arm;
He turns the arrows which else might
  harm,
And out of the storm he brings a calm.

—Susan Coolidge.

COME TO ME

Come to me, come to me, O my God;
  Come to me everywhere.
Let the trees mean thee, and the grassy sod,
  And the water and the air.

For thou art so far that I often doubt,
  As on every side I stare,
Searching within and looking without,
  If thou canst be anywhere.

How did men find thee in days of old?
  How did they grow so sure?
They fought in thy name, they were glad and bold,
  They suffered and kept themselves pure.

But now they say—neither above the sphere
  Nor down in the heart of man,
But only in fancy, ambition, and fear,
  The thought of thee began.

If only that perfect tale were true
  Which ages have not made old,
Of the endless many makes one anew,
  And simplicity manifold!

But he taught that they who did his word,
  The truth of it sure would know;
I will try to do it—if he be Lord
  Again the old faith will glow.

Again the old spirit-wind will blow
  That he promised to their prayer;
And obeying the Son, I too shall know
  His Father everywhere.

—George Macdonald.

Out of the hardness of heart and of will
Out of the longings which nothing could fill;
Out of the bitterness, madness, and strife,
Out of myself and all I called life,
Into the having of all things with Him!
Into an ecstacy full to the brim!
Wonderful loveliness, draining my cup!
Wonderful purpose that ne'er gave me up!
Wonderful patience, enduring and strong!
Wonderful glory to which I belong!

IF I HIM BUT HAVE

If I Him but have,
  If he be but mine—
If my heart, hence to the grave,
  Ne'er forgets his love divine—
Know I naught of sadness,
Feel I naught but worship, love, and gladness.

If I Him but have,
  Glad with all I part;
Follow on my pilgrim staff,
  My Lord only, with true heart;
Leave them, nothing saying,
On broad, bright, and crowded highways straying.

If I Him but have,
  Glad I fall asleep;
Aye the flood that his heart gave
  Strength within my heart shall keep;
And with soft compelling
Make it tender, through and through it swelling.

If I Him but have,
  Mine the world I hail!
Glad as cherub smiling, grave,
  Holding back the Virgin's veil.
Sunk and lost in seeing,
Earthly cares have died from all my being.

Where I have but Him
  Is my Fatherland,
And all gifts and graces come
  Heritage into my hand;
Brothers long deplored
I in his disciples find restored.

—George Macdonald.

Quiet from God! How beautiful to keep
  This treasure the All-merciful hath given;
To feel, when we awake or when we sleep,
  Its incense round us like a breath from heaven.

To sojourn in the world, and yet apart;
  To dwell with God, and still with man to feel;
To bear about forever in the heart
  The gladness which his spirit doth reveal.

—Sarah J. Williams.

HIS CHOSEN ONES

Some souls there are, beloved of God,
Who, following where the saints have trod,
Learn such surrender of the will
They seem insensible of ill.

Yet, finely strung and sensitive,
They live far more than others live,
And grief's and pain's experience
Must be to them far more intense.

O mystery—that such can know
A life impregnable to woe!
O paradox that God alone
In secret proveth to his own!

It must be that supremest grace
So nerves them for the heavenly race
Their litanies are turned to psalms,
Their crosses, even here, to palms.
—Harriet McEwen Kimball.

When, courting slumber,
The hours I number,
And sad cares cumber
My weary mind,
This thought shall cheer me:
That thou art near me,
Whose ear to hear me
Is still inclined.

My soul thou keepest,
Who never sleepest;
'Mid gloom the deepest
There's light above;
Thine eyes behold me,
Thine arms enfold me;
Thy word has told me
That God is love.

We are not angels, but we may
Down in earth's corners kneel,
And multiply sweet acts of love,
And murmur what we feel.
—Frederick William Faber.

Through thee, meseems, the very rose is red,
From thee the violet steals its breath in May,
From thee draw life all things that grow not gray,
And by thy force the happy stars are sped. —James Russell Lowell.

COME TO US, LORD

Come to us, Lord, as the daylight comes
When the darkling night has gone,
And the quickened East is tremulous
With the thrill of the wakened dawn.

Come to us, Lord, as the tide comes on
With the waves from the distant sea;
Come, till our desert places smile,
And our souls are filled with thee.

There are in this loud, stunning tide
Of human care and crime,
With whom the melodies abide
Of th' everlasting chime!
Who carry music in their heart
Through dusky lane and wrangling mart,
Plying their daily task with busier feet
Because their secret souls a holy strain repeat. —John Keble.

Earth's crammed with heaven,
And every common bush afire with God;
But only he who sees takes off his shoes.
The rest sit round it and pluck blackberries,
And daub their natural faces unaware
More and more from the first similitude.
— Elizabeth Barrett Browning.

O Name all other names above,
What art thou not to me,
Now I have learned to trust thy love
And cast my care on thee!
The thought of thee all sorrow calms;
Our anxious burdens fall;
His crosses turn to triumph palms
Who finds in God his all.
—Frederick Lucian Hosmer.

Far off thou art, but ever nigh,
I have thee still, and I rejoice,
I prosper circled with thy voice;
I shall not lose thee though I die.
—Alfred Tennyson.

Let the Loved One but smile on this poor heart of mine,
I will sell the two worlds for one drop of his wine.
—From the Persian.

CONFIDENCE

Thy presence, Lord, the place doth fill,
My heart is now thy throne,
Thy holy, just and perfect will
Now in my flesh is done.

My steadfast soul, from falling free,
Doth now no longer rove,
For Christ is all the world to me
And all my heart is love.
—Charles Wesley, altered by J. M.

Two worlds are ours; 'tis only sin
Forbids us to descry
The mystic heaven and earth within
Plain as the sea and sky.

Thou who hast given me eyes to see
And love this sight so fair,
Give me a heart to find out thee,
And read thee everywhere.
—John Keble.

Speak to him, thou, for he hears,
And spirit with spirit can meet;
Closer is he than breathing,
And nearer than hands and feet.
—Alfred Tennyson.

Heaven above is softer blue,
Earth around is sweeter green,
Something lives in every hue
Christless eyes have never seen.

Birds with gladder songs o'erflow,
Flowers with deeper beauties shine;
Since I knew, as now I know,
I am his and he is mine.

Unheard, because our ears are dull,
Unseen, because our eyes are dim,
He walks the earth, the Wonderful,
And all good deeds are done to him.
—John Greenleaf Whittier.

Where'er I look one Face alone I see,
With every attribute of beauty in it blent;
Still, still the Godhead's face entrances me,
Yielding transcendency of all that can be spent.
—From the Persian.

IMMANENCE

Not only in the cataract and the thunder
Or in the deeps of man's uncharted soul,
But in the dew-star dwells alike the wonder
And in the whirling dust-mite the control.
—Charles G. D. Roberts.

'Tis greatly wise to talk with our past hours
And ask them what report they bore to heaven.
—Edward Young.

A governed heart, thinking no thought but good,
Makes crowded houses holy solitude.
—Edwin Arnold.

But where will God be absent; in his face
Is light, and in his shadow healing, too.
—Robert Browning.

And good may ever conquer ill,
Health walk where pain has trod;
"As a man thinketh, so is he";
Rise, then, and think with God.

God is law, say the wise; O Soul, and let us rejoice,
For, if He thunder by law, the thunder is yet his voice.
—Alfred Tennyson.

Whatever road I take, it joins the street
Which leadeth all who walk it thee to meet.

O work thy works in God.
He can rejoice in naught
Save only in himself
And what himself hath wrought.

To live, to live, is life's great joy; to feel
The living God within—to look abroad,
And, in the beauty that all things reveal,
Still meet the living God.
—Robert Leighton.

JESUS

HIS PRECIOUSNESS, AND BEAUTY, AND LOVE

OUR MASTER

Immortal Love, forever full,
  Forever flowing free,
Forever shared, forever whole,
  A never-ebbing sea!

No fable old, nor mythic lore,
  Nor dream of bards and seers,
No dead fact stranded on the shore
  Of the oblivious years;—

But warm, sweet, tender, even yet
  A present help is he;
And faith has still its Olivet,
  And love its Galilee.

The healing of his seamless dress
  Is by our beds of pain;
We touch him in life's throng and press,
  And we are whole again.

Through him the first fond prayers are said
  Our lips of childhood frame,
The last low whispers of our dead
  Are burdened with his name.

O Lord and Master of us all!
  Whate'er our name or sign,
We own thy sway, we hear thy call,
  We test our lives by thine.

We faintly hear, we dimly see,
  In differing phrase we pray;
But, dim or clear, we own in thee
  The Light, the Truth, the Way!

To do thy will is more than praise,
  As words are less than deeds,
And simple trust can find thy ways
  We miss with chart of creeds.

No pride of self thy service hath,
  No place for me and mine;
Our human strength is weakness, death,
  Our life, apart from thine.

Apart from thee all gain is loss,
  All labor vainly done;
The solemn shadow of thy cross
  Is better than the sun.

Alone, O Love, ineffable!
  Thy saving name is given:
To turn aside from thee is hell,
  To walk with thee is heaven.

—John Greenleaf Whittier.

MY HEART IS FIXED

I'll not leave Jesus,—never, never!
  Ah, what can more precious be?
Rest and joy and light are ever
  In his hand to give to me.
All things that can satisfy,
Having Jesus, those have I.

Love has bound me fast unto him,
  I am his and he is mine;
Daily I for pardon sue him,
  Answers he with peace divine.
On that Rock my trust is laid,
And I rest beneath its shade.

Without Jesus earth would weary,
  Seem almost like hell to be;
But if Jesus I see near me
  Earth is almost heaven to me.
Am I hungry, he doth give
Bread on which my soul can live.

Spent with him, one little hour
  Giveth a year's worth of gain;
Grace and peace put forth their power,
  Joy doth wholly banish pain;
One faith-glance that findeth him
Maketh earthly crowns look dim.

O how light upon my shoulder
  Lies my cross, now grown so small!
For the Lord is my upholder,
  Fits it to me, softens all;
Neither shall it always stay,
Patience, it will pass away.

Those who faithfully go forward
  In his changeless care shall go,
Nothing's doubtful or untoward,
  To the flock who Jesus know.
Jesus always is the same;
True and faithful is his name.

CHRIST'S SYMPATHY

If Jesus came to earth again,
  And walked and talked in field and street,
Who would not lay his human pain
  Low at those heavenly feet?

And leave the loom, and leave the lute,
  And leave the volume on the shelf,
To follow him, unquestioning, mute,
  If 'twere the Lord himself?

How many a brow with care o'erworn,
  How many a heart with grief o'erladen,
How many a man with woe forlorn,
  How many a mourning maiden,

Would leave the baffling earthly prize,
  Which fails the earthly weak endeavor,
To gaze into those holy eyes
  And drink content forever!

His sheep along the cool, the shade,
  By the still watercourse he leads;
His lambs upon his breast are laid;
  His hungry ones he feeds.

And I where'er he went would go,
  Nor question where the paths might lead;
Enough to know that here below
  I walked with God indeed!

If it be thus, O Lord of mine,
  In absence is thy love forgot?
And must I, when I walk, repine
  Because I see thee not?

If this be thus, if this be thus,
  Since our poor prayers yet reach thee, Lord,
Since we are weak, once more to us
  Reveal the living Word!

O nearer to me, in the dark,
  Of life's low house, one moment stand;
And give me keener eyes to mark
  The moving of thy hand.

—Edward Bulwer Lytton.

There's not a craving in the mind
  Thou dost not meet and still;
There's not a wish the heart can have
  Which thou dost not fulfill.

—Frederick William Faber.

FINDING ALL IN JESUS

O Love that wilt not let me go,
  I rest my weary soul on thee;
I give thee back the life I owe,
That in thine ocean depth its flow
  May richer, fuller be.

O Light that followest all my way,
  I yield my flickering torch to thee;
My heart restores its borrowed ray,
That in thy sunshine's blaze its day
  May brighter, fairer be.

O Joy that seekest me through pain,
  I cannot close my heart to thee;
I trace the rainbow through the rain,
And feel the promise is not vain,
  That morn shall tearless be.

O Cross that liftest up my head,
  I dare not ask to fly from thee;
I lay in dust life's glory dead,
And from the ground there blossoms red
  Life that shall endless be.

—George Matheson.

EAST LONDON

'Twas August, and the fierce sun overhead
  Smote on the squalid streets of Bethnal Green,
  And the pale weaver, through his windows seen
In Spitalfields, look'd thrice dispirited.

I met a preacher there I knew, and said:
  "Ill and o'erworked, how fare you in this scene?"
  "Bravely!" said he; "for I of late have been
Much cheered with thoughts of Christ, *the living bread.*"

O human soul! as long as thou canst so
  Set up a mark of everlasting light
Above the howling senses' ebb and flow
To cheer thee, and to right thee if thou roam—
  Not with lost toil thou laborest thro' the night!
Thou mak'st the heaven thou hop'st indeed thy home.

—Matthew Arnold.

PRECIOUSNESS OF CHRIST

Jesus, the very thought of thee
  With sweetness fills the breast;
But sweeter far thy face to see,
  And in thy presence rest.

No voice can sing, no heart can frame,
  Nor can the memory find,
A sweeter sound than thy blest name,
  O Saviour of mankind!

O hope of every contrite heart!
  O joy of all the meek!
To those who ask how kind thou art,
  How good to those who seek!

But what to those who find? Ah, this
  Nor tongue nor pen can show;
The love of Jesus, what it is,
  None but his loved ones know.

Jesus, our only joy be thou,
  As thou our prize wilt be;
In thee be all our glory now,
  And through eternity.

—Bernard of Clairvaux, tr. by Edward Caswall.

A LITTLE TALK WITH JESUS

A little talk with Jesus,
  How it smooths the rugged road!
How it seems to help me onward,
  When I faint beneath my load;
When my heart is crushed with sorrow,
  And my eyes with tears are dim,
There is naught can yield me comfort
  Like a little talk with him.

Ah, this is what I'm wanting—
  His lovely face to see;
And, I'm not afraid to say it,
  I know he's wanting me.
He gave his life my ransom,
  To make me all his own,
And he'll ne'er forget his promise
  To me his purchased one.

I cannot live without him,
  Nor would I if I could;
He is my daily portion,
  My medicine and food.
He's altogether lovely,
  None can with him compare;
Chiefest among ten thousand,
  And fairest of the fair.

So I'll wait a little longer,
  Till his appointed time,
And along the upward pathway
  My pilgrim feet shall climb.
There in my Father's dwelling,
  Where many mansions be,
I shall sweetly talk with Jesus,
  And he will talk with me.

NOTHING TO WISH OR TO FEAR

His name yields the richest perfume,
  And sweeter than music his voice;
His presence disperses my gloom,
  And makes all within me rejoice;
I should, were he always thus nigh,
  Have nothing to wish or to fear;
No mortal so happy as I,
  My summer would last all the year.

Content with beholding his face,
  My all to his pleasure resigned,
No changes of season or place
  Would make any change in my mind;
While blest with a sense of his love
  A palace a toy would appear;
And prisons would palaces prove
  If Jesus would dwell with me there.

—John Newton.

THE HEART OF GOD

There is no love like the love of Jesus,
  Never to fade or fall
Till into the fold of the peace of God
  He has gathered us all.

There is no heart like the heart of Jesus,
  Filled with a tender lore;
Not a throb or throe our hearts can know
  But he suffered before.

There is no voice like the voice of Jesus;
  Ah! how sweet its chime,
Like the musical ring of some rushing spring
  In the summer-time!

O might we listen that voice of Jesus!
  O might we never roam
Till our souls should rest, in peace, on his breast,
  In the heavenly home!

—W. E. Littlewood.

THE TOUCH

"He touched her hand, and the fever left her."
He touched her hand as he only can,
With the wondrous skill of the Great Physician,
With the tender touch of the Son of man,
And the fever-pain in the throbbing temples
Died out with the flush on brow and cheek,
And the lips that had been so parched and burning
Trembled with thanks that she could not speak,
And the eyes where the fever light had faded
Looked up, by her grateful tears made dim,
And she rose and ministered in her household;
She rose and ministered unto him.

"He touched her hand, and the fever left her."
O blessed touch of the Man divine!
So beautiful to arise and serve him
When the fever is gone from your life and mine.
It may be the fever of restless serving
With heart all thirsty for love and praise,
And eyes all aching and strained with yearning
Toward self-set goals in the future days.
Or it may be fever of spirit anguish,
Some tempest of sorrow that does not down,
Till the cross at last is in meekness lifted
And the head stoops low for the thorny crown.
Or it may be a fever of pain and anger,
When the wounded spirit is hard to bear,
And only the Lord can draw forth the arrows
Left carelessly, cruelly rankling there.

Whatever the fever, his touch can heal it;
Whatever the tempest, his voice can still.
There is only a rest as we seek his pleasure,
There is only a rest as we choose his will.
And some day, after life's fitful fever,
I think we shall say, in the home on high,
"If the hands that he touched but did his bidding,
How little it matters what else went by!"
Ah, Lord, Thou knowest us altogether,
Each heart's sore sickness, whatever it be;
Touch thou our hands! Let the fever leave us,
And so shall we minister unto thee!

JESUS OUR JOY

Jesus, thou Joy of loving hearts!
Thou Fount of life! thou Light of men!
From the best bliss that earth imparts
We turn, unfilled, to thee again.

Thy truth unchanged hath ever stood;
Thou savest those that on thee call;
To them that seek thee thou art good,
To them that find thee, all in all.

We taste thee, O thou Living Bread,
And long to feast upon thee still;
We drink of thee, the Fountain Head,
And thirst our souls from thee to fill!

Our restless spirits yearn for thee
Where'er our changeful lot is cast;
Glad, when thy gracious smile we see,
Blest, when our faith can hold thee fast.

O Jesus, ever with us stay;
Make all our moments calm and bright;
Chase the dark night of sin away;
Shed o'er the world thy holy light.
—Bernard of Clairvaux, tr. by Ray Palmer.

FRIEND OF SOULS

O Friend of souls! how blest the time
When in thy love I rest!
When from my weariness I climb
E'en to thy tender breast!
The night of sorrow endeth there,
Thy rays outshine the sun;
And in thy pardon and thy care
The heaven of heavens is won.

The world may call itself my foe,
  Or flatter and allure,
I care not for the world—I go
  To this tried friend and sure.
And when life's fiercest storms are sent
  Upon life's wildest sea,
My little bark is confident
  Because it holdeth thee.

When the law threatens endless death
  Upon the awful hill,
Straightway from her consuming breath
  My soul goes higher still—
Goeth to Jesus, wounded, slain,
  And maketh him her home,
Whence she will not go out again,
  And where death cannnot come.

I do not fear the wilderness—
  Where thou hast been before;
Nay, rather will I daily press
  After thee, near thee, more.
Thou art my food, on thee I lean;
  Thou makest my heart sing;
And to thy heavenly pastures green
  All thy dear flock dost bring.

And if the gate that opens there
  Be dark to other men,
It is not dark to those who share
  The heart of Jesus then.
That is not losing much of life
  Which is not losing thee,
Who art as present in the strife
  As in the victory.

To others death seems dark and grim,
  But not, O Lord, to me;
I know thou ne'er forsakest him
  Who puts his trust in thee.
Nay, rather with a joyful heart
  I welcome the release
From this dark desert, and depart
  To thy eternal peace.
—Wolfgang C. Dessler.

MY LORD AND I

I have a Friend so precious,
  So very dear to me,
He loves me with such tender love,
  He loves so faithfully,
I could not live apart from him,
  I love to feel him nigh;
And so we dwell together,
  My Lord and I.

Sometimes I'm faint and weary;
  He knows that I am weak,
And as he bids me lean on him
  His help I gladly seek;
He leads me in the paths of light
  Beneath a sunny sky,
And so we walk together,
  My Lord and I.

He knows how much I love him,
  He knows I love him well,
But with what love he loveth me
  My tongue can never tell.
It is an everlasting love
  In ever rich supply,
And so we love each other,
  My Lord and I.

I tell him all my sorrows,
  I tell him all my joys,
I tell him all that pleases me,
  I tell him what annoys.
He tells me what I ought to do,
  He tells me how to try,
And so we talk together,
  My Lord and I.

He knows how I am longing
  Some weary soul to win,
And so he bids me go and speak
  The loving word for him.
He bids me tell his wondrous love,
  And why he came to die,
And so we work together,
  My Lord and I.

I have his yoke upon me,
  And easy 'tis to bear;
In the burden which he carries
  I gladly take a share;
For then it is my happiness
  To have him always nigh;
We bear the yoke together,
  My Lord and I.
—L. Shorey.

Ever, when tempted, make me see,
  Beneath the olive's moon-pierced shade,
My God alone, outstretched and bruised,
  And bleeding on the earth he made;
And make me feel it was my sin,
  As though no other sin there were,
That was to him who bears the world
  A load that he could scarcely bear.
—Frederick William Faber.

JESUS ALL-SUFFICIENT

If only he is mine—
If but this poor heart
Never more, in grief or joy,
May from him depart,
Then farewell to sadness;
All I feel is love, and hope, and gladness.

If only he is mine,
Then from all below,
Leaning on my pilgrim staff,
Gladly forth I go
From the crowd who follow,
In the broad, bright road, their pleasures false and hollow.

If only he is mine,
Then all else is given;
Every blessing lifts my eyes
And my heart to heaven.
Filled with heavenly love,
Earthly hopes and fears no longer tempt to move.

There, when he is mine,
Is my Fatherland,
And my heritage of bliss
Cometh from his hand.
Now I find again,
In his people, love long lost, and mourned in vain.

—Novalis.

JESUS SUPREME

Be thou supreme, Lord Jesus Christ,
Live o'er again in me,
That, filled with love, I may become
A Christ in my degree.

Be thou supreme, Lord Jesus Christ,
My inmost being fill;
So shall I think as thou dost think,
And will as thou dost will.

Be thou supreme, Lord Jesus Christ,
Thy life transfigure mine;
And through this veil of mortal flesh
Here may thy glory shine.

Be thou supreme, Lord Jesus Christ,
Thy love's constraint I feel,
Thy cross I see, and mind and heart
Obey its mute appeal.

Be thou supreme, Lord Jesus Christ,
And when this life is o'er
May I be with thee where thou art,
Like thee, forever more.

ALL FOR JESUS

What shall I sing for thee,
My Lord and Light?
What shall I bring to thee,
Master, to-night?
O for the strong desire!
O for the touch of fire!
Then shall my tuneful lyre
Praise thee aright.

Thou hast given all for me,
Saviour divine!
I would give all to thee,
Evermore thine!
Let my heart cling to thee,
Let my lips sing for thee,
Let me just bring to thee
All that is mine!

Didst thou not die for me,
Ransom for sin?
Ascending on high for me,
Pleading within?
All shall be dross for thee,
All shall be loss for thee,
Welcome the cross for thee
I, too, shall win!

What can I do for thee,
Glorious Friend?
Let me be true to thee
Right to the end!
Close to thy bleeding side,
Washed in the crimson tide,
On till the waves divide,
Till I ascend!

Then a still sweeter song,
Jesus, I'll bring;
Up 'mid the ransomed throng
Thee will I sing!
Never to leave thee now,
Never to grieve thee now,
Low at thy feet to bow,
Wonderful King!

—Henry Burton.

CHRIST OUR EXAMPLE

O who like thee, so calm, so bright,
Lord Jesus Christ, thou Light of light;
O who like thee did ever go
So patient through a world of woe?
O who like thee so humbly bore
The scorn, the scoffs of men, before;
So meek, so lowly, yet so high,
So glorious in humility?

Through all thy life-long weary years,
A Man of sorrows and of tears,
The cross, where all our sins were laid,
Upon thy bending shoulders weighed;
And death, that sets the prisoner free,
Was pang and scoff and scorn to thee;
Yet love through all thy torture glowed,
And mercy with thy life-blood flowed.

O wondrous Lord, our souls would be
Still more and more conformed to thee!
Would lose the pride, the taint of sin,
That burns these fevered veins within?
And learn of thee, the lowly One,
And, like thee, all our journey run,
Above the world, and all its mirth,
Yet weeping still with weeping earth.

Be with us as we onward go;
Illumine all our way of woe;
And grant us ever on the road
To trace the footsteps of our God;
That when thou shalt appear, arrayed
In light, to judge the quick and dead,
We may to life immortal soar
Through thee, who livest evermore.
—Arthur Cleveland Coxe.

IT PASSETH KNOWLEDGE

It passeth knowledge, that dear love of thine,
My Jesus! Saviour! Yet this soul of mine
Would of that love in all its depth and length,
Its height and breadth and everlasting strength,
Know more and more.

It passeth telling, that dear love of thine,
My Jesus! Saviour! yet these lips of mine
Would fain proclaim to sinners far and near
A love which can remove all guilty fear,
And love beget.

It passeth praises, that dear love of thine,
My Jesus! Saviour! yet this heart of mine
Would sing a love so rich, so full, so free,
Which brought an undone sinner, such as me,
Right home to God.

But ah! I cannot tell, or sing, or know,
The fulness of that love whilst here below,
Yet my poor vessel I may freely bring;
O thou who art of love the living spring,
My vessel fill.

I *am* an empty vessel! scarce one thought
Or look of love to thee I've ever brought;
Yet, I may come and come again to thee
With this—the contrite sinner's truthful plea—
"*Thou lovest me!*"

Oh! *fill* me, Jesus! Saviour! with thy love!
My woes but drive me to the fount above:
Thither may I in childlike faith draw nigh,
And never to another fountain fly
But unto thee!

And when, my Jesus, thy dear face I see,
When at that lofty throne I bend the knee,
Then of thy love—in all its breadth and length,
Its height and depth, and everlasting strength—
My soul shall sing.
—Mary Shekelnot.

SEEING JESUS

I would see Jesus. As I muse, and, thinking,
Grow amazed—bewildered with a strange delight,
My faith is roused, my spirit seemeth drinking
A foretaste of that ever-longed-for sight.

I know that I *shall* see him; in that hour
When he from fleshly bonds release doth give,
Earth's mists dispersing at his word of power,
Then shall I look upon my God and live!

O blessed hope! O glorious aspiration!
A little while and I the Christ shall see!
A patient waiting for the full salvation—
Then shall I know my Lord as he knows me.

I have seen the face of Jesus:
Tell me not of aught beside.
I have heard the voice of Jesus:
All my soul is satisfied.

SHE BROUGHT HER BOX OF ALABASTER

She brought her box of alabaster;
The precious spikenard filled the room
With honor worthy of the Master,
A costly, rare, and rich perfume.

Her tears for sin fell hot and thickly
On his dear feet, outstretched and bare;
Unconscious how, she wiped them quickly
With the long ringlets of her hair.

And richly fall those raven tresses
Adown her cheek, like willow leaves,
As stooping still, with fond caresses,
She plies her task of love, and grieves.

Oh may we thus, like loving Mary,
Ever our choicest offerings bring,
Nor grudging of our toil, nor chary
Of costly service to our King.

Methinks I hear from Christian lowly
Some hallowed voice at evening rise,
Or quiet morn, or in the holy
Unclouded calm of Sabbath skies;

I bring my box of alabaster,
Of earthly loves I break the shrine,
And pour affections, purer, vaster,
On that dear head, those feet of thine.

The joys I prized, the hopes I cherished,
The fairest flowers my fancy wove,
Behold my fondest idols perished,
Receive the incense of my love!

What though the scornful world, deriding,
Such waste of love, of service, fears?
Still let me pour, through taunt and chiding,
The rich libation of my tears.

I bring my box of alabaster;
Accepted let the offering rise!
So grateful tears shall flow the faster,
In founts of gladness from mine eyes!

—C. L. Ford.

Not I but Christ be honored, loved, exalted,
Not I but Christ be seen, be known, be heard,
Not I but Christ in every look and action,
Not I but Christ in every thought and word.

JESUS, I LOVE THEE

Jesus, I love thee, not because
I hope for heaven thereby,
Nor yet because, if I love not,
I must forever die.

I love thee, Saviour dear, and still
I ever will love thee,
Solely because my God, thou art,
Who first hast lovèd me.

For me to lowest depth of woe
Thou didst thyself abase;
For me didst bear the cross and shame,
And manifold disgrace;

For me didst suffer pain unknown,
Blood-sweat and agony—
Yea, death itself—all, all for me,
Who was thine enemy.

Then why, O blessed Saviour mine,
Should I not love thee well?
Not for the sake of winning heaven
Nor of escaping hell.

Not with the hope of gaining aught,
Nor seeking a reward;
But freely, fully, as thyself
Hast lovèd me, O Lord!

Even so I love thee, and will love,
And in thy praise will sing,
Solely because thou art my God
And my eternal king.

—Francis Xavier.

I'VE FOUND A JOY IN SORROW

I've found a joy in sorrow,
A secret balm for pain,
A beautiful to-morrow
Of sunshine after rain;
I've found a branch of healing
Near every bitter spring,
A whispered promise stealing
O'er every broken string.

I've found a glad hosanna
For every woe and wail,
A handful of sweet manna
When grapes of Eschol fail;
I've found a Rock of Ages
When desert wells were dry;
And, after weary stages,
I've found an Elim nigh—

An Elim with its coolness,
  Its fountains, and its shade;
A blessing in its fullness
  When buds of promise fade;
O'er tears of soft contrition
  I've seen a rainbow light;
A glory and fruition
  So near!—yet out of sight.

My Saviour, thee possessing,
  I have the joy, the balm,
The healing and the blessing,
  The sunshine and the psalm;
The promise for the fearful,
  The Elim for the faint,
The rainbow for the tearful,
  The glory for the saint!

PATIENCE OF JESUS

What grace, O Lord, and beauty shone
  Around thy steps below!
What patient love was seen in all
  Thy life and death of woe!

For ever on thy burdened heart
  A weight of sorrow hung;
Yet no ungentle, murmuring word
  Escaped thy silent tongue.

Thy foes might hate, despise, revile,
  Thy friends unfaithful prove;
Unwearied in forgiveness still,
  Thy heart could only love.

O give us hearts to love like thee,
  Like thee, O Lord, to grieve
Far more for others' sins than all
  The wrongs that we receive.

One with thyself, may every eye
  In us, thy brethren, see
That gentleness and grace that spring
  From union, Lord, with thee.
—Edward Denny.

True wisdom is in leaning
  On Jesus Christ, our Lord;
True wisdom is in trusting
  His own life-giving word;
True wisdom is in living
  Near Jesus every day;
True wisdom is in walking
  Where he shall lead the way.

✓TELL ME ABOUT THE MASTER

Tell me about the Master!
  I am weary and worn to-night,
The day lies behind me in shadow,
  And only the evening is light;
Light with a radiant glory
  That lingers about the west;
My poor heart is aweary, aweary,
  And longs, like a child, for rest.

Tell me about the Master!
  Of the hills he in loneliness trod,
When the tears and the blood of his anguish
  Dropped down on Judea's sod.
For to me life's numerous mile-stones
  But a sorrowful journey mark;
Rough lies the hill country before me,
  The mountains behind me are dark.

Tell me about the Master!
  Of the wrong he freely forgave:
Of his love and tender compassion,
  Of his love that is mighty to save;
For my heart is aweary, aweary
  Of the woes and temptations of life,
Of the error that stalks in the noonday,
  Of falsehood and malice and strife.

Yet I know that, whatever of sorrow
  Or pain or temptation befall,
The infinite Master has suffered,
  And knoweth and pitieth all.
So tell me the sweet old story,
  That falls on each wound like a balm,
And my heart that was bruised and broken
  Shall grow patient and strong and calm.

JESU

Jesu is in my heart, his sacred name
Is deeply carved there; but the other week
A great affliction broke the little frame,
E'en all to pieces; which I went to seek;
And first I found the corner where was J,
After where ES, and next where U was graved.
When I had got these parcels, instantly
I sat me down to spell them, and perceived
That to my broken heart he was I EASE YOU,
  And to my whole is JESU.
—George Herbert.

SEALED

I am thine own, O Christ-
Henceforth entirely thine;
And life from this glad hour,
New life, is mine!

No earthly joy shall lure
My quiet soul from thee;
This deep delight, so pure,
Is heaven to me.

My little song of praise
In sweet content I sing;
To thee the note I raise,
My King, my King!

I cannot tell the art
By which such bliss is given;
I know thou hast my heart,
And I—have heaven!

O peace! O holy rest!
O balmy breath of love!
O heart divinest, best,
Thy depth I prove.

I ask this gift of thee—
A life all lily fair,
And fragrant as the gardens be
Where seraphs are.
—Helen Bradley.

JESUS, MY GOD AND MY ALL

O Jesus! Jesus! dearest Lord!
Forgive me if I say
For very love thy sacred name
A thousand times a day.

I love thee so, I know not how
My transports to control;
Thy love is like a burning fire
Within my very soul.

O wonderful! that thou shouldst let
So vile a heart as mine
Love thee with such a love as this,
And make so free with thine.

The craft of this wise world of ours
Poor wisdom seems to me;
Ah! dearest Jesus! I have grown
Childish with love of thee!

For thou to me art all in all,
My honor and my wealth,
My heart's desire, my body's strength,
My soul's eternal health.

Burn, burn, O Love! within my heart
Burn fiercely night and day,
'Till all the dross of earthly loves
Is burned, and burned away.

O light in darkness, joy in grief,
O heaven begun on earth!
Jesus! my love! my treasure! who
Can tell what thou art worth?

O Jesus! Jesus! sweetest Lord!
What art thou not to me?
Each hour brings joys before unknown,
Each day new liberty!

What limit is there to thee, love?
Thy flight where wilt thou stay?
On! on! our Lord is sweeter far
To-day than yesterday.

O love of Jesus! blessed love!
So will it ever be;
Time cannot hold thy wondrous growth,
No, nor eternity.
—Frederick William Faber.

LOVE—JOY

As on a window late I cast mine eye,
I saw a vine drop grapes with J and C
Anneal'd on every bunch. One standing by
Ask'd what it meant. I (who am never loth
To spend my judgment) said it seem'd to me
To be the body and the letters both
Of Joy and Charity. Sir, you have not miss'd,
The man replied; it figures JESUS CHRIST.
—George Herbert.

WHY NOT?

Why not leave them all with Jesus—
All thy cares,
All the things that fret thee daily,
Earth's affairs?
Pour out all thy sin and longing;
He has felt
Need of human love as thou hast,
And has knelt
At his Father's feet, imploring,
For the day,
Strength to guard against temptation
By the way.

Why not leave them all with Jesus—
On his breast
Find a balm for all earth-suffering,
Peace and rest?
Ah! he knows that thou hast striven
To walk right;
Longs to make the thorny pathway
Clear and bright.
See, he bathes thy feet, all bleeding,
With his tears!
Give to him thyself, thy burden,
And thy fears.

JESUS ON THE SEA

When the storm of the mountains on Galilee fell
And lifted its waters on high—
And the faithless disciples were bound in the spell
Of mysterious alarm—their terrors to quell
Jesus whispered, "Fear not: it is I."

The storm could not bury that word in the wave,
For 'twas taught through the tempest to fly;
It shall reach his disciples in every clime,
And his voice shall be near, in each troublous time,
Saying, "Be not afraid: it is I."

When the spirit is broken with sickness or sorrow,
And comfort is ready to die;
The darkness shall pass and, in gladness to-morrow,
The wounded complete consolation shall borrow
From his life-giving word, "It is I."

When death is at hand, and the cottage of clay
Is left with a tremulous sigh,
The gracious forerunner is smoothing the way
For its tenant to pass to unchangeable day,
Saying, "Be not afraid: it is I."

When the waters are passed, and the glories unknown
Burst forth on the wondering eye,
The compassionate "Lamb in the midst of the throne"
Shall welcome, encourage, and comfort his own,
And say, "Be not afraid: it is I."

LET US SEE JESUS

We would see Jesus—for the shadows lengthen
Across the little landscape of our life;
We would see Jesus—our weak faith to strengthen
For the last weariness, the mortal strife.

We would see Jesus—for life's hand hath rested
With its dark touch on weary heart and brow;
And though our souls have many billows breasted
Others are rising in the distance now.

We would see Jesus—other lights are paling
Which for long years we have rejoiced to see;
The blessings of our pilgrimage are failing—
We would not mourn them, for we come to thee.

We would see Jesus—yet the spirit lingers
Round the dear object it has loved so long,
And earth from earth will scarce unclose its fingers,
Our love for thee makes not this love less strong.

We would see Jesus—the strong Rock-foundation
Whereon our feet are set by sovereign grace;
Not life or death, with all their agitation,
Can thence remove us if we seek his face.

We would see Jesus—sense is all too blinding,
And heaven appears too dim and far away;
We would see Jesus—to gain the sweet reminding
That thou hast promised our great debt to pay.

We would see Jesus—that is all we're needing,
Strength, joy, and willingness come with the sight;
We would see Jesus—dying, risen, pleading—
Then welcome day, and farewell mortal night!
—Anna B. Warner.

A SONG OF LOVE

To thee, O dear, dear Saviour!
  My spirit turns for rest;
My peace is in thy favor,
  My pillow on thy breast;
Though all the world deceive me,
  I know that I am thine,
And thou wilt never leave me,
  O blessed Saviour mine!

In thee my trust abideth,
  On thee my hope relies,
O thou whose love provideth
  For all beneath the skies!
O thou whose mercy found me,
  From bondage set me free,
And then forever bound me
  With threefold cords to thee!

My grief is in the dullness
  With which this sluggish heart
Doth open to the fullness
  Of all thou wouldst impart;
My joy is in thy beauty
  Of holiness divine,
My comfort in the duty
  That binds my life to thine.

Alas! that I should ever
  Have fail'd in love to thee,
The only One who never
  Forgot or slighted me.
O for a heart to love thee
  More truly as I ought,
And nothing place above thee
  In deed, or word, or thought.

O for that choicest blessing
  Of living in thy love,
And thus on earth possessing
  The peace of heaven above!
O for the bliss that by it
  The soul securely knows,
The holy calm and quiet
  Of faith's serene repose!
  —John Samuel Bewley Monsell.

THE UNFAILING FRIEND

O Jesus! Friend unfailing,
  How dear art thou to me!
Are cares and fears assailing?
  I find my strength in thee!
Why should my feet grow weary
  Of this my pilgrim way?
Rough though the path, and dreary,
  It ends in perfect day.

Naught, naught I count as treasure;
  Compared, O Christ, with thee!
Thy sorrow without measure
  Earned peace and joy for me.
I love to own, Lord Jesus,
  Thy claims o'er me and mine;
Bought with thy blood most precious,
  Whose can I be but thine?

What fills my soul with gladness?
  'Tis thine abounding grace!
Where can I look in sadness,
  But, Jesus, in thy face?
My all is thy providing;
  Thy love can ne'er grow cold;
In thee, my refuge, hiding,
  No good wilt thou withhold.

Why should I droop in sorrow?
  Thou'rt ever by my side:
Why, trembling, dread the morrow?
  What ill can e'er betide?
If I my cross have taken,
  'Tis but to follow thee;
If scorned, despised, forsaken,
  Naught severs me from thee!

Oh, worldly pomp and glory!
  Your charms are spread in vain!
I've heard a sweeter story,
  I've found a truer gain!
Where Christ a place prepareth,
  There is my loved abode;
There shall I gaze on Jesus,
  There shall I dwell with God!

For every tribulation,
  For every sore distress,
In Christ I've full salvation,
  Sure help, and quiet rest.
No fear of foes prevailing!
  I triumph, Lord, in thee!
O Jesus! Friend unfailing!
  How dear art thou to me!

THE SONG OF A HEATHEN

(Sojourning in Galilee, A. D. 32)

If Jesus Christ is a man—
  And only a man—I say
That of all mankind I cleave to him,
  And to him will I cleave alway.

If Jesus Christ is a God—
  And the only God—I swear
I will follow him through heaven and hell,
  The earth, the sea, the air.
  —Richard Watson Gilder.

"IT IS TOWARD EVENING"

Abide with me, O Christ; thou must not go,
For life's brief day is now far down the west;
In dark'ning clouds my sun is sinking low;
Lord, stay and soothe thy fretted child to rest.

Abide with me; ere I can fall on sleep
My throbbing head must on thy breast recline,
That I may hear anew thy voice, and feel
The thrill of thy pierced hands in touch with mine.

Abide with me; so then shall I have peace
The world can never give nor take from me;
Nor life nor death can that calm peace disturb,
Since life and death alike are gain through thee.

If life, 'tis well; for though in paths of pain,
In desert place afar, I'm led aside,
Yet here 'tis joy my Master's cup to share;
And so I pray, O Christ, with me abide.

'Tis gain if death; for in that far-off land—
No longer far—no veil of flesh will dim
For me the wondrous beauty of my King,
As he abides with me and I with him.

Abide with me; I have toiled gladly on,
A little while, in stir of care and strife;
The task is laid aside at thy command,
Make thou it perfect with thy perfect life.

THE BLESSED FACE

Jesus, these eyes have never seen
That radiant form of thine;
The veil of sense hangs dark between
Thy blessed face and mine.

I see thee not, I hear thee not,
Yet art thou oft with me;
And earth hath ne'er so dear a spot
As where I meet with thee.

Like some bright dream that comes unsought
When slumbers o'er me roll,
Thine image ever fills my thought
And charms my ravished soul.

Yet though I have not seen, and still
Must rest in faith alone,
I love thee, dearest Lord, and will,
Unseen but not unknown.

When death these mortal eyes shall seal,
And still this throbbing heart,
The rending veil shall thee reveal,
All-glorious as thou art.

—Ray Palmer.

TO THEE

I bring my sins to thee
The sins I cannot count,
That all may cleansed be
In thy once-opened fount.
I bring them, Saviour, all to thee;
The burden is too great for me.

My heart to thee I bring,
The heart I cannot read;
A faithless, wandering thing,
An evil heart indeed.
I bring it, Saviour, now to thee,
That fixed and faithful it may be

To thee I bring my care,
The care I cannot flee;
Thou wilt not only share,
But take it all for me.
O loving Saviour, now to thee,
I bring the load that wearies me.

I bring my grief to thee,
The grief I cannot tell;
No words shall needed be,
Thou knowest all so well.
I bring the sorrow laid on me,
O suffering Saviour! all to thee.

My joys to thee I bring,
The joys thy love has given,
That each may be a wing
To lift me nearer heaven.
I bring them, Saviour, all to thee,
Who hast procured them all for me.

My life I bring to thee,
I would not be my own;
O Saviour! let me be
Thine ever, thine alone!
My heart, my life, my all, I bring
To thee, my Saviour and my King.

WE LONG TO SEE JESUS

We would see Jesus! we have longed to see him
 Since first the story of his love was told;
We would that he might sojourn now among us,
 As once he sojourned with the Jews of old.

We would see Jesus! see the infant sleeping,
 As on our mother's knees we, too, have slept;
We would see Jesus! see him gently weeping,
 As we, in infancy, ourselves have wept.

We would behold him, as he wandered lowly—
 No room for him, too often, in the inn—
Behold that life, the beautiful, the holy,
 The only sinless in this world of sin.

We would see Jesus! we would have him with us,
 A guest beloved and honored at our board;
How blessèd were our bread if it were broken
 Before the sacred presence of the Lord!

We would see Jesus! we would have him with us,
 Friend of our households and our children dear,
Who still, should death and sorrow come among us,
 Would hasten to us, and would touch the bier.

We would see Jesus! not alone in sorrow,
 But we would have him with us in our mirth;
He, at whose right hand are joys forever,
 Doth not disdain to bless the joys of earth.

We would see Jesus! but the wish is faithless;
 Thou still art with us, who hast loved us well;
Thy blessed promise, "I am with you always,"
 Is ever faithful, O Immanuel!

—Anna E. Hamilton.

"TELL JESUS"

When thou wakest in the morning,
 Ere thou tread the untried way
Of the lot that lies before thee,
 Through the coming busy day,
Whether sunbeams promise brightness,
 Whether dim forebodings fall,
Be thy dawning glad or gloomy,
 Go to Jesus—tell him all!

In the calm of sweet communion
 Let thy daily work be done;
In the peace of soul outpouring,
 Care be banished, patience won;
And if earth, with its enchantments,
 Seek the spirit to enthrall,
Ere thou listen, ere thou answer,
 Turn to Jesus—tell him all.

Then, as hour by hour glides by thee,
 Thou wilt blessed guidance know;
Thine own burdens being lightened,
 Thou canst bear another's woe;
Thou canst help the weak ones onward,
 Thou canst raise up those that fall;
But remember, while thou servest,
 Still tell Jesus—tell him all!

And if weariness creep o'er thee
 As the day wears to its close,
Or if sudden fierce temptation
 Brings thee face to face with foes,
In thy weakness, in thy peril,
 Raise to heaven a trustful call;
Strength and calm for every crisis
 Come—in telling Jesus all.

ANYWHERE WITH JESUS

Anywhere with Jesus,
 Says the Christian heart;
Let him take me where he will,
 So we do not part.
Always sitting at his feet
 There's no cause for fears;
Anywhere with Jesus,
 In this vale of tears.

Anywhere with Jesus,
 Though he leadeth me
Where the path is rough and long,
 Where the dangers be;
Though he taketh from my heart
 All I love below,
Anywhere with Jesus
 Will I gladly go.

Anywhere with Jesus—
 Though he please to bring
Into floods or fiercest flames,
 Into suffering;
Though he bid me work or wait,
 Only bear for him—
Anywhere with Jesus,
 This shall be my hymn.

Anywhere with Jesus;
 For it cannot be
Dreary, dark, or desolate
 When he is with me;
He will love me to the end,
 Every need supply;
Anywhere with Jesus,
 Should I live or die.

OUR ROCK

If life's pleasures cheer thee,
 Give them not thy heart,
Lest the gifts ensnare thee
 From thy God to part;
His praises speak, his favor seek,
 Fix there thy hope's foundation,
Love him, and he shall ever be
 The Rock of thy salvation.

If sorrow e'er befall thee,
 Painful though it be,
Let not fear appall thee:
 To thy Saviour flee;
He, ever near, thy prayer will hear,
 And calm thy perturbation;
The waves of woe shall ne'er o'erflow
 The Rock of thy salvation.

Death shall never harm thee,
 Shrink not from his blow,
For thy God shall arm thee
 And victory bestow;
For death shall bring to thee *no sting*,
 The grave no desolation;
'Tis gain to die with Jesus nigh—
 The Rock of thy salvation.
—Francis Scott Key.

The dearest thing on earth to me
 Is Jesus' will;
Whate'er I do, where'er I be,
 To do his will.
Worldly pleasures cannot charm me,
Powers of evil cannot harm me,
Death itself cannot alarm me,
 For 'tis his will.

SWEET PROMISES

O Jesus, I have promised,
 To serve thee to the end;
Be thou forever near me,
 My Master and my Friend.
I shall not fear the battle
 If thou art by my side,
Nor wander from the pathway
 If thou wilt be my guide.

O let me feel thee near me;
 The world is ever near;
I see the sights that dazzle,
 The tempting sounds I hear;
My foes are ever near me,
 Around me and within;
But, Jesus, draw thou nearer,
 And shield my soul from sin.

O Jesus, thou hast promised
 To all who follow thee,
That where thou art in glory
 There shall thy servant be;
And, Jesus, I have promised
 To serve thee to the end;
O give me grace to follow
 My Master and my Friend.
—John E. Bode.

THE KING OF LOVE

The King of love my Shepherd is,
 Whose goodness faileth never;
I nothing lack if I am his,
 And he is mine forever.

Where streams of living water flow
 My ransomed soul he leadeth,
And where the verdant pastures grow
 With food celestial feedeth.

Perverse and foolish oft I strayed,
 But yet in love he sought me,
And on his shoulder gently laid,
 And home rejoicing brought me.

In death's dark vale I fear no ill,
 With thee, dear Lord, beside me;
Thy rod and staff my comfort still,
 Thy cross before to guide me.

And so, through all the length of day,
 Thy goodness faileth never;
Good Shepherd, may I sing thy praise
 Within thy house forever.
—Henry W. Baker.

WE WOULD SEE JESUS

We would see Jesus when our hopes are brightest
And all that earth can grant is at its best;
When not a drift of shadow, even the lightest,
Blurs our clear atmosphere of perfect rest.

We would see Jesus when the joy of living
Holds all our senses in a realm of bliss,
That we may know he hath the power of giving
Enduring rapture more supreme than this.

We would see Jesus when our pathway darkens,
Beneath the dread of some impending ill;
When the discouraged soul no longer harkens
To hope, who beckons in the distance still.

We would see Jesus when the stress of sorrow
Strains to their utmost tension heart and brain;
That he may teach us how despair may borrow
From faith the one sure antidote of pain.

We would see Jesus when our best are taken,
And we must meet, unshared, all shocks of woe;
Because he bore for us, alone, forsaken,
Burdens whose weight no human heart could know.

We would see Jesus when our fading vision,
Lost to the consciousness of earth and sky,
Has only insight for the far elysian;
We would see Jesus when we come to die! —Margaret J. Preston.

ALL THINGS IN JESUS

Jesus, the calm that fills my breast,
No other heart than thine can give;
This peace unstirred, this joy of rest,
None but thy loved ones can receive.

My weary soul has found a charm
That turns to blessedness my woe;
Within the shelter of thine arm
I rest secure from storm and foe.

In desert wastes I feel no dread,
Fearless I walk the trackless sea;
I care not where my way is led,
Since all my life is life with thee.

O Christ, through changeful years my Guide,
My Comforter in sorrow's night,
My Friend, when friendless—still abide,
My Lord, my Counsellor, my Light.

My time, my powers, I give to thee;
My inmost soul 'tis thine to move;
I wait for thy eternity,
I wait in peace, in praise, in love.
—Frank Mason North.

EVERYWHERE WITH JESUS

Everywhere with Jesus;
O how sweet the thought!
Filling all my soul with joy,
Deep with comfort fraught.
Never absent far from him,
Always at his side;
Everywhere with Jesus,
Trusting him to guide.

Everywhere with Jesus;
For no place can be
Where I may not find him near,
Very near to me;
Closer than the flesh I wear—
In my inmost heart—
Everywhere with Jesus;
We shall never part.

Everywhere with Jesus;
Do whate'er I may,
Work, or talk, or walk abroad,
Study, preach, or pray,
Still I find him, full of love,
Ready ere I call.
Everywhere with Jesus;
He's my all in all.

Everywhere with Jesus;
Let the world assail,
Naught can shake my sure repose,
He will never fail.
I am weak, but he is strong,
Mighty to defend;
Everywhere with Jesus,
Safe with such a friend.

Everywhere with Jesus;
  Careful should I be
Lest some secret thought of guile
  His pure eye may see.
Holy, harmless, undefiled,
  He no sin can know;
Everywhere with Jesus
  Spotless I may go.

Everywhere with Jesus
  Would that all might say;
Happy then beyond compare,
  Glad by night and day,
All would taste of joy sublime,
  Perfect peace and rest:
Everywhere with Jesus,
  Nothing could molest.
—James Mudge.

THE DEAREST FRIEND

Do not I love thee, O my Lord?
  Then let me nothing love;
Dead be my heart to every joy,
  When Jesus cannot move.

Is not thy name melodious still
  To mine attentive ear?
Doth not each pulse with pleasure bound
  My Saviour's voice to hear?

Hast thou a lamb in all thy flock
  I would disdain to feed?
Hast thou a foe before whose face
  I fear thy cause to plead?

Would not mine ardent spirit vie
  With angels round the throne
To execute thy sacred will,
  And make thy glory known?

Thou know'st I love thee, dearest Lord,
  But O I long to soar
Far from the sphere of mortal joys,
  And learn to love thee more.
—Philip Doddridge.

As by the light of opening day
  The stars are all concealed,
So earthly pleasures fade away
  When Jesus is revealed.

Creatures no more divide my choice;
  I bid them all depart:
His name, his love, his gracious voice,
  Have fixed my roving heart.
—John Newton.

FAIREST LORD JESUS

Fairest Lord Jesus!
  Ruler of all nature!
O thou of God and man the Son!
  Thee will I cherish,
  Thee will I honor,
Thee, my soul's glory, joy, and crown.

Fair are the meadows,
  Fairer still the woodlands,
Robed in the blooming garb of spring;
  Jesus is fairer,
  Jesus is purer,
Who makes the woeful heart to sing.

Fair is the sunshine,
  Fairer still the moonlight,
And all the twinkling starry host;
  Jesus shines brighter,
  Jesus shines purer
Than all the angels heaven can boast.
—From the German.

THE CALL OF JESUS

Jesus calls us; o'er the tumult
  Of our life's wild, restless sea,
Day by day his sweet voice soundeth,
  Saying, Christian, follow me!

Jesus calls us from the worship
  Of the vain world's golden store;
From each idol that would keep us;
  Saying, Christian, love me more!

In our joys and in our sorrows,
  Days of toil and hours of ease,
Still he calls, in cares and pleasures,
  Christian, love me more than these!

Jesus calls us! by thy mercies,
  Saviour, may we hear thy call;
Give our hearts to thy obedience,
  Serve and love thee best of all.
—Cecil Frances Alexander.

If washed in Jesus' blood,
  Then bear his likeness too,
And as you onward press
  Ask, What would Jesus do?
Be brave to do the right,
  And scorn to be untrue;
When fear would whisper, Yield,
  Ask, What would Jesus do?

LIFE

TIME, OPPORTUNITY, EXPERIENCE, CHARACTER

WITHOUT HASTE AND WITHOUT REST

Without haste and without rest;
Bind the motto to thy breast.
Bear it with thee as a spell,
Storm or sunshine, guard it well!
Heed not flowers that round thee bloom;
Bear it onward to the tomb!

Haste not—let no thoughtless deed
Mar the spirit's steady speed;
Ponder well, and know the right,
Onward, then, with all thy might;
Haste not—years can ne'er atone
For one reckless action done!

Rest not—life is sweeping by.
Do and dare before you die;
Something worthy and sublime
Leave behind to conquer time;
Glorious 'tis to live for aye,
When these forms have passed away.

Haste not—rest not. Calm in strife
Meekly bear the storms of life;
Duty be thy polar guide;
Do the right, whate'er betide;
Haste not—rest not. Conflicts past,
God shall crown thy work at last!

—Johann Wolfgang von Goethe.

WHY DO I LIVE?

I live for those who love me;
For those I know are true;
For the heaven that smiles above me
And awaits my spirit too;
For all human ties that bind me,
For the task my God assigned me,
For the bright hope left behind me,
And the good that I can do.

I live to learn their story
Who suffered for my sake,
To emulate their glory
And follow in their wake;
Bards, martyrs, patriots, sages,
The nobles of all ages,
Whose deeds crown History's pages
And time's great volume make.

I live to hail the season—
By gifted minds foretold—
When man shall live by reason,
And not alone for gold;
When man to man united,
And every wrong thing righted,
The whole world shall be lighted
As Eden was of old.

I live to hold communion
With all that is divine,
To feel that there is union
'Twixt nature's heart and mine;
To profit by affliction,
Reap truth from fields of fiction,
Grow wiser from conviction,
Fulfilling God's design.

I live for those who love me,
For those who know me true,
For the heaven that smiles above me
And awaits my spirit too;
For the wrongs that need resistance,
For the cause that needs assistance,
For the future in the distance,
And the good that I can do.

—George Linnæus Banks.

BEAUTIFUL THINGS

Beautiful faces are those that wear—
It matters little if dark or fair—
Whole-souled honesty printed there.

Beautiful eyes are those that show
Like crystal panes where hearth fires glow,
Beautiful thoughts that burn below.

Beautiful lips are those whose words
Leap from the heart like songs of birds,
Yet whose utterances prudence girds.

Beautiful hands are those that do
Work that is earnest, and brave, and true,
Moment by moment the long day through.

Beautiful feet are those that go
On kindly ministries to and fro—
Down lowliest ways, if God wills it so.

Beautiful shoulders are those that bear
Ceaseless burdens of homely care
With patient grace and daily prayer.

Beautiful lives are those that bless—
Silent rivers of happiness
Whose hidden fountain but few may
guess.

Beautiful twilight, at set of sun;
Beautiful goal, with race well won;
Beautiful rest, with work well done.

Beautiful graves, where grasses creep,
Where brown leaves fall, where drifts lie
deep
Over worn-out hands—O, beautiful
sleep.

AT SUNSET

It isn't the thing you do, dear,
It's the thing you've left undone
Which gives you a bit of heartache
At the setting of the sun.
The tender word forgotten,
The letter you did not write,
The flower you might have sent, dear,
Are your haunting ghosts to-night.

The stone you might have lifted
Out of a brother's way,
The bit of heartsome counsel
You were hurried too much to say,
The loving touch of the hand, dear,
The gentle and winsome tone
That you had no time or thought for,
With troubles enough of your own.

The little act of kindness,
So easily out of mind;
Those chances to be angels,
Which every mortal finds—
They come in night and silence—
Each chill, reproachful wraith—
When hope is faint and flagging,
And a blight has dropped on faith.

For life is all too short, dear,
And sorrow is all too great,
To suffer our slow compassion
That tarries until too late;
And it's not the thing you do, dear,
It's the thing you leave undone,
Which gives you the bit of heartache
At the setting of the sun.
—Margaret E. Sangster.

THE BUILDERS

All are architects of Fate,
Working in these walls of Time;
Some with massive deeds and great,
Some with ornaments of rhyme.

Nothing useless is, or low;
Each thing in its place is best;
And what seems but idle show
Strengthens and supports the rest.

For the structure that we raise
Time is with material filled;
Our to-days and yesterdays
Are the blocks with which we build.

Truly shape and fashion these;
Leave no yawning gaps between;
Think not, because no man sees,
Such things will remain unseen.

In the elder days of Art
Builders wrought with greatest care
Each minute and unseen part;
For the gods see everywhere.

Let us do our work as well,
Both the unseen and the seen;
Make the house where gods may dwell
Beautiful, entire, and clean;

Else our lives are incomplete,
Standing in these walls of Time,
Broken stairways, where the feet
Stumble as they seek to climb.

Build to-day, then, strong and sure,
With a firm and ample base;
And ascending and secure
Shall to-morrow find its place.

Thus alone can we attain
To those turrets where the eye
Sees the world as one vast plain
And one boundless reach of sky.
—Henry Wadsworth Longfellow.

The stars shall fade away, the sun him-
self
Grow dim with age, and Nature sink in
years,
But thou shalt flourish in immortal
youth,
Unhurt amid the war of elements,
The wreck of matter, and the crash of
worlds. —Joseph Addison.

RETROSPECTION

He was better to me than all my hopes,
He was better than all my fears;
He made a road of my broken works
And a rainbow of my tears.
The billows that guarded my sea girt path
But carried my Lord on their crest;
When I dwell on the days of my wilderness march
I can lean on his love for the rest.

He emptied my hands of my treasured store
And his covenant love revealed;
There was not a wound in my aching heart
But the balm of his breath hath healed.
Oh! tender and true was the chastening sore,
In wisdom, that taught and tried,
Till the soul that he sought was trusting in him
And in nothing on earth beside.

He guided by paths that I could not see,
By ways that I have not known,
The crooked was straight and the rough made plain,
As I followed the Lord alone.
I praise him still for the pleasant palms
And the water springs by the way;
For the glowing pillars of flame by night
And the sheltering clouds by day.

There is light for me on the trackless wild
As the wonders of old I trace,
When the God of the whole earth went before
To search me a resting place.
Has he changed for me? Nay! He changes not.
He will bring me by some new way,
Through fire and flood and each crafty foe,
As safely as yesterday.

And if to warfare he calls me forth,
He buckles my armor on;
He greets me with smiles and a word of cheer
For battles his sword hath won;
He wipes my brows as I droop and faint,
He blesses my hand to toil;
Faithful is he as he washes my feet,
From the trace of each earthly soil.
Never a watch on the dreariest halt
But some promise of love endears;
I read from the past that my future shall be
Far better than all my fears.
Like the golden pot of the wilderness bread,
Laid up with the blossoming rod,
All safe in the ark, with the law of the Lord,
Is the covenant care of my God.

—Anna Shipton.

ONE DAY'S SERVICE ✓

O to serve God for a day!
From jubilant morn to the peace and the calm of the night
To tread no path but his happy and blossoming way,
To seek no delight
But the joy that is one with the joy at heaven's heart;
Only to go where thou art,
O God of all blessing and beauty! to love, to obey
With obedience sweetened by love and love made strong by the right;
Not once, not once to be drunken with self,
Or to play the hypocrite's poisoned part,
Or to bend the knee of my soul to the passion for pelf,
Or the glittering gods of the mart;
Through each glad hour to lay on the wings of its flight
Some flower for the angels' sight;
Some fragrant fashion of service, scarlet and white—
White for the pure intent, and red where the pulses start.
O, if thus I could serve him, could perfectly serve him one day,
I think I could perfectly serve him forever—forever and aye!

—Amos R. Wells.

Life is a burden; bear it.
Life is a duty; dare it.
Life is a thorn crown; wear it.
Though it break your heart in twain,
Though the burden crush you down,
Close your lips and hide the pain;
First the cross and then the crown.

BETTER THINGS

Better to smell the violet cool than sip
the glowing wine;
Better to hark a hidden brook than
watch a diamond shine.

Better the love of gentle heart than
beauty's favors proud,
Better the rose's living seed than roses in
a crowd.

Better to love in loneliness than bask in
love all day;
Better the fountain in the heart than
the fountain by the way.

Better be fed by a mother's hand than
eat alone at will;
Better to trust in God than say, My
goods my storehouse fill.

Better to be a little wise than in knowl-
edge to abound;
Better to teach a child than toil to fill
perfection's round.

Better sit at a master's feet than thrill
a listening state;
Better suspect that thou art proud than
be sure that thou art great.

Better to walk in the realm unseen than
watch the hour's event;
Better the *well done* at the last than the
air with shoutings rent.

Better to have a quiet grief than a
hurrying delight;
Better the twilight of the dawn than
the noonday burning bright.

Better to sit at the water's birth than a
sea of waves to win;
To live in the love that floweth forth
than the love that cometh in.

Better a death when work is done than
earth's most favored birth;
Better a child in God's great house than
the king of all the earth.

—George Macdonald.

Time is indeed a precious boon,
But with the boon a task is given:
The heart must learn its duty well
To man on earth and God in heaven.

—Eliza Cook.

THE LENGTH OF LIFE

Are your sorrows hard to bear?
Life is short!
Do you drag the chain of care?
Life is short!
Soon will come the glad release
Into rest and joy and peace;
Soon the weary thread be spun,
And the final labor done.
Keep your courage! Hold the fort!
Life is short!

Are you faint with hope delayed?
Life is long!
Tarries that for which you prayed?
Life is long!
What delights may not abide—
What ambitions satisfied—
What possessions may not be
In God's great eternity?
Lift the heart! Be glad and strong!
Life is long!

—Amos R. Wells.

IS LIFE WORTH LIVING?

Is life worth living? Yes, so long
As there is wrong to right,
Wail of the weak against the strong,
Or tyranny to fight;
Long as there lingers gloom to chase,
Or streaming tear to dry,
One kindred woe, one sorrowing face,
That smiles as we draw nigh;
Long as at tale of anguish swells
The heart and lids grow wet,
And at the sound of Christmas bells
We pardon and forget;
So long as Faith with Freedom reigns
And loyal Hope survives,
And gracious Charity remains
To leaven lowly lives;
While there is one untrodden tract
For Intellect or Will,
And men are free to think and act,
Life is worth living still.

—Alfred Austin.

The Moving Finger writes, and having
writ
Moves on; nor all thy piety nor wit
Shall lure it back to cancel half a line,
Nor all thy tears wash out a word of it.

—Omar Khayyam.

LENGTH OF DAYS

He liveth long who liveth well;
  All other life is short and vain;
He liveth longest who can tell
  Of living most for heavenly gain.

He liveth long who liveth well;
  All else is being flung away;
He liveth longest who can tell
  Of true things truly done each day.

Waste not thy being; back to him
  Who freely gave it, freely give;
Else is that being but a dream;
  'Tis but to *be*, and not to *live*.

Be wise, and use thy wisdom well;
  Who wisdom *speaks* must *live* it too;
He is the wisest who can tell
  How first he lived, then spoke the true.

Be what thou seemest! live thy creed!
  Hold up to earth the torch divine;
Be what thou prayest to be made;
  Let the great Master's steps be thine.

Fill up each hour with what will last;
  Buy up the moments as they go;
The life above, when this is past,
  Is the ripe fruit of life below.

Sow truth if thou the true wouldst reap;
  Who sows the false shall reap the vain;
Erect and sound thy conscience keep;
  From hollow words and deeds refrain.

Sow love, and taste its fruitage pure;
  Sow peace and reap its harvest bright;
Sow sunbeams on the rock and moor,
  And find a harvest-home of light.

—Horatius Bonar.

REDEEMING THE TIME

We would fill the hours with the sweetest things
  If we had but a day;
We should drink alone at the purest springs
  In our upward way;
We should love with a lifetime's love in an hour
  If the hours were few;
We should rest not for dreams, but for fresher power
  To be and to do.

We should guide our wayward or wearied wills
  By the clearest light;
We should keep our eyes on the heavenly hills
  If they lay in sight;
We should trample the pride and the discontent
  Beneath our feet;
We should take whatever a good God sent,
  With a trust complete.

We should waste no moments in weak regret
  If the day were but one;
If what we remember and what we forget
  Went out with the sun;
We should be from our clamorous selves set free
  To work and to pray,
And to be what the Father would have us to be,
  If we had but a day.

—Mary Lowe Dickinson.

MORAL COSMETICS

Ye who would have your features florid,
Lithe limbs, bright eyes, unwrinkled forehead,
From age's devastation horrid,
    Adopt this plan—
'Twill make, in climate cold or torrid,
    A hale old man:

Avoid in youth luxurious diet;
Restrain the passion's lawless riot;
Devoted to domestic quiet,
    Be wisely gay;
So shall ye, spite of age's fiat,
    Resist decay.

Seek not in Mammon's worship pleasure,
But find your richest, dearest treasure
In God, his word, his work; not leisure.
    The mind, not sense,
Is the sole scale by which to measure
    Your opulence.

This is the solace, this the science,
Life's purest, sweetest, best appliance,
That disappoints not man's reliance,
    Whate'er his state;
But challenges, with calm defiance,
    Time, fortune, fate.

—Horace Smith.

STRENGTH FOR TO-DAY

Strength for to-day is all that we need,
As there never will be a to-morrow;
For to-morrow will prove but another to-day,
With its measure of joy and sorrow.

Then why forecast the trials of life
With such sad and grave persistence,
And watch and wait for a crowd of ills
That as yet have no existence?

Strength for to-day—what a precious boon
For the earnest souls who labor,
For the willing hands that minister
To the needy friend and neighbor.

Strength for to-day—that the weary hearts
In the battle for right may quail not,
And the eyes bedimmed with bitter tears
In their search for light may fail not.

Strength for to-day, on the down-hill track,
For the travelers near the valley,
That up, far up, the other side
Ere long they may safely rally.

Strength for to-day—that our precious youth
May happily shun temptation,
And build, from the rise to the set of the sun,
On a strong and sure foundation.

Strength for to-day, in house and home,
To practice forbearance sweetly;
To scatter kind deeds and loving words
Still trusting in God completely.

FAITHFUL

Like the star
That shines afar
Without haste
And without rest,
Let each man wheel with steady sway
Round the task that rules the day,
And do his best!
—Johann Wolfgang von Goethe.

Who learns and learns, and acts not what he knows,
Is one who plows and plows, but never sows.

MORNING

Lo here hath been dawning
Another blue day;
Think; wilt thou let it
Slip useless away?
Out of eternity
This new day is born;
Into eternity
At night will return.
Behold it aforetime
No eye ever did;
So soon it forever
From all eyes is hid.
Here hath been dawning
Another blue day;
Think; wilt thou let it
Slip useless away?
—Thomas Carlyle.

JUST FOR TO-DAY

Lord, for to-morrow and its needs
I do not pray;
Keep me, my God, from stain of sin
Just for to-day.
Help me to labor earnestly,
And duly pray;
Let me be kind in word and deed,
Father, to-day.

Let me no wrong or idle word
Unthinking say;
Set thou a seal upon my lips
Through all to-day.
Let me in season, Lord, be grave,
In season gay;
Let me be faithful to thy grace,
Dear Lord, to-day.

And if, to-day, this life of mine
Should ebb away,
Give me thy sacrament divine,
Father, to-day.
So for to-morrow and its needs
I do not pray;
Still keep me, guide me, love me, Lord,
Through each to-day.
—Ernest R. Wilberforce.

That life is long which answers life's great end;
The time that bears no fruit deserves no name;
The man of wisdom is the man of years.
—Edward Young.

JUST ONE DAY

If I could live to God for just one day,
One blessed day, from rosy dawn of light
Till purple twilight deepened into night,
A day of faith unfaltering, trust complete,
Of love unfeigned and perfect charity,
Of hope undimmed, of courage past dismay,
Of heavenly peace, patient humility—
No hint of duty to constrain my feet,
No dream of ease to lull to listlessness,
Within my heart no root of bitterness,
No yielding to temptation's subtle sway,
Methinks, in that one day would so expand
My soul to meet such holy, high demand
That never, never more could hold me bound
This shriveling husk of self that wraps me round.
So might I henceforth live to God alway.

—Susan E. Gammons.

NOW

Forget the past and live the present hour;
Now is the time to work, the time to fill
The soul with noblest thoughts, the time to will
Heroic deeds, to use whatever dower
Heaven has bestowed, to test our utmost power.
Now is the time to live, and, better still,
To serve our loved ones; over passing ill
To rise triumphant; thus the perfect flower
Of life shall come to fruitage; wealth amass
For grandest giving ere the time be gone.
Be glad to-day—to-morrow may bring tears;
Be brave to-day; the darkest night will pass
And golden days will usher in the dawn;
Who conquers now shall rule the coming years.

—Sarah Knowles Bolton.

THE HOURS

The hours are viewless angels,
That still go gliding by,
And bear each minute's record up
To him who sits on high;
And we who walk among them,
As one by one departs,
See not that they are hovering
Forever round our hearts.

Like summer bees that hover
Around the idle flowers,
They gather every act and thought,
Those viewless angel-hours;
The poison or the nectar
The heart's deep flower cups yield,
A sample still they gather swift,
And leave us in the field.

And some flit by on pinions
Of joyous gold and blue,
And some flag on with drooping wing
Of sorrow's darker hue;
But still they steal the record
And bear it far away;
Their mission-flight, by day and night,
No magic power can stay.

And as we spend each minute
That God to us has given,
The deeds are known before his throne,
The tale is told in heaven.
Those bee-like hours we see not,
Nor hear their noiseless wings;
We often feel—too oft—when flown
That they have left their stings.

So teach me, heavenly Father,
To meet each flying hour,
That as they go they may not show
My heart a poison flower!
So, when death brings its shadows,
The hours that linger last
Shall bear my hopes on angels' wings,
Unfettered by the past.

—Christopher Pearse Cranch.

TO-DAY

The hours of rest are over,
The hours of toil begin;
The stars above have faded,
The moon has ceased to shine.
The earth puts on her beauty
Beneath the sun's red ray;
And I must rise to labor.
What is my work to-day?

To search for truth and wisdom,
 To live for Christ alone,
To run my race unburdened,
 The goal my Father's throne;
To view by faith the promise,
 While earthly hopes decay;
To serve the Lord with gladness—
 This is my work to-day.

To shun the world's allurements,
 To bear my cross therein,
To turn from all temptation,
 To conquer every sin;
To linger, calm and patient,
 Where duty bids me stay,
To go where God may lead me—
 This is my work to-day.

To keep my troth unshaken,
 Though others may deceive;
To give with willing pleasure,
 Or still with joy receive;
To bring the mourner comfort,
 To wipe sad tears away;
To help the timid doubter—
 This is my work to-day.

To bear another's weakness,
 To soothe another's pain;
To cheer the heart repentant,
 And to forgive again;
To commune with the thoughtful,
 To guide the young and gay;
To profit all in season—
 This is my work to-day.

I think not of to-morrow,
 Its trial or its task;
But still, with childlike spirit,
 For present mercies ask.
With each returning morning
 I cast old things away;
Life's journey lies before me;
 My prayer is for TO-DAY.

LIFE'S MIRROR

There are loyal hearts, there are spirits brave,
 There are souls that are pure and true;
Then give to the world the best you have.
 And the best will come back to you,

Give love, and love to your life will flow,
 And strength in your inmost needs;
Have faith, and a score of hearts will show
 Their faith in your work and deeds.

Give truth, and your gifts will be paid in kind,
 And song a song will meet;
And the smile which is sweet will surely find
 A smile that is just as sweet.

Give pity and sorrow to those who mourn;
 You will gather in flowers again
The scattered seeds from your thought outborne,
 Though the sowing seemed in vain.

For life is the mirror of king and slave,
 'Tis just what we are and do;
Then give to the world the best you have
 And the best will come back to you.
 —Madeline S. Bridges.

WHEN I HAVE TIME

When I have time so many things I'll do
To make life happier and more fair
For those whose lives are crowded now with care;
I'll help to lift them from their low despair
 When I have time.

When I have time the friend I love so well
Shall know no more these weary, toiling days;
I'll lead her feet in pleasant paths always
And cheer her heart with words of sweetest praise,
 When I have time.

When you have time! The friend you hold so dear
May be beyond the reach of all your sweet intent;
May never know that you so kindly meant
To fill her life with sweet content
 When you had time.

Now is the time! Ah, friend, no longer wait
To scatter loving smiles and words of cheer
To those around whose lives are now so drear;
They may not need you in the coming year—
 Now is the time!

SOME RULES OF LIFE

Have Faith in God

What though the dark close round, the storm increase,
Though friends depart, all earthly comforts cease;
Hath He not said, I give my children peace?
Believe his word.

Complain of Naught

To murmur, fret, repine, lament, bemoan—
How sinful, stupid, wrong! God's on the throne,
Does all in wisdom, ne'er forgets his own.
Be filled with praise.

Watch Unto Prayer

Think much of God, 'twill save thy soul from sin;
Without his presence let no act begin;
Look up, keep vigil, fear not; thou shalt win.
See him in all.

Go Armed with Christ

He said, "I come, O God, to do thy will."
Shall we not, likewise, all his word fulfill,
And find a weapon firm 'gainst every ill?
Put on the Lord.

Be True, Be Sweet

Let not the conflict make thee sour or sad;
Swerve not from battle: faithful, loyal, glad—
The likeness of our Saviour may be had.
Aim high, press on!

—James Mudge.

Forenoon and afternoon and night,—Forenoon,
And afternoon, and night,—Forenoon, and—what?
The empty song repeats itself. No more?
Yea, that is Life: make this forenoon sublime,
This afternoon a psalm, this night a prayer,
And Time is conquered, and thy crown is won.

—Edward Rowland Sill.

I PACK MY TRUNK

What shall I pack up to carry
From the old year to the new?
I'll leave out the frets that harry,
Thoughts unjust and doubts untrue.

Angry words—ah, how I rue them!
Selfish deeds and choices blind;
Any one is welcome to them!
I shall leave them all behind.

Plans? the trunk would need be double.
Hopes? they'd burst the stoutest lid.
Sharp ambitions? last year's stubble!
Take them, old year! Keep them hid!

All my fears shall be forsaken,
All my failures manifold;
Nothing gloomy shall be taken
To the new year from the old.

But I'll pack the sweet remembrance
Of dear Friendship's least delight;
All my jokes—I'll carry *them* hence;
All my store of fancies bright;

My contentment—would 'twere greater!
All the courage I possess;
All my trust—there's not much weight there!
All my faith, or more, or less;

All my tasks; I'll not abandon
One of these—my pride, my health;
Every trivial or grand one
Is a noble mine of wealth.

And I'll pack my choicest treasures:
Smiles I've seen and praises heard,
Memories of unselfish pleasures,
Cheery looks, the kindly word.

Ah, my riches silence cavil!
To my rags I bid adieu!
Like a Crœsus I shall travel
From the old year to the new!

—Amos R. Wells.

The stars shine over the earth,
The stars shine over the sea;
The stars look up to the mighty God,
The stars look down on me.
The stars have lived for a million years
A million years and a day;
But God and I shall love and live
When the stars have passed away.

OPPORTUNITY RENEWED

They do me wrong who say I come no more
When once I knock and fail to find you in;
For every day I stand outside your door
And bid you wake and ride to fight and win.
Wail not for precious chances passed away,
Weep not for golden ages on the wane!
Each night I burn the records of the day;
At sunrise every soul is born again.
Laugh like a boy at splendors that have sped,
To vanished joys be blind and deaf and dumb;
My judgments seal the dead past with its dead
But never bind a moment yet to come.
Though deep in mire, wring not your hands and weep;
I lend my arm to all who say "I can!"
No shamefaced outcast ever sank so deep
But yet might rise and be again a man.
Dost thou behold thy lost youth all aghast?
Dost reel from righteous retribution's blow?
Then turn from blotted archives of the past
And find the future's pages white as snow.
Art thou a mourner? Rouse thee from thy spell!
Art thou a sinner? Sins may be forgiven!
Each morning gives thee wings to flee from hell,
Each night a star to guide thy feet to heaven.

—Walter Malone.

Though life is made up of mere bubbles
'Tis better than many aver,
For while we've a whole lot of troubles
The most of them never occur.

—Nixon Waterman.

A happy lot must sure be his—
The lord, not slave, of things—
Who values life by what it is
And not by what it brings.

—John Sterling.

A BUILDER'S LESSON

"How shall I a habit break?"
As you did that habit make.
As you gathered you must lose;
As you yielded, now refuse.

Thread by thread the strands we twist
Till they bind us neck and wrist;
Thread by thread the patient hand
Must untwine ere free we stand.
As we builded, stone by stone,
We must toil—unhelped, alone—
Till the wall is overthrown.

But remember: as we try,
Lighter every test goes by;
Wading in, the stream grows deep
Toward the center's downward sweep;
Backward turn—each step ashore
Shallower is than that before.

Ah, the precious years we waste
Leveling what we raised in haste;
Doing what must be undone
Ere content or love be won!
First across the gulf we cast
Kite-borne threads, till lives are passed,
And habit builds the bridge at last!

BUILDING

We are building every day
In a good or evil way,
And the structure, as it grows,
Will our inmost self disclose,

Till in every arch and line
All our faults and failings shine;
It may grow a castle grand,
Or a wreck upon the sand.

Do you ask what building this
That can show both pain and bliss,
That can be both dark and fair?
Lo, its name is character!

Build it well, whate'er you do;
Build it straight and strong and true;
Build it clear and high and broad;
Build it for the eye of God.

—I. E. Dickenga.

Nor love thy life, nor hate; but what thou livest
Live well, how long or short permit to heaven.

—John Milton.

HOLY HABITS

Slowly fashioned, link by link,
Slowly waxing strong,
Till the spirit never shrink,
Save from touch of wrong,

Holy habits are thy wealth,
Golden, pleasant chains;
Passing earth's prime blessing—health,
Endless, priceless gains.

Holy habits give thee place
With the noblest, best,
All most godlike of thy race,
And with seraphs blest.

Holy habits are thy joy,
Wisdom's pleasant ways,
Yielding good without alloy,
Lengthening, too, thy days.

Seek them, Christian, night and morn;
Seek them noon and even;
Seek them till thy soul be born
Without stains—in heaven.

—Thomas Davis.

MAKE HASTE, O MAN! TO LIVE

Make haste, O man! to live,
For thou so soon must die;
Time hurries past thee like the breeze;
How swift its moments fly.
Make haste, O man! to live.

Make haste, O man! to do
Whatever must be done,
Thou hast no time to lose in sloth,
Thy day will soon be gone.
Make haste, O man! to live.

To breathe, and wake, and sleep,
To smile, to sigh, to grieve,
To move in idleness through earth,
This, this is not to live.
Make haste, O man! to live.

The useful, not the great;
The thing that never dies,
The silent toil that is not lost,
Set these before thine eyes.
Make haste, O man! to live.

Make haste, O man! to live.
Thy time is almost o'er;
Oh! sleep not, dream not, but arise,
The Judge is at the door.
Make haste, O man! to live.

—Horatius Bonar.

TEACH ME TO LIVE

Teach me to live! 'Tis easier far to die—
Gently and silently pass away—
On earth's long night to close the heavy eye
And waken in the glorious realms of day.

Teach me that harder lesson—how to live;
To serve thee in the darkest paths of life;
Arm me for conflict now, fresh vigor give,
And make me more than conqueror in the strife.

Teach me to live thy purpose to fulfill;
Bright for thy glory let my taper shine;
Each day renew, remold this stubborn will;
Closer round thee my heart's affections twine.

Teach me to live for self and sin no more;
But use the time remaining to me yet;
Not mine own pleasure seeking as before,
Wasting no precious hours in vain regret.

Teach me to live; no idler let me be,
But in thy service hand and heart employ.
Prepared to do thy bidding cheerfully—
Be this my highest and my holiest joy.

Teach me to live—my daily cross to bear,
Nor murmur though I bend beneath its load.
Only be with me, let me feel thee near,
Thy smile sheds gladness on the darkest road.

Teach me to live and find my life in thee,
Looking from earth and earthly things away.
Let me not falter, but untiringly
Press on, and gain new strength and power each day.

Teach me to live with kindly words for all,
Wearing no cold repulsive brow of gloom,
Waiting with cheerful patience till thy call
Summons my spirit to her heavenly home.

OPPORTUNITY

Master of human destinies am I,
Fame, love, and fortune on my footsteps wait,
Cities and fields I walk; I penetrate
Deserts and seas remote, and, passing by
Hovel and mart and palace, soon or late
I knock, unbidden, once at every gate!
If sleeping, wake—if feasting, rise—before
I turn away. It is the hour of fate,
And they who follow me reach every state
Mortals desire, and conquer every foe
Save death; but those who doubt, or hesitate,
Condemned to failure, penury, and woe,
Seek me in vain and uselessly implore;
I answer not, and I return no more.
—John James Ingalls.

THREE DAYS

So much to do; so little done!
Ah! yesternight I saw the sun
Sink beamless down the vaulted gray—
The ghastly ghost of yesterday.

So little done; so much to do!
Each morning breaks on conflicts new;
But eager, brave, I'll join the fray,
And fight the battle of to-day.

So much to do; so little done!
But when it's o'er—the victory won—
O then, my soul, this strife and sorrow
Will end in that great, glad to-morrow!
—James Roberts Gilmore.

JUSTICE

Three men went out one summer night;
No care had they or aim.
They dined and drank. Ere we go home
We'll have, they said, a game.

Three girls began that summer night
A life of endless shame,
And went through drink, disease, and death
As swift as racing flame.

Lawless, homeless, foul, they died;
Rich, loved, and praised, the men.
But when they all shall meet with God,
And Justice speaks, what then?
—Stopford Augustus Brooke.

OPPORTUNITY IMPROVED

This I beheld, or dreamed it in a dream:
There spread a cloud of dust along a plain;
And underneath the cloud, or in it, raged
A furious battle, and men yelled, and swords
Shocked upon swords and shields. A prince's banner
Wavered, then staggered backward, hemmed by foes.
A craven hung along the battle's edge,
And thought, "Had I a sword of keener steel—
That blue blade that the king's son bears—but this
Blunt thing——!" he snapt and flung it from his hand,
And lowering crept away and left the field.
Then came the king's son, wounded, sore bestead,
And weaponless, and saw the broken sword,
Hilt-buried in the dry and trodden sand,
And ran and snatched it and, with battle-shout
Lifted afresh, he hewed his enemy down,
And saved a great cause that heroic day.
—Edward Rowland Sill.

DUM VIVIMUS VIVAMUS

Live while you live, the epicure would say,
And seize the pleasures of the passing day!
Live while you live, the sacred preacher cries,
And give to God each moment as it flies!
Lord, in my views let both united be;
I live in pleasure when I live to thee.
—Philip Doddridge.

It is bad to have an empty purse,
But an empty head is a whole lot worse.
—Nixon Waterman.

Shut your mouth, and open your eyes,
And you're sure to learn something to make you wise.
—Nixon Waterman.

THE COMMON LOT

Once, in the flight of ages past,
There lived a man, and who was he?
Mortal! howe'er thy lot be cast,
That man resembled thee.

Unknown the region of his birth;
The land in which he died unknown;
His name has perished from the earth;
This truth survives alone:

That joy and grief and hope and fear,
Alternate triumphed in his breast;
His bliss and woe—a smile, a tear!
Oblivion hides the rest.

He suffered—but his pangs are o'er;
Enjoyed—but his delights are fled;
Had friends—his friends are now no more;
And foes—his foes are dead.

He saw whatever thou hast seen;
Encountered all that troubles thee;
He was—whatever thou hast been;
He is—what thou shalt be.

The rolling seasons, day and night,
Sun, moon, and stars, the earth and man,
Erewhile his portion, life, and light,
To him exist in vain.

The clouds and sunbeams, o'er his eye
That once their shades and glory threw,
Have left in yonder silent sky
No vestige where they flew.

The annals of the human race,
Their ruins, since the world began,
Of him afford no other trace
Than this—there lived a man.
—James Montgomery.

Happy the man, and happy he alone,
He who can call to-day his own;
He who, secure within, can say,
"To-morrow, do thy worst; for I have lived to-day.
Be fair or foul, or rain or shine,
The joys I have possessed, in spite of fate, are mine.
Not heaven itself upon the past has power,
But what has been has been, and I have had my hour."
—Horace, tr. by John Dryden.

PROEM

If this little world to-night
Suddenly should fall through space
In a hissing, headlong flight,
Shriveling from off its face,
As it falls into the sun,
In an instant every trace
Of the little crawling things—
Ants, philosophers, and lice,
Cattle, cockroaches, and kings,
Beggars, millionaires, and mice,
Men and maggots—all as one
As it falls into the sun—
Who can say but at the same
Instant, from some planet far,
A child may watch us and exclaim,
"See the pretty shooting star!"
—Oliver Herford.

DOING AND BEING

Think not alone to *do* right, and fulfill
Life's due perfection by the simple worth
Of lawful actions called by justice forth,
And thus condone a world confused with ill!
But fix the high condition of thy will
To *be* right, that its good's spontaneous birth
May spread like flowers springing from the earth
On which the natural dews of heaven distill;
For these require no honors, take no care
For gratitude from men—but more are blessed
In the sweet ignorance that they are fair;
And through their proper functions live and rest,
Breathing their fragrance out with joyous air,
Content with praise of bettering what is best.
—William Davies.

And, since we needs must hunger, better for man's love
Than God's truth! better for companions sweet
Than great convictions! let us bear our weights
Preferring dreary hearths to desert souls.
—Elizabeth Barrett Browning.

RICHES

Since all the riches of this world
May be gifts from the devil and earthly kings,
I should suspect that I worshiped the devil
If I thanked my God for worldly things.
—William Blake.

Trust to the Lord to hide thee,
Wait on the Lord to guide thee,
So shall no ill betide thee
Day by day.
Rise with his fear before thee,
Tell of the love he bore thee,
Sleep with his shadow o'er thee,
Day by day.

Four things a man must learn to do
If he would make his record true:
To think without confusion clearly;
To love his fellow-men sincerely;
To act from honest motives purely;
To trust in God and heaven securely.
—Henry van Dyke.

Each moment holy is, for out from God
Each moment flashes forth a human soul.
Holy each moment is, for back to him
Some wandering soul each moment home returns.
—Richard Watson Gilder.

At thirty man suspects himself a fool;
Knows it at forty, and reforms his plan;
At fifty chides his infamous delay,
Pushes his prudent purpose to resolve;
In all the magnanimity of thought
Resolves, and re-resolves; then dies the same.
—Edward Young.

Abundance is the blessing of the wise;
The use of riches in discretion lies;
Learn this, ye men of wealth: a heavy purse
In a fool's pocket is a heavy curse.
—From the Greek.

FRIEND AND FOE

Dear is my friend, but my foe too
Is friendly to my good;
My friend the thing shows I *can* do,
My foe the thing I should.
—Johann C. F. von Schiller.

How does the soul grow? Not all in a minute;
Now it may lose ground, and now it may win it;
Now it resolves, and again the will faileth;
Now it rejoiceth, and now it bewaileth;
Now its hopes fructify, then they are blighted;
Now it walks sunnily, now gropes benighted;
Fed by discouragements, taught by disaster,
So it goes forward, now slower, now faster;
Till, all the pain past and failure made whole,
It is full grown, and the Lord rules the soul.
—Susan Coolidge.

Life is too short to waste
In critic peep or cynic bark,
Quarrel, or reprimand.
'Twill soon be dark;
Up! mind thine own aim, and
God speed the mark!
—Ralph Waldo Emerson.

Pleasures are like poppies spread,
You seize the flower, its bloom is shed;
Or like the snow-fall in the river,
A moment white—then melts forever;
Or like the borealis race,
That flit ere you can point their place;
Or like the rainbow's lovely form,
Evanishing amid the storm.
—Robert Burns.

I saw a farmer plow his land who never came to sow;
I saw a student filled with truth to practice never go;
In land or mind I never saw the ripened harvest grow.
—Saadi, tr. by James Freeman Clarke.

CARES AND DAYS

To those who prattle of despair
 Some friend, methinks, might wisely say:
Each day, no question, has its care,
 But also every care its day.
 —John Sterling.

What imports
Fasting or feasting? Do thy day's work; dare
Refuse no help thereto; since help refused
Is hindrance sought and found.
 —Robert Browning.

I go to prove my soul!
I see my way as birds their trackless way.
I shall arrive! What time, what circuit first,
I ask not; but unless God send his hail
Or blinding fireballs, sleet or stifling snow,
In some time, his good time, I shall arrive:
He guides me and the bird. In his good time.
 —Robert Browning.

Art thou in misery, brother? Then, I pray,
Be comforted; thy grief shall pass away.

Art thou elated? Ah! be not too gay;
Temper thy joy; this, too, shall pass away.

Whate'er thou art, where'er thy footsteps stray,
Heed the wise words: "This, too, shall pass away."

We live in deeds, not years; in thoughts, not breaths,
In feelings, not in figures on a dial.
We should count time by heart-throbs. He most lives
Who thinks most, feels the noblest, acts the best.
Life's but a means unto an end; that end
Beginning, mean, and end to all things—God.
 —Philip James Bailey.

WE DEFER THINGS

We say, and we say, and we say,
 We promise, engage, and declare,
Till a year from to-morrow is yesterday
 And yesterday is—where?
 —James Whitcomb Riley.

To be sincere. To look life in the eyes
 With calm, undrooping gaze. Always to mean
 The high and truthful thing. Never to screen
Behind the unmeant word the sharp surprise
Of cunning; never tell the little lies
 Of look or thought. Always to choose between
 The true and small, the true and large, serene
And high above Life's cheap dishonesties.

The soul that steers by this unfading star
Needs never other compass. All the far,
Wide waste shall blaze with guiding light, though rocks
 And sirens meet and mock its straining gaze.
Secure from storms and all Life's battle-shocks
 It shall not veer from any righteous ways.
 —Maurice Smiley.

The lily's lips are pure and white without a touch of fire;
The rose's heart is warm and red and sweetened with desire.
In earth's broad fields of deathless bloom the gladdest lives are those
Whose thoughts are as the lily and whose love is like the rose.
 —Nixon Waterman.

We shape ourselves the joy or fear
 Of which the coming life is made,
And fill our future's atmosphere
 With sunshine or with shade.

The tissue of the life to be
 We weave with colors all our own,
And in the field of destiny
 We reap as we have sown.
 —John Greenleaf Whittier.

THE ROUND OF THE WHEEL

The miller feeds the mill, and the mill
the miller;
So death feeds life, and life, too, feeds its
killer. —John Sterling.

If I were dead I think that you would
come
And look upon me, cold and white,
and say,
"Poor child! I'm sorry you have gone
away."

But just because my body has to live
Through hopeless years, you do not
come and say,
"Dear child, I'm glad that you are
here to-day."

Who heeds not experience, trust him
not; tell him
The scope of our mind can but trifles
achieve;
The weakest who draws from the mine
will excel him—
The wealth of mankind is the wisdom
they leave.
—John Boyle O'Reilly.

A pious friend one day of Rabia asked
How she had learned the truth of
Allah wholly;
By what instructions was her memory
tasked?
How was her heart estranged from the
world's folly?

She answered, "Thou who knowest God
in parts
Thy spirit's moods and processes
canst tell:
I only know that in my heart of hearts
I have despised myself and loved him
well."

There is a tide in the affairs of men
Which, taken at the flood, leads on to
fortune;
Omitted, all the voyage of their life
Is bound in shallows and in miseries.
—William Shakespeare.

THE DESERT'S USE

Why wakes not life the desert bare and
lone?
To show what all would be if she were
gone.
—John Sterling.

So live that, when thy summons comes
to join
The innumerable caravan which moves
To that mysterious realm where each
shall take
His chamber in the silent halls of death,
Thou go not like the quarry slave at
night
Scourged to his dungeon; but, sustained
and soothed
By an unfaltering trust, approach thy
grave
Like one who wraps the drapery of his
couch
About him and lies down to pleasant
dreams.
—William Cullen Bryant.

The time is short.
If thou wouldst work for God it must
be now.
If thou wouldst win the garlands for thy
brow,
Redeem the time.

I sometimes feel the thread of life is
slender;
And soon with me the labor will be
wrought;
Then grows my heart to other hearts
more tender;
The time is short.

The man who idly sits and thinks
May sow a nobler crop than corn;
For thoughts are seeds of future deeds,
And when God thought, the world was
born. —George John Romanes.

Thought is deeper than all speech,
Feeling deeper than all thought;
Souls to souls can never teach
What unto themselves was taught.
—Christopher Pearse Cranch.

That thou mayst injure no man dove-like be,
And serpentlike that none may injure thee.

The poem hangs on the berry bush
When comes the poet's eye.
The street begins to masquerade
When Shakespeare passes by.
—William C. Gannett.

Be thou a poor man and a just
And thou mayest live without alarm;
For leave the good man Satan must,
The poor the Sultan will not harm.
—From the Persian.

Diving, and finding no pearls in the sea,
Blame not the ocean; the fault is in thee!
—From the Persian.

All habits gather by unseen degrees;
As brooks make rivers, rivers run to seas. —John Dryden.

Habits are soon assumed, but when we strive
To strip them off 'tis being flayed alive.
—William Cowper.

So live that when the mighty caravan,
Which halts one night-time in the Vale of Death,
Shall strike its white tents for the morning march,
Thou shalt mount onward to the Eternal Hills,
Thy foot unwearied, and thy strength renewed
Like the strong eagle's for the upward flight.

And see all sights from pole to pole,
And glance and nod and bustle by,
And never once possess our soul
Before we die.
—Matthew Arnold.

Catch, then, O catch the transient hour;
Improve each moment as it flies;
Life's a short summer—man a flower.
—Dr. Samuel Johnson.

This world's no blot for us
Nor blank; it means intensely, and means good:
To find its meaning is my meat and drink. —Robert Browning.

What is life?
'Tis not to stalk about, and draw fresh air,
Or gaze upon the sun. 'Tis to be free.
—Joseph Addison.

I see the right, and I approve it too,
Condemn the wrong, and yet the wrong pursue. —Ovid.

God asks not "To what sect did he belong?"
But, "Did he do the right, or love the wrong?" —From the Persian.

Ships that pass in the night, and speak each other in passing,
Only a signal shown and a distant voice in the darkness;
So on the ocean of life we pass and speak one another,
Only a look and a voice, then darkness again and a silence.
—Henry Wadsworth Longfellow.

One wept all night beside a sick man's bed:
At dawn the sick was well, the mourner dead. —From the Persian.

'Tis life whereof our nerves are scant,
O life, not death, for which we pant;
More life and fuller that I want.
—Alfred Tennyson.

AGE AND DEATH

MATURITY, VICTORY, HEAVEN

A DEFIANCE TO OLD AGE

Thou shalt not rob me, thievish Time,
Of all my blessings or my joy;
I have some jewels in my heart
Which thou art powerless to destroy.

Thou mayest denude mine arm of strength,
And leave my temples seamed and bare;
Deprive mine eyes of passion's light,
And scatter silver o'er my hair.

But never, while a book remains,
And breathes a woman or a child,
Shalt thou deprive me whilst I live
Of feelings fresh and undefiled.

No, never while the earth is fair,
And Reason keeps its dial bright,
Whate'er thy robberies, O Time,
Shall I be bankrupt of delight.

Whate'er thy victories o'er my frame,
Thou canst not cheat me of this truth:
That, though the limbs may faint and fail,
The spirit can renew its youth.

So, thievish Time, I fear thee not;
Thou'rt powerless on this heart of mine;
My precious jewels are my own,
'Tis but the settings that are thine.

—Charles Mackay.

SIMPLE FAITH

You say, "Where goest thou?" I cannot tell
And still go on. If but the way be straight
I cannot go amiss! Before me lies
Dawn and the Day! the Night behind me; that
Suffices me: I break the bounds: I see,
And nothing more; believe, and nothing less.
My future is not one of my concerns.

A MORNING THOUGHT

What if some morning, when the stars were paling,
And the dawn whitened, and the East was clear,
Strange peace and rest fell on me from the presence
Of a benignant Spirit standing near,

And I should tell him, as he stood beside me,
"This is our Earth—most friendly Earth, and fair;
Daily its sea and shore through sun and shadow
Faithful it turns, robed in its azure air;

"There is blest living here, loving and serving,
And quest of truth, and serene friendships dear;
But stay not, Spirit! Earth has one destroyer—
His name is Death; flee, lest he find thee here!"

And what if then, while the still morning brightened,
And freshened in the elm the summer's breath,
Should gravely smile on me the gentle angel,
And take my hand and say, "My name is Death."

—Edward Rowland Sill.

On parent knees, a naked, new-born child,
Weeping thou sat'st while all around thee smiled:
So live that, sinking in thy last long sleep,
Calm thou may'st smile while all around thee weep.

—From the Persian.

EMMAUS

Abide with us, O wondrous guest!
A stranger still, though long possessed;
Our hearts thy love unknown desire,
And marvel how the sacred fire
Should burn within us while we stray
From that sad spot where Jesus lay.

So when our youth, through bitter loss
Or hopes deferred, draws near the cross,
We lose the Lord our childhood knew
And God's own word may seem untrue;
Yet Christ himself shall soothe the way
Towards the evening of our day.

And though we travel towards the west
'Tis still for toil, and not for rest;
No fate except that life is done;
At Emmaus is our work begun;
Then let us watch lest tears should hide
The Lord who journeys by our side.

NOT NOW BUT THEN

Take the joys and bear the sorrows—neither with extreme concern!
Living here means nescience simply; 'tis next life that helps to learn.
Shut those eyes next life will open—stop those ears next life will teach
Hearing's office; close those lips next life will give the power of speech!
Or, if action more amuse thee than the passive attitude,
Bravely bustle through thy being, busy thee for ill or good,
Reap this life's success or failure! Soon shall things be unperplexed,
And the right or wrong, now tangled, lie unraveled in the next.

—Robert Browning.

CHEERFUL OLD AGE

Ah! don't be sorrowful, darling,
And don't be sorrowful, pray;
For taking the year together, my dear,
There isn't more night than day.

'Tis rainy weather, my darling;
Time's waves they heavily run;
But taking the year together, my dear,
There isn't more cloud than sun.

We are old folks now, my darling,
Our heads are growing gray;
And taking the year together, my dear,
You will always find the May.

We have had our May, my darling,
And our roses long ago;
And the time of year is coming, my dear,
For the silent night and snow.

And God is God, my darling,
Of night as well as day,
And we feel and know that we can go
Wherever he leads the way.

Ay, God of night, my darling;
Of the night of death so grim;
The gate that leads out of life, good wife,
Is the gate that leads to him.

For age is opportunity no less
Than youth itself, though in another dress,
And as the evening twilight fades away
The sky is filled with stars invisible by day.

At sixty-two life has begun;
At seventy-three begin once more;
Fly swifter as thou near'st the sun,
And brighter shine at eighty-four.
At ninety-five
Shouldst thou arrive,
Still wait on God, and work and thrive.

—Oliver Wendell Holmes.

For what is age but youth's full bloom,
A riper, more transcendent youth?
A weight of gold is never old.

Thy thoughts and feelings shall not die,
Nor leave thee, when gray hairs are nigh,
A melancholy slave;
But an old age serene and bright,
And lovely as a Lapland night,
Shall lead thee to thy grave.

—William Wordsworth.

Fill, brief or long, my granted years
Of life with love to thee and man;
Strike when thou wilt, the hour of rest,
But let my last days be my best.

—John Greenleaf Whittier.

An age so blest that, by its side,
Youth seems the waste instead.

—Robert Browning.

ON THE EVE OF DEPARTURE

At the midnight, in the silence of the sleep-time,
When you set your fancies free,
Will they pass to where—by death, fools think, imprisoned—
Low he lies who once so loved you, whom you love so,
—Pity me?

O to love so, be so loved, yet so mistaken!
What had I on earth to do
With the slothful, with the mawkish, the unmanly?
Like the aimless, helpless, hopeless, did I drivel
—Being—who?

One who never turned his back, but marched breast forward,
Never doubted clouds would break,
Never dreamed, though right were worsted, wrong would triumph,
Held we fall to rise, are baffled to fight better,
Sleep to wake.

No, at noonday, in the bustle of man's work-time,
Greet the unseen with a cheer!
Bid him forward, breast and back as either should be,
"Strive and thrive!" cry, "Speed,—fight on, fare ever
There as here!"
—Robert Browning.

Let no one till his death
Be called unhappy. Measure not the work
Until the day's out and the labor done;
Then bring your gauges.
—Elizabeth Barrett Browning.

I WOULD LIVE LONGER

Phil. i. 23.

O I would live longer, I gladly would stay,
Though "storm after storm rises dark o'er the way";
Temptations and trials beset me, 'tis true,
Yet gladly I'd stay where there's so much to do.

O I would live longer—not "away from my Lord"—
For ever he's with me, fulfilling his word;
In sorrow I lean on his arm, for he's near,
In darkness he speaks, and my spirit doth cheer.

Yes, I would live longer some trophy to win,
Some soul to lead back from the dark paths of sin;
Some weak one to strengthen, some faint one to cheer,
And heaven will be sweeter for laboring here.

But—would I live longer? How can I decide,
With Jesus in glory, still here to abide?
O Lord, leave not the decision to me,
Where best I can serve thee, Lord, there let me be.
—L. Kinney.

THERE IS NO DEATH

There is no death! the stars go down
To rise upon some fairer shore,
And bright in heaven's jeweled crown
They shine forever more.

There is no death! the dust we tread
Shall change, beneath the summer showers,
To golden grain, or mellow fruit,
Or rainbow-tinted flowers.

There is no death! the leaves may fall,
The flowers may fade and pass away—
They only wait, through wintry hours,
The warm sweet breath of May.

There is no death! the choicest gifts
That Heaven hath kindly lent to earth
Are ever first to seek again
The country of their birth;

And all things that, for grief or joy,
Are worthy of thy love and care,
Whose loss has left us desolate,
Are safely garnered there.

* * * * *

They are not dead! they have but passed
Beyond the mists that blind us here,
Into the new and larger life
Of that serener sphere.

They have but dropped their robe of
clay
To put their shining raiment on;
They have not wandered far away—
They are not "lost" or "gone."

Though disenthralled and glorified,
They still are here and love us yet;
The dear ones they have left behind
They never can forget.
—J. C. McCreery.

PROSPICE (LOOK FORWARD)

Fear death?—to feel the fog in my
throat,
The mist in my face;
When the snows begin, and the blasts
denote
I am nearing the place,
The power of the night, the press of the
storm,
The post of the foe;
Where he stands, the Arch Fear in a
visible form?
Yet the strong man must go;
For the journey is done and the summit
attained,
And the barriers fall—
Though a battle's to fight ere the guer-
don be gained,
The reward of it all.
I was ever a fighter, so—one fight more,
The best and the last!
I would hate that death bandaged my
eyes, and forbore,
And bade me creep past.
No! let me taste the whole of it, fare
like my peers,
The heroes of old,
Bear the brunt, in a minute pay glad
life's arrears
Of pain, darkness, and cold.
For sudden the worst turns the best to
the brave,
The black minute's at end,
And the elements' rage, the fiend voices
that rave,
Shall dwindle, shall blend,
Shall change: shall become first a peace
out of pain,
Then a light, then thy breast,
O thou soul of my soul! I shall clasp
thee again,
And with God be the rest!
—Robert Browning.

OUR HOME ABOVE

We thank thee, gracious Father,
For many a pleasant day,
For bird and flower, and joyous hour,
For friends, and work, and play.
Of blessing and of mercy
Our life has had its share;
This world is not a wilderness,
Thou hast made all things fair.

But fairer still, and sweeter,
The things that are above;
We look and long to join the song
In the land of light and love.
We trust the Word which tells us
Of that divine abode;
By faith we bring its glories nigh,
While hope illumes the road.

So death has lost its terrors;
How can we fear it now?
Its face, once grim, now leads to him
At whose command we bow.
His presence makes us happy,
His service is delight,
The many mansions gleam and glow,
The saints our souls invite.

We welcome that departure
Which brings us to our Lord;
We hail with joy the blest employ
Those wondrous realms afford.
We call it home up yonder;
Down here we toil and strain
As in some mine's dark, danksome
depths;
There sunshine bright we gain.

To God, then, sound the timbrel!
There's naught can do us harm;
Our greatest foe has been laid low;
What else can cause alarm?
For freedom and for victory
Our hearts give loud acclaim;
Whate'er befall, on him we call;
North, South, East, West, in him we
rest;
All glory to his name!
—James Mudge.

AT LAST

When on my day of life the night is
falling,
And, in the winds from unsunned
spaces blown,
I hear far voices out of darkness calling
My feet to paths unknown;

Thou who hast made my home of life so pleasant,
Leave not its tenant when its walls decay;
O Love Divine, O Helper ever present,
Be thou my strength and stay!

Be near me when all else is from me drifting:
Earth, sky, home's pictures, days of shade and shine,
And kindly faces to my own uplifting
The love which answers mine.

I have but Thee, my Father! let thy spirit
Be with me then to comfort and uphold;
No gate of pearl, no branch of palm I merit,
Nor street of shining gold.

Suffice it if—my good and ill unreckoned,
And both forgiven through thy abounding grace—
I find myself by hands familiar beckoned
Unto my fitting place.

Some humble door among thy many mansions,
Some sheltering shade where sin and striving cease,
And flows forever through heaven's green expansions
The river of thy peace.

There, from the music round about me stealing,
I fain would learn the new and holy song,
And find at last, beneath thy trees of healing,
The life for which I long.
—John Greenleaf Whittier.

READY

I would be ready, Lord,
My house in order set,
None of the work thou gavest me
To do unfinished yet.

I would be watching, Lord,
With lamp well trimmed and clear,
Quick to throw open wide the door,
What time thou drawest near.

I would be waiting, Lord,
Because I cannot know
If in the night or morning watch
I may be called to go.

I would be waking, Lord,
Each day, each hour for thee;
Assured that thus I wait thee well,
Whene'er thy coming be.

I would be living, Lord,
As ever in thine eye;
For whoso lives the nearest thee
The fittest is to die.
—Margaret J. Preston.

THALASSA! THALASSA!

I stand upon the summit of my life,
Behind, the camp, the court, the field, the grove,
The battle and the burden; vast, afar
Beyond these weary ways, behold the Sea!
The sea, o'erswept by clouds and winds and waves;
By thoughts and wishes manifold; whose breath
Is freshness and whose mighty pulse is peace.

Palter no question of the horizon dim—
Cut loose the bark! Such voyage, it is rest;
Majestic motion, unimpeded scope,
A widening heaven, a current without care,
Eternity! Deliverance, promise, course,
Time-tired souls salute thee from the shore.
—Brownlee Brown.

AT END

At end of love, at end of life,
At end of hope, at end of strife,
At end of all we cling to so,
The sun is setting—must we go?

At dawn of love, at dawn of life,
At dawn of peace that follows strife,
At dawn of all we long for so,
The sun is rising—let us go!
—Louise Chandler Moulton.

WHAT IS DEATH

It is not death to die—
To leave this weary road,
And, 'mid the brotherhood on high,
To be at home with God.

It is not death to close
The eye long dimmed by tears,
And wake in glorious repose
To spend eternal years.

It is not death to bear
The wrench that sets us free
From dungeon chain, to breathe the air
Of boundless liberty.

It is not death to fling
Aside this sinful dust,
And rise on strong exulting wing
To live among the just.

Jesus, thou Prince of life,
Thy chosen cannot die!
Like thee they conquer in the strife
To reign with thee on high.
—Abraham H. C. Malan, tr. by George Washington Bethune.

UPHILL

Does the road wind uphill all the way?
Yes, to the very end.
Will the day's journey take the whole long day?
From morn to night, my friend.

But is there for the night a resting-place?
A roof for when the slow dark hours begin.
May not the darkness hide it from my face?
You cannot miss the inn.

Shall I meet other wayfarers at night?
Those who have gone before.
Then must I knock or call when just in sight?
They will not keep you standing at the door.

Shall I find comfort, travel-sore and weak?
Of labor you shall find the sum.
Will there be beds for me and all who seek?
Yes, beds for all who come.
—Christina G. Rossetti.

ON SECOND THOUGHT

The end's so near,
It is all one
What track I steer,
What work's begun,
It is all one
If *nothing's* done,
The end's so near!

The end's so near,
It is all one
What track thou steer,
What work's begun—
Some deed, *some* plan,
As thou'rt a man!
The end's so near!
—Edward Rowland Sill.

THE VOICE CALLING

In the hush of April weather,
With the bees in budding heather,
And the white clouds floating, floating, and the sunshine falling broad;
While my children down the hill
Run and leap, and I sit still,
Through the silence, through the silence art thou calling, O my God?

Through my husband's voice that prayeth,
Though he knows not what he sayeth,
Is it thou who, in thy holy word, hast solemn words for me?
And when he clasps me fast,
And smiles fondly o'er the past,
And talks hopeful of the future, Lord, do I hear only thee?

Not in terror nor in thunder
Comes thy voice, although it sunder
Flesh from spirit, soul from body, human bliss from human pain;
All the work that was to do,
All the joys so sweet and new,
Which thou shew'dst me in a vision, Moses-like, and hid'st again.

From this Pisgah, lying humbled,
The long desert where I stumbled
And the fair plains I shall never reach seem equal, clear, and far:
On this mountain-top of ease
Thou wilt bury me in peace;
While my tribes march onward, onward unto Canaan and to war.

In my boy's loud laughter ringing,
In the sigh, more soft than singing,
Of my baby girl that nestles up unto this mortal breast,
After every voice most dear,
Comes a whisper, "Rest not here."
And the rest thou art preparing, is it best, Lord, is it best?

Lord, a little, little longer!
Sobs the earth love, growing stronger;
He will miss me, and go mourning through his solitary days,
And heaven were scarcely heaven
If these lambs that thou hast given
Were to slip out of our keeping and be lost in the world's ways.

Lord, it is not fear of dying,
Nor an impious denying
Of thy will—which evermore on earth, in heaven, be done;
But a love that, desperate, clings
Unto these, my precious things,
In the beauty of the daylight, and glory of the sun.

Ah! thou still art calling, calling,
With a soft voice unappalling;
And it vibrates in far circles through the everlasting years;
When thou knockest, even so!
I will arise and go:
What, my little ones, more violets? nay, be patient; mother hears!

—Dinah Maria Mulock Craik.

THE "SILVER CORD IS LOOSED"

In the June twilight, in the soft, gray twilight,
The yellow sun-glow trembling through the rainy eve,
As my love lay quiet, came the solemn fiat,
"All these things for ever, for ever thou must leave."

My love she sank down quivering like a pine in tempest shivering,
"I have had so little happiness as yet beneath the sun;
I have called the shadow sunshine, and the merest frosty moonshine
I have, weeping, blessed the Lord for as if daylight had begun.

"Till he sent a sudden angel, with a glorious sweet evangel,
Who turned all my tears to pearl-gems, and crowned *me*—so little worth;
Me! and through the rainy even changed my poor earth into heaven
Or, by wondrous revelation, brought the heavens down to earth.

"O the strangeness of the feeling!—O the infinite revealing,—
To think how God must love me to have made me so content!
Though I would have served him humbly, and patiently, and dumbly,
Without any angel standing in the pathway that I went."

In the June twilight, in the lessening twilight,
My love cried from my bosom an exceeding bitter cry:
"Lord, wait a little longer, until my soul is stronger!
O wait till thou hast taught me to be content to die!"

Then the tender face, all woman, took a glory superhuman,
And she seemed to watch for something, or see some I could not see:
From my arms she rose full-statured, all transfigured, queenly-featured,—
"As thy will is done in heaven, so on earth still let it be!"

I go lonely, I go lonely, and I feel that earth is only
The vestibule of places whose courts we never win;
Yet I see my palace shining, where my love sits amaranths twining,
And I know the gates stand open, and I shall enter in!

—Dinah Maria Mulock Craik.

CROSSING THE BAR

Sunset and evening star,
And one clear call for me!
And may there be no moaning of the bar
When I put out to sea,

But such a tide as, moving, seems asleep,
Too full for sound and foam,
When that which drew from out the boundless deep
Turns again home.

Twilight and evening bell,
  And after that the dark!
And may there be no sadness of farewell
  When I embark;

For though from out our bourne of Time
    and Place
  The flood may bear me far,
I hope to see my Pilot face to face
  When I have crossed the bar.
—Alfred Tennyson.

LAUS MORTIS

Nay, why should I fear Death,
Who gives us life, and in exchange takes
    breath?

He is like cordial spring,
That lifts above the soil each buried
    thing;

Like autumn, kind and brief,
The frost that chills the branches frees
    the leaf;

Like winter's stormy hours,
That spread their fleece of snow to save
    the flowers;

The lordliest of all things!—
Life lends us only feet, Death gives us
    wings.

Fearing no covert thrust,
Let me walk onward, armed in valiant
    trust;

Dreading no unseen knife,
Across Death's threshold step from life
    to life!

O all ye frightened folk,
Whether ye wear a crown or bear a yoke,

Laid in one equal bed,
When once your coverlet of grass is
    spread,

What daybreak need you fear?
The Love will rule you there that guides
    you here.

Where Life, the sower, stands,
Scattering the ages from his swinging
    hands,

Thou waitest, reaper lone,
Until the multitudinous grain hath
    grown.

Scythe-bearer, when thy blade
Harvests my flesh, let me be unafraid.

God's husbandman thou art,
In his unwithering sheaves, O, bind my
    heart!
—Frederic Lawrence Knowles.

IMMANUEL'S LAND

The sands of time are sinking,
  The dawn of heaven breaks,
The summer morn I've sighed for—
  The fair, sweet morn awakes.
Dark, dark hath been the midnight,
  But dayspring is at hand,
And glory, glory dwelleth
  In Immanuel's land.

I've wrestled on toward heaven
  'Gainst storm, and wind, and tide,
Now, like a weary traveler
  That leaneth on his guide,
Amid the shades of evening,
  While sinks life's lingering sand,
I hail the glory dawning
  From Immanuel's land.

Deep waters crossed life's pathway;
  The hedge of thorns was sharp;
Now these lie all behind me.
  O for a well-tuned harp!
O to join the Hallelujah
  With yon triumphant band
Who sing where glory dwelleth—
  In Immanuel's land!

With mercy and with judgment
  My web of time he wove,
And aye the dews of sorrow
  Were lustered with his love;
I'll bless the hand that guided,
  I'll bless the heart that planned,
When throned where glory dwelleth—
  In Immanuel's land.
—Annie R. Cousin.

The grave itself is but a covered bridge
Leading from light to light through a
  brief darkness.
—Henry Wadsworth Longfellow.

I hold that, since by death alone
  God bids my soul go free,
In death a richer blessing is
  Than all the world to me.
—Scheffler, tr. by Frederic Rowland
Marvin.

DEATH

Fearest the shadow? Keep thy trust;
  Still the star-worlds roll.
Fearest death? sayest, "Dust to dust"?
  No; say "Soul to Soul!"
—John Vance Cheney.

THE TENANT

This body is my house—it is not I;
Herein I sojourn till, in some far sky,
I lease a fairer dwelling, built to last
Till all the carpentry of time is past.
When from my high place viewing this lone star,
What shall I care where these poor timbers are?
What though the crumbling walls turn dust and loam—
I shall have left them for a larger home.
What though the rafters break, the stanchions rot,
When earth has dwindled to a glimmering spot!
When thou, clay cottage, fallest, I'll immerse
My long-cramp'd spirit in the universe.
Through uncomputed silences of space
I shall yearn upward to the leaning Face.
The ancient heavens will roll aside for me,
As Moses monarch'd the dividing sea.
This body is my house—it is not I.
Triumphant in this faith I live, and die.
—Frederic Lawrence Knowles.

TO OUR BELOVED

It singeth low in every heart,
We hear it, each and all—
A song of those who answer not,
However we may call;
They throng the silence of the breast,
We see them as of yore—
The kind, the brave, the true, the sweet,
Who walk with us no more.

'Tis hard to take the burden up
When these have laid it down;
They brightened all the joy of life,
They softened every frown;
But, O, 'tis good to think of them
When we are troubled sore!
Thanks be to God that such have been,
Though they are here no more.

More homelike seems the vast unknown
Since they have entered there;
To follow them were not so hard,
Wherever they may fare;
They cannot be where God is not,
On any sea or shore;
Whate'er betides, thy love abides,
Our God, for evermore.
—John White Chadwick.

A DEATH BED

As I lay sick upon my bed
I heard them say "in danger";
The word seemed very strange to me
Could any word seem stranger?

"In danger"—of escape from sin
For ever and for ever!
Of entering that most holy place
Where evil entereth never!

"In danger"—of beholding him
Who is my soul's salvation!
Whose promises sustain my soul
In blest anticipation!

"In danger"—of soon shaking off
Earth's last remaining fetter!
And of departing hence to be
"With Christ," which is far better!

It *is* a solemn thing to die,
To face the king Immortal,
And each forgiven sinner should
Tread softly o'er the portal.

But when we have confessed our sins
To him who can discern them,
And God has given pardon, peace,
Tho' we could ne'er deserve them,

Then, dying is no dangerous thing;
Safe in the Saviour's keeping,
The ransomed soul is gently led
Beyond the reach of weeping.

So tell me with unfaltering voice
When Hope is really dawning;
I should not like to sleep away
My few hours till the morning.

Yet Love will dream and Faith will trust,
(Since he who knows our need is just,)
That somehow, somewhere meet we must.
Alas for him who never sees
The stars shine through his cypress trees!
Who hopeless lays his dead away,
Nor looks to see the breaking day
Across the mournful marbles play;
Who hath not learned in hours of faith
This truth to flesh and sense unknown;
That Life is ever lord of death,
And Love can never lose its own!

—John Greenleaf Whittier.

AFTERWARD

There *is* no vacant chair. The loving meet—
A group unbroken—smitten, who knows how?
One sitteth silent only, in his usual seat;
We gave him once that freedom. Why not now?

Perhaps he is too weary, and needs rest;
He needed it too often, nor could we
Bestow. God gave it, knowing how to do it best.
Which of us would disturb him? Let him be.

There is no vacant chair. If he will take
The mood to listen mutely, be it done.
By his least mood we crossed, for which the heart must ache,
Plead not nor question! Let him have this one.

Death is a mood of life. It is no whim
By which life's Giver wrecks a broken heart.
Death is life's reticence. Still audible to him,
The hushed voice, happy, speaketh on, apart.

There is no vacant chair. To love is still
To have. Nearer to memory than to eye,
And dearer yet to anguish than to comfort, will
We hold him by our love, that shall not die,

For while it doth not, thus he cannot. Try!
Who can put out the motion or the smile?
The old ways of being noble all with him laid by?
Because we love he is. Then trust awhile.

—Elizabeth Stuart Phelps Ward.

OUR TWO GIFTS

Two gifts God giveth, and he saith
One shall be forfeit in the strife—
The one no longer needed: life,
No hand shall take the other, death.

—John Vance Cheney.

ATHANASIA

The ship may sink,
And I may drink
A hasty death in the bitter sea;
But all that I leave
In the ocean grave
Can be slipped and spared, and no loss to me.

What care I
Though falls the sky
And the shriveling earth to a cinder turn;
No fires of doom
Can ever consume
What never was made nor meant to burn!

Let go the breath!
There is no death
To a living soul, nor loss, nor harm.
Not of the clod
Is the life of God—
Let it mount, as it will, from form to form.

—Charles Gordon Ames.

LIFE

Life! I know not what thou art,
But know that thou and I must part;
And when, or how, or where we met
I own to me's a secret yet.

But this I know—when thou art fled,
Where'er they lay these limbs, this head,
No clod so valueless shall be
As all that there remains of me.
O whither, whither dost thou fly?
Where bend unseen thy trackless course?
And in this strange divorce,
Ah, tell where I must seek this compound, I?

Life! we've been long together,
Through pleasant and through cloudy weather;
'Tis hard to part when friends are dear.
Perhaps 'twill cost a sigh, a tear;
Then steal away, give little warning,
Choose thine own time;
Say not "Good Night," but in some brighter clime
Bid me "Good Morning."

—Anna Letitia Barbauld.

THE STRUGGLE

"Body, I pray you, let me go!"
(It is a soul that struggles so.)
"Body, I see on yonder height
Dim reflex of a solemn light;
A flame that shineth from the place
Where Beauty walks with naked face;
It is a flame you cannot see—
Lie down, you clod, and set me free.

"Body, I pray you, let me go!"
(It is a soul that striveth so.)
"Body, I hear dim sounds afar
Dripping from some diviner star;
Dim sounds of joyous harmony,
It is my mates that sing, and I
Must drink that song or break my heart—
Body, I pray you, let us part.

"Comrade, your frame is worn and frail,
Your vital powers begin to fail;
I long for life, but you for rest;
Then, Body, let us both be blest.
When you are lying 'neath the dew
I'll come sometimes, and sing to you;
But you will feel no pain nor woe—
Body, I pray you, let me go."

Thus strove a Being. Beauty fain,
He broke his bonds and fled amain.
He fled: the Body lay bereft,
But on its lips a smile was left,
As if that spirit, looking back,
Shouted upon his upward track,
With joyous tone and hurried breath,
Some message that could comfort Death. —Danske Dandridge.

THE THREE FRIENDS

Man in his life hath three good friends—
Wealth, family, and noble deeds;
These serve him in his days of joy
And minister unto his needs.

But when the lonely hour of death
With sad and silent foot draws nigh,
Wealth, then, and family take their wings,
And from the dying pillow fly.

But noble deeds in love respond,
"Ere came to thee the fatal day,
We went before, O gentle friend,
And smoothed the steep and thorny way."

—From the Hebrew, tr. by
Frederic Rowland Marvin.

AN OLD LATIN HYMN

How far from here to heaven?
Not very far, my friend;
A single hearty step
Will all thy journey end.

Hold, there! where runnest thou?
Know heaven is *in* thee!
Seek'st thou for God elsewhere?
His face thou'lt never see.

Go out, God will go in;
Die thou, and let him live;
Be not, and he will be;
Wait, and he'll all things give.

I don't believe in death.
If hour by hour I die,
'Tis hour by hour to gain
A better life thereby.

—Angelus Silesius, A.D. 1620.

The chamber where the good man meets his fate
Is privileged beyond the common walk
Of virtuous life, quite in the verge of heaven. —Edward Young.

Life-embarked, out at sea, 'mid the wave-tumbling roar,
The poor ship of my body went down to the floor;
But I broke, at the bottom of death, through a door,
And, from sinking, began for ever to soar. —From the Persian.

Truths that wake to perish never;
Which neither listlessness, nor mad endeavor,
Nor man, nor boy,
Nor all that is at enmity with joy
Can utterly abolish or destroy!
Hence in a season of calm weather,
Though inland far we be,
Our souls have sight of that immortal sea
Which brought us hither;
Can in a moment travel thither
And see the children sport upon the shore,
And hear the mighty waters rolling evermore.

—William Wordsworth.

APPENDIX

MISCELLANEOUS SELECTIONS

BE STRONG![1]

Be strong!
We are not here to play, to dream, to drift,
We have hard work to do, and loads to lift.
Shun not the struggle, face it, 'tis God's gift.

Be strong!
Say not the days are evil—who's to blame?
And fold the hands and acquiesce—O shame!
Stand up, speak out, and bravely, in God's name.

Be strong!
It matters not how deep intrenched the wrong,
How hard the battle goes, the day, how long;
Faint not, fight on! To-morrow comes the song.

—Maltbie D. Babcock.

NOT TO BE MINISTERED UNTO

O Lord, I pray
That for this day
I may not swerve
By foot or hand
From thy command,
Not to be served, but to serve.

This, too, I pray,
That for this day
No love of ease
Nor pride prevent
My good intent,
Not to be pleased, but to please.

And if I may
I'd have this day
Strength from above
To set my heart
In heavenly art,
Not to be loved, but to love.

—Maltbie D. Babcock.

COMPANIONSHIP

No distant Lord have I,
Loving afar to be;
Made flesh for me, he cannot rest
Unless he rests in me.

Brother in joy and pain,
Bone of my bone was he,
Now—intimacy closer still,
He dwells himself in me.

I need not journey far
This dearest Friend to see;
Companionship is always mine,
He makes his home with me.

I envy not the twelve,
Nearer to me is he;
The life he once lived here on earth
He lives again in me.

Ascended now to God,
My witness there to be,
His witness here am I, because
His Spirit dwells in me.

O glorious Son of God,
Incarnate Deity,
I shall forever be with thee
Because thou art with me.

—Maltbie D. Babcock.

"WHAT SHALL IT PROFIT?"

If I lay waste and wither up with doubt
The blessed fields of heaven where once my faith
Possessed itself serenely safe from death;
If I deny the things past finding out;
Or if I orphan my own soul of One
That seemed a Father, and make void the place
Within me where He dwelt in power and grace,
What do I gain that am myself undone?

—William Dean Howells.

[1] The poems by the Rev. Maltbie D. Babcock on this and the following page are reprinted, by special permission, from "Thoughts for Every Day Living," copyright, 1901, by Charles Scribner's Sons.

EMANCIPATION

Why be afraid of Death as though your life were breath!
Death but anoints your eyes with clay. O glad surprise!

Why should you be forlorn? Death only husks the corn.
Why should you fear to meet the thresher of the wheat?

Is sleep a thing to dread? Yet sleeping, you are dead
Till you awake and rise, here, or beyond the skies.

Why should it be a wrench to leave your wooden bench,
Why not with happy shout run home when school is out?

The dear ones left behind! O foolish one and blind.
A day—and you will meet,—a night—and you will greet!

This is the death of Death, to breathe away a breath
And know the end of strife, and taste the deathless life,

And joy without a fear, and smile without a tear,
And work, nor care nor rest, and find the last the best.
—Maltbie D. Babcock.

SCHOOL DAYS

Lord, let me make this rule:
To think of life as school,
And try my best
To stand each test,
And do my work
And nothing shirk.

Should some one else outshine
This dullard head of mine,
Should I be sad?
I will be glad.
To do my best
Is thy behest.

If weary with my book
I cast a wistful look
Where posies grow,
Oh, let me know
That flowers within
Are best to win.

Dost take my book away
Anon to let me play,
And let me out
To run about?
I grateful bless
Thee for recess.

Then recess past, alack,
I turn me slowly back,
On my hard bench,
My hands to clench,
And set my heart
To learn my part.

These lessons thou dost give
To teach me how to live,
To do, to bear,
To get and share,
To work and pray
And trust alway.

What though I may not ask
To choose my daily task,
Thou hast decreed
To meet my need.
What pleases thee
That shall please me.

Some day the bell will sound,
Some day my heart will bound,
As with a shout,
That school is out,
And, lessons done,
I homeward run.
—Maltbie D. Babcock.

CATHOLIC LOVE

Weary of all this wordy strife,
These notions, forms, and modes, and names,
To Thee, the Way, the Truth, the Life,
Whose love my simple heart inflames,
Divinely taught, at last I fly,
With Thee, and Thine, to live and die.

Redeemed by Thine almighty grace,
I taste my glorious liberty,
With open arms the world embrace,
But cleave to those who cleave to Thee;
But only in thy saints delight,
Who walk with God in purest white.

My brethren, friends, and kinsmen these,
Who do my heavenly Father's will;
Who aim at perfect holiness,
And all Thy counsels to fulfill,
Athirst to be whate'er Thou art
And love their God with all their heart.
—Charles Wesley.

WHAT MATTER

What matter, friend, though you and I
May sow and others gather?
We build and others occupy,
Each laboring for the other?
What though we toil from sun to sun,
And men forget to flatter
The noblest work our hands have done—
If God approves, what matter?

What matter, though we sow in tears,
And crops fail at the reaping?
What though the fruit of patient years
Fast perish in our keeping?
Upon our hoarded treasures, floods
Arise, and tempests scatter—
If faith beholds, beyond the clouds,
A clearer sky, what matter?

What matter, though our castles fall,
And disappear while building;
Though "strange handwritings on the wall"
Flame out amid the gilding?
Though every idol of the heart
The hand of death may shatter,
Though hopes decay and friends depart,
If heaven be ours, what matter?

—H. W. Teller.

JOHN WESLEY

In those clear, piercing, piteous eyes behold
The very soul that over England flamed!
Deep, pure, intense; consuming shame and ill;
Convicting men of sin; making faith live;
And,—this the mightiest miracle of all,—
Creating God again in human hearts.

What courage of the flesh and of the spirit!
How grim of wit, when wit alone might serve!
What wisdom his to know the boundless might
Of banded effort in a world like ours!
How meek, how self-forgetful, courteous, calm!
A silent figure when men idly raged
In murderous anger; calm, too, in the storm,—
Storm of the spirit, strangely imminent,
When spiritual lightnings struck men down
And brought, by violence, the sense of sin,
And violently oped the gates of peace.

O hear that voice, which rang from dawn to night,
In church and abbey whose most ancient walls
Not for a thousand years such accents knew!
On windy hilltops; by the roaring sea;
'Mid tombs, in market-places, prisons, fields;
'Mid clamor, vile attack,—or deep-awed hush,
Wherein celestial visitants drew near
And secret ministered to troubled souls!

Hear ye, O hear! that ceaseless-pleading voice,
Which storm, nor suffering, nor age could still—
Chief prophet voice through nigh a century's span!
Now silvery as Zion's dove that mourns,
Now quelling as the Archangel's judgment trump,
And ever with a sound like that of old
Which, in the desert, shook the wandering tribes,
Or, round about storied Jerusalem,
Or by Gennesaret, or Jordan, spake
The words of life.

Let not that image fade
Ever, O God! from out the minds of men,
Of him thy messenger and stainless priest,
In a brute, sodden, and unfaithful time,
Early and late, o'er land and sea, on-driven;
In youth, in eager manhood, age extreme,—
Driven on forever, back and forth the world,
By that divine, omnipotent desire—
The hunger and the passion for men's souls!

—Richard Watson Gilder.

"WITH WHOM IS NO VARIABLENESS"

It fortifies my soul to know
That, though I perish, Truth is so:
That, howsoe'er I stray and range,
Whate'er I do, Thou dost not change.
I steadier step when I recall
That, if I slip, Thou dost not fall.

—Arthur Hugh Clough.

HER GLADNESS

My darling went
Unto the seaside long ago. Content
I stayed at home, for O, I was so glad
Of all the little outings that she had!
I knew she needed rest. I loved to stay
At home a while that she might go away.
"How beautiful the sea! How she enjoys
The music of the waves! No care annoys
Her pleasures," thought I; "O, it is so good
That she can rest a while. I wish she could
Stay till the autumn leaves are turning red."
"Stay longer, sister," all my letters said.
"If you are growing stronger every day,
I am so very glad to have you stay."

My darling went
To heaven long ago. Am I content
To stay at home? Why can I not be glad
Of all the glories that she there has had?
She needed change. Why am I loath to stay
And do her work and let her go away?
The land is lovely where her feet have been;
Why do I not rejoice that she has seen
Its beauties first? That she will show to me
The City Beautiful? Is it so hard to be
Happy that she is happy? Hard to know
She learns so much each day that helps her so?
Why can I not each night and morning say,
"I am so glad that she is glad to-day?"

"OUT OF REACH"

You think them "out of reach," your dead?
Nay, by my own dead, I deny
Your "out of reach."—Be comforted;
'Tis not so far to die.

O by their dear remembered smiles,
And outheld hands and welcoming speech,
They wait for us, thousands of miles
This side of "out of reach."

—James Whitcomb Riley.

SORROWFUL, YET REJOICING

I lift my head and walk my ways
Before the world without a tear,
And bravely unto those I meet
I smile a message of good cheer;
I give my lips to laugh and song,
And somehow get me through each day;
But, oh, the tremble in my heart
Since she has gone away!

Her feet had known the stinging thorns,
Her eyes the blistering tears;
Bent were her shoulders with the weight
And sorrow of the years;
The lines were deep upon her brow,
Her hair was thin and gray;
And, oh, the tremble in my heart
Since she has gone away!

I am not sorry; I am glad;
I would not have her here again;
God gave her strength life's bitter cup
Unto the bitterest dreg to drain;
I will not have less strength than she,
I proudly tread my stony way;
But, oh, the tremble in my heart
Since she has gone away!

IN THE HOSPITAL

I lay me down to sleep
With little thought or care
Whether my waking find
Me here or there.

A bowing, burdened head,
That only asks to rest,
Unquestioning, upon
A loving breast.

My good right hand forgets
Its cunning now;
To march the weary march
I know not how.

I am not eager, bold,
Nor strong—all that is past;
I'm ready not to do
At last, at last.

My half-day's work is done,
And this is all my part;
I give a patient God
My patient heart,

And grasp his banner still,
Though all its blue be dim;
These stripes, no less than stars,
Lead after Him.

—M. W. Howland.

FATHER OF MERCIES

Father of mercies, thy children have wandered
Far from thy bosom, their home;
Most of their portion of goods they have squandered;
Farther and farther they roam.

We are thy children, and we have departed
To the lone country afar,
We would arise, we come back broken-hearted;
Take us back just as we are.

Not for the ring or the robe we entreat thee,
Nor for high place at the feast;
Only to see thee, to touch thee, to greet thee,
Ranked with the last and the least.

But for thy mercy we dare not accost thee,
But for thy Son who has come
Seeking his brothers who left thee and lost thee,
Seeking to gather them home.

Father of mercies, thy holiness awes us;
Yet thou dost wait to receive!
Jesus, the light of thy countenance charms us,
Father of him, we believe.

Back in the home of thy heart, may we labor
Others to bring from the wild,
Counting each creature that needs us our neighbor,
Claiming each soul as thy child.

—Robert F. Horton.

ANGELS

How shall we tell an angel
From another guest?
How, from common worldly herd,
One of the blest?

Hint of suppressed halo,
Rustle of hidden wings,
Wafture of heavenly frankincense—
Which of these things?

The old Sphinx smiles so subtly:
"I give no golden rule—
Yet would I warn thee, World: treat well
Whom thou call'st fool."

—Gertrude Hall.

HIS PILGRIMAGE

Give me my scallop-shell of quiet,
My staff of faith to walk upon,
My scrip of joy, immortal diet,
My bottle of salvation,
My gown of glory, hope's true gage;
And thus I'll take my pilgrimage.

Blood must be my body's balmer;
No other balm will there be given;
Whilst my soul, like quiet palmer,
Traveleth toward the land of heaven;
Over the silver mountains,
Where spring the nectar fountains,
There will I kiss
The bowl of bliss,
And drink mine everlasting fill
Upon every milken hill.
My soul will be a-dry before;
But after, it will thirst no more.

Then by that happy, blissful day,
More peaceful pilgrims I shall see,
That have cast off their rags of clay,
And walk appareled fresh like me.
I'll take them first
To quench their thirst
And taste of nectar suckets,
At those clear wells
Where sweetness dwells,
Drawn up by saints in crystal buckets.

—Sir Walter Raleigh.

OUR WORDS

O Sentinel at the loose-swung door of my impetuous lips,
Guard close to-day! Make sure no word unjust or cruel slips
In anger forth, by folly spurred or armed with envy's whips;
Keep clear the way to-day.

And Watchman on the cliff-scarred heights that lead from heart to mind,
When wolf-thoughts clothed in guile's soft fleece creep up, O be not blind!
But may they pass whose foreheads bear the glowing seal-word, "kind";
Bid them Godspeed, I pray.

And Warden of my soul's stained house, where love and hate are born,
O make it clean, if swept must be with pain's rough broom of thorn!
And quiet impose, so straining ears with world-din racked and torn,
May catch what God doth say.

A GOOD MAN

A good man never dies—
In worthy deed and prayer,
And helpful hands, and honest eyes,
If smiles or tears be there;
Who lives for you and me—
Lives for the world he tries
To help—he lives eternally.
A good man never dies.

Who lives to bravely take
His share of toil and stress,
And, for his weaker fellows' sake
Makes every burden less—
He may, at last, seem worn—
Lie fallen—hands and eyes
Folded—yet, though we mourn and mourn,
A good man never dies.
—James Whitcomb Riley.

THE IMMANENT GOD

Each in His Own Tongue

A fire-mist and a planet,
A crystal and a cell,
A jellyfish and a saurian,
And caves where the cavemen dwell;
Then a sense of law and beauty,
And a face turned from the clod—
Some call it Evolution
And others call it God.

A haze on the far horizon,
The infinite, tender sky,
The ripe, rich tint of the cornfields,
And the wild geese sailing high—
And all over upland and lowland
The charm of the golden rod—
Some of us call it Autumn,
And others call it God.

Like tides on a crescent sea beach,
When the moon is new and thin,
Into our hearts high yearnings
Come welling and surging in—
Come from the mystic ocean,
Whose rim no foot has trod—
Some of us call it Longing,
And others call it God.

A picket frozen on duty—
A mother starved for her brood—
Socrates drinking the hemlock,
And Jesus on the rood;
And millions who, humble and nameless,
The straight, hard pathway trod—
Some call it Consecration,
And others call it God.
—William Herbert Carruth.

THE HIGHER FELLOWSHIP

Do you go to my school?
Yes, you go to my school,
And we've learned the big lesson—Be strong!
And to front the loud noise
With a spirit of poise,
And drown down the noise with a song.
We have spelled the first line in the Primer of Fate;
We have spelled it, and dare not to shirk—
For its first and its greatest commandment to men
Is "Work, and rejoice in your work."
Who is learned in this Primer will not be a fool—
You are one of my classmates. You go to my school.

You belong to my club?
Yes, you're one of my club,
And this is our program and plan:
To each do his part
To look into the heart
And get at the good that's in man.
Detectives of virtue and spies of the good
And sleuth-hounds of righteousness we.
Look out there, my brother! we're hot on your trail,
We'll find out how good you can be.
We would drive from our hearts the snake, tiger, and cub;
We're the Lodge of the Lovers. You're one of my club.

You belong to my church?
Yes, you go to my church—
Our names on the same old church roll—
The tide-waves of God
We believe are abroad
And flow into the creeks of each soul.
And the vessel we sail on is strong as the sea
That buffets and blows it about;
For the sea is God's sea as the ship is God's ship,
So we know not the meaning of doubt;
And we know howsoever the vessel may lurch
We've a Pilot to trust in. You go to my church.
—Sam Walter Foss.

Never elated while one man's oppressed;
Never dejected while another's blessed.
—Alexander Pope.

THE OTHER FELLOW'S JOB

There's a craze among us mortals that is cruel hard to name;
Wheresoe'er you find a human you will find the case the same;
You may seek among the worst of men or seek among the best,
And you'll find that every person is precisely like the rest:
Each believes his real calling is along some other line
Than the one at which he's working—take, for instance, yours and mine.
From the meanest "me-too" creature to the leader of the mob,
There's a universal craving for "the other fellow's job."

There are millions of positions in the busy world to-day,
Each a drudge to him who holds it, but to him who doesn't, play;
Evey farmer's broken-hearted that in youth he missed his call,
While that same unhappy farmer is the envy of us all.
Any task you care to mention seems a vastly better lot
Than the one especial something which you happen to have got.
There's but one sure way to smother Envy's heartache and her sob:
Keep too busy at your own to want "the other fellow's job."

—Strickland W. Gilliland.

THE SCORN OF JOB

"If I have eaten my morsel alone,"
The patriarch spoke in scorn.
What would he think of the Church were he shown
Heathendom—huge, forlorn,
Godless, Christless, with soul unfed,
While the Church's ailment is fullness of bread,
Eating her morsel alone?

"Freely as ye have received, so give,"
He bade who hath given us all.
How shall the soul in us longer live
Deaf to their starving call,
For whom the blood of the Lord was shed,
And his body broken to give them bread,
If we eat our morsel alone?

—Archbishop Alexander.

GREATNESS

What makes a man great? Is it houses and lands?
Is it argosies dropping their wealth at his feet?
Is it multitudes shouting his name in the street?
Is it power of brain? Is it skill of hand?
Is it writing a book? Is it guiding the State?
Nay, nay, none of these can make a man great.

The crystal burns cold with its beautiful fire,
And is what it is; it can never be more;
The acorn, with something wrapped warm at the core,
In quietness says, "To the oak I aspire."
That something in seed and in tree is the same—
What makes a man great is his greatness of aim.

What is greatness of aim? Your purpose to trim
For bringing the world to obey your behest?
O no, it is seeking God's perfect and best,
Making something the same both in you and in him.
Love what he loves, and, child of the sod,
Already you share in the greatness of God.

—Samuel V. Cole.

A SAFE FIRM

When the other firms show dizziness
Here's a house that does not share it.
Wouldn't you like to join the business?
Join the firm of Grin and Barrett?
Give your strength that does not murmur,
And your nerve that does not falter,
And you've joined a house that's firmer
Than the old rock of Gibraltar.
They have won a good prosperity;
Why not join the firm and share it?
Step, young fellow, with celerity;
Join the firm of Grin and Barrett.
Grin and Barrett,
Who can scare it?
Scare the firm of Grin and Barrett?

—Sam Walter Foss.

JOHN MILTON

Milton! thou shouldst be living at this hour:
England hath need of thee: she is a fen
Of stagnant waters: altars, sword, and pen,
Fireside, the heroic wealth of hall and bower,
Have forfeited their ancient English dower
Of inward happiness. We are selfish men.
O! raise us up, return to us again;
And give us manners, virtue, freedom, power.
Thy soul was like a Star, and dwelt apart:
Thou hadst a voice whose sound was like the sea:
Pure as the naked heavens, majestic, free,
So didst thou travel on life's common way,
In cheerful godliness; and yet thy heart
The lowliest duties on herself did lay.
—William Wordsworth.

SUMMUM BONUM

For radiant health I praise not when I pray,
Nor for routine of toil well-pleasing every way,
Though these gifts, Lord, more priceless grow each day.

Not for congenial comrades, garnered store
Of worldly wealth, nor vision that sees o'er
Such sordid mass, mind's plumèd eagles soar.

Not even, Lord, for love that eases stress
Of storm, contention, hope's unconquerableness,
Nor faith's abiding peace, nor works that bless.

But this, dear Lord, stir inner depths divine,
That day by day, though slowly! line on line
My will begins—begins—to merge in thine.
—Charles L. Story.

THE AIM

O Thou who lovest not alone
The swift success, the instant goal,
But hast a lenient eye to mark
The failures of the inconstant soul,

Consider not my little worth—
The mean achievement, scamped in act—
The high resolve and low result,
The dream that durst not face the fact.

But count the reach of my desire—
Let this be something in thy sight;
I have not, in the slothful dark,
Forgot the vision and the height.

Neither my body nor my soul
To earth's low ease will yield consent.
I praise thee for the will to strive;
I bless thy goad and discontent.
—Charles G. D. Roberts.

SAY SOMETHING GOOD

When over the fair fame of friend or foe
The shadow of disgrace shall fall, instead
Of words of blame or proof of thus and so,
Let something good be said!

Forget not that no fellow-being yet
May fall so low but love may lift his head;
Even the cheek of shame with tears is wet,
If something good be said.

No generous heart may vainly turn aside
In ways of sympathy; no soul so dead
But may awaken, strong and glorified,
If something good be said.

And so I charge ye, by the thorny crown,
And by the cross on which the Saviour bled,
And by your own soul's hope of fair renown,
Let something good be said!
—James Whitcomb Riley.

WHEN TO BE HAPPY

Why do we cling to the skirts of sorrow?
Why do we cloud with care the brow?
Why do we wait for a glad to-morrow—
Why not gladden the precious Now?
Eden is yours! Would you dwell within it?
Change men's grief to a gracious smile,
And thus have heaven here this minute
And not far-off in the afterwhile.

Life, at most, is a fleeting bubble,
Gone with the puff of an angel's breath.
Why should the dim hereafter trouble
Souls this side of the gates of death?
The crown is yours! Would you care to win it?
Plant a song in the hearts that sigh,
And thus have heaven here this minute
And not far-off in the by-and-by.

Find the soul's high place of beauty,
Not in a man-made book of creeds,
But where desire ennobles duty
And life is full of your kindly deeds.
The bliss is yours! Would you fain begin it?
Pave with love each golden mile,
And thus have heaven here this minute
And not far-off in the afterwhile.
—Nixon Waterman.

Love thyself last: cherish those hearts that hate thee;
Corruption wins not more than honesty.
Still in thy right hand carry gentle peace,
To silence envious tongues. Be just, and fear not:
Let all the ends thou aim'st at be thy country's,
Thy God's, and truth's.
—William Shakespeare.

Sweet are the uses of adversity;
Which, like the toad, ugly and venomous,
Wears yet a precious jewel in his head;
And this our life, exempt from public haunt,
Finds tongues in trees, books in the running brooks,
Sermons in stones, and good in everything.
—William Shakespeare.

WORSHIP

But let my due feet never fail
To walk the studious cloister's pale,
And love the high embowèd roof
With antique pillars massy proof,
And storied windows richly dight,
Casting a dim religious light.
There let the pealing organ blow,
To the full-voiced choir below,
In service high, and anthems clear,
As may with sweetness, through mine ear,
Dissolve me into ecstasies,
And bring all Heaven before mine eyes.
—John Milton.

Give us men!
Strong and stalwart ones:
Men whom highest hope inspires,
Men whom purest honor fires,
Men who trample Self beneath them,
Men who make their country wreathe them
As her noble sons,
Worthy of their sires,
Men who never shame their mothers,
Men who never fail their brothers;
True, however false are others:
Give us Men—I say again,
Give us Men!
—Bishop of Exeter.

I will not doubt though all my ships at sea
Come drifting home with broken masts and sails,
I will believe the Hand which never fails,
From seeming evil worketh good for me;
And though I weep because those sails are tattered,
Still will I cry, while my best hopes lie shattered,
"I trust in Thee."

The wounds I might have healed,
The human sorrow and smart!
And yet it never was in my soul
To play so ill a part.
But evil is wrought by want of thought
As well as want of heart.
—Thomas Hood.

DON'T FEAR—GOD'S NEAR!

Feel glum? Keep mum.
Don't grumble. Be humble.
Trials cling? Just sing.
Can't sing? Just cling.
Don't fear—God's near!
Money goes—He knows.
Honor left—Not bereft.
Don't rust—Work! Trust!
—Ernest Bourner Allen.

A rose to the living is more
Than sumptuous wreaths to the dead;
In filling love's infinite store,
A rose to the living is more,
If graciously given before
The hungering spirit is fled—
A rose to the living is more
Than sumptuous wreaths to the dead.
—Nixon Waterman.

Canst thou see no beauty nigh?
Cure thy dull, distempered eye.
Canst thou no sweet music hear?
Tune thy sad, discordant ear.
Earth has beauty everywhere
If the eye that sees is fair.
Earth has music to delight
If the ear is tuned aright.
—Nixon Waterman.

Anew we pledge ourselves to Thee,
To follow where thy Truth shall lead;
Afloat upon its boundless sea,
Who sails with God is safe indeed.

O, though oft depressed and lonely
All my fears are laid aside,
If I but remember only
Such as these have lived and died.

It was only a glad "Good morning,"
As she passed along the way;
But it spread the morning's glory
Over the livelong day.

For the right against the wrong,
For the weak against the strong,
For the poor who've waited long,
For the brighter age to be.

RECOMPENSE

The gifts that to our breasts we fold
Are brightened by our losses.
The sweetest joys a heart can hold
Grow up between its crosses.
And on life's pathway many a mile
Is made more glad and cheery,
Because, for just a little while,
The way seemed dark and dreary.
—Nixon Waterman.

Wherever now a sorrow stands,
'Tis mine to heal His nail-torn hands.
In every lonely lane and street,
'Tis mine to wash His wounded feet—
'Tis mine to roll away the stone
And warm His heart against my own.
Here, here on earth I find it all—
The young archangels, white and tall,
The Golden City and the doors,
And all the shining of the floors!

I sent my soul through the Invisible,
Some letter of that After-life to spell;
And by and by my soul returned to me,
And answered, "I myself am Heaven and Hell."
—Omar Khayyam.

Count that day really worse than lost
You might have made divine,
Through which you scattered lots of frost
And ne'er a speck of shine.
—Nixon Waterman.

O, the little birds sang east, and the little birds sang west,
And I smiled to think God's greatness flowed around our incompleteness,
Round our restlessness, His rest.
—Elizabeth Barrett Browning.

If by one word I help another,
A struggling and despairing brother,
Or ease one bed of pain;
If I but aid some sad one weeping,
Or comfort one, lone vigil keeping,
I have not lived in vain.

INDEX TO AUTHORS

INDEX TO TITLES

INDEX TO FIRST LINES

INDEX TO FIRST LINES IN APPENDIX

BAD DIVORCE

BILLIONAIRE'S CLUB BOOK 5

ELISE FABER

BAD DIVORCE
BY ELISE FABER
Newsletter sign-up

BAD DIVORCE

Print ISBN-13: 978-1-946140-27-2
Ebook ISBN-13: 978-1-946140-26-5
Cover Art by Jena Brignola